WHAT IS AN *Aspen RoadMap?*

Aspen RoadMaps™ are comprehensive course outlines that lead you, step by step, through your law school courses—helping you prepare for class and study for exams. With a clean, modern design that is as easy to use as it is visually appealing, your RoadMap will guide you from the "big picture" to the details you need to know.

WHAT MAKES THE *ASPEN ROADMAP*™ FOR TORTS THE BEST?

The Aspen RoadMap™ for Torts:

- Represents the newest, most up-to-date outline available.
- Is brought to you by the publishers of the successful *Examples and Explanations Series*, and the author of *Evidence: Examples and Explanations*.
- Is informed by the insights and teaching methods of Professor Arthur Best, one of America's best classroom teachers of Torts.
- Explains the basic rules of torts that most courts apply—and the reasons that support the rules.
- Offers the most complete set of study tools available to help you reinforce your learning and prepare for exams.
- Incorporates the policy, politics, and analysis that help you apply and critique the rules.

THE PRACTICAL COMPONENTS OF YOUR *ASPEN ROADMAP*™

- ***The Casebook Correlation Chart*** helps you match sections of your casebook to this *RoadMap*™.
- ***The RoadMap™ Capsule Summary***, cross-referenced to the outline text, provides a "big picture" view anytime you need it.
- ***Chapter Overviews,*** each no more than two pages long, highlight key concepts.
- ***Minority Positions*** are clearly explained and the effects of rival approaches clarified.
- ***Hypotheticals*** are interwoven throughout to help further clarify important concepts.
- ***Examples***—complete with accompanying analyses—are included in each chapter to provide lively and memorable illustrations of key points.
- ***Chapter Review Questions***—complete with answers—reinforce your understanding.
- ***Exam Tips*** help you target what you really need to know in order to maximize your study time and do well on exams.
- ***Sample Exam Questions***, presented as short essays, are accompanied by model answers.

ASPEN LAW & BUSINESS Educational Division

Dear Student,

I'd like to take this opportunity to welcome you to the *Aspen RoadMap™* for Torts. I am Arthur Best, a professor at the University of Denver College of Law. I have been teaching Torts since 1976. From what students have told me over the years, I have developed specific approaches and effective techniques for teaching Torts which I think will help to guide you through this interesting course of study.

The challenge in Torts is to be able to develop legally sound reasons for your position on a case that usually involves injury—for example, medical malpractice. Your reasons have to be based on current and traditional rules, as well as on the common-sense ideas that support those rules. You also have to be consistent with social policy as it is recognized by the court. You have a number of considerations, and that's why there are a number of approaches to be taken in the study of Torts. But not to worry! Your *RoadMap™* can help explain and put all of these approaches into context—giving you confidence and perspective regardless of which tack your professor chooses to take.

Here's why. Your *RoadMap™* gives you a clear statement of the basic rules that most courts apply. It explains the reasons that support those rules and gives you lots of hypotheticals and exercises to test your mastery of the material. It will help you understand how courts deal with tort law problems. It will prepare you to discuss social and policy issues by explaining the main policy justifications that support the basic doctrines. Unfold your *RoadMap™*, and feel confident about your ability to find your way successfully through cases, classes, and exams.

Good luck, and please remember that this book is not intended to replace your casebook and assigned primary material, but rather to help you orient yourself in your study of Torts. Torts is an exciting field, full of train wrecks, car crashes, fisticuffs, and the like. Armed against mishap with your *RoadMap™*, you ought to be able to enjoy Torts even more.

Sincerely,

Arthur Best
Professor of Law

P.S. I'd welcome your suggestions for making the *RoadMap™* even more useful. Please write to me at Aspen Law & Business, Law School Division, One Liberty Square, 10th floor, Boston, MA 02109 or e-mail me at j.barmack@aspenpubl.com

Aspen Publishers, Inc. A Wolters Kluwer Company
1185 Avenue of the Americas, New York, NY 10036

Torts

Arthur Best

Professor of Law
University of Denver College of Law

ASPEN LAW & BUSINESS
A Division of Aspen Publishers, Inc.

Permissions
Aspen Law & Business
1185 Avenue of the Americas
New York, NY 10036

Printed in the United States of America

Library of Congress Cataloging-in-Publication Data

Best, Arthur.
Torts / Arthur Best.
p. cm.
Includes index.
ISBN 1-56706-487-6
1. Torts—United States. I. Title.
KF1250.B43 1997
346.7303—dc21

97-19844
CIP

ACKNOWLEDGMENTS

Thanks are due to Mark Russell for thoughtful and supportive editorial supervision. Also, I am grateful to Randy Lee for providing a thorough and creative critique of the entire manuscript. I appreciate having had the benefit of comments on smaller portions of the book by Alan Chen and Sheila Hyatt.

I am indebted, also, to Eli Best and Rachel Best for proofreading and other technical help, and to Lee Barrow, Jared Blank, Eli Kuhlmann, and David Rubin for the example they set of intellectual rigor and clarity in communication.

SUMMARY OF CONTENTS

CONTENTS

4 INTENTIONAL TORTS AGAINST PROPERTY 45

13 Defenses 211

18 Nuisance 297

19 MISREPRESENTATION 305

20 Defamation 315

Casebook Correlation

Aspen RoadMap	Epstein, **Cases and Materials on Torts** (6th ed. 1995)	Franklin, Rabin, **Tort Law and Alternatives** (6th ed. 1996)	Prosser, Wade, Schwartz, **Torts** (9th ed. 1994)	Robertson, Powers, Anderson, **Torts** (1989)
1. INTRODUCTION		1-21		
A. What is Tort Law?	3-4	1-2	1	
B. Goals of Tort Law			1-2	
C. Relationship of Tort Law to Other Fields				
D. Categories of Tort Causes of Action				
E. Historical Patterns in Tort Law Development			3-16	
F. Procedural Context		9-14		2-6
2. INTENTIONAL TORTS: BACKGROUND CONCEPTS				
A. Elements of Intention	8-9	802-811	17-20	7-8
B. Recurring Intent Issues	33-35		20-27	
C. Transferred Intent	9		27-29	
D. Distinction Between Intentional and Unintentional Conduct				
3. INTENTIONAL TORTS AGAINST PEOPLE				
A. Battery	4-31, 70-72	811-813	29-33	8-18
B. Assault	66-70	811-813	33-36	18-22
C. False Imprisonment	72-81	814-820	36-47	22-27
D. Infliction of Emotional Distress	82-91	820-835	47-62	28-36
4. INTENTIONAL TORTS AGAINST PROPERTY				
A. Trespass to Land	9-11	588-594	62-74	37-45
B. Conversion and Trespass to Chattels	11-12	1077-1078	74-89	45-48

Aspen RoadMap	Epstein, **Cases and Materials on Torts** (6th ed. 1995)	Franklin, Rabin, **Tort Law and Alternatives** (6th ed. 1996)	Prosser, Wade, Schwartz, **Torts** (9th ed. 1994)	Robertson, Powers, Anderson, **Torts** (1989)
5. DEFENSES TO INTENTIONAL TORT LIABILITY				
A. Introduction				49
B. Consent	12-31, 80-81	835-838, 843, 844	90-102	49-60
C. Defense of Human Beings	35-39	838-841, 844-845	102-106	60-63
D. Defense of Property	40-49	841-843, 845-846	106-111	63-67
E. Recapture of Property	50-53		112-117	67-70
F. Necessity	53-66	846-852	118-124	71-80
G. Arrest			124-125	
H. Discipline			125-127	
I. Justification			127-129	
J. Procedural Treatment of Consent and Privileges				
6. NEGLIGENCE				
A. Introduction	165-167	22-30	130-131	81-83
B. Basic Elements of Negligence			131-143	83-84
C. Standards of Care	167-250	31-48	143-199	84-110
D. Standards from Statutes (Negligence Per Se)	250-275	63-75	205-227	110-126
E. Standards from Judicial Precedents	275-291	48-58	200-205	
F. Inferred Negligence: Res Ipsa Loquitur	292-317	80-97	231-254	128-135
7. CAUSATION IN FACTS				
A. Basic Problem	467			
B. Categories of Analysis	467-468	293		136
C. Basic Cause in Fact Test	469-491	293-345	255-259	137-142
D. Proof of Cause in Fact			259-263	
E. Scientific Evidence	475-482	321-322	266-273	
F. Loss of a Chance	482-489		263-266	142-148
G. Increased Risk of Future Harm	488-490	311-319		
H. Difficulty in Identifying the Defendant	400-424	325-341	276-283	149-157, 527-534
I. Difficulty in Identifying the Plaintiff				

Aspen RoadMap	Epstein, **Cases and Materials on Torts** (6th ed. 1995)	Franklin, Rabin, **Tort Law and Alternatives** (6th ed. 1996)	Prosser, Wade, Schwartz, **Torts** (9th ed. 1994)	Robertson, Powers, Anderson, **Torts** (1989)
8. PROXIMATE CAUSE				
A. Basic Issue	491-542-543	345	284-285	163-168
B. Usually a Jury Question	491			175-176
C. Directness Test	491-501	352-353	295-297	168-174
D. Foreseeability Test	501-536	353-358, 366-378	297-312	174-194
E. Flexibility of the Foreseeability Approach	536-539	358		
F. Conventional Applications of Foreseeability Analysis	506-509, 539-542	348-350, 375-381	293-295, 314-315, 328-332	
G. Restatement Postion on Foreseeability		364	313, 318	
H. Intervening Events: General Rule	497-501	358	315-319	178, 191-192
I. Risk of Intervening Event Was Part of Definition of Defendant's Negligence		359	319-321	
J. Standard Intervening-Cause Situations	502-506	349-352	323-328, 333-342	581-612
K. Third-Party Criminal Conduct			321-323	
L. Third Person's Failure to Prevent Harm: Usually Not Superseding		360-364	342-343	
9. MULTIPLE PARTY CASES				
A. Issues in Multiple Party Cases	399-400			
B. Indivisible Injuries			347-353	
C. Varied Treatments of Joint and Several Liability	424-450	322-325	344-347	521-534
D. Contribution	435, 437-438	399-400	364-368	534-539
E. Doctrinal Restrictions on Contribution			368-369	
F. Amount of Contribution Permitted	441-447		369-370	
G. Settlements	447-450	400-401	353-364	539-580
H. Indemnity: General Rule		399-400	371	534-539
I. Indemnity and Comparative Fault			370-373	
J. Contractual and Judicially Imposed Indemnity			373-384	

Aspen RoadMap	Epstein, **Cases and Materials on Torts** (6th ed. 1995)	Franklin, Rabin, **Tort Law and Alternatives** (6th ed. 1996)	Prosser, Wade, Schwartz, **Torts** (9th ed. 1994)	Robertson, Powers, Anderson, **Torts** (1989)
10. DUTY AND LIMITED-DUTY RULES				
A. Function of Duty in Tort Law	559-560	116-140	385-386	161-168, 194-196
B. Court and Jury Roles				
C. Emotional Distress	542-558	226-257, 274-276	386-403	241-259
D. Failure to Act	561-578, 631-640		403-421	211-228
E. Mere Economic Loss		268-292	448-460	228-241
F. Preconception and Prenatal Injuries		257-268	421-436	259-274
G. Promises as a Basis for Tort Duties			436-437	196-211
H. Misfeasance as a Basis for Tort Duties	573	129-133	437-448	196-211
I. Tort Remedy for Contracting Party's Lack of Good Faith and Fair Dealing	602-619		1176-1189	
11. LAND OCCUPIERS' DUTIES				
A. Special Rules for Landowners and Land Occupiers				
B. Injuries Outside the Land			461-467	274-279
C. Injuries on the Land: Duty Related to Plaintiff's Status	578-601	165-168, 172-178	467-494	274, 280-289
D. Duty to Trespassers	578-585	168, 170-171	467-471, 482-486	289-294
E. Definition of Licensee	586	166	471	288
F. Duty to Licensee	585-598	168, 171	471-474	287-289
G. Definition of Invitee	586	166	475-489	287-288
H. Duty to Invitee	585-598	168, 169	474-482	287-289
I. Duty in Modern Two Category Jurisdictions				
J. Duty in Modern One Category Jurisdictions		172-179	489-492	
K. Summary of General Land Entrant Doctrines				
L. Landlords' Obligations to Tenants and Other Entrants	621-631	178-180	495-506	294-298

Aspen RoadMap	Epstein, **Cases and Materials on Torts** (6th ed. 1995)	Franklin, Rabin, **Tort Law and Alternatives** (6th ed. 1996)	Prosser, Wade, Schwartz, **Torts** (9th ed. 1994)	Robertson, Powers, Anderson, **Torts** (1989)
12. DAMAGES				
A. Fundamental Principles	863-864		507	299-301
B. Economic and Non-economic Damages Distinguished	870-871, 892-893	613-614, 623-627		
C. Categories of Damages	865-897	613-621	508, 512-518	
D. Calculating Past and Future Losses	871-874	621-623	508-518	302-309
E. Adjustments to the Jury's Damages Findings	875-914	627-628	514-515, 518-522	309-326
F. Plaintiff's Obligation to Mitigate Damages	712-713, 894-897	645-650	526-528	380-396
G. Periodic Payments			525	
H. Loss of Consortium	920-922	247-251, 397-398	523	326-337
I. Wrongful Death and Survival Actions	915-920	398, 632-645	546-565	326-337
J. Punitive Damages	922-928	650-667	530-545	338-355
K. Conditional New Trial Orders: Additur and Remittitur	890-891	628-629	518	306-308
13. DEFENSES				
A. Plaintiff's Negligent Conduct	320-348, 373-398	382-405	566-581	356-380
B. Assumption of Risk	354-373	405-430	581-598	397-414
C. Statutes of Limitations and Repose			599-604	415-429
D. Immunities	939-977	197-225	604-637	461-520
14. VICARIOUS LIABILITY				
A. General Definition		17		430-431
B. Main Instances of Vicarious Liability		17-18		
C. Rationale for Vicarious Liability	450-459	18-19		430-431
D. Respondeat Superior	450-458	90-97	638-645	431-442
E. Independent Contractors: Allocation of Responsibility for Their Torts	459-466	19-20	646-650	435-442
F. Joint Enterprises			651-655	
G. Vehicular Injuries and Vicarious Liability			658	449-457
H. Parental Liability for Children's Torts	353-354			442-448
I. Imputed Contributory Negligence	349-354	385-387	660-663	448-460

Aspen RoadMap	Epstein, **Cases and Materials on Torts** (6th ed. 1995)	Franklin, Rabin, **Tort Law and Alternatives** (6th ed. 1996)	Prosser, Wade, Schwartz, **Torts** (9th ed. 1994)	Robertson, Powers, Anderson, **Torts** (1989)
15. TRADITIONAL STRICT LIABILITY				
A. General Definition		431	664	613
B. Coverage of Strict Liability				
C. Distinguished from Negligence	114-163, 205-206			
D. Economic Analysis of Strict Liability	118-120	454-472		
E. Harms Caused by Animals	651-659		664-669	613-614
F. Injuries Caused by Abnormally Dangerous Activities	659-681	443-450	669-686	614-623
G. Causation			686-690	
H. Plaintiff's Negligence			690-693	
I. Plaintiff's Assumption of Risk		452		
16. PRODUCT LIABILITY				
A. Introduciton	727-730	473	694-695	624
B. Negligence	730-750	473-479	695-699	624-626
C. Warranty Liability	750-755	479-486	700-712	626-627
D. Strict Liability	755-862	586-587	713-809	628-688
17. WORKERS' COMPENSATION AND OTHER ALTERNATIVE COMPENSATION SYSTEMS	1013-1014		1190	
A. Workers' Compensation	1014-1047	726-753	1191-1197	
B. Automobile Injury Compensation Systems (No-fault Systems)	1048-1064	753-780	1197-1208	
C. Childhood Vaccine Injuries		783-784	1191	
18. NUISANCE				
A. Definitions			810-811	689
B. Private Nuisance: Elements	682-717	596-598	811-824	689-698
C. Coming to the Nuisance	700-706		836-838	
D. Remedies for Private Nuisance	706-717	598-612	824-838	
E. Public Nuisance: Elements	717-725	594-596	810-811	698-703
F. Nuisance and Trespass Distinguished	686-687	598		
G. Comparative Negligence Defense				

Aspen RoadMap	Epstein, **Cases and Materials on Torts** (6th ed. 1995)	Franklin, Rabin, **Tort Law and Alternatives** (6th ed. 1996)	Prosser, Wade, Schwartz, **Torts** (9th ed. 1994)	Robertson, Powers, Anderson, **Torts** (1989)
19. MISREPRESENTATION				
A. Introduction	1285-1286		1013-1015	797-798
B. Categories				
C. Intentional Misrepresentation	1286-1315	1119-1139	1015-1027	798-817, 831-848
D. Negligent Misrepresentation	1315-1328	1139-1140	1027-1062	817-831
E. Innocent Misrepresentation		1139	1062-1064	
20. DEFAMATION				
A. Introduction	1083-1085	876	842-844	
B. Common Law Defamation in Cases with No Public Attributes	1085-1169	876-928	844-875	704-727
C. Constitutional Requirements	1169-1214	929-997	875-933	727-758
21. INVASION OF PRIVACY				
A. Four Causes of Action	1222-1223	1028		
B. Appropriation	1223-1241	1092-1117	948-953	788-796
C. Public Disclosure of Private Facts	1241-1260	1028-1059	954-958	759-773
D. Unreasonable Intrusion	1268-1284	1069-1092	958-968	773-778
E. False Light in the Public Eye	1260-1268	1059-1069	968-979	778-787
22. MISUSE OF LEGAL PROCEDURE				
A. Causes of Action				
B. Malicious Prosecution			996-1003	887-906
C. Wrongful Institution of Civil Proceedings			1003-1011	
D. Abuse of Process			1011-1012	906-915
23. INTERFERENCE WITH ADVANTAGEOUS RELATIONS				
A. Interference with Contract	1330-1340	1140-1146, 1162-1164	1085-1121	849-876
B. Interference with Prospective Advantage	1341-1355	1146-1165	1085-1121	876-886
C. Injurious Falsehood	1380-1381	1156-1157	1073-1085	

CAPSULE SUMMARY

Bracketed page numbers refer to main outline.

1 INTRODUCTION

A. WHAT IS TORT LAW?

Tort law is a group of doctrines that establish and control causes of action for individuals who are harmed by the actions of others. **[p. 2]**

B. GOALS OF TORT LAW

Tort law resolves individual cases fairly. It also serves the goals of compensation, deterrence, and the defining of societal norms. **[p. 2]**

1. Compensation

The successful plaintiff in a tort action receives money from the defendant. **[p. 2]**

2. Deterrence

A defendant who is liable in tort must pay money to the plaintiff. To avoid this potential injurers may use care. **[p. 3]**

3. Definition of Societal Norms

Tort law doctrines represent and communicate a consensus about how people and institutions should act. **[p. 3]**

C. RELATIONSHIP OF TORT LAW TO OTHER FIELDS

1. Criminal Law

In criminal law the state imposes penalties on wrongdoers. A government employee, the prosecutor, decides when and how to litigate cases. **[p. 3]**

2. **Contract Law**

Contract law governs relationships between people who have agreed to act toward each other in ways they specify in their contracts. Tort cases do not usually involve prior agreements. **[p. 4]**

D. CATEGORIES OF TORT CAUSES OF ACTION

Tort law imposes liability for intentional misconduct, negligent conduct, or conduct for which responsibility is imposed without regard to the quality of the defendant's conduct. **[p. 4]**

1. **Types of Conduct Treated**

In an intentional tort case the plaintiff must show intentional conduct by the defendant. For negligence the plaintiff must show that the defendant's conduct fell short of a recognized standard of care. For strict liability harmful conduct is the basis for recovery regardless of whether the defendant acted intentionally, recklessly, or negligently. **[p. 4]**

2. **Consequences of Categorization**

a. **Statutes of limitations.** There may be different periods of time for different categories of tort suits. **[p. 5]**

b. **Range of consequences for which a defendant may be liable.** A defendant who was only negligent pays for fewer consequences than a defendant whose conduct was intentional or whose conduct was subject to strict liability. **[p. 5]**

c. **Types of damages.** In all torts cases plaintiffs are entitled to recover damages, called compensatory damages, for actual harm. In intentional torts cases plaintiffs are also entitled to nominal and punitive damages. Nominal damages are a token or symbolic sum of money awarded to a plaintiff who is unable to prove any actual damages. Punitive damages are money taken from the defendant and given to the plaintiff entirely to punish the defendant. **[p. 5]**

E. HISTORICAL PATTERNS

1. **Early Strict Liability**

Early common law held that if you directly touched or otherwise injured another person, you were liable for damages. This was strict liability called "trespass." **[p. 6]**

2. **Indirect Harm and Fault**

Another cause of action called "trespass on the case" developed for indirect harm caused by a defendant. It required the plaintiff to show that the defendant had been at fault. Fault meant that the defendant's conduct was blameworthy or substandard. **[p. 6]**

3. Direct Harm and Fault

Weaver v. Ward established that a defendant whose conduct had directly injured a plaintiff was protected from liability if the defendant could show that the injury had occurred "utterly without his fault." **[p. 7]**

4. Modern Strict Liability

Strict liability now applies for injuries caused by a defective product or for injuries resulting from a defendant's abnormally dangerous activity. **[p. 7]**

F. PROCEDURAL CONTEXT

To be entitled to judgment a plaintiff must provide evidence that can support a jury's conclusion that each element of the plaintiff's prima facie case is established. The defendant is entitled to judgment as a matter of law if the plaintiff's case fails to have that support for each element. **[p. 8]**

Two other procedural concepts are important: the burdens of production and persuasion. The burden of production is the obligation to produce evidence on an aspect of a claim. At the start of a trial, the plaintiff bears this burden. At the close of a case, if the jury is not persuaded by either side, then whichever party bears the persuasion burden (or the risk of nonpersuasion) loses the case. **[p. 9]**

2 INTENTIONAL TORTS: BACKGROUND CONCEPTS

A. ELEMENTS OF INTENTION

For every intentional tort the plaintiff must show that the defendant did some volitional act and intended certain consequences. **[p. 15]**

1. Volitional Act

The defendant must have moved in some way as a result of a conscious decision to movc. **[p. 16]**

2. Defendant's Mental State with Regard to Consequences of Volitional Act

The plaintiff must show that the defendant intended his or her action to have a consequence that tort law prohibits. The plaintiff can show that the defendant acted with: 1. willful purpose or 2. substantial certainty in regard to the consequence. **[p. 16]**

B. RECURRING INTENT ISSUES

The intent requirement can be satisfied even when a defendant did not mean to hurt the plaintiff, was not aware that the law forbids certain conduct, or was mentally ill. **[p. 17]**

C. TRANSFERRED INTENT

Transferred intent applies to five intentional torts: assault, battery, false imprisonment, trespass to land, and trespass to chattels. An actor's intent to commit any one of those intentional torts against a particular person is equivalent to an intent: 1. to commit the same tort against a different person; 2. to commit a different one of those five torts against the same person; or 3. to commit a different one of those five torts against a different person. **[p. 18]**

3 INTENTIONAL TORTS AGAINST PEOPLE

A. BATTERY

One commits a battery if one: 1. commits a volitional act; 2. with the intent to cause a contact with another person; and 3. causes such a contact either directly or indirectly; if 4. the contact is either harmful or offensive. **[p. 24]**

1. Intent

The plaintiff must show that the defendant committed a volitional act and intended that act to cause a contact with the plaintiff. Transferred intent doctrines apply to battery. **[p. 24]**

2. Touchings That Constitute Battery

To be a battery a touching has to cause physical harm or be contrary to a reasonable sense of dignity. **[p. 25]**

a. **Unconsented.** There are two types of consent to conduct that would otherwise be a battery: express consent and implied consent. Consent is implied for touchings people ordinarily expect in our society. To be a battery the contact must be outside the scope of generally accepted contacts. **[p. 25]**

b. **Objective standard for offensiveness.** An objective societal standard applies to the issue of whether a touching is offensive, **[p. 25]** unless

CAPSULE SUMMARY

the defendant knows or has reason to know that the plaintiff is specially sensitive. **[p. 25]**

c. **Touching something other than the plaintiff's body.** Touching the plaintiff's horse while the plaintiff is riding or touching something the plaintiff is holding can be equivalent to touching the plaintiff. **[p. 25]**

d. **Touching unknown to the plaintiff.** The Restatement provides that a person commits a battery by kissing a woman while she is asleep. **[p. 26]**

3. Unusual Results of a Defendant's Action

A defendant whose conduct supports liability for battery is liable for all the consequences of the act regardless of their foreseeability or the defendant's intent to cause them. **[p. 26]**

4. Damages

Battery plaintiffs can win actual (or compensatory), nominal damages, and punitive damages. **[p. 27]**

B. ASSAULT

Assault is an intentional tort. The phrase *assault and battery* confuses two separate torts, assault and battery. **[p. 27]** One commits an assault by: 1. committing a volitional act; 2. with intent to cause a person to expect an imminent battery; and 3. such apprehension results either directly or indirectly. This tort does not require proof that a touching happened. **[p. 27]**

1. Intent

a. **Intent to cause expectation of contact, not harm.** Intent to make the plaintiff expect an unpermitted touching is required, not intent to touch or harm the plaintiff. **[p. 27]**

b. **Jokes and friendly acts.** A joke or act of friendship can be an assault if it makes the plaintiff believe a harmful or offensive touching is about to happen. **[p. 28]**

c. **Transferred intent.** Transferred intent applies to assault. **[p. 28]**

2. Apprehension of Imminent Contact

The plaintiff must show that he or she had an apprehension of immediate contact. **[p. 29]** To be an assault a threat must convey the meaning that the defendant will commit a battery in the very near future. **[p. 29]** The traditional view requires the plaintiff to show that the defendant took an action in addition to speaking. Under the Restatement words alone may constitute an assault if the plaintiff reasonably anticipates an imminent harmful or offensive touching. **[p. 29]**

a. **Defendant's capability.** The plaintiff must reasonably believe that the defendant can carry out the threatened conduct. **[p. 29]**

b. **Plaintiff's awareness.** The plaintiff must be aware of the defendant's threat. **[p. 30]**

c. **Extortionate threat can be assault.** If a defendant makes a threat like "your money or your life," tort law treats it as a threat to kill and therefore as an assault. **[p. 30]**

d. **Terminated assault is assault.** If a defendant acts in a way that satisfies the definition of assault but then stops the act, the defendant has committed an assault. **[p. 30]**

e. **Expectation, not fear, is required for assault.** Apprehension of an imminent battery means expectation or belief, not fear. **[p. 30]**

3. Attempted Battery

Some attempted batteries satisfy the definition of assault, and some attempted batteries are not assaults. Conduct outside the definition of attempted battery also can be assault. **[p. 31]**

4. Damages

Assault plaintiffs can win actual (or compensatory) damages, nominal damages, and punitive damages. **[p. 31]**

C. FALSE IMPRISONMENT

One commits the tort of false imprisonment if one: 1. commits a volitional act; 2. with intent to confine a person within boundaries set by the actor; 3. the person is confined within those boundaries; and 4. the person is aware of his or her confinement. **[p. 32]**

1. Intent

The defendant must act with the intention of limiting someone's ability to leave a place. The transferred intent doctrine also applies. **[p. 32]**

2. Place of Imprisonment or Confinement

The plaintiff must be aware of genuine confinement in a defined place with no reasonable escape. **[p. 32]**

3. Method of Restraint

Many restraints can support a false imprisonment action, such as locking the plaintiff in a room, using threats, or denying access to a means of leaving a place. A request or a command unaccompanied by an explicit or implied threat does not constitute a restraint. **[p. 33]**

a. **Merchants and shoplifters.** Many statutes authorize merchants to impose reasonable restraints on persons suspected of shoplifting. **[p. 35]**

b. **Arrest.** Telling the plaintiff that he or she is under arrest can satisfy the restraint element of false imprisonment. **[p. 35]**

c. **Instigating arrest.** Instigating an improper arrest by police can render a defendant liable for false imprisonment. **[p. 35]**

4. Damages

False imprisonment plaintiffs can win actual (or compensatory), nominal, and punitive damages. **[p. 35]**

D. INFLICTION OF EMOTIONAL DISTRESS

A defendant commits the tort of infliction of emotional distress by: 1. intentionally or recklessly 2. doing something extreme and outrageous that 3. causes 4. the plaintiff to feel severe emotional or mental distress. **[p. 36]**

1. Recklessness

Reckless conduct is done with deliberate disregard of a high degree of probability that an injury will result. **[p. 36]**

2. Recovery By Plaintiffs Other Than the Defendant's Intended Victim

Transferred intent does not apply, but other rules produce similar results in certain situations.

a. **Presence of family member known to defendant.** In many states a defendant who commits an outrageous act against a member of the plaintiff's family is liable for emotional distress to the plaintiff if the defendant acts in the known presence of the plaintiff. **[p. 37]**

b. **Restatement positions.** Under the Restatement the defendant who commits an outrageous act against a relative of the plaintiff is liable for emotional distress to the plaintiff if the defendant acts in the known presence of the plaintiff. The Restatement also allows recovery by anyone who suffers bodily harm from observing the defendant's conduct. **[p. 37]**

c. **Emotional harms related to other intentional torts.** A defendant who is liable for assault, battery, or false imprisonment is liable for emotional harms those torts may cause. **[p. 38]**

3. Conduct Constituting Infliction of Emotional Distress

Conduct must be "extreme and outrageous," in the Restatement's terms, to constitute infliction of emotional distress. It must be "utterly intolerable in a civilized community." **[p. 38]**

a. **Policy issues related to mental effects.** Courts have been concerned that this tort might allow too many interpersonal interactions to become the subject of litigation and that it can be manipulated with perjured testimony. This has led some jurisdictions to impose requirements to deter illegitimate cases. **[p. 38]**

b. **Required evidence.** A plaintiff's claim of mental harm must be supported by evidence, usually proof of medical treatment. In some states the plaintiff must show physical harm like an ulcer or a rash. The Restatement does not require proof of physical consequences, but it suggests that a court may give greater emphasis to the requirement that the defendant's conduct be outrageous in cases where the plaintiff has no physical manifestations of the claimed distress. **[p. 39]**

c. **Reasonable, not idiosyncratic, reaction.** A defendant's conduct is outrageous only if it would cause serious distress to a typical community member. If a defendant knows about a plaintiff's unusual sensitivity, however, the defendant is subject to liability for acting in a way that causes the unusual harm the defendant knows the plaintiff might suffer. **[p. 39]**

d. **Effect of plaintiff's characteristics.** A plaintiff's status may affect his or her response to a defendant's actions. Examples include a defendant who in the role of school principal embarrasses a student and a defendant who, impersonating a police officer, frightens a plaintiff. Many cases involve efforts by debt collectors to upset debtors, although the straightforward presentation of a legal claim cannot be the basis for a tort claim. **[p. 39]**

4. Duty of Hotels, Common Carriers, and Public Utilities

If an employee of a hotel, common carrier, or a public utility directs a gross insult toward a patron, the employer is liable for any resultant emotional distress. The employee must act (in other ways) within the scope of employment for the hotel, common carrier, or public utility to be liable. **[p. 41]**

5. Damages

Intentional infliction of emotional distress plaintiffs can win actual (or compensatory), nominal, and punitive damages. **[p. 41]**

6. First Amendment Restrictions

The First Amendment restricts the right of "public figures" to recover for defamation. Similar restrictions apply to a public figure's effort to use intentional infliction of emotional distress doctrines to recover for harms caused by a publication. **[p. 41]**

4 INTENTIONAL TORTS AGAINST PROPERTY

A. TRESPASS TO LAND

One commits a trespass to land if one: 1. commits a volitional act; 2. with intent to cause a physical invasion of the plaintiff's land; and 3. causes such an invasion directly or indirectly. The presence of a person or an object is an invasion. The term *trespass* refers to a situation where a defendant causes an entry intentionally. **[p. 45]**

1. Intent: Common Law

Intent was not required at early common law. This was **strict liability**, where the plaintiff had no obligation to prove anything about the defendant's mental state or style of conduct. **[p. 46]** There was no trespass action, however, against a person who came to be on the plaintiff's land without committing any voluntary act.

2. Intent: Modern Requirement

At present the plaintiff must show that the defendant had some intent to make the entry, unless the claim is based on the consequences of a defendant's abnormally dangerous activity. **[p. 46]**

a. **Intent to cause harm not required.** The plaintiff need not show that the defendant meant to cause any harm or that the defendant knew he or she had no right to be on the plaintiff's land. **[p. 46]**

3. Types of Invasion

Trespass law deals with the presence of people or things on the plaintiff's property. The following invasions can constitute a trespass: human being on the land without permission; human being enters land with permission but stays after permission is revoked; object put on land by defendant; object put on land by defendant with permission but not removed after permission is revoked; blasting or other conduct that affects someone else's land through vibration or concussion (under modern doctrines, not at common law); defendant's actions put dust or gas on the plaintiff's land (some jurisdictions require accumulation, others recognize microscopic entry). **[p. 47]**

a. **Above the land's surface.** Common law treated a landowner as having possession from the depths to the sky. Now federal law preempts any action seeking damages for flights over land that conform to federal regulations. For other flights law of nuisance applies and the reasonableness of the defendant's conduct is examined. **[p. 49]**

b. **Below the land's surface.** Entry under a plaintiff's land is usually a trespass. **[p. 50]**

c. **Continuous entry.** Something placed on the plaintiff's land may be defined as a continuing trespass. The plaintiff is permitted to seek past and future damages in a single lawsuit or to sue only for past damages (with a chance to sue again if the defendant continues the trespass). **[p. 50]**

4. **Plaintiff Must Be Land Possessor**

The plaintiff in a trespass case must possess, not necessarily own, the land on which the defendant has allegedly trespassed. An owner who is not in possession of the land may not seek damages for trespass (but may sue for damage to the right of reversion). **[p. 50]**

a. **No trespass claim against wrongful possessor.** A wrongful possessor who has a plausible claim to ownership may not be sued for trespass by an allegedly rightful owner. **[p. 50]**

5. **Damages**

Trespass damages may be nominal or actual, but nominal damages are less available at present than at early common law. **[p. 50]** If a defendant's conduct causes unpredictable harms or affects individuals whose injury was unlikely, a defendant is ordinarily responsible for such remote or unforeseeable harms. **[p. 50]**

B. **CONVERSION AND TRESPASS TO CHATTELS**

One commits a trespass to a chattel when one: 1. commits a volitional act; 2. with the intent to cause an interference with the plaintiff's chattel; and 3. causes such an interference directly or indirectly. **[p. 51]** One commits a conversion when one: 1. commits a volitional act; 2. with the intent to cause an interference with the plaintiff's chattel; and 3. causes destruction of the chattel or serious interference with it directly or indirectly. **[p. 51]**

1. **Difference Between Trespass to Chattels and Conversion**

Trespass to chattels applies when the defendant's conduct imposes a minor interference with the plaintiff's possession or use of his or her property. Conversion applies when a defendant inflicts a significant harm to a plaintiff's interest in his or her property. **[p. 51]**

2. **Different Remedies**

For trespass to chattels the plaintiff is ordinarily entitled to compensation only for harm done to the thing. The remedy for conversion is a judgment for the market value of the item. Because conversion permits larger recoveries, it is a more important cause of action at present than trespass to chattels. **[p. 51]**

3. Intent

The defendant must act intentionally. Careless or negligent conduct is not a trespass or conversion. The intent must be to do something to the chattel, not necessarily to harm it or deprive the plaintiff of a right to it. **[p. 52]**

4. Characterization of Conduct as Trespass or Conversion

Factors used by courts to decide whether conduct is a trespass or a conversion include: amount of the defendant's control over or interference with the chattel; the defendant's intention to assert a right inconsistent with the plaintiff's right to control it; the defendant's good faith; harm to the thing; and the plaintiff's expense and inconvenience. **[p. 52]**

5. Damages

For trespass to a chattel the plaintiff is entitled to compensation for actual harm to the chattel or harm suffered from the brief deprivation of the use of it. There are no nominal damages. **[p. 52]** For conversion the plaintiff is entitled to the full value of the chattel. **[p. 53]**

a. **Return of the item.** In a trespass to chattels case a defendant's return of the item reduces damages. In conversion cases the defendant is not entitled to mitigation for returning the chattel (a minority view permits mitigation if the defendant acted in good faith, if the item suffered no damage, and if the plaintiff had no related additional damages). **[p. 53]**

6. Possible Plaintiffs

A plaintiff may be one who had possession, was about to have possession, or was entitled to future possession of a chattel. **[p. 53]**

a. **Liability to a person entitled to future possession.** Modern decisions and the Restatement allow recovery of the value of a plaintiff's future interest impaired by the defendant's conduct. **[p. 53]**

7. Methods of Committing a Trespass Against a Chattel

a. **Dispossession.** Dispossession includes taking a chattel, obtaining it by fraud or duress, blocking someone else from access to it, destroying it, or taking it into the custody of the law. **[p. 54]**

b. **Use or meddling.** Meddling is defined as intentionally causing a contact with something that belongs to the plaintiff. **[p. 54]**

8. Methods of Committing a Conversion

a. **Gaining possession.** Conversion can be done by stealing, using fraud, or using apparent legal authority to obtain possession of something. **[p. 54]**

i. **Belief in right to possession.** A defendant's belief in a right to the thing taken has no bearing on the definition of conversion. It may support a defense of privilege. **[p. 54]**

ii. **Bona fide purchasers.** A bona fide (good faith) purchase can be a conversion. **[p. 55]**

(a) **Restatement modification.** Under the Restatement a bona fide purchaser may reduce damages by returning the item. **[p. 55]**

(b) **Bona fide purchaser from fraudulent possessor.** A bona fide purchaser of something from a person who obtained it by fraud has no liability for conversion unless he or she fails to return it when requested to its rightful owner. **[p. 55]**

(c) **Bona fide purchasers of negotiable instruments.** A person who obtains a negotiable instrument in good faith is not treated as having committed a conversion. **[p. 55]**

b. **Destruction or alteration.** Conversion can be done by destroying or significantly altering a chattel. **[p. 55]**

c. **Use.** A defendant can commit a conversion by using something in a way that seriously violates another person's right to control its use or by using it in a way that exceeds permission granted by the owner. **[p. 55]**

i. **Proof of excessive use.** To establish excessive use the owner must show that the defendant refused a request for its return. **[p. 55]**

d. **Storing or transporting.** A person who agrees to keep or transport something is liable for conversion only if he or she has reason to know that a third person is entitled to immediate possession of the item. **[p. 56]**

e. **Agent or employee's possession.** An agent or employee who negotiates a transaction is liable for conversion if the transaction cannot transfer the ownership interest it purports to transfer. An agent or employee who accepts something without having negotiated about it is free from liability for conversion if he or she is reasonably unaware that the transferor cannot transfer it. **[p. 56]**

f. **Misdelivery by agent, employee, or bailee.** An unauthorized delivery by an agent, employee, or bailee is a conversion, unless it is a delivery to a rightful immediate possessor of the item. **[p. 57]**

5 DEFENSES TO INTENTIONAL TORT LIABILITY

A. EFFECT OF CONSENT AND PRIVILEGES

A defendant is protected from liability for an intentional tort by a plaintiff's consent or a defendant's privilege. **[p. 60]**

B. CONSENT

A plaintiff's consent can be express or implied.

1. Express Consent

Express consent is an oral or written agreement in which the plaintiff grants the defendant permission to do conduct that might harm the plaintiff. **[p. 60]**

2. Implied Consent

The law sometimes implies consent based on a reasonable evaluation of circumstances.

a. **Defendant's reasonable belief.** A defendant's reasonable belief that the plaintiff consented is a complete defense. It may be based on objective manifestations, customs, or the plaintiff's failure to object. **[p. 60]**

b. **Plaintiff's uncommunicated grant of permission.** An individual's expressed willingness for the defendant to act in a certain way is a defense even if the defendant did not know about it. **[p. 60]**

3. Consent Based on a Mistake

Consent based on a plaintiff's mistake is a valid defense, unless it was induced by the defendant in connection with a significant (noncollateral) topic. **[p. 61]**

4. Consent Under Duress

A plaintiff's consent has no effect if the defendant induced it by threatening immediate harm. **[p. 62]**

5. Consent to Criminal Acts

Consent to an illegal act is not a defense. The Restatement adopts a minority position that does recognize consent to illegal acts except where the conduct (such as statutory rape) is made illegal to protect vulnerable individuals. **[p. 62]**

6. People Incapable of Consenting

Consent is implied or allowed to be given by representatives in some cases involving minors, disabled people, or very sick people. **[p. 62]**

a. **Person in need of treatment.** Health care practitioners may treat a patient without actual consent if the patient is incapacitated, is in an emergency situation, has not shown unwillingness to consent, and a reasonable person in that situation would consent. **[p. 63]**

   i. **Parents and other relatives.** A court or the parents or close relatives of a minor or an incapacitated adult can consent to medical procedures on the person's behalf. **[p. 63]**

b. **Procedure to benefit another person.** Sometimes a medical procedure on a person incapable of giving consent could benefit another person. A court ordinarily requires that the incapacitated person receive a benefit from any procedure; courts differ on what constitutes such a benefit. **[p. 63]**

7. Scope of Consent

A consent is valid only for the acts it authorizes.

a. **Consent covers conduct regardless of the result.** Regardless of consequences consent is a valid defense if the defendant's conduct was the type of conduct to which the plaintiff agreed. **[p. 63]**

b. **Medical cases.** A plaintiff's consent to surgery covers that operation and treatment of emergency or related problems discovered during the surgery. **[p. 64]**

   i. **Operation on different part of body.** If a patient consents to an operation on a particular part of the body, an operation on some significantly different part of the body is outside the scope of the consent. **[p. 64]**

   ii. **Misrepresentation.** Consent based on false information from a physician is not a defense. **[p. 64]**

   iii. **Informed consent.** For significant medical procedures physicians must obtain informed consent, giving the patient adequate information about the proposed treatment. Most courts use a negligence analysis to evaluate these disclosures. **[p. 64]**

c. **Professional athletes.** Consent rules can apply to professional sports. A professional football player can obtain intentional tort damages from an opposing player who intentionally hits him in a way that is clearly outside the rules of the game. **[p. 64]**

C. DEFENSE OF HUMAN BEINGS

Self-defense or the defense of others can justify conduct that might otherwise support liability for an intentional tort. **[p. 65]**

1. Self-Defense

A person may use force against another person reasonably believed to be committing or about to commit an intentional tort against him or her. The self-defender must establish that circumstances justified the use of force and that the amount of force was reasonable. **[p. 65]**

2. Defense of Others

A person may use force to counter an attack on someone else if that force would be permitted in response to the same attack directed against him or her. **[p. 65]**

3. Circumstances Justifying Use of Force

The privilege has limits based on the idea that everyone's physical safety is valuable. **[p. 65]**

a. **Reasonable belief that force is necessary.** A person may use force based on a reasonable belief that the other person is about to harm or is harming him or her. **[p. 65]** For mistakes connected to an actor's defense of someone else, the majority rule rejects privilege if the actor is mistaken about whether that individual is really being threatened. A minority and the Restatement apply the privilege if there is a reasonable belief that the third person is being threatened. **[p. 66]**

4. Future Harm

Self-defense is not allowed to stop future (nonimminent) harm. **[p. 66]**

5. Amount of Force Allowed

Self-defense force must be roughly equal to or less than the force it resists. **[p. 67]**

a. **Punishment.** Self-defense does not allow force to punish someone for a past wrong. **[p. 67]**

b. **No physical response to threatening words.** Force is not usually allowed in response to threatening words. **[p. 67]**

c. **Helpless attacker.** Force may not be used against an attacker who has stopped attacking or has become helpless. **[p. 67]**

d. **Deadly force.** Deadly force is usually allowed only to defend against threats of death or serious bodily harm (including a sexual assault). **[p. 67]**

i. **Retreat.** The traditional view was that no retreat was necessary prior to a threatened person's use of deadly force to meet deadly force. Under an alternative view, outside his or her home an individual must use an available safe retreat instead of deadly force to meet deadly force. Under the Restatement: outside one's home deadly force is not privileged if a safe retreat is available; inside one's home deadly force against someone else who lives there is not privileged if retreat is available; and inside one's home deadly force against someone who does not live there is privileged whether or not retreat is available. **[p. 67]**

ii. **Antifelony privilege.** A privilege to use deadly force to stop a felony does not require retreat. It applies whether or not the one using force is personally in danger of physical harm. **[p. 68]**

6. Harm To Third Parties

A third person who suffers an injury from a self-defender's negligent action can recover damages. **[p. 68]**

D. DEFENSE OF PROPERTY

Individuals may use reasonable nondeadly force to defend property. A separate privilege covers the use of force to prevent a felony. This antifelony privilege has traditionally allowed the use of deadly force. **[p. 69]**

1. Mistake About Right to Use Force

There is no privilege to defend property against a person privileged to use it. A defender of property mistaken in this context is liable for any harm inflicted. **[p. 69]**

2. Mistake About Amount of Force

A reasonable error about the amount of force appropriate in a situation where some force is permissible allows the operation of the privilege. **[p. 69]**

3. Type of Force

Only reasonable force may be used. If mere words might be effective, a person is obligated to try that method first. Warnings are often required for dangerous methods of protection, such as barbed wire, unless a warning would be superfluous due to local customs. Deadly force is never allowed just to protect property but may be legitimized by a privilege to stop a felony or protect life. **[p. 70]**

a. **Nonhuman force.** If guard dogs, mechanical devices, or barriers harm an intruder, the property owner is liable for that harm unless he or she would have been privileged to inflict the same harm in person. **[p. 70]**

CAPSULE SUMMARY

i. **Warnings.** The privilege to use nondeadly devices is subject usually to a requirement of a warning, but a warning is not prerequisite to the privilege to use deadly force. **[p. 70]**

E. RECAPTURE OF PROPERTY

A property owner has a fresh-pursuit right to act quickly with reasonable force to regain possession of property wrongfully taken. **[p. 71]**

1. Amount of Force

Reasonable force is allowed for the recapture of property, but deadly force is never justified. **[p. 72]**

2. Entry on Another's Land

A property owner may enter another's land to recapture property. The entry must be reasonable with respect to time and type. **[p. 72]**

a. **Landowner not responsible for the presence of item on land.** The item's owner is privileged to enter the land to recapture it but must pay for any damage caused to the land. **[p. 72]**

b. **Item owner responsible for presence of item on landowner's land.** If the item is on someone's land due to the fault of the owner of the item, there is no privilege to enter that land to recapture it. **[p. 72]**

3. Wrongful or Fraudulent Possession

The recapture privilege applies only to property that a person has taken wrongfully (as by theft or fraud). **[p. 72]**

4. Mistake

Mistakes about whether the target of a recapture attempt possesses the recapturer's goods and about the appropriate amount of force both destroy the privilege. **[p. 72]**

5. Storekeepers

Storekeepers in many jurisdictions are privileged to detain briefly persons reasonably suspected of shoplifting. **[p. 73]**

a. **Limitations on merchant's privilege.** The privilege does not allow detention for coercing payment, arresting the suspected thief, or extracting a confession. **[p. 73]**

b. **Privilege in store or beyond store.** Some jurisdictions apply the privilege only to conduct within the stores' premises. **[p. 73]**

6. Real Estate

At common law an owner could use reasonable force to eject a former tenant wrongfully in possession of land. Most states now prohibit this. **[p. 73]**

F. NECESSITY

Use of another's property is privileged when it protects an individual or society from a harm greater than that inflicted on the person's property. This is called "public necessity" when the actor is the government and "necessity" when the actor is an individual. **[p. 74]**

1. Compensation

An individual who uses another person's property must pay damages for any harm caused. The government has no parallel obligation under the public necessity privilege. **[p. 74]**

a. **Statutes.** Some state statutes require payment in public necessity cases. **[p. 74]**

2. Rules for Private Necessity

The privilege is available only when the danger an actor seeks to avoid is greater than the risk the actor imposes on the stranger's property. The privilege claimant must pay for any harm he or she inflicts. **[p. 75]**

G. ARREST

The common-law arrest privilege is the most important instance of privilege for acting under authority of law. Statutes replace or supplement its doctrines in most places. **[p. 75]**

1. Warrant

Under common law an arrest warrant with no obvious flaws justifies an arrest. **[p. 75]**

a. **Arrest of wrong person.** Mistaken identity, even if reasonable, eliminates the privilege. **[p. 75]**

b. **Trespass *ab initio*.** The trespass *ab initio* doctrine provides that an error in any part of the arrest process voids the arrest privilege for all parts of the arrest. **[p. 76]**

2. Absence of a Warrant

Arrest without a warrant may be privileged. **[p. 76]**

a. **Present for imminent felony.** Anyone may arrest a person who has committed a felony or is about to commit a felony in his or her presence. **[p. 76]**

b. **Past felony.** An officer may arrest someone in connection with a past felony, if the officer reasonably believes it did occur and the person arrested committed it. **[p. 76]**

3. **Force**

Only reasonable force is justified by the arrest privilege. **[p. 76]**

a. **Stopping a felony.** Deadly force is permitted where a felony threatens death or serious injury. **[p. 76]**

b. **Arrest for past felony.** Deadly force is allowed only if the target of the arrest presents a significant threat of death or serious physical injury to others. **[p. 76]**

H. DISCIPLINE

A person in authority over another has a privilege to use force for discipline. This force must be appropriate. **[p. 77]**

I. JUSTIFICATION

Where imposing liability for an intentional tort seems highly inappropriate, a court may refer to justification as an overriding privilege. **[p. 77]**

J. PROCEDURAL TREATMENT OF CONSENT AND PRIVILEGES

An intentional tort defendant is responsible for pleading privilege and supporting it with proof. For intentional torts other than trespass to land, the plaintiff is required to plead and prove the absence of consent. **[p. 77]**

6 NEGLIGENCE

A. NEGLIGENCE: INTRODUCTION

Negligent conduct is conduct less careful than an applicable standard of care requires. It is not an intentional tort, so proof of the defendant's intent is not required. **[p. 82]**

B. BASIC ELEMENTS

The elements of negligence are: duty, breach, causation, and damages.

1. **Duty**

The plaintiff must show that the defendant owed the plaintiff a duty to act or refrain from acting in a certain way. **[p. 82]**

2. **Breach**

The plaintiff must show that the defendant breached a duty by failing to conform to the required quality of care. **[p. 83]**

3. Causation

The plaintiff must show that the defendant's conduct caused an injury to the plaintiff in terms of cause in fact and proximate cause. **[p. 83]**

4. Damages

The plaintiff must show actual damages and may sometimes be entitled to punitive damages **[p. 84]**

C. STANDARDS OF CARE

The trier of fact must compare the defendant's actual conduct to a standard of care that defines how the defendant should have acted. **[p. 84]**

1. Reasonable Prudent Person

The usual standard is the reasonable prudent person. **[p. 84]**

a. **Objective test.** The standard of comparison is objective: the conduct of a hypothetical typically reasonable person. **[p. 84]**

   i. **Easy to apply.** The test is easier to apply than one that requires estimating each actor's own particular level of skill. **[p. 84]**

b. **Knowledge.** The reasonable prudent person is assumed to have knowledge typical of people in the community. **[p. 85]** Some courts and the Restatement require a person additionally to use any superior qualities or knowledge he or she possesses. **[p. 85]**

c. **Physical disabilities.** For a person with a physical disability, the jury applies the standard of care of a reasonable prudent person with that person's disability. **[p. 86]**

d. **Mental illness.** A person with a mental illness is required to act as reasonably as a person with ordinary mental health. **[p. 86]**

e. **Low intelligence.** Traditional common law denies any special standard to people with mental disabilities or mental weakness. This differs from the treatment of physical disabilities. Many factors may support the result. Degrees of mental power are difficult to identify, so it would be hard for a judge to know when to replace the usual reasonable prudent person test with a special test dealing with mental weakness. Also, jurors may be unfamiliar with different degrees of mental weakness. Finally, using the reasonable prudent person standard may encourage those who can influence the conduct of the mentally weak person to have that person avoid activities that risk injuries to others. **[p. 86]**

f. **Intoxication.** A person who is intoxicated is expected to act as well as a person who is sober. **[p. 87]**

g. **Custom.** Proof that a defendant's conduct complied with general customs for that activity is always relevant. It is a complete defense in professional standard cases. In other cases compliance with an industry custom is not necessarily a defense. **[p. 88]**

h. **Emergencies.** Some jurisdictions allow a sudden-emergency instruction, emphasizing to jurors that people in emergency situations may not act less carefully than in normal situations. A defendant who created an emergency situation cannot rely on that situation as a basis for a sudden-emergency instruction. **[p. 88]**

i. **Learned Hand test: *United States v. Carroll Towing Co.*** Judge Learned Hand suggested an algebraic formula to determine how a reasonable prudent person should act. He called precautions or carefulness a "burden," and treated anticipated losses with two concepts: expected cost of an injury ("loss") and likelihood of the loss happening ("probability"). His formula multiplies the loss times the probability to calculate the likely cost of injuries that conduct might cause. He defined negligence as acting without a precaution if the burden would have been less than the expected loss. He expressed this as $B < PL$. **[p. 89]**

   i. **Theoretical only.** The test is never used explicitly by juries, but appellate courts may use it to decide whether a jury's finding about negligence was adequately supported. Courts recognize that the test is not precise because it involves guesses about probabilities. **[p. 89]**

2. **Child Standard**

A child's conduct is evaluated under the standard of what a child of similar age, experience, and intelligence would have done. **[p. 89]**

a. **Rationale.** This doctrine developed in part to moderate the effects of contributory negligence in cases with child plaintiffs. Other ideas also support the standard. Encouraging children to be active helps their development. The injuries children may inflict are likely to be small. Judges are able to decide easily whether a particular person's conduct should be judged by the standard, since ages are easy to determine. Jurors are likely to apply the standard well, since all people have experience with children. **[p. 90]**

b. **Age limits.** The child's standard of care applies to people younger than the age of majority. **[p. 90]**

c. **No application to adult activities.** The child's standard does not apply if the child is doing something primarily performed by adults or requiring special skill or training, such as driving a motor vehicle. **[p. 90]**

CAPSULE SUMMARY

3. Professional Standard

The professional standard of care replaces the reasonable prudent person standard for evaluating the conduct of a professional person such as a doctor or a lawyer. If the professional acts in conformity with typical professional performance, he or she is free from negligence. If his or her conduct does not conform with what typical professionals would do, then it is negligent. **[p. 91]**

a. **Professions covered.** The professional standard of care always applies to doctors and lawyers. Factors such as the degree of independence in the work, the need for specialized knowledge, and whether organizations within the field seek to maintain high standards control whether it is applied to other occupations. **[p. 92]**

b. **Expert testimony.** A court usually requires expert testimony to enable the jury to determine the standard as a factual inquiry. **[p. 92]**

   i. **Lay knowledge exception.** For a claimed error within common knowledge, no expert testimony is required. **[p. 92]**

c. **National or locality standard.** The locality rule requires expert testimony showing the practice for professionals in the defendant's precise locality. Many jurisdictions have liberalized the rule. **[p. 93]**

   i. **Broad locality.** Some states broaden the definition of "locality" from the actual community in which the professional works to the same or similar community. **[p. 93]**

   ii. **National standard.** Some jurisdictions require all medical personnel to conform to a national standard. **[p. 93]**

   iii. **Standard related to type of practice.** Some jurisdictions apply a national standard to specialists and a locality standard for general practitioners. **[p. 93]**

   iv. **Local circumstances.** In applying a national standard a jurisdiction considers local circumstances. **[p. 93]**

d. **Informed consent.** Physicians must obtain informed consent from patients before treating them. Patients must be told about risks and alternatives. **[p. 94]**

   i. **Professional or lay standard.** A physician might fail to describe a risk because of not knowing about it or because of believing it is not necessary to tell the patient about it. Most jurisdictions apply a professional standard of care to both circumstances. A minority view applies the professional standard to whether the doctor's knowledge was adequate and applies a lay standard to whether the doctor's choice about what to tell the patient was appropriate. **[p. 94]**

ii. **Causation in informed consent.** The plaintiff must establish that with better information he or she would not have undergone the procedure that caused injury. Most jurisdictions use objective tests for this, while some allow plaintiffs to show what they personally would have done with fuller information. **[p. 94]**

D. STANDARDS FROM STATUTES (NEGLIGENCE PER SE)

When an actor's conduct violates a safety statute, usually the statute is used to define the standard of care. Violation of the statute is called negligence per se. Conduct in violation of the statute is defined as negligent regardless of how reasonable it might seem to the jury. **[p. 95]**

1. Majority Rule

The plaintiff must establish that the injury suffered is of the type the statute was adopted to prevent and that the plaintiff is a member of the class the legislature intended to protect. **[p. 95]**

2. Minority Rules

One minority rule treats statutory violations as only evidence of negligence. In some other jurisdictions, plaintiffs who introduce evidence showing statutory violation are entitled to presumptions that the defendants were negligent. **[p. 96]**

3. Types of Statutes

Violation-of-statute doctrines always apply when defendants have violated state statutes. Violations of local statutes and ordinances are usually treated only as evidence of negligence. **[p. 96]**

4. Statutory Purpose Inquiry

Ignoring a statutory violation unless the kind of injury the plaintiff suffered is the kind of injury the legislature meant to avert and the plaintiff is the type of person the legislature meant to benefit is consistent with the basic theory of the negligence per se doctrine. The doctrine relies on the legislature's judgment about how people should act. If the legislature has not considered a situation like the one in which the plaintiff is injured, there is no legislative "wisdom" available for the tort litigation. **[p. 96]**

5. Causation

The negligence per se doctrine characterizes the defendant's conduct as negligent. The plaintiff must also establish causation. **[p. 97]**

6. **Excused Violations**

No excuses are permitted for violation of a statute meant to protect specially weak classes of individuals or to protect all people from particularly significant dangers. For other violations there are two methods of treating a claim of excuse. **[p. 98]**

a. **Excuse as evidence.** An excuse may be considered by the jury along with the evidence of statutory violation. The Restatement takes this position. **[p. 98]**

b. **Presumption.** Another approach applies a presumption that a defendant who violated an applicable statute was negligent. **[p. 98]**

c. **Types of excuses.** Jurisdictions following the Restatement recognize only excuses that fit certain general categories: reasonable ignorance, reasonable attempt to obey the statute, emergency not the fault or responsibility of the defendant, greater risk would be incurred by obeying the statute than by disobeying it. **[p. 98]**

E. STANDARDS FROM PRECEDENTS

Courts sometimes attempt to develop precedents requiring particular behavior in specific situations. In *Baltimore & Ohio v. Goodman* Justice Holmes sought to establish "stop, look, and get out to see better if necessary" as a requirement at railroad crossings. Seven years later the United States Supreme Court essentially rejected that effort in *Pokora v. Wabash Ry. Co.* **[p. 99]**

F. INFERRED NEGLIGENCE: *RES IPSA LOQUITUR*

The *res ipsa loquitur* doctrine prevents a defendant from winning dismissal of the plaintiff's claim on the ground that the plaintiff does not have adequate evidence to support a finding in the plaintiff's favor. **[p. 99]**

1. ***Byrne v. Boadle:* The Original Example**

In *Byrne v. Boadle* a barrel came out of a second-story window and hit the plaintiff as he walked past the window. The court stated that the accident "speaks for itself." **[p. 100]**

2. **Elements of *Res Ipsa Loquitur***

a. **Incident usually involves negligence.** The plaintiff must show that the type of event that hurt the plaintiff usually occurs due to negligence. **[p. 100]**

b. **Defendant's exclusive control or likely responsibility.** Traditionally the plaintiff had to show that the instrumentality that caused the plaintiff's injury was under the control of the defendant at that time. Modern courts apply this element with some flexibility. **[p. 100]**

c. **Plaintiff's freedom from responsibility.** Many courts require plaintiffs to show freedom from responsibility for their injuries. This requirement is weakened by the nearly universal adoption of comparative negligence, which permits recovery by negligent plaintiffs. In some states the plaintiff's-freedom-from-responsibility element is only an aspect of the need to show a high likelihood that the defendant caused the plaintiff's injury. **[p. 101]**

d. **Plaintiff's ignorance of defendant's actual conduct.** A minority of courts require that plaintiffs have no information about the details of the defendants' conduct. **[p. 101]**

3. **Specific Proof of Defendant's Negligent Acts**

If plaintiffs who seek the *res ipsa loquitur* inference also introduce some proof that provides details about the defendants' actions, some courts refuse to apply the doctrine. Others hold that the introduction of specific evidence can be consistent with the idea that the types of injuries the plaintiffs suffered usually are caused by negligence. They do not withdraw the doctrine. **[p. 102]**

4. **Multiple-Defendant Cases**

Where there are multiple defendants, the plaintiff cannot show that one defendant caused the injury. In many cases this deprives the plaintiffs of access to the *res ipsa loquitur* doctrine. A minority approach applies the doctrine but offers each defendant an opportunity to avoid liability. **[p. 102]**

5. **Procedural Effect of *Res Ipsa Loquitur***

The *res ipsa loquitur* doctrine protects the plaintiff from a defendant's motion for directed verdict on the basis of inadequate evidence of negligence. Under a minority view it entitles a plaintiff to judgment as a matter of law unless the defendant introduces evidence to rebut a finding of negligence. Under another view it shifts the burden of persuasion to the defendant. **[p. 103]**

7 CAUSATION IN FACT

A. INTRODUCTION

Causation involves separate analyses of cause in fact and legal cause. **[p. 109]**

B. CATEGORIES OF ANALYSIS

Cause in fact asks the historical question: Was the defendant's conduct a cause of the plaintiff's injury? Legal cause (also called "proximate cause") makes a second inquiry: Is there a reason to protect the defendant from having to pay for the plaintiff's injury? **[p. 110]**

C. BASIC CAUSE IN FACT TEST

The test for cause in fact is usually the but for test. The test asks whether the defendant's conduct was essential in the sequence of events that caused the plaintiff's injury. The jury decides whether the plaintiff would have been all right except for the fact that the defendant did what he or she did. **[p. 110]**

1. Not Completely Factual

The test compares what the trier of fact believes really happened with what it believes would have happened if the defendant's conduct had been different. A defendant's conduct can be a cause in fact of the plaintiff's injury even if there is a chance that the injury would have happened in the absence of the defendant's conduct, since the plaintiff is required to prove the but for test only by a preponderance of the evidence. **[p. 111]**

2. Substantial Factor Test: Twin Fires and Other Concurrent Causes

A substantial factor test usually applies where the but for test produces an unsatisfactory answer. Primarily these are cases where two events combine to produce an injury. The classic example involves two fires started by different people merging just prior to burning the plaintiff's property. Applying the but for test to either fire, a jury would conclude that it was not a cause in fact of the plaintiff's loss, since the loss would have occurred even without that fire. The substantial factor test asks whether an event that happened to coincide with another event was a substantial factor in causing the plaintiff's injury. **[p. 112]**

D. PROOF OF CAUSE IN FACT

Cause in fact can be established with eyewitness testimony or with circumstantial evidence. **[p. 112]**

E. SCIENTIFIC EVIDENCE

Expert testimony can provide an adequate basis for a finding of cause in fact.

1. Physician's Expert Testimony

Physicians may testify about the cause of an injury. **[p. 113]**

2. Experiments and Scientific Analyses

When a party seeks to introduce scientific evidence, particularly if it is based on experiments or scientific analyses, a court applies either the *Frye* test or the *Daubert* test. Under *Frye* the plaintiff must show that the methodology on which the scientific evidence is based has received general acceptance in some relevant scientific community. Under *Daubert* the proponent must establish that the evidence meets scientific standards, such as peer review, publication, general acceptance in a scientific community, and the replicability of the results. **[p. 113]**

F. LOSS OF A CHANCE

In loss-of-a-chance cases the plaintiff claims that the defendant's conduct caused a decedent to lose a chance of survival. **[p. 114]**

1. Traditional Treatment

Under traditional doctrines, to permit recovery testimony must show that the defendant's conduct more likely than not caused the death. If the victim had less than a 50-percent chance of survival, testimony cannot show that more likely than not the defendant's conduct caused the death. **[p. 115]**

2. Proportional Recovery

Some states avoid this causation problem by seeking to determine the cause of a lost chance of survival instead of a death. If testimony supports a finding that the defendant's conduct more likely than not deprived the decedent of a chance of survival, recovery is allowed for the value of that lost chance. Recovery is reduced in proportion to the amount of chance the plaintiff lost. Standard wrongful death damages are multiplied by the percentage of the lost chance. **[p. 115]**

G. INCREASED RISK OF FUTURE HARM

Conduct that allegedly has given the plaintiff an increased risk of some future adverse consequence also involves causation problems. **[p. 116]**

1. Traditional Treatment

If proof shows that future harms are more likely than not to occur, the majority of jurisdictions permit full recovery for them. If evidence shows only that there is a less-than-50-percent chance of the consequence occurring, the majority of jurisdictions deny all recovery. **[p. 116]**

a. **Precautionary future medical expenses.** Most courts allow recovery for medical monitoring that is reasonable due to a chance of future medical complications. **[p. 116]**

2. Proportional Recovery

A few jurisdictions allow proportional recovery if the plaintiffs' evidence shows by a preponderance that the likelihood of the future harm's occurrence is less than 50 percent. The court multiplies the standard damages that would be awarded if the future consequence were more likely than not to occur by the percentage of likelihood established by the proof. **[p. 116]**

3. Full Application of Proportional Recovery

A jurisdiction that applies proportional recovery to predicted future consequences when the plaintiff's evidence shows that the odds of their occurrence are 50 percent or less might logically apply proportional calculations to injuries with odds of future occurrence that are greater than 50 percent. **[p. 117]**

H. DIFFICULTY IN IDENTIFYING THE DEFENDANT

In some unusual cases a plaintiff who is unable to identify the defendant that caused a harm is allowed to sue a group of defendants on the theory that at least one of them caused the injury. **[p. 117]**

1. Double Fault and Alternative Liability

In *Summers v. Tice* the plaintiff was allowed to obtain a judgment against two hunters who both had shot in his direction, even though there was no way to prove which one had hit him. Each defendant had contributed to a circumstance that deprived the plaintiff of the ability to identify the hunter whose shot had hit him. The court decided that the defendants should appropriately suffer the consequences of that lack of information, rather than the blameless plaintiff. **[p. 117]**

2. DES and Market Share Liability

In cases involving injuries from the drug DES, some courts use market-share theories to compensate injured plaintiffs. A victim is permitted to recover damages from any company that manufactured the drug in proportion to its past share of the market for the drug. **[p. 117]**

a. **Individual liability.** Courts applying the market-share theory tend to impose individual (or several) liability, with each defendant responsible for a share of damages equal to its percentage of market share. **[p. 118]**

b. **Exculpatory evidence.** If a defendant can show that it did not produce the pills the plaintiff's mother used, that defendant is free from liability in all jurisdictions except New York. **[p. 118]**

c. **Narrow applicability of market share theory.** Plaintiffs seeking to use the market-share theory in cases involving injuries other than DES-related injuries have faced significant resistance. **[p. 119]**

8 PROXIMATE CAUSE

A. BASIC ISSUE

Every jurisdiction requires the plaintiff to satisfy a proximate cause (or legal cause) requirement. **[p. 123]**

B. USUALLY A JURY QUESTION

The issue of proximate cause is usually a question for the jury under instruction reflecting the jurisdiction's proximate cause doctrines. The issue can be decided by the court when it is so clear that only one decision is supportable. **[p. 124]**

C. DIRECTNESS TEST

The directness test is one main approach to proximate cause. Conduct is a proximate cause of an injury if the injury followed directly from the defendant's conduct. An injury is not a direct result of conduct where a superseding cause occurs between the conduct and the injury.

1. Example: Risk a Dent, Pay for a Fire

The *Polemis* case illustrates the directness method. The defendant's employee carelessly dropped a plank into a ship's hold. In a way that no one could have predicted, that caused a spark that ignited inflammable vapors. The ship was destroyed. The court reasoned that conduct which risked some harm of one type should logically be a basis for liability when the same conduct caused some harm of a different type. **[p. 124]**

2. Natural and Probable Consequence Test

In many jurisdictions defendants' conduct is a proximate cause of any results that are natural and probable consequences of the conduct. **[p. 125]**

3. Policy Analysis of Directness Test

Opponents argue that it does not allow any reasonable limit on the scope of a defendant's liability. Supporters argue that it is a fair response to a situation involving a blameworthy defendant and a blameless plaintiff who has suffered an unexpected loss. It may also be true that many defendants whose conduct causes a lot of consequences are large enterprises with ability to spread the loss. **[p. 125]**

D. FORESEEABILITY TEST

Under the foreseeability test a defendant is responsible for all the foreseeable consequences of his or her actions. Scope-of-the-risk analysis is another version of the general foreseeability test. A defendant is responsible for consequences that involve the type of risk that is the basis for characterizing the defendant's conduct as negligent **[p. 126]**

1. Example: Risk a Smudge, Cause a Fire for Free

A leading case for the foreseeability test is *Wagon Mound No. 1.* The defendant was negligent to spill oil in the harbor because that risked smudging or fouling equipment used there. Unexpectedly the oil caught fire and burned the plaintiff's dock. The appellate court held that it would be wrong to make the defendant pay for fire damage, since (on the facts as proved in the case) no one would have anticipated a fire from the spill. **[p. 126]**

2. *Palsgraf* and the Unforeseeable Plaintiff

Palsgraf involved the unforeseeability of a plaintiff. The defendant railroad's employees jostled a passenger they were trying to push onto a train, causing a package he was carrying to fall to the platform floor. The package exploded, and the plaintiff was injured at a distant point on the station platform when a scale fell on her. **[p. 126]**

a. ***Palsgraf* majority.** Judge Cardozo held that there could be no liability since the defendant railroad owed no duty to a person unless its employees could have foreseen that their conduct might injure that person. **[p. 126]**

b. ***Palsgraf* dissent.** Judge Andrews argued that once a defendant has been negligent, the legal system should hold that person responsible for most of the consequences of that negligence. He recommended a foreseeability inquiry that assumes the immediate results of the negligence and then examines whether any further consequences should be the defendant's responsibility. **[p. 127]**

c. **Contemporary understanding of *Palsgraf*.** The majority's reasoning, although expressed in terms of duty, is consistent with the usual foreseeability approach to proximate cause. The dissent's reasoning is consistent with the direct causation approach, although it limits that approach with considerations of foreseeability and other factors. **[p. 127]**

E. FLEXIBILITY OF THE FORESEEABILITY APPROACH

The foreseeability approach compares characterizations of what the defendant risked and what the plaintiff suffered. If the characterizations are phrased very generally, they will seem similar and the foreseeability test will be satisfied. If either one is made highly specific, there will probably be a discrepancy between the descriptions of what the defendant risked and what the plaintiff suffered, and the foreseeability test will produce a finding of no proximate cause. **[p. 127]**

1. Very Slight Foreseeability

The Wagon Mound incident led to another trial with a different plaintiff. The evidence showed that there was very small foreseeability of fire risk from the spilled furnace oil. Liability was approved since a small risk of fire, while perhaps not severe enough to have made the spilling of the oil negligent, was nonetheless a fact that justified imposing liability for fire losses on the oil spiller. **[p. 129]**

F. CONVENTIONAL APPLICATIONS OF FORESEEABILITY ANALYSIS

1. Eggshell-Skull Plaintiff

A plaintiff may have a particular weakness, such as an "eggshell" skull. Courts often say that "the defendant takes the plaintiff as he finds him." **[p. 129]**

2. Rescuers

If a defendant's conduct puts a person in peril, rescuers' presence and rescuers' conduct are foreseeable. **[p. 129]** *Wagner v. International Ry. Co.*, contains Judge Cardozo's famous sentence: "Danger invites rescue." **[p. 129]**

3. Same Class of Harm

Foreseeability jurisdictions may impose liability on defendants for unforeseeable injuries if they involve risks or forces that are the basis of defining the defendants' conduct as negligent. *Kinsman Transport Co.* illustrates this. **[p. 130]**

G. RESTATEMENT POSITION

For unforeseeability to block liability under the Restatement, a person looking back from the harm to the defendant's conduct must consider it highly extraordinary that the conduct caused the harm. **[p. 130]**

H. INTERVENING EVENTS: GENERAL RULE

Natural forces or acts by others may occur between the defendant's conduct and the plaintiff's injury. The defendant is insulated from responsibility if those events are characterized as superseding. The general rule is that only unforeseeable subsequent events can be superseding causes, and even those events do not insulate the defendant from liability if they lead to a type of harm that could have been foreseen. **[p. 130]**

I. RISK OF INTERVENING EVENT IS PART OF THE DEFINITION OF DEFENDANT'S NEGLIGENCE

If the defendant's conduct was negligent because it made the subsequent injurious event possible or more likely, the subsequent event is not a superseding cause of an injury. **[p. 132]**

J. STANDARD INTERVENING CAUSE SITUATIONS

1. Bad Medical Treatment

Medical malpractice, other than grossly negligent treatment, is not a superseding cause of the victim's ultimate injury. **[p. 133]**

2. Injuries During Evasion of Initial Threat

The defendant is responsible for injuries a plaintiff suffers while trying to avoid a risk of injury posed by the defendant. **[p. 133]**

3. Additional Injury Due to Original Harm

When a defendant's conduct weakens the plaintiff, consequences of that weakness are the defendant's responsibility. **[p. 133]**

4. Suicide

If the victim of the defendant's accidentally injurious behavior suffers psychological consequences that lead to suicide, the defendant is responsible for the death. **[p. 133]**

5. Injuries Due to Drunkenness

When a defendant negligently serves liquor to a minor or to an adult who is intoxicated, and the drunken person then injures someone else (usually by driving while drunk), modern decisions tend to reject the idea that the intoxicated individual is the sole cause of the ultimate harm. **[p. 133]**

K. THIRD PARTY CRIMINAL CONDUCT

Criminal conduct by a third party is superseding in cases where it is characterized as unforeseeable. **[p. 134]**

1. Theft

A defendant whose negligent conduct immobilizes a vehicle containing valuable freight is likely to be liable for the loss of the freight to thieves. **[p. 134]**

2. Negligent Driving of Stolen Vehicle

Most states have decided keys-in-the-car cases. In such a case the defendant leaves a motor vehicle with its keys in the ignition, a thief steals the car, and, while driving the car, the thief injures the plaintiff. Some jurisdictions hold that one of the foreseeable risks of theft is that a thief will injure someone by driving carelessly. Others hold that the risk involved is only loss of the vehicle, so a thief's bad driving is superseding. In some states the juries must decide whether the likelihood of theft was significant enough to make an injury by a thief foreseeable. **[p. 134]**

L. THIRD PERSON'S FAILURE TO PREVENT HARM: USUALLY NOT SUPERSEDING

If an actor negligently creates a situation that presents a danger to the plaintiff, a third person's failure to correct what the first actor did is not usually a superseding cause of eventual harm. **[p. 135]**

1. Responsibility Shifts in Rare Cases

a. **Responsibility shift by agreement.** An original wrongdoer may be protected from liability if an agreement that is not against public policy transfers full responsibility to another person. **[p. 135]**

b. **Responsibility shift reflecting degrees of fault and status of third person.** Courts sometimes treat subsequent conduct as superseding because of the degree of fault it represented and the relationship of the subsequent actors to the victims. **[p. 136]**

9 MULTIPLE PARTY CASES

A. INDIVISIBLE INJURIES

Under joint and several liability each defendant is subject to a judgment for the whole amount of a plaintiff's indivisible damages. **[p. 140]**

1. Indivisible Injury Definition

An injury is indivisible if more than one defendant caused the injury and no one can prove that a particular defendant is responsible for a particular part of the injury. **[p. 140]**

2. Divisible Injury Definition

A plaintiff's injuries are divisible if there is proof that a particular defendant is responsible individually for a particular part of the injuries. **[p. 140]**

3. Action in Concert

People who agree to carry out a particular type of conduct together act in concert. Each is responsible for any harms the joint effort causes. **[p. 141]**

4. Death

Death is an indivisible injury. **[p. 141]**

5. Fire Loss

The loss of property due to fire is an indivisible injury. **[p. 141]**

6. Burden of Proof on Divisibility

The burden of proof on divisibility of damages is usually on the defendant who seeks to avoid responsibility for the entire injury. **[p. 141]**

B. VARIED TREATMENTS OF JOINT AND SEVERAL LIABILITY

Where two or more defendants have contributed to an indivisible injury, most jurisdictions apply joint and several liability.

1. Traditional Rule

Each defendant is subject to a judgment for the plaintiff's entire damages. The plaintiff may enforce the judgment against any one or more of the defendants and can collect all or part of it from any one of them. The plaintiff may collect a total amount of money that is equal to the total judgment. **[p. 141]**

2. Applied to Economic, Not Noneconomic Damages

Some jurisdictions require the jury to identify damage amounts as economic (such as past and future medical expenses and lost income) and noneconomic (such as pain and suffering) damages. Joint and several liability applies to economic damages but not to noneconomic damages. **[p. 142]**

3. Particular Limitations

States employ a wide array of treatments of joint and several liability, including applying it only in cases with small total damages, applying it only to defendants with specified percentages of overall responsibility for the plaintiff's harm, or applying it only to environmental torts or cases where defendants have acted in concert. **[p. 142]**

4. Abolished

About ten states have completely eliminated joint and several liability. In these states a factual finding is made, assigning a percentage of responsibility to each defendant. Each defendant is liable for a judgment based on his or her percentage share of responsibility. **[p. 143]**

C. CONTRIBUTION

Under joint and several liability a plaintiff may enforce a judgment against any one or more of the defendants. Contribution is the process through which a defendant who has paid too much of a judgment can sue other defendants to be reimbursed. Contribution may also be obtained from parties who could have been but were not defendants in the plaintiff's original suit. **[p. 143]**

D. DOCTRINAL RESTRICTIONS ON CONTRIBUTION

Contribution is not available to intentional tortfeasors; nor is it available from actors with no liability to the original plaintiff (such as parties protected from liability by immunity). **[p. 144]**

E. AMOUNT OF CONTRIBUTION PERMITTED

A jurisdiction that permits contribution ordinarily defines a defendant's ultimate liability on the basis of the percentage share of responsibility assigned to the defendant at trial under the jurisdiction's comparative negligence system. If there is no such system, a defendant's share is determined by dividing the total judgment equally among all defendants. **[p. 144]**

1. No Contribution Where Joint and Several Liability is Abolished

Since contribution is only possible where joint and several liability has led to a defendant's paying more than his or her share to a plaintiff, there can never be contribution in a jurisdiction where joint and several liability does not apply. **[p. 145]**

F. SETTLEMENTS

When a plaintiff settles with one of two or more parties who injured him or her, tort law should protect the nonsettling defendant from bearing an unfair amount of responsibility for the injury but should not discourage settlements. **[p. 145]**

1. **Common Law**

A party who settled with the plaintiff was still liable to a contribution lawsuit brought against him or her by some other party who ultimately paid a judgment to the plaintiff. **[p. 146]** A party who settled was entitled to contribution from other parties if those defendants could have been liable to the plaintiff and the settlement amount paid to the plaintiff was reasonable. **[p. 146]**

2. **Modern Statutes**

Most states now control contribution by statute. **[p. 146]**

a. **1955 Uniform Contribution Among Tortfeasors Act.** A release or covenant not to sue does not release any other tortfeasor from liability. Any plaintiff's judgment must be reduced by the amount of any good-faith settlement. A settling party will have no further liability in the case. **[p. 146]**

b. **1977 Uniform Comparative Fault Act.** This act is similar to the 1955 act, except that the amount by which any plaintiff's judgment must be reduced to reflect a settlement is based on the released party's share of responsibility. **[p. 146]** The act also contains a method of determining the amount of contribution to which an overpaying defendant is entitled. **[p. 146]**

3. **Mary Carter Settlements**

Mary Carter agreements require the settling defendant to pay the plaintiff a certain amount of money unless the plaintiff's ultimate recovery from the nonsettling defendant reaches a specified amount. The settling defendant participates in the trial, with incentives to make the nonsettling defendant seem bad and the plaintiff seem good. **[p. 148]**

a. **Disclosure.** Most jurisdictions require that the parties reveal a Mary Carter settlement to the court. Some permit its existence to be disclosed to the jury. **[p. 148]**

b. **Prohibition.** Some jurisdictions prohibit these agreements. **[p. 148]**

G. INDEMNITY: GENERAL RULE

Indemnity is a complete transfer of the entire burden of a judgment that one party has paid. This seems fair when a defendant has been liable to the plaintiff even though the defendant was completely free from fault. **[p. 148]**

H. INDEMNITY AND COMPARATIVE FAULT

As jurisdictions have adopted comparative negligence, some have developed comparative or proportional indemnity principles. The amount a defendant is able to shift to another defendant is calculated with reference to the comparative responsibility of each defendant. **[p. 148]**

1. Gross Negligence as a Basis for Indemnity

A minority view entitles a defendant whose negligence was relatively slight to full indemnity from another defendant whose negligence was gross or whose misconduct was intentional. **[p. 149]**

I. CONTRACTUAL AND JUDICIALLY IMPOSED INDEMNITY

Some businesses provide for indemnity by contract. In other instances courts impose indemnity. **[p. 149]**

1. Vicarious Liability

An employer is responsible for torts by an employee occurring within the scope of employment. When an employer pays a judgment in this situation, the worker is liable to the employer for the full amount of the judgment the employer paid. **[p. 149]**

2. Failure to Discover Contractor's Hazard

In many jurisdictions if a contractor acts negligently and creates a dangerous condition on someone's land, the landowner is entitled to indemnity from the contractor if the landowner pays a judgment to someone injured due to the dangerous condition. **[p. 149]**

3. Failure to Discover Manufacturer's Hazard

Under traditional doctrines a retailer may obtain indemnity from a manufacturer if a customer obtains damages for an injury suffered because of a flaw in the manufacturer's product. **[p. 149]**

4. Liability for Subsequent Tortfeasor's Conduct

Partial indemnity is sometimes available where a defendant's conduct harms a plaintiff, but the damages are increased by another party's subsequent negligence. This scenario is exemplified when a first defendant's bad driving is followed by a second defendant's medical malpractice. **[p. 149]**

10 DUTY AND LIMITED-DUTY RULES

A. FUNCTION OF DUTY IN TORT LAW

To recover damages for an injury a plaintiff must show that the defendant had a duty to avoid inflicting that type of harm on the plaintiff or a person like the plaintiff. **[p. 153]**

1. **Typical Definition**

Courts typically state that one has a duty to avoid creating risks of foreseeable harm to foreseeable individuals. **[p. 154]**

2. **Duty as a Limitation on Liability**

A no-duty or limited-duty rule establishes that a defendant had no duty or only a limited duty to avoid inflicting injury on a particular plaintiff or to avoid inflicting a particular type of injury on anyone. **[p. 154]**

a. **Rationale and effect of no-duty and limited-duty rules.** These rules are supported by many of the same social factors that support proximate cause doctrines. The rules govern situations in which it seems unfair to make a defendant pay for the consequences of his or her conduct. **[p. 154]**

b. **Overlap between duty and proximate cause.** A court can use duty or proximate cause concepts for the same purpose: limiting the consequences of a defendant's actions for which the defendant may be required to pay. **[p. 154]**

B. COURT AND JURY ROLES

In theory the issue of duty is a legal question for the court. **[p. 155]**

C. EMOTIONAL DISTRESS

If someone's negligent conduct causes a person to suffer "mere" emotional distress, the victim may have no cause of action because there is usually no duty to avoid negligent conduct that leads another person to suffer only emotional consequences. **[p. 155]**

1. **Intentional Misconduct**

Courts recognize a cause of action for intentional infliction of emotional distress. **[p. 155]**

2. **Parasitic Damages**

When a defendant's conduct is negligent and the plaintiff suffers some physical injuries as a result, the plaintiff is also entitled to emotional distress damages, called "parasitic damages", associated with the injury. **[p. 155]**

3. **Initial Physical Impact**

Under traditional common law principles recovery for emotional distress was allowed only if the plaintiff could show an impact as part of the allegedly tortious conduct by the defendant. **[p. 156]**

4. **Zone of Danger (Near-Miss Cases)**

In most states a plaintiff who was in a zone of danger, where physical harm could have resulted from the defendant's conduct, may recover for negligent infliction of emotional distress if the plaintiff had a harmful emotional reaction to the event, whether or not the plaintiff suffered an initial physical impact. **[p. 156]**

a. **Fear of fraud.** The fact that feelings are hard to verify is the main justification for limiting recovery for emotional distress in the absence of other injuries. **[p. 156]**

b. **Ultimate physical consequences or manifestation usually required.** Traditional common law doctrines required that the plaintiff have some physical manifestation of the claimed emotional distress. **[p. 157]**

   i. **Exceptions to physical consequences requirement.** Some jurisdictions do not impose the physical consequences requirement for claims based on negligent transmission of a telegram about a relative's death and mishandling of a corpse. **[p. 157]**

   ii. **Minority rejection of physical consequences requirement.** A number of jurisdictions reject the requirement of a physical manifestation and allow the juries to decide whether emotional distress really exists. **[p. 157]**

5. Bystander Recovery

Under a minority view, a bystander outside the zone of danger may recover for emotional distress caused by observing conduct by defendant that harms the bystander's grandparent, parent, spouse, sibling, or child. **[p. 157]**

a. **Presence at scene.** The emotional distress plaintiff must see the injury directly. **[p. 158]**

b. **Awareness of injury.** The plaintiff must also be aware of the injury to the loved one at the time the plaintiff witnesses the defendant's conduct. **[p. 158]**

D. FAILURE TO ACT

A failure to help a person who would benefit from that help is usually not actionable, but in some situations, tort law imposes a duty to be helpful to others. **[p. 158]**

1. Special Relationship with Plaintiff

A special relationship supports duties to render aid and provide reasonable protection against harms that might be inflicted by third parties or forces of nature. **[p. 158]**

a. **Common carriers, innkeepers, and other businesses.** Common carriers and innkeepers are obligated to act reasonably to protect their passengers and guests from hazards created by third parties or by forces of nature. **[p. 158]**

b. **Employers.** An employer has a duty to act reasonably in response to a worker's injury in the course of the worker's employment. **[p. 159]**

c. **Schools.** A school has a duty to protect its students, but a university need not supervise students' private lives. **[p. 159]**

d. **Coventurers.** People who embark on an activity together may be obligated to act reasonably in the event that one of them needs assistance. **[p. 159]**

2. Defendant Caused Plaintiff's Peril

If a defendant's negligent conduct has caused the plaintiff to need assistance, the defendant is often under a duty to act reasonably in response to that need. **[p. 159]** In many jurisdictions and under the Restatement, people whose non-negligent conduct puts others in peril are obligated to act reasonably in response to those others' needs. **[p. 159]**

3. Assumed Duty

A defendant who begins to give help to an imperiled plaintiff must use reasonable care in his or her actions. The defendant may stop the assistance unless the plaintiff's position would then be worse than it was when the defendant intervened. One who customarily provides a helpful service may be liable for injuries caused by ceasing to provide the service. **[p. 160]**

a. **Promise to help.** A mere promise to offer assistance cannot be a basis for imposing a duty. Courts may impose a duty, however, where a promise is combined with some small act by the defendant or with reliance by the plaintiff. **[p. 160]**

b. **Inspections and examinations.** Courts are divided on whether an insurance company that conducts an inspection has a duty to individuals who are employed in the inspected location to perform the inspection with due care. If the insurance company has motives other than its own financial interests, a duty is usually imposed. **[p. 161]**

4. Special Relationship with Third Party

Psychotherapists, some other health care providers, and vehicle owners sometimes have a duty to protect others from potential injury by third parties. They owe that duty to individuals who are the foreseeable victims of misconduct by that potential injurer. **[p. 161]**

5. Good Samaritan Statutes

Good Samaritan statutes in most states immunize health care professionals from liability for negligent acts committed while rendering aid in emergency situations without payment. **[p. 162]**

6. **Vermont Duty-to-Aid Statute**

   A Vermont statute requires people to give aid to others in grave physical danger where they can do so without personal risk. The statute immunizes someone who gives aid from liability for negligence. **[p. 162]**

E. MERE ECONOMIC LOSS

Recovery is usually prohibited in a mere-economic-harm case where a defendant's conduct causes the plaintiff to lose money, but the plaintiff does not suffer any bodily harm or property damage. **[p. 162]**

1. **Economic Harm Plus Additional Harm, Distinguished**

   If a defendant's conduct causes the plaintiff to suffer economic harm in combination with harm to property or some personal injury, the plaintiff may recover damages for the economic harms subject to proximate cause limits. **[p. 163]**

2. **Economic Harm Without Other Harm: Modern View**

   A minority approach allows recovery for pure economic harms if the plaintiff can establish the particular foreseeability of the harm. **[p. 162]** A special relationship between the plaintiff and defendant may also support recovery of damages for pure economic harm. **[p. 162]**

F. PRECONCEPTION AND PRENATAL INJURIES

A variety of causes of action relate to harms to fetuses and the birth of children after negligent sterilization procedures or negligent genetic counseling. **[p. 164]**

1. **Abrogation of Common Law No-Duty Rule**

   Common law denied a cause of action by or on behalf of a child allegedly injured by the defendant prior to the child's birth. Virtually all jurisdictions have abrogated this common law no-duty rule. **[p. 164]**

   a. **Viable at time of injury.** A minority view requires proof that the fetus was viable when the defendant's conduct occurred. **[p. 164]**

   b. **Born alive.** Some jurisdictions require that an allegedly injured fetus be born alive, rather than stillborn, to apply a tort remedy. **[p. 164]**

2. **Duty to Child for Preconception Conduct**

   Courts are divided on whether a child may recover for harms caused by a doctor's or a drug company's conduct in connection with the child's mother prior to the time the child was conceived. **[p. 165]**

   a. **Drug company's duty.** In cases involving harm to children of mothers who took the drug DES during their pregnancies, the majority of courts have allowed the children to seek relief against the drug makers. **[p. 165]**

b. **Doctor's duty.** Where a doctor's negligence in connection with a woman's RH-negative status led to harm to a later-born child, one jurisdiction allowed a cause of action by the child against the allegedly negligent physician. **[p. 165]**

3. Wrongful Conception

Wrongful conception is a cause of action by the parents of an unwanted child born free from birth defects, seeking damages for a negligently performed sterilization procedure. **[p. 165]** All courts allow damages for the economic costs and pain and suffering associated with pregnancy and childbirth. Some allow damages for the costs of supporting the child to the age of majority (benefits the parents receive from the child's existence are offset from the damage award). **[p. 165]**

4. Wrongful Birth

Wrongful birth is a cause of action by parents whose child is born with birth defects, seeking damages on the theory that the child would not have been conceived or would have been aborted if the defendant had provided proper genetic counseling or other prenatal health care. **[p. 166]** All courts allow damages for the economic costs and pain and suffering associated with pregnancy and childbirth. The majority also allow parents to recover the expected costs of providing whatever unusual care is needed due to the birth defects. **[p. 166]**

a. **Damages for child's adult life.** In a state that recognizes damages for extraordinary child-rearing costs, and where parents are obligated to provide care for a disabled adult child, the parents' damages are calculated to reflect that obligation. **[p. 166]**

5. Wrongful Life

Wrongful life is a child's cause of action for the injury of being born with birth defects instead of not being born at all. Most jurisdictions reject this action. A minority allow damages for expenses not covered in a parents' wrongful birth suit. **[p. 166]**

G. PROMISE AS A BASIS FOR TORT DUTY

Promises or contracts may support tort duties to promisees or to third parties. The common law rule, however, is that one who makes a gratuitous promise is never liable in tort for consequences of the failure to fulfill the promise. Similarly, no tort duty is imposed on a person who breaches a contractual obligation by failing to take actions required under the contract. **[p. 167]**

1. Nonfeasance

Failure to act, in the context of either a gratuitous promise or a contract, is usually not a basis for tort liability. **[p. 167]**

H. MISFEASANCE AS A BASIS FOR TORT DUTY

The careless performance of an act, in the context of a gratuitous promise, a contract, or even in the absence of either a promise or a contract, can support tort liability. **[p. 167]**

1. Significance of Contract Context

If an actor's misfeasance involves a contractual obligation, a plaintiff usually prefers a tort cause of action, since damages are free from the strict foreseeability rules of contract damages. **[p. 167]**

2. Standard Negligence Analysis

Once someone begins to act in accordance with a contract, standard negligence doctrines control liability to anyone who suffers an injury related to those actions. **[p. 168]**

I. TORT REMEDY FOR CONTRACTING PARTY'S LACK OF GOOD FAITH AND FAIR DEALING

Contract law requires contracting parties to act in good faith and deal fairly. This duty is sometimes enforceable under tort doctrines. **[p. 168]**

1. Insurance Bad-Faith Litigation

In many states insurance companies are subject to tort remedies in favor of their insureds if they act in bad faith concerning opportunities to settle claims against their insureds. **[p. 168]**

2. Unlawful Discharge

Many jurisdictions recognize tort actions for unlawful discharge of at-will employees discharged in retaliation for obtaining workers' compensation benefits or for refusing to violate laws. **[p. 168]**

11 LAND OCCUPIERS' DUTIES

A. INJURIES OUTSIDE THE LAND

A landowner owes a duty to use reasonable care to protect people outside his or her land from risks related to its condition or activities on it. **[p. 173]**

1. Natural Conditions

There is usually no duty to remove or otherwise control natural hazards present on the land without human intervention **[p. 174]**

a. **Urban-rural distinction.** Some courts impose duty if a defendant's land is urban. **[p. 174]**

2. **Conduct by People on the Land**

A landowner also has a duty to protect people off the land from foreseeable injuries caused by conduct of people on the land. **[p. 175]**

B. INJURIES ON THE LAND: PLAINTIFF'S STATUS

When a plaintiff is injured on the defendant's land, many jurisdictions define a defendant's duty according to a plaintiff's status as a trespasser, a licensee (social visitor), or an invitee (business visitor). **[p. 175]**

1. **Traditional Three-Category Jurisdictions**

Traditional common law jurisdictions use all three status categories. **[p. 175]**

2. **Modern Two-Category Jurisdictions**

Some jurisdictions use two categories: trespasser and nontrespasser. **[p. 175]**

3. **Modern One-Category Jurisdictions**

Some jurisdictions include all entrants in a single category. **[p. 175]**

C. DUTY TO TRESPASSERS

A landowner must refrain from committing an intentional tort and from willful, wanton, or reckless conduct that could harm a trespasser. **[p. 176]**

1. **Discovered Trespassers**

A landowner must use reasonable care for the safety of a discovered trespasser. This rule applies with respect to conduct and artificial conditions on the land. Its application to natural conditions is not clear. **[p. 176]**

2. **Frequent or Tolerated Trespassers**

A landowner has a duty to frequent or tolerated trespassers to make the premises safe or to provide a warning of dangers they are unlikely to discover. **[p. 176]**

3. **Child Trespassers**

The attractive nuisance doctrine increases the duty a landowner owes a trespassing child to a duty of reasonable care with respect to artificial conditions on the land. **[p. 177]**

4. **Elements of Attractive Nuisance**

a. **Likelihood of trespass.** The landowner knows or should know children are likely to go to the place of danger. **[p. 177]**

b. **Danger.** The landowner knows or should know that the place is unreasonably dangerous to children. **[p. 177]**

c. **Child's ignorance.** The child must be unaware of the danger because of his or her youth. **[p. 177]**

d. **Utility.** The utility of the condition or activity must be less than the risk it imposes. **[p. 177]**

e. **Landowner's conduct.** Failure to reduce the risk must be unreasonable. **[p. 177]**

5. Age Limits

A modern decision usually compares the child's degree of knowledge to the type of risk, so a child close to the age of majority can still be entitled to application of the doctrine if the risk was unknown to him or her. **[p. 177]**

6. Natural Conditions

The Restatement takes no position on applying the doctrine to natural conditions. Some case law limits it to artificial conditions. **[p. 177]**

7. Conduct by Landowner

For injuries related to active operations, a trespassing child is treated in the same way as a trespassing adult. **[p. 178]**

D. DEFINITION OF LICENSEE

A licensee is someone the landowner invites or allows on the land for social purposes of no economic value to the landowner. Being invited socially does not make a person an invitee. **[p. 178]**

1. Mixed Business and Social Purposes

An entrant for a combination of social and other purposes is usually a licensee. **[p. 178]**

2. Automobile Passenger

In some jurisdictions the licensee category includes a guest in someone's vehicle. **[p. 179]**

3. Firefighters and Police Officers

Firefighters and police officers are licensees if they enter a landowner's premises in an emergency. **[p. 179]**

E. DUTY TO LICENSEE

A landowner owes limited duties to a licensee. Under common law a guest must tolerate whatever level of safety the host ordinarily provides for the host's own safety. **[p. 179]**

1. **Warn of Known-Dangerous Conditions**

   A host must warn a licensee about any known-dangerous condition if the host knows or should know that the guest may not discover it. **[p. 179]**

2. **Natural Conditions**

   The duty to warn covers natural conditions. **[p. 179]**

3. **No Duty to Repair**

   The host has no duty to make the land or premises safe. **[p. 179]**

4. **No Duty to Inspect**

   The host has no duty to inspect the land or premises. **[p. 179]**

5. **Distinction Between Conditions and Activities**

   In most jurisdictions that use the licensee category for land entrant cases, the limited-duty rules apply only to conditions on the land. For risks related to activities on the land, a licensee is owed a duty of reasonable care. **[p. 179]**

6. **Recreational-Use Immunity Statutes**

   Most states have a recreational-use immunity statute providing that a person allowed to enter another's land for recreational purposes does not have the status of licensee or invitee. **[p. 180]**

F. DEFINITION OF INVITEE

A person a landowner invites onto the land to transact business is an invitee. The majority of jurisdictions define "invitee" to include a "public invitee," someone who enters land for a purpose for which it is held open to the public. **[p. 180]**

1. **Typical Invitee**

   Invitees include a defendant's customer, someone who uses a bathroom in a store, a door-to-door salesperson invited to enter a house, and public employees doing routine work. **[p. 180]**

2. **Time and Space Limits**

   Limits on the landowner's invitation are determined by the entrant's reasonable beliefs. **[p. 181]**

G. DUTY TO INVITEE

A landowner owes a duty of reasonable care to an invitee. **[p. 181]**

1. **Duty to Inspect**

   A reasonably prudent landowner is expected to inspect the land or premises. **[p. 181]**

2. **Warnings**

Sometimes reasonable care requires only that a landowner give a warning to an invitee. **[p. 181]**

3. **Open and Obvious Dangers**

At common law a landowner has no obligation to remove or to warn about an open and obvious danger. A few modern decisions allow a cause of action for a plaintiff injured by such a danger, using comparative negligence doctrines to take account of the plaintiff's probable carelessness. **[p. 182]**

4. **Protection from Crime**

Landowners may owe invitees a duty of protection from criminal conduct by third persons. Cases often involve customers injured by those attempting to rob businesses. **[p. 182]**

a. **No-duty position.** Some jurisdictions treat criminal conduct as superseding or apply no-duty rules for public policy reasons. **[p. 182]**

b. **Foreseeability analysis.** Other jurisdictions allow liability based on patterns of past crimes at certain locations. **[p. 183]**

i. **Same location rule.** Some jurisdictions require a plaintiff to show that there had previously been a significant number of past crimes at the specific establishment where the plaintiff's injury occurred. **[p. 183]**

ii. **Totality of circumstances rule.** Other jurisdictions allow a plaintiff to show that the totality of circumstances made an attack foreseeable. **[p. 183]**

5. **Danger Known to Invitee**

If an invitee knows about a danger, there is usually no obligation to remove it or warn about it. Some modern decisions, however, treat the invitee's knowledge as just a factor relevant to the invitee's comparative negligence. **[p. 183]**

H. DUTY IN MODERN TWO-CATEGORY JURISDICTIONS

In jurisdictions that treat entrants with two categories, trespasser and all other entrants, a trespasser is owed the traditional common law duty, and all other entrants are owed reasonable care. **[p. 183]**

I. DUTY IN MODERN ONE-CATEGORY JURISDICTIONS

In jurisdictions that have abolished the three categories of trespasser, licensee, and invitee, a landowner owes a duty of reasonable care to all entrants on the land. **[p. 184]**

FIGURE 1

SUMMARY OF GENERAL LAND ENTRANT DOCTRINES

Type of Entrant	*Type of Hazard: Intentional or Reckless Conduct*	*Type of Hazard: Active Operations*	*Type of Hazard: Latent Conditions*
Trespasser	DUTY TO REFRAIN FROM CONDUCT	NO DUTY	NO DUTY
Discovered Trespasser	DUTY TO REFRAIN FROM CONDUCT	DUTY OF REASONABLE CARE	Restatement: DUTY OF REASONABLE CARE Alternate view: NO DUTY
Licensee	DUTY TO REFRAIN FROM CONDUCT	Traditional common law: DUTY OF REASONABLE CARE if: 1. defendant should expect that licensee will not realize the danger; and 2. licensee actually does not know or have reason to know the danger Modern view: DUTY OF REASONABLE CARE	DUTY TO MAKE CONDITION SAFE OR GIVE WARNING if: 1. defendant should expect that licensee will not realize the danger; 2. licensee actually does not know or have reason to know the danger; and 3. defendant knows or has reason to know of the danger
Invitee	DUTY TO REFRAIN FROM CONDUCT	DUTY OF REASONABLE CARE	DUTY OF REASONABLE CARE

1. Factual Significance of Status

An entrant's status is significant when a jury considers the facts of a case to apply the reasonable person test. **[p. 184]**

J. SUMMARY OF GENERAL LAND ENTRANT DOCTRINES

See Figure 1, above.

K. LANDLORDS' OBLIGATIONS TO TENANTS AND OTHER ENTRANTS

A landlord generally has a no-duty defense to a tenant's suit for injuries caused by conditions on the land. Some exceptions to the limited-duty rule can impose a duty of reasonable care owed to tenants and their licensees and invitees. **[p. 184]**

1. Dangers Present at Start of Lease

A landlord has a duty of reasonable care with respect to danger that is present on the premises at the start of the lease if the landlord knows or should know about the risk and the tenant is reasonably unaware of it. **[p. 186]**

2. **Common Areas**

A landlord owes a duty of reasonable care for conditions in common areas (like a lobby) that remain in the landlord's control. **[p. 186]**

3. **Public Invited**

A landlord who knows that a tenant will invite the public to the premises is liable to a member of the public injured by a dangerous condition if the landlord knew the premises might be open before the dangerous condition was repaired. **[p. 186]**

4. **Repair Promises and Efforts**

If a landlord is obligated by the lease to maintain the leased premises or has promised to make a repair, a duty of reasonable care is imposed for that maintenance or repair. **[p. 186]**

a. **Tenant's knowledge of hazard.** The majority of jurisdictions impose liability on landlords for inept or partial repairs only if the tenants are ignorant of the dangers. **[p. 187]**

5. **Modern Full-Duty Rule**

Some states impose a general duty of reasonable care on landlords with respect to all hazards and all entrants on leased premises. **[p. 187]** This parallels the reform abolishing use of the trespasser, licensee, and invitee categories for general entrant on land cases.

6. **Protection from Third-Party Criminal Acts**

In some jurisdictions a landlord has a duty to take reasonable care to protect tenants from foreseeable criminal acts by third parties. **[p. 187]**

12 Damages

A. FUNDAMENTAL PRINCIPLES

In most cases plaintiffs must prove physical injury. This can be property damage (physical injury to something that belongs to the plaintiff) or personal injury (physical injury to the plaintiff's body). **[p. 192]**

B. ECONOMIC AND NONECONOMIC DAMAGES, DISTINGUISHED

Some jurisdictions categorize damages as economic (losses that can be quantified by reference to past and anticipated earnings or costs) and noneconomic (losses for harms that are not tangible, such as pain and suffering). **[p. 192]**

1. Joint and Several Liability

Some jurisdictions apply joint and several liability only to economic damages. **[p. 192]**

2. Damages Caps

Some jurisdictions limit the amount of noneconomic damages plaintiffs may recover. **[p. 192]**

C. CATEGORIES OF DAMAGES

Courts analyze damages in specific categories. Juries are likely to award more damages, in total, if they can calculate amounts for many categories. When an appellate court reviews an award, the chance of affirmance is greater if the plaintiff established a basis for damages in many separate categories. **[p. 192]**

1. Economic Damages

Conventional economic damages are medical expenses, lost income, and the cost of hiring employees for functions the plaintiff formerly did personally. **[p. 193]**

2. Noneconomic Damages

Conventional noneconomic damages are pain and suffering, including amounts for physical pain, fright, shock, embarrassment, sadness, depression, worry, and anxiety. **[p. 193]**

a. **Theoretical criticism.** Pain cannot be measured accurately. Also, our society ordinarily does not have a market basis for evaluating the cost of pain. **[p. 193]**

b. **Responses to criticism.** Money is the best our society has to offer the victim of painful injuries. Also, pain and suffering awards may be an approximate method of reimbursing the plaintiff for attorney's fees. **[p. 193]**

c. **Hedonic damages.** Hedonic damages are damages for loss of the enjoyment of life. Some jurisdictions allow them as a separate category. Others treat them as part of pain and suffering. **[p. 194]**

d. **Victim's awareness.** All jurisdictions require plaintiffs to be aware of pain and suffering to be entitled to damages for it. Some jurisdictions allow hedonic damages regardless of a plaintiff's state of awareness (this increases damages for a victim who is comatose). **[p. 194]**

D. CALCULATING PAST AND FUTURE LOSSES

A plaintiff usually can sue a defendant only once for damages related to a specific injury. Proof of damages in a typical case, therefore, covers past damages and anticipated future damages. **[p. 195]**

1. **Degree of Certainty for Future Losses**

Damages for future harm must be based on evidence showing that more likely than not the future harm will occur. Expert testimony usually involving actuarial concepts can support these findings. **[p. 195]**

2. **Per Diem Argument**

Some plaintiffs' lawyers have developed a per diem argument that asks jurors to assign a small value to a minute of suffering and then to multiply that value by the victim's life expectancy in minutes. Most jurisdictions allow this argument. **[p. 195]**

E. ADJUSTMENTS TO A JURY'S DAMAGES FINDINGS

1. **Inflation**

Some courts allow expert testimony on the expected effects of inflation on the value of future losses. Others reject this evidence. **[p. 196]**

2. **Present Value of Money**

Most courts require juries to reduce estimates of plaintiffs' future economic harm to present value. **[p. 196]**

3. **Offset Inflation and Present Value Concept**

Some courts disregard possible future inflation and the concept of reducing damages to present value, on the theory that the errors these concepts introduce offset each other. **[p. 196]**

4. **Taxes**

Considering damages for a plaintiff's lost income, tort law must recognize that income would have been subject to taxation if the plaintiff had earned it, but personal injury damages awards are not taxed. **[p. 196]**

a. **Lost income and taxation.** Juries are ordinarily instructed to consider taxation when they calculate damages for past lost income. For predicted future lost income, however, future tax rates are unknown. For this reason most courts have juries ignore taxation in calculating future lost income for typical plaintiffs. **[p. 196]**

i. **Federal tort causes of action.** In a case tried in federal court on federal causes of action, the jury must consider future taxation in calculating the amount of future income the plaintiff has lost. **[p. 197]**

b. **Nontaxability of personal injury damage awards.** There are three views on telling juries that personal injury awards are nontaxable. Some jurisdictions require giving a jury this information, some allow it, and some forbid it. **[p. 197]**

5. **Statutory Ceilings on Damages**

Some state statutes limit the damages tort plaintiffs may receive. The most common type of statute limits noneconomic damages. **[p. 198]**

a. **Informing the jury about a damages ceiling.** Jurisdictions differ on whether a jury may be informed about a ceiling on damages. **[p. 00]**

6. **Payments from Third Parties (Collateral Source Rule)**

The collateral source rule requires that a plaintiff receive the full damages found by the jury, even if some of those costs have already been paid to the plaintiff from other sources. About 25 states reject this rule. **[p. 198]** They reduce judgments to reflect payments the plaintiffs have received in connection with their injuries. **[p. 198]**

a. **Reform proposal.** An American Law Institute study proposes that a plaintiff's judgment be reduced to reflect payments received by the plaintiff from insurance but that the defendant be required to reimburse the plaintiff for some of the insurance premiums that kept the policy in effect. **[p. 199]**

F. PLAINTIFF'S OBLIGATION TO MITIGATE DAMAGES

A plaintiff must act reasonably to lessen the effects of the defendant's wrongdoing. This is mitigation of damages. **[p. 200]**

1. **Failure to Use an Available Seat Belt**

In some states if a plaintiff injured in a vehicular accident had failed to use an available seat belt, that plaintiff is not entitled to damages for any injuries that would have been avoided by using it. Many state statutes decrease a plaintiff's recovery through comparative fault principles, limiting the amount of reduction to a fairly small percentage. **[p. 200]**

G. PERIODIC PAYMENTS

Some state statutes allow a defendant to pay a judgment through periodic payments instead of a single payment to the plaintiff. The plaintiff receives payments on a regular schedule for the remainder of his or her life. The payments stop when the plaintiff dies, and no payments are made to the plaintiff's estate. **[p. 200]**

H. LOSS OF CONSORTIUM

When a tortfeasor injures someone who has a spouse, children, or parents, the tortfeasor may be liable to those people for loss of consortium damages. **[p. 201]**

1. **Spousal Consortium**

Damages for loss of spousal consortium are meant to compensate the husband or wife for the loss of companionship, sexual relations, household services, and other benefits previously received from the injured spouse. **[p. 201]**

2. Child's Loss of Parental Consortium

Most states reject actions for children's loss of parental consortium. **[p. 202]**

a. **Large liability.** Parental loss of consortium actions might present the risk of large liability for defendants since victims could have large numbers of children. **[p. 202]**

b. **Duplicative recovery.** A parent's own damages award includes money to replace the services the parent would have been able to provide to his or her children. **[p. 202]**

c. **Approved by minority.** Some states allow children's loss of parental consortium actions. **[p. 202]**

3. Parent's Loss of Consortium with Child

Some states allow a parent to recover for the loss of companionship with a child if injuries make the child less able to participate in family life and familial emotional relationships. **[p. 203]**

I. WRONGFUL DEATH AND SURVIVAL ACTIONS

Wrongful death actions and survival actions are suits to recover damages for deaths. **[p. 203]**

1. Wrongful Death Action Defined

A wrongful death action can be brought against a tortfeasor by individuals specified in a wrongful death statute. The action seeks compensation for the victim's death. Wrongful death beneficiaries ordinarily are entitled to damages for loss of support and loss of companionship. **[p. 203]**

2. Survival Action Defined

A survival action is brought against a tortfeasor on behalf of the original victim's estate, seeking damages for claims that the original victim would have been allowed to make personally if he or she had not died. **[p. 203]**

3. Beneficiaries

a. **Wrongful death beneficiaries.** Wrongful death beneficiaries are usually the spouse and children of the victim. Most statutes allow a victim's parents to be beneficiaries if the victim had no spouse or children. Stepchildren and illegitimate children are ordinarily not beneficiaries. **[p. 204]**

b. **Survival action beneficiary.** The beneficiary in a survival action is the estate of the victim. **[p. 204]**

4. **Damages**

Damages in all jurisdictions include medical and related expenses, funeral expenses, and the loss of victims' future earnings. States are split on availability of compensation for grief and the loss of companionship with a victim. **[p. 204]**

a. **Statutory limits.** Some wrongful death statutes limit total awards or limit the amount that members of particular classes of beneficiaries may receive. **[p. 204]**

b. **Death of a child.** Damages for the death of a child are affected by whether a jurisdiction recognizes noneconomic damages as well as economic damages. **[p. 204]**

i. **Only economic damages recognized.** A child's death may not cause any real economic loss. Some jurisdictions stretch the meaning of economic loss to recognize monetary value for anticipated companionship. **[p. 205]**

ii. **Economic and noneconomic damages recognized.** In a jurisdiction that allows recovery for noneconomic losses such as mental anguish or loss of companionship, a case involving a child's death is similar to a case involving an adult's death. **[p. 205]**

c. **Damages to estate rule.** A minority of jurisdictions calculate damages in terms of the loss to a decedent's estate. This method estimates the amount the decedent would have earned had he or she lived a normal period of time and then deducts from that amount an estimate of the amounts he or she would have spent personally. **[p. 205]**

d. **Spouse's remarriage.** Most jurisdictions prohibit informing a jury that a victim's widow or widower has remarried prior to the time of the wrongful death suit. **[p. 205]**

5. **Defenses**

Negligence by the victim or beneficiary is a defense in a wrongful death or survival action under comparative negligence principles. **[p. 205]**

J. PUNITIVE DAMAGES

In exceptional cases juries are permitted to award punitive damages in addition to compensatory damages. Punitive damages are taken from a defendant as a punishment. Usually the plaintiff must show reckless or willful and wanton conduct by the defendant. The punitive damages award is ordinarily given to the plaintiff, but some states require that a portion of punitive damages be paid to the state. **[p. 205]**

1. **Multiple Judgments Against a Single Defendant**

   A single defendant might be subject to punitive damages awards if there are many similarly injured plaintiffs. This risk has led some manufacturers to bankruptcy. **[p. 206]**

2. **Constitutional Rules**

   The United States Supreme Court has ruled that punitive damages in general do not violate due process but that some punitive awards may be too high to be constitutional. **[p. 206]**

   a. **Multiple-state conduct.** A state court jury may only consider a defendant's conduct in that state in assessing punitive damages. **[p. 207]**

   b. **Reprehensible conduct.** Conduct that represents a good-faith choice among possible courses of action is not reprehensible enough to support a large punitive damages award. **[p. 207]**

   c. **Compensatory to punitive ratio.** The ratio between compensatory and punitive damages must not be too large. **[p. 207]**

   d. **Relationship to civil or criminal penalties.** A punitive damages award can be supported by a showing that it is similar in size to civil or criminal penalties that a state might impose for the defendant's type of conduct. **[p. 207]**

3. **Insurance for Punitive Damages**

   Some insurance policies explicitly exclude coverage for punitive damages. Some courts also prohibit such coverage, since it would negate the punitive effect of the damages. **[p. 207]**

4. **Statutory Restrictions**

   State statutes may control punitive damages awards. Some require that portions of punitive awards be paid to the state rather than to the plaintiffs. Some also impose ceilings or heighten the evidentiary standards for plaintiffs' proof. **[p. 207]**

K. CONDITIONAL NEW-TRIAL ORDERS: ADDITUR AND REMITTITUR

Additur and remittitur are orders by a trial judge that a new trial will be held unless the party who has opposed a motion for new trial accepts a judgment in a lesser (remittitur) or greater (additur) amount set by the judge. **[p. 208]**

13 DEFENSES

A. PLAINTIFF'S NEGLIGENT CONDUCT

Tort law treats a plaintiff's negligent conduct as a defense with the doctrines of contributory negligence and comparative negligence. **[p. 212]**

1. Contributory Negligence Defined

Under contributory negligence a plaintiff whose own negligence contributes in any way to his or her injury is prohibited from recovering damages. **[p. 212]**

a. **Contemporary significance.** Only Alabama, Maryland, North Carolina, Virginia, and the District of Columbia use the contributory negligence doctrine. **[p. 213]**

b. **Rationales.** The basic rationale is that no one else should pay for a person's own wrong. Another rationale is that the plaintiff's conduct is the proximate cause of the plaintiff's harm. **[p. 213]**

c. **Application.** To apply the contributory negligence doctrine it is necessary to evaluate the plaintiff's conduct. Standards of care used for this evaluation are essentially the same as the standards used to evaluate the conduct of a defendant. **[p. 213]**

i. **Child's standard of care.** Some scholars suggest that the special child's standard of care was developed to protect children from being found negligent and thus barred from recoveries. **[p. 213]**

ii. **Causation.** A defendant who sought to use the contributory negligence defense was obligated to show that the plaintiff's negligence had a cause-in-fact and a proximate-cause relationship to the plaintiff's injury. **[p. 214]**

d. **Exceptions to the contributory negligence defense.**

i. **Last clear chance doctrine.** In a case where the defendant had the last clear chance to avoid an injury, the contributory negligence doctrine is withdrawn and the plaintiff is entitled to full recovery. **[p. 214]**

ii. **Unavailable as a defense to certain types of misconduct by defendants.** A plaintiff's contributory negligence did not bar recovery if the defendant's conduct was an intentional tort, was reckless or willful and wanton, or was a violation of a safety statute adopted for the protection of individuals like the plaintiff. **[p. 215]**

2. **Comparative Negligence**

Under the comparative negligence doctrine a plaintiff's negligence is not automatically a bar to recovery. **[p. 215]**

a. **Contemporary significance.** Forty-six states use comparative negligence to deal with a plaintiff's contribution to his or her own injury. Another name for the doctrine is comparative fault. **[p. 216]**

b. **Contrast with contributory negligence.** Under contributory negligence a negligent plaintiff recovers nothing and a blameless plaintiff recovers full damages. Under comparative negligence a plaintiff who was partly responsible for his or her injury is not necessarily barred from recovery but may be entitled to damages that are reduced to reflect the plaintiff's responsibility. **[p. 215]**

c. **Application.** All comparative negligence systems require determinations of the amount of a plaintiff's damages and the percentage of the plaintiff's responsibility for the damages. **[p. 216]**

i. **Meaning of "plaintiff's percentage."** Jurors are usually told to assign a percentage of negligence or responsibility to each party whose conduct they are required to evaluate. **[p. 216]**

(a) **Quality or causal significance of actor's conduct.** The percentage of responsibility could be based on the jury's conclusion about how bad the plaintiff's conduct was or on a conclusion about causal significance. Only a few jurisdictions specifically require the casual approach. **[p. 216]**

d. **Types of comparative negligence.**

i. **Pure.** In pure comparative negligence a plaintiff may recover if his or her negligence is less than 100 percent of the total negligence involved in the injury. Total damages are reduced by the plaintiff's percentage of responsibility. **[p. 217]**

ii. **Modified, 50-percent form.** In the 50-percent form of modified comparative negligence, a plaintiff may recover if his or her negligence is 50 percent or less of the total negligence involved in the injury. Total damages are reduced by the plaintiff's percentage of responsibility. A plaintiff whose negligence is 51 percent or more recovers nothing. **[p. 217]**

iii. **Modified, 49-percent form.** In the 49-percent form of modified comparative negligence, a plaintiff may recover if his or her negligence is 49 percent or less of the total negligence involved in the injury. Total damages are reduced by the plaintiff's percentage of responsibility. A plaintiff whose negligence is 50 percent or more recovers nothing. **[p. 217]**

e. **Modified forms and 50-50 cases.** The difference between the 49-percent and 50-percent forms of modified comparative negligence is only significant if a jury finds that the plaintiff and defendant were equally at fault. If the jury finds that the parties were equally at fault (50 percent and 50 percent), the plaintiff recovers damages (reduced by 50 percent) in a 50-percent, modified comparative negligence jurisdiction but recovers nothing in a 49-percent, modified comparative negligence jurisdiction. **[p. 218]**

f. **Illustrative chart.** Plaintiff's recovery under forms of comparative negligence by plaintiff's percentage of responsibility (assuming damages of $100,000): **[p. 218]**

	Plaintiff's percentage of responsibility		
Form	0 to 49	50	51 to 100
pure	$100,000 to $51,000	$50,000	$49,000 to zero
modified, 50-percent form	$100,000 to $51,000	$50,000	zero
modified, 49-percent form	$100,000 to $51,000	zero	zero

g. **Multiple-party cases.**

i. **Unit or individual rule.** In modified comparative negligence jurisdictions a plaintiff may recover only if his or her negligence is equal to or less than the defendant's. Some courts and legislatures have failed to specify whether a plaintiff's negligence should be compared to the negligence of each defendant separately or to the total of negligence assigned to all the defendants. These methods are called the individual rule and the unit rule, respectively. The vast majority of jurisdictions use the unit rule. **[p. 218]**

ii. **Nonparties' conduct.** Under comparative negligence some jurisdictions have eliminated or limited the joint and several liability doctrine, giving defendants incentive to offer proof about other parties' possible negligence. A defendant is free from responsibility for any share the jury may assign to any other party.

(a) **Phantom parties.** In some states a defendant is entitled to give notice to the plaintiff that he or she will seek to have the jury consider the negligence of phantom, or nonparty, actors. The jury is allowed to assign a percentage of responsibility to the phantoms, reducing the original defendant's share of responsibility. The plaintiff thus may receive a smaller amount of damages than in a system that precludes consideration of the conduct of nonparties. **[p. 220]**

h. **Rationale for comparative negligence.** The strongest impetus for the adoption of comparative negligence was dissatisfaction with the total bar of contributory negligence. Reluctance to "reward" careless plaintiffs was overcome by a belief that it was wrong to allow negligent defendants to avoid all the costs of the injuries they partly caused. **[p. 220]**

   i. **Fairness to plaintiffs.** Pure comparative negligence can be described as fair to all plaintiffs. A negligent plaintiff always bears some of the cost of the injury, since compensation from a defendant only covers part of the cost. **[p. 220]** Modified comparative negligence fails to compensate plaintiffs whose own negligence exceeds the 49-percent or 50-percent threshold. **[p. 220]**

   ii. **Serve the deterrence goal.** Pure comparative negligence deters all individuals from acting negligently because all negligent individuals bear the cost of their negligence. Modified forms similarly deter plaintiffs and defendants in all cases in which the plaintiffs' negligence does not exceed the forms' threshold amounts. In a case where a plaintiff's negligence is greater than the threshold amounts, however, the plaintiff recovers nothing. Such a case provides no deterrence to defendants. **[p. 221]**

   iii. **Increase compensation to deserving plaintiffs.** All forms of comparative negligence increase the availability of compensation to plaintiffs. Modified forms make compensation available to many plaintiffs who would have been excluded from recovery by the contributory negligence doctrine, but they continue to treat some plaintiffs' negligence as a full defense (negligence that exceeds the systems' thresholds of either 49 or 50 percent). **[p. 221]**

i. **Effect on traditional contributory negligence doctrines.**

   i. **Last clear chance.** Every jurisdiction that has adopted comparative negligence and has considered the continued applicability of the last clear chance doctrine has rejected it. A jury considers the facts that formerly supported application of the doctrine when it assigns percentages of negligence. **[p. 221]**

ii. **Sudden emergency.** Jurisdictions are divided on whether the sudden emergency doctrine should continue under comparative negligence. **[p. 221]**

iii. **Defendant's willful and wanton or intentional misconduct.** Under contributory negligence a plaintiff's negligence was not a defense to liability based on a defendant's intentional tort or reckless or willful and wanton conduct. A few comparative negligence jurisdictions still refuse to reduce a defendant's liability to a negligent plaintiff in such a case. Many allow the jury to compare a plaintiff's negligence with a defendant's conduct even if the defendant's conduct is worse than negligent. **[p. 222]**

iv. **Open and obvious danger.** A few jurisdictions have rejected the rule that an entrant on land has no cause of action against the landowner for an injury caused by an encounter with an open and obvious hazard. They treat an entrant's conduct as a factor for evaluation under comparative negligence principles. **[p. 222]**

v. **Safety statutes.** In most states a defendant who violated a statute enacted for the safety of a class of individuals that includes the plaintiff is prohibited from relying on the plaintiff's own negligence as a defense. **[p. 222]**

j. **Nonuse of available seat belt.**

i. **Not relevant.** A few jurisdictions prohibit consideration of a plaintiff's failure to use an available seat belt. **[p. 222]**

ii. **Plaintiff bears total cost of avoidable injuries.** In some jurisdictions a plaintiff bears the total cost of the injuries he or she would have avoided through use of the available seat belt. **[p. 222]**

iii. **Plaintiff's fault related to entire incident applies to all injuries.** The jury determines a percentage of fault that encompasses all aspects of the plaintiff's conduct. That percentage is used to reduce all damages, including those that might have been avoided with use of a seat belt. **[p. 223]**

iv. **Plaintiff's fault related to nonuse of seat belt applies only to avoidable injuries.** A minority of jurisdictions require juries to make findings of fault specifically for failure to use available seat belts. The negligence percentage with regard to failure to use a seat belt is applied to damages related to that failure. **[p. 223]**

v. **Statutes.** Many state statutes set an upper limit on the percentage of negligence that a jury may assign for that conduct. **[p. 223]**

B. ASSUMPTION OF RISK

Assumption of risk traditionally was a complete defense when a defendant established that it applied to a plaintiff. In the contributory negligence era the law recognized express assumption of risk and two kinds of implied assumption of risk. At present the majority of jurisdictions recognize express assumption of risk and only one kind of implied assumption of risk. **[p. 223]**

1. Express Assumption of Risk

Express assumption of risk is a plaintiff's agreement to suffer the consequences of someone's conduct without seeking redress for any injuries. Courts enforce such agreements when they are very explicit (usually in writing). **[p. 223]**

a. **Prohibited assumptions of risk.**

i. **Recklessness and intentional torts.** Courts refuse to enforce promises not to seek damages for the defendant's willful and wanton, reckless, or intentional torts. **[p. 224]**

ii. **Health care.** Health care providers are generally not allowed to have their patients assume the risk of negligent treatment. **[p. 224]**

iii. **Public services.** Common carriers and public utilities are not permitted to rely on express assumption of risk agreements as defenses against liability to their customers. **[p. 224]**

2. Implied Primary Assumption of Risk

Implied primary assumption of risk describes a situation about which a court holds that a defendant owes either no duty or a reduced duty of care to a plaintiff. Common examples are the activities of attending professional sports games or participation in sports. The bar to recovery applies whether the prospective plaintiff was aware or was not aware of the risk that ultimately injured him or her. This makes it more like a no-duty rule than true assumption of risk. **[p. 225]**

3. Implied Secondary Assumption of Risk

A second type of implied assumption of risk is called "implied secondary assumption of risk." The term describes the situation from which a jury can infer that the plaintiff chose to assume the risks connected with his or her conduct. Most jurisdictions no longer treat implied secondary assumption of risk as a full defense. **[p. 226]**

a. **Elements of implied secondary assumption of risk.** The defendant must show that the plaintiff: 1. knew and understood the risk; 2. voluntarily subjected himself or herself to the risk; and 3. acted in a way that showed that consent. **[p. 226]**

   i. **Voluntariness.** A plaintiff who relies on a defendant's assurances of safety is not treated as assuming the risks of the activity. Also, a plaintiff who reasonably encounters a defendant's hazard because of necessity is not treated as assuming the risk. **[p. 227]**

   ii. **Manifestation of consent.** The plaintiff's conduct must manifest consent. **[p. 228]**

4. **Assumption of Risk Under Comparative Negligence Doctrines**

a. **Express assumption of risk.** The concept of express assumption of risk continues to apply in the context of comparative negligence. **[p. 228]**

b. **Implied primary assumption of risk.** Implied primary assumption of risk continues to apply in the context of comparative negligence. **[p. 228]**

c. **Implied secondary assumption of risk.** Implied secondary assumption of risk can be reasonable or unreasonable.

   i. **Rejection of implied secondary unreasonable assumption of risk.** Conduct that involves a knowing and unreasonable encounter with a risk is a full defense in contributory negligence jurisdictions. Comparative negligence jurisdictions have rejected the doctrine of implied secondary unreasonable assumption of risk, because comparative negligence generally rejects the idea of treating imprudent conduct as a full defense. **[p. 229]**

   ii. **Rejection of implied secondary reasonable assumption of risk.** Conduct that involves a knowing and reasonable encounter with a risk is a full defense in contributory negligence jurisdictions. Comparative negligence jurisdictions reject that result. If a plaintiff whose knowing and unreasonable encounter with a risk is no longer barred automatically from recovery, it seems wrong to impose that bar on a plaintiff whose encounter was actually reasonable. **[p. 229]**

5. **Summary of Modern Status of Assumption of Risk**

[p. 230]

Type of Assumption of Risk	*Contributory Negligence Jurisdiction*	*Comparative Negligence Jurisdiction*
Express (plaintiff actually agrees not to seek damages for any injuries caused by the defendant)	Full defense	Full defense
Implied primary (plaintiff has no cause of action for injuries from activity in which courts have held that defendant owes plaintiff limited duty or no duty of care)	Full defense	Full defense
Implied secondary unreasonable (plaintiff encounters risk voluntarily, with full knowledge of risk, for a purpose that makes encountering the risk unreasonable)	Full defense	Possible defense (conduct evaluated under comparative negligence doctrines)
Implied secondary reasonable (plaintiff encounters risk voluntarily, with full knowledge of risk, for a purpose that makes encountering the risk reasonable)	Full defense	No defense (conduct treated as reasonable under comparative negligence doctrines)

C. STATUTES OF LIMITATION AND REPOSE

A statute of limitations provides a defendant with a full defense if the plaintiff fails to commence litigation within the time period specified in the statute. The time period begins when the defendant injures the plaintiff. A statute of repose similarly provides a full defense to any action brought later than a time defined in the statute. The time period begins prior to any injury. **[p. 230]**

1. Rationales for Limitations and Repose Statutes

The statutes protect people from litigation about events that are so old that accurate records or accurate testimony may no longer be available. **[p. 231]**

2. Expansion of Time Limits in Statutes of Limitations

a. **Discovery rule.** For medical malpractice cases the discovery rule sets the beginning of the statutory time period at the time when the plaintiff discovered or should have discovered the injury. **[p. 232]**

i. **Foreign objects only.** Some states apply the discovery rule only to cases involving objects left in a plaintiff's body. **[p. 232]**

ii. **Discovery of harm and suspicion of negligence.** In some states the statutory time period begins when the plaintiff discovers or should have discovered a harm and suspects or should have suspected that the defendant's negligence caused it. **[p. 232]**

b. **Continuous treatment doctrine.** The statutory period starts running at the conclusion of a course of continuous treatment by the defendant (rather than earlier, when the defendant committed the allegedly negligent act). **[p. 233]**

c. **Minority or incapacity.** The statute of limitations is tolled (stopped from running) for any period during which a plaintiff was a minor or was incapacitated. **[p. 233]**

d. **Repressed memory cases.** Some courts have developed pro-plaintiff doctrines for limitations in sexual assault cases where delay in filing claims is allegedly due to the victims' having repressed memory of the incidents.

i **Discovery rule with corroboration.** Some courts treat these claims under the discovery rule if a plaintiff provides corroborating evidence of the allegedly tortious conduct. **[p. 233]**

ii. **Discovery rule regardless of corroboration.** Other courts apply the discovery rule regardless of corroborating evidence. **[p. 233]**

iii. **Discovery of consequences of remembered sexual abuse.** In some cases courts have allowed suits to proceed under the discovery rule where the plaintiffs did not repress recollections of alleged sexual abuse but did not relate the abuse to its alleged emotional consequences until the statute of limitations period had expired. **[p. 233]**

D. IMMUNITIES

Immunities protect their holders from all tort law responsibility for conduct that would otherwise be a basis for liability.

1. Governmental Immunity

Governmental (or sovereign) immunity can apply when the defendant is a governmental unit, official, or employee. **[p. 233]**

2. Federal Tort Claims Act

The Federal Tort Claims Act (FTCA) allows individuals to seek tort damages from the federal government.

a. **Basic provisions.** When a federal employee acting within the scope of his or her employment negligently injures someone, the victim may recover damages from the United States if a private entity or person would be liable under the law of the state where the injury occurs.

[p. 234] When a plaintiff seeks damages under the FTCA, no claim is permitted against the employee personally.

i. **Respondeat superior.** The federal government is liable for injuries only in circumstances in which a private employer would be liable under respondeat superior doctrines. **[p. 234]**

ii. **Discretionary functions excluded from FTCA coverage.** The FTCA does not allow liability for injuries arising out of discretionary functions that involve significant judgment and policy making. **[p. 234]**

iii. **Negligent exercise of discretionary functions.** Even if the discretion involved in carrying out a discretionary function is exercised carelessly, the FTCA prohibits recovery for any resultant injuries. **[p. 235]**

iv. **Tests for discretionary functions.** One test for identifying discretionary functions treats planning as discretionary and work involved in carrying out a plan as nondiscretionary. A more general inquiry into whether the conduct involves considerations of public policy is currently required under United States Supreme Court decisions. **[p. 235]**

v. **Reasonable enforcement of statute or regulation.** The FTCA excludes liability for reasonable actions to enforce a statute or regulation. **[p. 236]**

vi. **Intentional torts excluded from FTCA coverage.** Liability for intentional torts is excluded. This exclusion is withdrawn, however, for law enforcement officers. A victim may obtain damages for assault, battery, false imprisonment, false arrest, abuse of process, or malicious prosecution committed by law enforcement or investigative officers. **[p. 236]**

vii. **Strict liability excluded from FTCA coverage.** The FTCA has been interpreted to forbid suits on strict liability theories. **[p. 236]**

3. States as Defendants

Traditionally state governments were immune from suit under the same theory that supported federal government immunity. Currently only a small number of states preserve full immunity. Factors leading to the erosion of immunity include the availability of insurance and a growing belief that all citizens, through taxation, should pay for harms the state inflicts on individuals. **[p. 236]**

a. **Discretionary functions.** Where immunity is abrogated, states still prohibit suits based on discretionary conduct. **[p. 237]**

b. **State tort claims statutes.**

i. **Exposure linked to insurance.** Some statutes expose the state to suit only if the state is insured for the loss. **[p. 237]**

ii. **Suit permitted for categories of conduct.** Some statutes allow suit only for conduct in specific categories, such as operation of motor vehicles or operation of real estate. **[p. 237]**

4. Local Government Units as Defendants

Counties and cities may also be defendants. Their immunity once covered only governmental functions. At present many states have lessened or eliminated even that narrow immunity. **[p. 237]**

a. **Governmental/proprietary distinction.** In attaching immunity to governmental functions, courts have denied immunity for proprietary activities (functions that a government might perform but that a private entity could also perform). **[p. 237]**

b. **Immunity rejected for insured risks.** In some states local government immunity is rejected for conduct covered by insurance. **[p. 237]**

c. **Limited-duty rules as a substitute for immunity.** As municipalities have lost immunity, courts have developed other methods to shield certain types of activity from tort scrutiny. For claims based on inadequate police protection, in particular, courts are likely to define the duty quite narrowly. **[p. 237]**

d. **Practices violative of federal rights.** A local government entity may be sued under a federal statute, the Civil Rights Act of 1871 (42 U.S.C. §1983), for a policy, custom, or practice that violates federally guaranteed rights under color of state law. **[p. 238]**

5. Officials and Employees as Defendants

Government officials and employees often have immunity from tort liability. The extent of immunity varies depending on the individual's rank and the type of activity. **[p. 238]**

a. **Legislators, judges, and prosecutors.** Legislators, judges, and prosecutors at all levels of government ordinarily receive absolute immunity for any conduct within the scope of their official duties. **[p. 238]** Qualified immunity may apply for acts outside the scope of official duties.

b. **Federal executive and administrative officials.**

i. **Claims based on state law.** Federal officials have absolute immunity against claims based on state law for acts within the scope of their official duties. **[p. 238]**

ii. **Claims based on federal law.** When a plaintiff claims that an injury was caused by a federal official's violation of his or her rights under the United States Constitution, the official has only a qualified immunity. The immunity is defeated with a showing that the defendant acted unreasonably. **[p. 239]**

c. **State executive and administrative officials.**

i. **Claims based on state law.** In most states there is no immunity for ministerial acts (acts that do not involve discretion). For acts that involve discretion most states grant officials a qualified immunity that is defeated with a showing of malice or bad faith. **[p. 239]**

ii. **Claims based on federal law.** Legislators, judges, and prosecutors have absolute immunity from claims based on federal law in connection with their legislative or judicial roles, but other officials have only qualified immunity. **[p. 239]**

d. **Governmental employees other than officials.** Qualified immunity applies to employees alleged to have violated a plaintiff's federal constitutional or statutory rights, unless the violation occurred in the context of purely ministerial functions. **[p. 239]**

6. **Charitable Immunity**

Charitable institutions such as hospitals and schools once received immunity from negligence liability in almost all states. Virtually all jurisdictions have now eliminated this doctrine. **[p. 240]**

7. **Familial Immunity**

a. **Claims against spouses.** A common law interspousal immunity has mostly been rejected or limited. Typical limits reject its application for: 1. intentional torts, 2. automobile accidents, 3. injuries prior to the marriage, or 4. litigation commenced after the termination of the marriage. **[p. 240]**

b. **Litigation between parents and children.** Common law doctrines traditionally prohibited parent-child suits. Primarily influenced by the availability of insurance, many states have eliminated or limited these immunities. **[p. 241]**

i. **Doctrines to limit immunity.** Even if a general immunity is available, many states reject it for: 1. intentional torts, 2. automobile accidents, 3. business or property disputes, 4. actions seeking damages for the death of parents, and 5. actions brought by adults against parents. **[p. 241]**

ii. **Parental standards of care.** Jurisdictions have established standards of care for parent-child interactions. **[p. 241]**

(a) **Reasonable parent standard.** Some jurisdictions use reasonable prudent parent tests. **[p. 241]**

(b) **No duty to provide reasonable supervision.** Some courts have held that parents have no tort duty to provide reasonable supervision of their children. **[p. 241]**

14 VICARIOUS LIABILITY

A. GENERAL DEFINITION

In some circumstances a non-negligent individual must pay for the consequences of someone else's negligent conduct. This is called "vicarious liability." A common example is the employer-employee relationship. **[p. 245]**

B. RATIONALE FOR VICARIOUS LIABILITY

1. Deep Pocket

It helps an injury victim to have as a defendant an enterprise, not just its employee. This increases the chance that money will be available to pay a judgment. **[p. 246]**

2. Deterrence and Loss-Spreading Rationales

An employer can spread injury costs to all customers and ought, morally, to be the one who suffers losses related to injuries. **[p. 246]**

3. Ambiguity of Deterrence Rationale

Defendants who are vicariously liable pay judgments where there is no proof that they have been negligent or blameworthy in any way. This makes it hard to claim that the doctrine encourages careful conduct. **[p. 246]**

C. RESPONDEAT SUPERIOR

Respondeat superior is a doctrine that makes an employer liable for an employee's torts. It applies when an employee injures someone while acting within the scope of employment. **[p. 247]**

1. Tests for Employment Status

The crucial question in a respondeat superior case is often whether the negligent person was an employee or an independent contractor. A person who employs an independent contractor is free from responsibility for harms that person causes. **[p. 247]**

a. **Control test.** The basic distinction between an employee and an independent contractor is that an employee is subject to significant control and supervision, but an independent contractor has freedom to decide how to work. An independent contractor may do work for many employers, is paid to accomplish a result rather than to work in any particular way, and may supply the needed tools personally. **[p. 247]**

2. **Scope of Employment**

One test defines scope of employment as acts that further the employer's business purpose. **[p. 248]**

a. **Mixed business and pleasure.** A worker's acts that combine business and pleasure are usually within the scope of employment. **[p. 248]**

b. **Travel to and from workplace.** Travel from home to work is always defined as outside the scope of employment. Travel from work to home is sometimes within the scope of employment. **[p. 248]**

c. **Side trips.** Common law courts used the expression *frolic and detour* for a side trip an employee took to serve his or her own need while en route for a work-related purpose. They usually treated the side trip as outside the scope of employment. Modern courts use a foreseeability analysis for this issue. **[p. 249]**

d. **Smoking and other personal conduct.** Modern courts usually impose liability on employers for negligent injuries employees inflict while smoking or while walking to a bathroom. **[p. 249]**

e. **Intentional torts.** If an employee commits an intentional tort, the employer is usually liable if the worker did it to further the employer's enterprise. **[p. 249]**

i. **Special employers.** Some employers are liable even for personally motivated intentional torts by employees if the employer and the victim have a special relationship such as passenger-common carrier or innkeeper-guest. **[p. 249]**

ii. **Facilitation of intentional tort.** Some business operations may facilitate the commission of intentional torts. A courts sometimes makes an employer liable for an employee's intentional torts in this circumstance. **[p. 250]**

iii. **General foreseeability test.** A minority of courts make employers liable for a foreseeable intentional tort by employees. **[p. 250]**

iv. **Dangerous instrumentalities.** A minority of courts impose liability on employers for employees' intentional torts committed using dangerous instrumentalities related to the employees' work. **[p. 250]**

D. INDEPENDENT CONTRACTORS: RESPONSIBILITY FOR THEIR TORTS

The client or employer of an independent contractor usually has no responsibility for harms that contractor may inflict. **[p. 250]**

1. Test for Independent Contractor Status

The test for independent contractor status is the mirror image of the test for employee status. **[p. 250]**

2. Injuries to Employees of Contractor

Most jurisdictions hold that a worker has no cause of action against the employer of a contractor, even if exceptions to the usual rules of independent contractor liability make the employer of the contractor responsible for injuries the contractor or its workers inflict on other individuals. **[p. 250]**

3. Vicarious Liability for Independent Contractors' Torts

a. **Nondelegable duties.** Some safety responsibilities, called "nondelegable duties," are so important that an individual who fulfills them by hiring a contractor is nonetheless responsible for injuries caused by the contractor's negligent acts. **[p. 251]** Typical nondelegable duties are the obligations to keep streets in repair and to make sure that a motor vehicle is in good working order. **[p. 251]**

b. **Inherently dangerous activities.** When an independent contractor does inherently dangerous work, the the contractor's employer is liable for injuries related to the activity's special risks if the contractor would be responsible for them under theories of negligence or strict liability. An inherently dangerous activity is one that presents a high degree of danger to others unless special precautions are taken. **[p. 251]**

i. **Doctrine limited to special risks.** This doctrine imposes vicarious liability only for injuries related to the special risks that qualify the activity as inherently dangerous. **[p. 251]**

E. JOINT ENTERPRISES

People who collaborate for a particular purpose are sometimes called "joint venturers" within a "joint enterprise." Each participant in a joint enterprise is responsible for any negligence by any participant. **[p. 252]**

1. Elements of Joint Enterprise

A joint enterprise is defined by express or implied agreement, common purpose, common pecuniary or business interest in that purpose, and equal rights to control the enterprise. **[p. 252]**

a. **Common pecuniary or business interest.** Under the Restatement sharing expenses of a trip is not enough to satisfy the common pecuniary or business interest element. **[p. 252]**

b. **Equal rights to control.** Automobile passengers who have a business purpose in common with the driver and who ride under an express or implied agreement are usually found to have enough control over the vehicle to satisfy the joint enterprise definition. **[p. 252]**

F. VEHICULAR INJURIES AND VICARIOUS LIABILITY

In addition to the joint enterprise concept, other methods of imposing vicarious liability in vehicular injury cases are automobile consent statutes and the family purpose doctrine. **[p. 253]**

1. Automobile Consent Statutes

A typical statute provides that if an automobile owner gives someone permission to use his or her car, the owner is liable for any injuries the driver may cause through negligence or other tortious conduct. **[p. 253]**

2. Family Purpose Doctrine

This doctrine imposes vicarious liability when a vehicle owner allows members of his or her family to use the vehicle. **[p. 253]**

G. PARENTAL LIABILITY FOR CHILDREN'S TORTS

At common law parents had no responsibility for their children's torts. Currently many states have changed this doctrine by statute. **[p. 254]**

1. Limited Liability for Willful or Malicious Acts

Many statutes impose liability on parents for the consequences of their children's willful or malicious acts, with a moderate ceiling on liability. **[p. 254]**

2. Liability for Negligent Acts

Some statutes make parents responsible even for their children's negligent acts. **[p. 254]**

H. IMPUTED CONTRIBUTORY NEGLIGENCE

Under the both-ways test, if someone would be vicariously liable for another person's negligence, the person subject to vicarious liability is charged with any contributory negligence by that other person in any suit where contributory negligence is relevant. The imputed contributory negligence doctrine has less importance as jurisdictions develop comparative negligence principles that tend to restrict any party's liability to a proportion of the injury related to that party's fault. **[p. 254]**

15 TRADITIONAL STRICT LIABILITY

A. GENERAL DEFINITION

A defendant who is strictly liable must pay for a plaintiff's injuries regardless of how carefully the defendant has acted. **[p. 257]**

B. ECONOMIC ANALYSIS OF STRICT LIABILITY

Strict liability can be understood in comparison to liability for negligence. Negligence doctrines seek to have society spend money on the less costly of either injury occurrence or injury avoidance. In contrast strict liability makes an enterprise pay for all injuries related to its activities, even if preventing them would cost more than the costs they represent. Some suggest that placing all the costs of injuries on the enterprise makes sense when the enterprise is in the best position to evaluate all the costs and risks. The enterprise can use its special knowledge to decide what volume of the activity to undertake. **[p. 258]**

C. HARMS CAUSED BY ANIMALS

1. Trespassing Animals

The traditional rule makes an animal's owner strictly liable for property damage it causes on another's land. **[p. 259]** Domestic animals such as cats and dogs are excluded from this rule.

a. **Statutes.** The common law rule has been superseded by fencing-out statutes and fencing-in statutes, primarily in the west. A fencing-out statute provides that a landowner has a strict liability action against the owner of trespassing animals only if the landowner has constructed a fence to keep animals out. A fencing-in statute provides that a landowner has a strict liability action against the owner of trespassing animals only if the animal owner has failed to construct a fence to keep the animals in. **[p. 259]**

2. Personal Injuries by Animals

Strict liability applies to personal injuries caused by wild animals and by domestic animals in certain circumstances. **[p. 259]**

a. **Classification of animals.** Domestic animals are those traditionally used for the service of mankind, such as cats, dogs, cows, horses, and bees. Wild animals are any nondomestic animals. **[p. 259]**

b. **Injuries caused by wild animals.** The owner or keeper of a wild animal is strictly liable for any harms that the animal inflicts related to its general propensities or any particular propensities known to the owner. **[p. 259]**

c. **Injuries caused by domestic animals.** The owner or keeper of a domestic animal is strictly liable for any harms that the animal inflicts if the owner knows or has reason to know of the animal's dangerous nature. Some state statutes impose strict liability on dog owners for their dogs' bites, precluding liability only if the owner can show that the plaintiff provoked the dog's conduct. **[p. 260]**

D. INJURIES CAUSED BY ABNORMALLY DANGEROUS ACTIVITIES

Strict liability applies to injuries caused by a defendant's abnormally dangerous activity. **[p. 260]**

1. Abnormally Dangerous Definition

Courts define these activities by evaluating six factors: high likelihood of risk; dangerousness of risk; risk cannot be eliminated by reasonable care; not a matter of common usage; appropriateness of location; community value. **[p. 261]**

2. Typical Abnormally Dangerous Activities

Usually classified as abnormally hazardous are the following: use of explosives and fireworks, crop dusting, and nuclear installations. Sometimes classed as abnormally dangerous but sometimes not so classed are aviation and transport of hazardous materials. **[p. 262]**

E. CAUSATION

The plaintiff in a strict liability case must establish cause in fact and proximate cause. **[p. 263]**

F. PLAINTIFF'S NEGLIGENCE

Under contributory negligence a plaintiff's negligence was not a defense to a claim based on strict liability. Under comparative negligence the majority position treats all aspects of a plaintiff's conduct as factors to be used by the jury in its assessment of comparative negligence, including conduct that might have formerly been characterized as assumption of risk. **[p. 264]**

16 PRODUCT LIABILITY

A. OVERVIEW

Theories of negligence, warranty, and strict liability can all apply to cases in which plaintiffs seek damages for injuries caused by products. **[p. 267]**

B. NEGLIGENCE

A person who suffers a product-related injury can establish a negligence cause of action against a defendant who produced or marketed the product by showing that: 1. the defendant owed the person a duty of reasonable care; 2. the defendant breached that duty; 3. the person suffered an injury; and 4. the defendant's conduct was a proximate cause of the injury. **[p. 268]**

1. Privity

Plaintiffs were once required to establish that they were in privity with the defendant in a products case. **[p. 269]**

a. **Definition.** If a person buys a product from a retailer, the buyer and the retailer are in privity. **[p. 269]**

b. ***MacPherson v. Buick Motor Co.*** The opinion rejected the privity requirement in any case where something was "reasonably certain to place life and limb in peril when negligently made." **[p. 270]**

c. **Modern range of allowable plaintiffs.** In all states negligence actions may be maintained against manufacturers by those who suffer personal injury proximately caused by negligence. **[p. 270]**

2. Duty of Reasonable Care

a. **Manufacturer.** The duty to act as a reasonable prudent person (the duty of due care) applies to designing a product, selecting raw materials and component parts, examining or testing materials and parts (if reasonable), manufacturing the product, inspecting and testing it, packing, shipping, and providing necessary instructions or warnings. **[p. 270]**

b. **Retailer.** The duty to act as a reasonable prudent person (the duty of due care) applies to all aspects of a retailer's actions. Retailers who sell things manufactured by others can meet the duty easily. **[p. 270]**

   i. **Inspections.** In most jurisdictions a retailer is obligated to inspect a product only if there is a particular reason to think that the product may be dangerous. **[p. 271]**

3. Proximate Cause

Each jurisdiction applies its proximate cause rules to negligence cases involving product-related injuries. **[p. 271]**

C. WARRANTY LIABILITY

If a seller sells something that turns out not to be as good as the seller claimed it would, the buyer has a contract-based, warranty remedy for that deficiency. Relief is based on proof of a discrepancy between the product as it is and the product as it was supposed to be, without regard to why it is deficient. The discrepancy is called a "breach" of the warranty. **[p. 271]**

1. Express Warranties

An express warranty is a seller's specific statement about a product's features or attributes. **[p. 272]**

a. **U.C.C. provisions.** The Uniform Commercial Code covers express warranties in §2-313. It provides that a seller can give an express warranty by: affirming a fact, promising something, describing the product, or showing a model or sample. **[p. 272]**

   i. **Reliance.** The U.C.C. requires that the warranty be part of the "basis of the bargain," which usually means that the statement must have been made during or prior to the sale transaction. **[p. 272]**

2. Implied Warranty of Merchantability

The U.C.C. implies a warranty of merchantability in sales of goods by merchants for that type of goods who regularly sell them. The goods must be "fit for the ordinary purposes for which such goods are used." U.C.C. §§2-314(1) and (2). **[p. 272]**

a. **Transactions covered.** The implied warranty of merchantability applies to food and drink as well as to sales of durable goods. It applies to sales by retailers, wholesalers, or manufacturers. **[p. 272]**

3. Implied Warranty of Fitness for a Particular Purpose

The U.C.C. implies a warranty of fitness for a particular purpose when: a buyer wants goods for a purpose that is not typical; the seller knows about that purpose; the seller recommends certain goods; and the buyer relies on the seller's recommendation. U.C.C. §2-315. **[p. 273]**

4. Privity

A traditional privity requirement has been relaxed by judicial action and legislative adoption of U.C.C. provisions. **[p. 273]**

a. **Judicial action.** *Henningsen v. Bloomfield Motors, Inc.* allowed a plaintiff who had been injured in a vehicular accident to sue the car's retailer and manufacturer on an implied warranty theory, even though she was not the purchaser of the car. **[p. 273]**

b. **U.C.C. and privity.** The U.C.C. provides states with three options.

i. **Alternative *A*.** A warranty claim that a purchaser would have may also be made by a member of the purchaser's household or a guest in the household if it is reasonable to expect that the person might be affected by the goods. **[p. 274]**

ii. **Alternative *B*.** A warranty claim that a purchaser would have may also be made by any natural person who may reasonably be expected to suffer personal injury from the goods. **[p. 274]**

iii. **Alternative *C*.** Alternative *C* expands on Alternative *B* by adding non-natural plaintiffs (such as business entities) and property damage claims. **[p. 274]**

5. **Defenses**

Certain traditional warranty defenses have been rejected by the U.C.C., by federal law, and by courts. These include disclaimers in some instances, limitations on damages, and requirements of notice of breach. **[p. 274]**

D. STRICT LIABILITY

Under strict liability the plaintiff must show that the product had a manufacturing defect (product failed to meet manufacturer's specifications), a design defect (design was not adequately safe), or a defect in warnings or instructions (it lacked information required to make its use less dangerous). The plaintiff does not have to show that the defendant acted unreasonably in producing or selling it. **[p. 275]**

1. **Comparison with Negligence Liability**

Strict liability for product cases is similar in many ways to negligence liability. **[p. 275]**

a. **Relationship to *res ipsa loquitur*.** The *res ipsa loquitur* doctrine allows a jury to infer negligence; the strict liability theory allows a jury to impose liability without finding that any negligence occurred. **[p. 275]**

b. **Range of defendants.** Strict liability allows plaintiffs to obtain redress from more defendants than would usually be subject to liability under a negligence analysis. **[p. 275]**

c. **Reasonably produced dangerous product.** In a rare case a manufacturer might act reasonably and still produce a dangerous product. **[p. 275]**

FIGURE 2

Restatement Language	*Issues and Explanations*
§402A Special Liability of Seller of Product for Physical Harm to User or Consumer	The "special liability" is strict liability.
One who sells	The defendant must be one who sells the product. Manufacturers and wholesalers, as well as retailers, are product sellers.
any product	§402A covers products, not services.
in a defective condition unreasonably dangerous	"[D]efective condition unreasonably dangerous" is a term of art interpreted in a variety of ways.
to the user or consumer or to his property	Injury to a person or to property can be a basis for recovery.
is subject to liability for physical harm thereby caused to the ultimate user or consumer, or to his property, if	§402A applies only if an injury produces physical damages. It does not apply to a case with only economic damages.
(a) the seller is engaged in the business of selling such a product, and	The defendant must regularly sell the product. Sellers of used goods may be outside of this definition if they sell many different types of goods.
(b) it is expected to and does reach the user or consumer without substantial change in the condition in which it is sold.	A seller is free from responsibility if injuries result from significant product alterations that the seller could not reasonably foresee.
(2) The rule stated in Subsection (1) applies although	The two statements following this introductory clause represent the two pro-plaintiff elements from negligence law and warranty law that §402A incorporates.
(a) the seller has exercised all possible care in the preparation and sale of this product, and	Liability is strict (as in warranty cases). Even the best possible care is no defense if the product was defective.
(b) the user or consumer has not bought the product from or entered into any contractual relation with the seller.	Privity between the victim and the defendant is not required (as in negligence cases after *MacPherson v. Buick*).

d. **Defective designs.** The analysis of strict liability for defective designs in most jurisdictions uses concepts that are highly similar to negligence concepts. **[p. 276]**

2. **Restatement §402A**

Restatement §402A, promulgated in the mid-1960s, provides strict liability for product injuries. It was subsequently adopted in most states. **[p. 276]**

a. **§402A text.** Figure 2, opposite, sets out the text of the Restatement section in the left-hand column. The right-hand column explains the main significance of each portion of the text. **[p. 276]**

b. **Identifying the defendant or defendants.** In most states a victim of a product-related injury may obtain damages from any individual or entity with any role in the manufacture, distribution, or sale of the product. **[p. 278]**

i. **Contemporary modifications.** Some states allow strict liability claims only against a product's manufacturer. Others apply that limitation generally but allow suits against wholesalers and retailers if the manufacturer is not solvent or is not subject to state jurisdiction. **[p. 278]**

c. **Manufacturing defect.** A product has a manufacturing defect if there is a difference between its condition when it leaves the manufacturer's possession and the manufacturer's specifications. **[p. 278]**

d. **Design defect.** Most product liability cases involve products sold in exactly the condition that the manufacturer intended. The plaintiff must show that such a product was in a "defective condition unreasonably dangerous," in the language of Restatement §402A, because of its design. **[p. 279]**

i. **Consumer expectation.** The consumer expectation test asks whether the product is dangerous "to an extent beyond that which would be contemplated by the ordinary consumer who purchases it, with the ordinary knowledge common to the community as to its characteristics." Restatement §402A, comment *i.* **[p. 279]**

ii. **Risk-benefit.** Many jurisdictions use a risk-benefit test to ask whether the design selected was reasonable in light of its risks and benefits. Courts use many different factors in applying a risk-benefit analysis. A seven-part test suggested by the late John Wade is used in many jurisdictions. Its factors are:

- the product's usefulness and desirability as designed;
- likely occurrence and severity of injury;

- availability of safer alternative design or product;
- manufacturer's ability to eliminate danger without impairing its usefulness or making it too expensive;
- user's ability to avoid the danger;
- user's anticipated awareness of the danger; and
- feasibility of manufacturer's spreading the risk through insurance or pricing. **[p. 279]**

iii. **Alternative tests: consumer expectation or risk-benefit.** In some states a plaintiff is permitted to show defective design with either the consumer expectation test or the risk-benefit test. **[p. 280]**

iv. **Feasible alternative.** To prove that defendants' products were defective, plaintiffs in some jurisdictions must prove that they failed the risk-benefit test and that feasible, safer alternatives existed. An American Law Institute study, prepared as a possible replacement for the Restatement (Second) of Torts, adopts this view. **[p. 280]**

v. **Unavoidably unsafe products.** §402A includes comment *k* on unavoidably unsafe products. A dangerous product that is socially useful is outside the scope of strict liability if: 1. the product's benefits outweigh its dangers; and 2. the seller provides adequate warnings along with the product. **[p. 281]**

e. **Warnings or instructions defect.** A product that is free from manufacturing or design defects may be defective if safety could have been increased by better warnings or instructions for use. **[p. 281]**

i. **Standard for warnings and instructions.** The standard for adequacy of a product's warnings or instructions is essentially a negligence standard. If the cost of a warning or particular instruction is less than the cost of the injuries it might prevent, then the warning or instruction should be provided. **[p. 281]**

ii. **Learned intermediary doctrine.** For prescription drugs manufacturers are permitted to satisfy the obligation to warn by providing warnings to doctors. Those learned intermediaries are expected to convey the warning information to their patients. **[p. 282]**

iii. **Heeding presumption.** In most jurisdictions it may be presumed that a plaintiff would have heeded a proper warning or instruction. **[p. 282]**

f. **Factual context for all cases.**

i. **General rule: Consider only facts knowable when product manufactured.** The overwhelming weight of authority excludes from consideration information that was not within the scope of human knowledge at the time the defendant made the product. **[p. 283]**

ii. **Liability based on later-known facts.** In *Beshada v. Johns-Manville Products Corp.* the court imposed responsibility on a defendant for its failure to warn about risks that were scientifically unknowable at the time the defendant marketed its product. **[p. 283]**

g. **All defects: present when defendant released product.** A defendant has strict liability only for defects that were present at the time the defendant released the product into the stream of commerce. **[p. 283]**

i. **Responsibility for anticipated modifications.** If a seller provides a product and knows that the user is likely to modify it in a particular way, strict liability may be imposed on the seller if that modification makes the product defective. **[p. 283]**

3. **Compliance with State of the Art, Statutes, or Regulations**

a. **Common law.** A jury may reject the custom of an industry or a regulatory or statutory requirement and decide that under the applicable tort law standards the defendant should be liable. **[p. 284]**

b. **State statutes.** Under some state statutes defendants are protected from liability if their products complied with applicable regulations or statutes or with the state of the art at the time they were made. **[p. 284]**

c. **Pre-emption by federal statutes and regulations.** As a matter of constitutional law, some federal statutes pre-empt the right of states to impose common law, statutory, or regulatory controls on certain activities. **[p. 284]**

i. **Application dependent on statutory interpretation.** Application of the pre-emption doctrine depends on statutory interpretation. In recent cases, for example, federal statutes have been held to pre-empt some but not all state-based remedies for injuries caused by cigarettes and pacemakers. **[p. 285]**

d. **Government contractor defense.** A defendant who supplies a product to the federal government for military use has no liability for injuries the product causes if it complies with government specifications. **[p. 285]**

4. **Causation**

The plaintiff must establish that the product's defect was a cause in fact and a proximate cause of his or her injury. **[p. 285]**

5. **Plaintiff's Conduct**

During the early development of strict liability for product-related injuries, misuse was a defense but ordinary negligence by the plaintiff was not. The majority of states now apply comparative negligence principles to a plaintiff's ordinary negligence but may treat misuse as a full defense under certain circumstances. **[p. 285]**

a. **Ordinary negligence.**

i. **Restatement (contributory negligence era).** Restatement §402A states that ordinary contributory negligence is not a defense. It also states that assumption of the risk is a full defense. **[p. 285]**

ii. **Current treatment (comparative negligence).** In almost all jurisdictions now a jury compares a plaintiff's negligence with a defendant's stict liability. **[p. 286]**

b. **Misuse.** When a plaintiff has allegedly misused a product, a defendant can argue: 1. there was no defect in the product; 2. the strange use of the product caused the harm; or 3. the plaintiff's negligence should reduce or bar recovery. **[p. 286]**

i. **Duty.** A product seller has a duty to provide a product that is not defective for foreseeable uses. Thus, the decision about whether a product was defective must necessarily include a decision about what use the product was meant to have. **[p. 286]**

(a) **Crashworthy vehicles.** Car manufacturers once claimed that cars were made for ordinary driving, not for crashes. All courts currently require cars to be "crashworthy." **[p. 286]**

ii. **Causation.** A defendant may be able to show that the product's defect did not cause the injury because the real cause of the injury was the plaintiff's misuse of the product. **[p. 287]**

iii. **Comparative negligence.** Some conduct that a defendant might characterize as "misuse" is treated as plaintiff's carelessness. **[p. 287]**

6. Evidentiary Issues

a. **Subsequent remedial measures.** A nearly universal rule in negligence cases prohibits use of evidence of a defendant's postaccident remedial measures to prove negligence. Most courts apply that rule to strict liability. A minority admit evidence of subsequent remedial measures in strict liability cases as relevant to defectiveness. **[p. 287]**

b. **Epidemiological data.** A few courts require plaintiffs to introduce epidemiological data to support claims that environmental hazards caused illnesses or that a harm was related to a particular drug. **[p.288]**

17 Workers' Compensation and Other Alternative Compensation Systems

A. WORKERS' COMPENSATION

State statutes grant employers immunity from suits by employees seeking damages for workplace injuries but require them to pay specified amounts for injuries that occur in the course of and arising out of employment. **[p. 293]**

1. Intentional Misconduct Exception

An employee continues to have a right to seek redress from an employer under any common law theory for intentional misconduct. **[p. 294]**

2. Actions Against Others Involved in Workplace Injury

Workers injured in accidents that involve equipment often seek to obtain damages from the suppliers of the equipment. Workers' compensation statutes do not prevent recovery from others whose conduct contributed to the injury. **[p. 295]**

B. AUTOMOBILE INJURY COMPENSATION SYSTEMS (NO-FAULT SYSTEMS)

Under no-fault statutes for automobile injuries, insurance provides benefits for injuries that are within the statutes' definitions of coverage, and there is no litigation to determine anyone's fault. **[p. 295]**

C. CHILDHOOD VACCINE INJURIES

A federal statute provides a compensation system for victims of injuries related to childhood vaccines, with no requirement that the victims prove fault. **[p. 295]**

18 NUISANCE

A. DEFINITIONS

1. Private Nuisance

A private nuisance is a thing or activity that substantially and unreasonably interferes with a plaintiff's use and enjoyment of his or her land or interest in land. **[p. 298]**

2. Public Nuisance

A public nuisance is an unreasonable interference with a right possessed by the general public. **[p. 298]**

3. Injury, Not Tort

A nuisance is a harm to a plaintiff's interest in land, but the plaintiff must establish duty, breach, and causation to win a remedy. **[p. 298]**

B. PRIVATE NUISANCE: ELEMENTS

The plaintiff in a private nuisance case must show that: the defendant's conduct was intentional, reckless, negligent, or connected with an abnormally dangerous activity; the plaintiff suffered substantial and unreasonable interference with the enjoyment of his or her land or interest in land; and the defendant's conduct caused the interference. **[p. 298]**

1. Defendant's Conduct

A plaintiff may use many types of proof to show that the defendant's conduct involved an abnormally dangerous activity, was negligent, or was reckless. To show that it was intentional, a plaintiff might show that the defendant continued it after learning about its effects on the plaintiff's land. **[p. 298]**

2. Substantial Harm

The defendant's conduct must have an effect on the plaintiff's land or interest in land that would be significant to a typical person in the community or would have a significant effect on land in the community being used in a typical way. **[p. 299]**

3. Unreasonableness

To determine unreasonableness of the defendant's effect on the plaintiff's land, a court usually compares the harm to the plaintiff with the utility of the defendant's conduct. The Restatement also asks whether the defendant's activity would be economically feasible if the defendant had to pay for the activity's impact on the plaintiff. **[p. 299]**

C. COMING TO THE NUISANCE

Proving that the plaintiff had come to the nuisance by buying land near the defendant's was once a complete defense. A plaintiff's choice to move near the alleged nuisance is now just one factor in evaluating whether a defendant's activity is appropriate in its place. **[p. 300]**

D. REMEDIES FOR PRIVATE NUISANCE

1. Damages

A plaintiff is entitled to money damages for the harm inflicted on his or her enjoyment of the use of the affected property. **[p. 301]**

2. Injunction

An injunction is an order requiring the defendant to stop or modify the offensive activity. **[p. 301]**

3. Permanent Damages

Ordinarily a plaintiff may seek and be awarded damages many times against the same defendant if the defendant repeatedly commits acts that satisfy the elements of a nuisance claim. In *Boomer v. Atlantic Cement Co., Inc.* the court refused to enjoin the defendant's activities because they had great social value; instead it awarded a remedy of permanent damages. This was a damage award calculated to compensate the plaintiff for past and future harms from the defendant's activity. **[p. 301]**

4. Purchased Injunction

In *Spur Industrics v. Dcl E. Wcbb Dcvclopmcnt Co.* thc court grantcd an injunction to the plaintiff real estate developer conditioned on the developer's payment to the defendant of thc co3t3 thc dcfcndant would incur in rclocating its business. This remedy is called a "purchased injunction." **[p. 301]**

E. PUBLIC NUISANCE: ELEMENTS

The plaintiff must show the defendant has interfered with a right common to the public, inflicting a type of harm on the plaintiff different from the harm to the public. **[p. 301]**

1. Harms to Public Rights

Conduct that harms public rights includes: maintaining a brothel or unlicensed bar, creating a health hazard, or blocking a street. **[p. 301]**

2. **Plaintiff's Special Harm**

An individual is entitled to damages for a public nuisance only if he or she has suffered a harm of a type that is different from the harm that the nuisance inflicts on the general public. **[p. 302]**

a. **Rationale for special harm requirement.** The requirement that the plaintiff's harm be different from the general harm protects defendants from being sued by a huge number of citizens. **[p. 302]**

F. NUISANCE AND TRESPASS, DISTINGUISHED

Trespass cases involve a physical invasion of the plaintiff's land. Nuisance actions treat interference with the use or enjoyment of the land. **[p. 302]**

G. COMPARATIVE NEGLIGENCE DEFENSE

Comparative negligence principles generally apply to private and public nuisance cases. **[p. 302]**

19 MISREPRESENTATION

A. INTRODUCTION

Misrepresentation is a cause of action to redress economic harm caused by a communication that conveyed false information to the plaintiff. **[p. 305]**

B. INTENTIONAL MISREPRESENTATION

The plaintiff must establish: defendant's false communication; defendant's scienter as either intentional or reckless with regard to the truth of the communication; defendant's intent to have the plaintiff rely on the misrepresentation; plaintiff's justifiable reliance; and damages. **[p. 306]**

1. **Types of False Communication**

Statements, half-truths, actions, and concealment can be the basis for a claim of misrepresentation. **[p. 306]**

a. **Nondisclosure.** At early common law silence was not actionable. Modern decisions establish a number of exceptions to this rule. **[p. 307]**

i. **Fiduciary relationships.** In a fiduciary relationship there is often a duty to disclose material facts. **[p. 307]**

ii. **Incomplete statements.** A defendant who communicates a half-truth must furnish supplementary information that allows the statement to be understood accurately. **[p. 307]**

iii. **New information.** A defendant might obtain information after a communication to the plaintiff. If it makes the earlier communication untrue and the defendant believes the plaintiff is acting on the earlier information, the defendant must tell the plaintiff the new information. **[p. 307]**

iv. **Discovered reliance.** A statement cannot be a misrepresentation unless the defendant has intended that the plaintiff rely on it. If a defendant discovers that a plaintiff is relying on a false statement that the defendant has made to the plaintiff, the defendant must disclose the untruth to the plaintiff. **[p. 307]**

v. **Basic facts.** A defendant must disclose essential facts to a plaintiff if the defendant has special access, if nondisclosure would be unconscionable, or if other factors make the plaintiff reasonably expect disclosure. **[p. 307]**

b. **Opinions.** Under a traditional rule if a defendant says that something is his or her opinion, there is no liability even if the statement is false. **[p. 308]**

i. **Puffing.** The term *puffing* is used for commercial representations that are in the form of opinion. Courts refuse to base relief on false statements that are puffing on the theory that everyone knows sellers tell lies. **[p. 308]**

ii. **Modern classes of actionable opinion statements.**

(a) **Expert.** If the seller claims to have special knowledge on the topic, his or her opinion statements can be a basis for a misrepresentation claim. **[p. 308]**

(b) **Fiduciary relationship.** In a fiduciary relationship even statements of opinion can be treated as misrepresentations. **[p. 308]**

(c) **Plaintiff's reliance.** Opinion statements are subject to treatment as misrepresentations if the defendant knows of a plaintiff's special vulnerability to false statements. **[p. 308]**

c. **Statements about law.** If a statement about a legal standard implies something factual, the statement can be a basis for a misrepresentation action. **[p. 308]**

d. **Predictions.** Predictions are equivalent to opinions. They can be a basis for a misrepresentation claim only if they are made in a context in which opinion statements can be actionable. **[p. 309]**

e. **Intentions.** Statements about the speaker's intentions are treated as statements of fact. **[p. 309]**

2. Defendant's State of Mind

A plaintiff must show the defendant's scienter, or state of mind, with proof that the defendant: 1. knew or believed his or her statement was false; 2. did not have confidence in the accuracy of his or her express or implied statement; or 3. knew he or she did not have a basis for the statement. **[p. 309]**

3. Allowable Plaintiffs

A defendant who makes a misrepresentation can be liable to any individual to whom the defendant makes the misrepresentation. Under modern doctrines there can sometimes be liability to third persons for statements made in commercial documents or statements on which others might foreseeably rely. **[p. 309]**

4. Reliance

The plaintiff must show justifiable reliance. The misrepresentation must have been a substantial factor in the plaintiff's choice of action. **[p. 309]**

5. Damages

Damages for intentional misrepresentation are measured either in terms of reliance or benefit of the bargain. **[p. 310]**

C. NEGLIGENT MISREPRESENTATION

The elements of a cause of action in negligent misrepresentation are identical to those for intentional misrepresentation, with the exception of the scienter, or intent, requirement. Instead of proving intention the plaintiff in a negligent misrepresentation case must prove negligent action. **[p. 311]**

1. Defendant's Pecuniary Interest

The defendant must have a pecuniary interest in the transaction. **[p. 311]**

2. Allowable Plaintiffs

The defendant may be liable to any individual to whom he or she meant to give the incorrect information. Additional individuals may be permitted to recover if the defendant knew they would receive and rely upon the information. **[p. 311]**

a. **Communications likely to be used by third parties.** These statements include those made by a public weigher, a land surveyor, a will-drafting lawyer, or an accountant. **[p. 311]**

3. Physical Harm

If a defendant's negligent misrepresentation causes physical harm, the plaintiff may bring a cause of action under ordinary negligence principles. **[p. 312]**

D. INNOCENT MISREPRESENTATION

Liability for innocent misrepresentation may be available for: physical harm from products and monetary loss in a sale, rental, or exchange transaction. **[p. 312]**

1. Physical Harm from Product

Restatement §402B makes a defendant who is in the business of selling a product strictly liable for physical harm caused by a misrepresentation to the public about the product. **[p. 312]**

2. Monetary Loss in Sale, Rental, or Exchange

Another Restatement provision, §552C, applies strict liability for an innocent misrepresentation when it is made by someone in the negotiation of a sale, rental, or exchange transaction. **[p. 313]**

20 DEFAMATION

A. INTRODUCTION

Cases involving public figures or public topics are controlled by significant constitutional doctrines. In other cases traditional common law can apply. **[p. 316]**

B. COMMON LAW DEFAMATION IN CASES WITH NO PUBLIC ATTRIBUTES

Restatement §558 defines four elements for liability for defamation: a false and defamatory statement about another, unprivileged publication to a third party, fault, and damages. **[p. 316]**

1. Defamatory Statement

A defamatory statement is one that has a tendency to harm the plaintiff's reputation. **[p. 317]**

a. **Reputation in small group.** A statement with the capacity to injure the plaintiff's reputation within some relatively small group in society is defamatory if the group is respectable. **[p. 317]**

b. **Living person.** A statement must refer to a living person to be defamatory. **[p. 317]**

c. **Legal entity.** A legal entity such as a corporation or partnership can be defamed. **[p. 318]**

2. **Judge and Jury Roles**

If a judge decides that at least one reasonable interpretation of a statement is defamatory, then a jury will decide whether any individual actually did interpret the statement that way. **[p. 318]**

a. **Defamatory only in context of additional information.** Some statements are defamatory only if the people to whom they are communicated have additional information. The common law uses technical terms for the process of providing context. **[p. 318]**

i. **Inducement.** A statement of extra facts relevant to understanding the statement. **[p. 318]**

ii. **Innuendo.** A statement explaining how the inducement makes it possible for the statement to have a defamatory meaning. **[p. 318]**

iii. **Colloquium.** Proof that the statement could be interpreted as referring to the plaintiff. **[p. 318]**

b. **Group references.** References to large groups of people are not defamatory. A reference to a relatively small group may defame a single member of the group. **[p. 318]**

c. **Statements of opinion.** A statement that only expresses an opinion is never defamatory. However, a statement of opinion that seems to contain a representation about a fact may be defamatory. **[p. 319]**

3. **Truth**

The truth of a statement is a full defense to defamation. A statement with a minor error of fact is treated as substantially true. **[p. 319]** At common law the defendant bears the burden of proving the truth of the statement. **[p. 302]**

4. **Publication**

The plaintiff in a defamation case must prove that the statement was "published," meaning that it was communicated to at least one person. **[p. 320]**

a. **Defendant communicates with the plaintiff.** Communicating a defamatory statement about the plaintiff to the plaintiff does not satisfy the publication requirement. **[p. 320]**

b. **Special cases of defendant's communication.** The publication requirement is met if the defendant dictates a defamation to a stenographer or if a person includes a defamation in a will and an executor reads the will. **[p. 320]**

c. **Repeater.** A person who repeats a defamatory statement is subject to liability for defamation. **[p. 321]**

d. **Single publication rule.** A single edition of a book, newspaper, or magazine is treated as a single publication. **[p. 321]**

5. **Intent**

Defamation is a strict liability tort under the common law, although constitutional decisions prohibit strict liability in many cases. **[p. 321]**

6. **Damages and the Libel/Slander Distinction**

The common law recognizes two types of defamation: libel and slander. Damages for most types of slander require a showing of pecuniary harm, while damages for most types of libel can be presumed. **[p. 321]**

a. **Definitions.** In general a defamatory statement that is printed is a libel, and a defamatory statement that is spoken is a slander. **[p. 321]**

b. **Presumed damages for libel available at common law.** A private person harmed by a private defendant's libel may recover presumed damages. **[p. 322]**

c. **Pecuniary harm required for some slander damages.** The general rule for slander damages is that the plaintiff is entitled only to actual damages. **[p. 322]**

d. **Pecuniary harm requirement waived for specified slanders.** For certain types of slander, the pecuniary harm requirement is withdrawn. Called ''slander per se,'' these statements relate the plaintiff to crime, loathsome disease, lack of fitness for business or trade, or sexual impropriety. **[p. 322]**

e. **Punitive damages.** Common law allows punitive damages for libel or slander. **[p. 322]**

7. **Defenses**

Consent, privilege, and truth are defenses. In most cases at present, falsity is a factor that the plaintiff must cstablish. **[p. 322]**

a. **Privilege.** A defendant who would otherwise be liable for defamation may be immune from liability because of a privilege.

i. **Absolute privileges.** Absolute privileges provide total protection from liability for conduct that would otherwise support liability for defamation. They cover executive communications by federal and state officials, legislative communications, judicial communications, and spousal communications. **[p. 323]**

ii. **Conditional privileges.** A conditional privilege, sometimes called a qualified privilege, protects a beneficiary, unless the beneficiary has acted in a way that causes the privilege to be withdrawn.

Conditional privileges cover reports of public proceedings and statements about matters of public interest, among others. **[p. 323]**

iii. **Loss of conditional privilege.** A conditional privilege is overcome with proof of the defendant's lack of belief in truth of statement or of a purpose inconsistent with the purpose of the privilege. **[p. 324]**

C. CONSTITUTIONAL REQUIREMENTS

New York Times v. Sullivan introduced First Amendment concepts to the law of defamation, requiring analysis of the type of plaintiff and the topic of the allegedly defamatory statement. Supreme Court decisions seem to allow operation of the common law doctrines only in a case with a private plaintiff and a private-interest topic. The Court has reserved judgment on whether some of its requirements announced in cases where the defendants were media defendants might apply only to defendants of that type. **[p. 325]**

1. Actual Malice Requirement for Public Official Cases

In *New York Times v. Sullivan* the Court held that a public official plaintiff must show that the defendant acted with "actual malice." **[p. 325]**

a. **Actual malice: Primary definition.** *New York Times v. Sullivan* defined actual malice as "knowledge that [the statement] was false or with reckless disregard of whether it was false or not." **[p. 325]**

2. Actual Malice Requirement for Public Figure Cases

In *Curtis Publishing Co. v. Butts* and *Associated Press v. Walker* the Court held that a public figure is someone who is intimately involved in the resolution of important public questions or who has so much fame that he or she shapes events in areas of concern to the public. The actual malice requirement applies to such plaintiffs. **[p. 325]**

3. Fault Requirements for Private Figure Cases Involving Public Issues

In *Gertz v. Robert Welch, Inc.* the plaintiff was a private figure and the defendant was a magazine publisher. The court held that even a private figure plaintiff cannot be allowed to have a strict liability defamation action. States must require such a plaintiff to show negligence, recklessness, or actual malice. **[p. 326]** The court also held that to recover presumed or punitive damages the plaintiff must be required to show actual malice. **[p. 326]**

4. Fault Requirement for Private Figure Cases Involving Private Issues

In *Dun & Bradstreet v. Greenmoss Builders* the plaintiff and defendant were private parties. The Court held that where the topic of the defamation is of no public interest, it would not apply the *Gertz* requirement of a showing of actual malice for presumed or punitive damages. **[p. 326]**

5. Burden of Proof on Truth or Falsity

In *Philadelphia Newspapers v. Hepps* a private figure plaintiff sought defamation damages from a newspaper. The Court held that the plaintiff was required to establish that the statement was false. **[p. 326]**

6. Illustrative Chart

SUMMARY OF CONSTITUTIONAL ASPECTS OF DEFAMATION LAW

Type of Plaintiff	*Topic of Statement*	*Proof for Actual Damages*	*Proof for Presumed Damages*	*Proof for Punitive Damages*
Public official or public figure	Public topic	Actual malice	Actual malice	Actual malice
Private figure	Public topic	State's choice of negligence or more pro-defendant requirement	Actual malice	Actual malice
Private figure	Private topic	State's choice, not currently restricted by Supreme Court decisions	State's choice	State's choice

21 INVASION OF PRIVACY

A. FOUR CAUSES OF ACTION

Invasion of privacy cases are usually analyzed in a framework of four causes of action. These are: 1. appropriation, 2. public disclosure of private facts, 3. unreasonable intrusion, and 4. false light in the public eye. **[p. 331]**

B. APPROPRIATION

Appropriation requires a defendant's use without authorization of the plaintiff's identity for a commercial purpose. It is sometimes called "misappropriation of identity" or "invasion of a right of publicity." **[p. 331]**

1. Damages

Compensatory and punitive damages are available for appropriation of identity. Compensatory damages are measured by the value of the appropriated use. **[p. 332]**

C. PUBLIC DISCLOSURE OF PRIVATE FACTS

The elements of the tort of public disclosure of private facts are a defendant's disclosure to the public of private facts about the plaintiff; the disclosure must be "highly offensive to a reasonable person" (Restatement §652D); and it must not be a subject of legitimate public interest. **[p. 332]**

1. Disclosure to Public

The disclosure must be to the public. **[p. 332]**

2. Private Facts

This tort applies only to facts that are private. **[p. 332]**

3. Public Interest

If a person's life has become a matter of public interest, disclosure of facts that are private is not a basis for recovery. **[p. 333]**

4. Constitutional Limits on Recovery

The First Amendment limits the public disclosure of private facts cause of action, prohibiting a cause of action for disclosure of public record facts. Newsworthy facts not on the public record may be protected through a defamation action, but the constitutional requirements are not clear. **[p. 333]**

5. Damages

Damages include compensatory and punitive damages. Mental distress is an allowable component of these compensatory damages. **[p. 333]**

D. UNREASONABLE INTRUSION

The elements of the tort of unreasonable intrusion are an intrusion into a plaintiff's seclusion that would be highly offensive to a reasonable person. **[p. 334]**

1. Types of Intrusion

This tort covers intrusions such as planting of electronic listening devices or obtaining ordinarily private information about the plaintiff from third persons. **[p. 334]**

2. Seclusion

The conduct must affect the plaintiff in some private place. **[p. 334]**

3. Damages

Damages include compensatory and punitive damages. Mental distress is an allowable component of these compensatory damages. **[p. 334]**

E. FALSE LIGHT IN THE PUBLIC EYE

The false light tort requires public presentation of the plaintiff in a false light in a way that would be highly offensive to a reasonable person. **[p. 334]**

1. **Different from Defamation**

   Information that presents a person in a false light need not be defamatory. **[p. 334]**

2. **Constitutional Limits on Recovery**

   Current doctrine requires that a false light plaintiff show actual malice to be entitled to recovery, even if the plaintiff is a private figure. **[p. 335]**

   a. **Argument for relaxing the actual malice requirement.** In defamation cases the *New York Times* actual malice requirement has been rejected where the plaintiff is a private figure. A similar evolution of the actual malice requirement may occur for false light cases. **[p. 335]**

22 MISUSE OF LEGAL PROCEDURE

A. CAUSES OF ACTION

Three tort causes of action redress misuse of legal procedures: malicious prosecution, wrongful institution of civil proceedings, and abuse of process. **[p. 339]**

B. MALICIOUS PROSECUTION

Malicious prosecution requires: institution of a criminal proceeding for an improper purpose and without probable cause, malice, resolution of the proceeding in favor of the plaintiff, and damages. **[p. 339]**

1. **Institution of Criminal Proceedings**

   The defendant must take a significant action that brings about a criminal prosecution of the plaintiff. **[p. 339]**

2. **Improper Purpose**

   Improper purpose can be shown if the defendant's main purpose in instituting the criminal proceeding is something other than a desire to bring the offender to justice. **[p. 340]**

3. **No Probable Cause**

   A defendant has probable cause to instigate a criminal proceeding only if he or she reasonably believes that the plaintiff committed acts that constitute the charged crime. **[p. 340]**

   a. **Plaintiff's proof.** The plaintiff can seek to establish that the defendant did not have probable cause with an objective test or a subjective test. **[p. 340]**

b. **Consultation with lawyer or prosecutor.** When defendants institute criminal proceedings on advice from lawyers or prosecutors, most jurisdictions treat this advice as conclusive evidence of probable cause **[p. 340]**

4. **Outcome Favorable to Plaintiff**

The plaintiff must establish a favorable outcome of the criminal proceeding. **[p. 340]**

5. **Damages**

At common law presumed damages are permitted for malicious prosecution. It is unconstitutional to permit presumed damages in some defamation cases now, but it is unclear whether that limitation will be imposed on malicious prosecution cases. **[p. 341]**

C. WRONGFUL INSTITUTION OF CIVIL PROCEEDINGS

The tort of wrongful institution of civil proceedings is similar to the tort of malicious prosecution. **[p. 341]**

1. **No Probable Cause**

In the civil context a finding of probable cause can be based on weaker evidence than is required in the malicious prosecution context. **[p. 342]**

D. ABUSE OF PROCESS

Abuse of process is the intentional misuse of a judicial process for a purpose different from the purpose for which that process is intended. **[p. 342]**

1. **Favorable Termination Not Relevant**

Abuse of process cases do not involve an element of favorable termination of an earlier proceeding. **[p. 342]**

23 INTERFERENCE WITH ADVANTAGEOUS RELATIONS

A. INTERFERENCE WITH CONTRACT

Interference with contract cases involve at least three parties: a plaintiff who had a contract with a second party and a defendant alleged to have induced the second party to breach the contract. The plaintiff must establish that: 1. the plaintiff and the second party had a valid contract; 2. the defendant knew about it; 3. the defendant intended to interfere with it; 4. the defendant did interfere with it; and 5. the plaintiff suffered damages. **[p. 345]**

2. Particular Contracts

a. **Illegal, unenforceable, or contract to marry.** Interference with contract actions are not permitted in the context of these contracts. **[p. 346]**

b. **Employment at will.** The common law did not recognize an action for interference with an at-will contract. The Restatement and many modern courts do allow a cause of action. **[p. 346]**

3. Defendant's Conduct

A defendant is privileged to protect his or her own prior financial interests and to protect the financial interests of others. **[p. 346]**

4. Knowledge and Intention

The plaintiff must show that the defendant knew about the contract that someone breached and that the defendant intended to influence that person to breach it. **[p. 347]**

B. INTERFERENCE WITH PROSPECTIVE ADVANTAGE

The tort of interference with prospective advantage is similar to the tort of interference with contract, except it applies to business dealings that have not yet developed into a contract. **[p. 347]**

1. Privilege to Protect Defendant's Interest

The privilege to protect one's financial interests is applied more favorably to defendants in prospective advantage cases than in contractual interference cases. **[p. 348]**

C. INJURIOUS FALSEHOOD

A defendant who makes a false statement about a person's business or property with the intention of causing economic injury to that person is liable for injurious falsehood (or trade libel). **[p. 348]**

1. Attributes of Statement

The plaintiff must show that the statement was false and that it referred to the plaintiff. **[p. 348]**

2. Distinct from Defamation

A injurious falsehood need not be defamatory. **[p. 348]**

3. **Damages**

The plaintiff must show that the defendant's statement caused economic harm, such as a general loss of business. **[p. 348]**

4. **Defenses**

Consent is a full defense. Privileges available are those applicable to defamation and a privilege for fair competition. **[p. 349]**

1 INTRODUCTION

CHAPTER OVERVIEW

- This chapter describes tort law's basic definitions, some of its history, and its modern division into three main categories of causes of action.
- Tort law is a group of doctrines that allow individuals to recover damages for injuries others inflict upon them. These doctrines define harms and set limits on the consequences of actions for which defendants are responsible.
- The three main goals of tort law are: 1. to compensate deserving plaintiffs who have suffered loss; 2. to deter individuals from injuring others by making them pay for the harm they cause; and 3. to establish societal definitions of acceptable and unacceptable interactions.
- Contract law is different from tort law. Contract law generally involves negotiated arrangements between parties and the consequences of failure to follow those arrangements. In contrast, tort law generally involves parties who are strangers or who have not given any detailed description of how they will act toward each other.
- Criminal law is different from tort law. Criminal law is the state's method of controlling antisocial conduct. In contrast, tort law offers individuals the chance to deter antisocial conduct and obtain compensation for injuries it has caused.
- **Causes of action** in tort are usually categorized as based on: 1. intentional misconduct; 2. negligent misconduct; or 3. strict liability.

- **Intentional misconduct** is a defendant's intentionally acting in a way that tort law forbids, causing a type of injury for which tort law requires a defendant to compensate a plaintiff.
- **Negligent misconduct** is a defendant's acting less carefully than a reasonably prudent person would act, causing a type of injury for which tort law requires a defendant to compensate a plaintiff.
- **Strict liability** is a theory that allows an injured plaintiff to obtain compensation from a defendant without any proof of intentional or negligent misconduct, by showing that: 1. the defendant engaged in a type of activity to which strict liability applies; and 2. the activity caused the plaintiff to suffer an injury.
- The concepts of strict liability and faulty (or blameworthy) conduct have had different relative importance at different periods of the development of common law.
- For every tort, legal doctrines define a "prima facie case." This expression refers to the facts the plaintiff must establish to be entitled to a judgment against the defendant.
- For a jury to be permitted to consider a plaintiff's case, the plaintiff must introduce evidence on every element of the prima facie case for the tort claim on which the plaintiff seeks a judgment. The amount of evidence the plaintiff must introduce is whatever amount the judge believes is adequate to support a jury's conclusion that the element existed.

A. WHAT IS TORT LAW?

Tort law is a group of doctrines that establish and control causes of action for individuals who are harmed by the actions of others. Tort doctrines define what the law will recognize as harms in many types of situations. Tort doctrines also separate the nearly infinite consequences of people's actions into two groups: those for which the actor is responsible and those for which the actor is free from responsibility. Tort law has a number of general themes, but it is also a collection of a great many unrelated special rules.

B. GOALS OF TORT LAW

In addition to providing fair results in particular cases, tort law may serve certain more general societal goals. These are usually described as compensation, deterrence, and the definition of societal norms.

1. Compensation

The successful plaintiff in a tort action receives money from the defendant. This represents one of the main functions of tort law. It provides compensation to plaintiffs in situations where they have suffered losses that society believes they should not have to bear.

2. Deterrence

A defendant who is liable in tort pays money to the plaintiff. This is the flip side of the compensation effect of tort law. In theory, tort law deters dangerous conduct because defendants who would like to avoid having to pay money to plaintiffs will avoid actions that could lead to tort liability. More specifically, tort doctrines usually make defendants pay for damages when their conduct causes risk of injury more costly than the value of the risky conduct itself. For society as a whole, it is economically efficient to discourage conduct that will cause harms that are greater than the benefits it can produce.

3. Definition of Societal Norms

Tort law doctrines, established by judicial decisions or by statutes, serve two functions with regard to defining societal norms. They represent a consensus about how people and institutions should act in various recurring situations. Also, they communicate that societal consensus to the general population. Thus, they define and communicate ideas about what conduct is proper and what conduct is wrongful.

Example and Analysis

How does knowing about the goals of tort law help anaylze a torts problem? Sometimes it can be very helpful. For example, battery (discussed in Chapter 3) is the tort of intentionally causing an offensive or harmful contact with another person. You could justify tort law's having such a cause of action in terms of the three goals. Battery victims need compensation, because they often have sudden and unexpected medical bills. Battery defendants need to be deterred, because we don't want people committing unpermitted touchings on other people. Finally, it's good for society to reaffirm through the legal system that we respect individuals' bodily integrity.

C. RELATIONSHIP OF TORT LAW TO OTHER FIELDS

Tort law can apply to events that might also be treated by criminal law or contract law. An injury to a plaintiff involving tort law also might involve criminal law or contract law.

1. Criminal Law

Tort law is separate from criminal law. Criminal law is a system in which the state imposes penalties on wrongdoers, requiring them to pay fines, go to jail, or make amends in some other way for violating criminal statutes. A government employee, the prosecutor, decides when to bring cases and how to litigate them. The government bears the costs of prosecution, and the defendant bears the cost of defense.

In contrast, tort law is part of our civil system. A person who commits a tortious act may be required to pay money to a plaintiff or may be forbidden to do the act in the future, but tort law has no criminal penalties. Private individuals, as plaintiffs, begin tort cases and decide how to litigate them. The parties bear the costs of litigation.

2. Contract law

Contract law governs the relationships between people who have agreed to act toward each other in ways that they have specified in their contracts. Tort cases do not usually involve parties who have made an agreement to have a relationship. Tort cases usually involve strangers whose only relationship is the injurious event that has become the subject of litigation. When someone is hit by a car, tort law can resolve the economic consequences of that event. When a car buyer has a dispute with a car seller, contract law and its doctrines apply.

D. CATEGORIES OF TORT CAUSES OF ACTION

When a plaintiff claims that a defendant's conduct has injured him or her in a way that tort law recognizes as a basis for giving the plaintiff a remedy, our legal system usually characterizes the plaintiff's claim as involving intentional misconduct, negligent conduct, or conduct for which liability is imposed without regard to the quality of the defendant's conduct.

1. Three Main Categories

For most situations in which a person thinks that he or she has been injured by the conduct of another, tort law provides a means for possible recovery. There are three generally recognized categories of tort liability: **intentional torts, negligence,** and **strict liability.** The plaintiff in an intentional tort case must show intentional conduct by the defendant. In a negligence case the plaintiff must show that the defendant's conduct fell short of a recognized standard of care. In strict liability cases harmful conduct is the basis for recovery regardless of whether the defendant acted intentionally, recklessly, or negligently concerning the risk that harmed the plaintiff.

E&A EXAMPLES AND ANALYSIS

What are examples of tort actions that fit each of the categories (intentional torts, negligence, and strict liability)? Battery is an intentional tort. An easy example is an uninvited punch in the nose. A negligence cause of action involves a defendant's conduct that is unreasonable and that exposes someone to a foreseeable risk of significant harm. A storekeeper's failure to pick up a banana peel from the floor supports a negligence cause of action if a customer slips on the peel and gets hurt. Strict liability applies to certain types of activity by defendants who must pay for the harms they inflict regardless of intent or negligence. If a nuclear power plant blows up and injures a person, that person is entitled to damages without proving intentional harm or negligence (if the lawyers and the legal system survive the explosion).

---

2. Consequences of Categorization

The lines between the three causes of action are sometimes unclear. For example, a person who sells products without inspecting them may "know" that a certain number of injuries will likely occur. In a way, if that person continues to sell those products, it might be said that he or she intends to inflict injuries. Nonetheless, the label "intentional tort" is usually reserved for a situation involving clearer intent, like someone punching another in the nose. Despite the vagueness of lines drawn between categories of tort action, significant consequences follow from the designation of a cause of action as one based on intentional tort, negligence, or strict liability.

a. **Statute of limitations.** A statute of limitations requires that a plaintiff begin a lawsuit within a specified period of time following the occurrence of some event. State statutes may use different periods of time for the three different categories of tort suit.

b. **Range of consequences for which a defendant may be liable.** A defendant's conduct usually causes many results, some fairly predictable and some fairly remote. In deciding for which consequences a defendant should have to pay, a court may be influenced by the quality of the defendant's conduct. A defendant who was only negligent (or careless) will have to pay for fewer consequences than one whose conduct was intentional or one whose conduct was subject to strict liability.

c. **Types of damages.** In all types of tort cases, plaintiffs are entitled to recover damages, called **compensatory damages,** for actual harm. Actual harm is measured in dollar amounts intended to equal the value of the plaintiff's past and future pain and suffering, lost income, and actual expenses due to the injury. In intentional tort cases plaintiffs are also entitled to nominal and punitive damages. **Nominal damages** are a token or symbolic sum of money awarded to a plaintiff who is unable to prove any "actual" harm. **Punitive damages** are a sum of money taken from the defendant and given to the plaintiff entirely to punish the defendant, without being closely limited to the amount of actual damages proved by the plaintiff.

   i. **Nominal damages.** Nominal damages are a symbolic award that vindicates the plaintiff's right to be protected from the type of conduct the defendant carried out. The amount may be as small as one dollar.

ii. **Punitive damages.** Punitive damages may be very large amounts of money, but they are available only when the plaintiff shows that the defendant's intentional or reckless conduct was especially blameworthy (outrageous or malicious) and should therefore be deterred by a financial penalty imposed in addition to damages based on actual loss.

E. HISTORICAL PATTERNS IN TORT LAW DEVELOPMENT

Tort law began with the concept of strict liability and evolved to include the concept of liability based on fault. Both concepts are part of contemporary tort law.

1. Early Strict Liability

The earliest common law applied rules that minimized the need for interpretation and judgment. If you directly touched or otherwise injured another person, you were liable for damages. This was an application of strict liability. The plaintiff's cause of action was generally called "trespass."

Illustration: In Anonymous, K.B. 1466, Y.B. 5 Edw. IV, folio 7, placitum 18, the court stated that a person who raised a stick to protect himself from an attack would be liable to someone whom he struck accidentally, such as a person who had been standing behind him when he moved the stick to protect himself.

2. Development of the "Fault" Concept

The concept of fault involves making a decision that a person's conduct was blameworthy or substandard in a way that should affect the person's legal liability for the consequences of the conduct.

a. **Trespass on the case.** While trespass causes of action allowed strict liability, another type of cause of action known as "trespass on the case" developed at early common law. Liability for trespass on the case had to be based on proof of the defendant's fault.

i. **Distinction between trespass and trespass on the case.** An action seeking damages for a defendant's direct harm to the plaintiff was known as trespass. An action for damages caused indirectly by the defendant's conduct was known as tresspass on the case.

E&A EXAMPLE AND ANALYSIS

In common law times, if a defendant's carriage hit a plaintiff, an action could be brought in trespass. If a plaintiff ran into a broken carriage that partly blocked a road, resulting harm would be described as indirect, and the plaintiff's action would be known as "trespass on the case."

---

b. **Introduction of the fault principle as a defense to trespass claims:** Weaver v. Ward, 80 Eng. Rep. 284 (K.B. 1616). Originally, strict liability applied to actions in trespass, but the 1616 case of *Weaver v. Ward* established that a defendant whose conduct directly injured a plaintiff would be protected from liability if the defendant could show that the injury occurred "utterly without his fault." In this case the defendant shot a musket and wounded the plaintiff. The court treated it as a trespass case but ruled that the defendant could have avoided liability if he had been able to show that he had been completely free from blameworthy conduct.

c. **Adoption of the fault principle in trespass cases as part of the plaintiff's required proof:** Brown v. Kendall, 60 Mass. 292 (1850). Beginning in the 19th century, to recover in a negligence action, a plaintiff has been required to show that the defendant was at fault. This is illustrated by Brown v. Kendall, in which two people were trying to separate fighting dogs, and the defendant hit the plaintiff with a stick as he raised it over his shoulder. The court held that, in order to recover damages from the defendant, the plaintiff would be required to show that the defendant acted without reasonable care.

3. Modern Strict Liability

While the fault principle governs most tort cases involving accidental injuries, in certain situations strict liability now applies, excusing the plaintiff from having to show negligence or fault. There is strict liability for injuries caused by defective products. Strict liability also applies to injuries resulting from a defendant's abnormally dangerous activity. Defining an activity as "abnormally dangerous" involves consideration of a wide range of factors. There is a consensus that blasting and other uses of explosives are abnormally dangerous activities, but other endeavors may also be placed in this category.

Illustration: Spano v. Perini Corp., 25 N.Y.2d 11, 302 N.Y.S.2d 527, 250 N.E.2d 31, *on remand,* 33 A.D.2d 516, 304 N.Y.S.2d 15 (1969). The defendant's blasting destroyed the plaintiff's garage. The plaintiff was entitled to recover damages without showing any blameworthy or negligent conduct by the defendant, since the defendant's conduct was within the category of "absolute" or strict liability activities. This decision rejected prior New York doctrine that applied strict liability for blasting only if there had been a physical invasion of the plaintiff's property. This brought New York's law on strict liability for blasting damage into line with the majority view.

F. PROCEDURAL CONTEXT

To understand many aspects of tort law, a student needs to understand the context of civil procedure. This introduction describes the most important aspects of procedure for tort law: the concepts of prima facie case and judgment as a matter of law.

1. Prima Facie Case

To be entitled to judgment, a plaintiff must support a claim with evidence that can properly be a basis for a jury's conclusion that the plaintiff established each required element of the tort on which he or she has based the claim.

2. Elements of Prima Facie Case

There are different elements in the prima facie case for different tort causes of action. They are described in this text's discussion of each type of tort claim. Although different torts have different required elements of proof, for every tort it is a basic rule that the plaintiff must have evidence (or an excuse for a lack of evidence) adequate to support a jury's conclusion that the plaintiff has proved what each element requires the plaintiff to prove.

E&A EXAMPLE AND ANALYSIS

To recover for the intentional tort of battery, the plaintiff must prove that: 1. the defendant committed a volitional act; 2. the defendant intended by that act to touch the plaintiff in a harmful or offensive way; 3. a harmful or offensive contact with the plaintiff occurred; and 4. the defendant's act caused the harmful or offensive contact. There are many ways the plaintiff might produce proof about all these elements, but the crucial fact to remember is that the plaintiff must have proof related to each element in order to be entitled to a remedy. What if a plaintiff were to prove only that: a defendant ran toward the plaintiff with a knife, that the defendant meant to stab the plaintiff, and that the defendant slipped and fell before being able to touch or stab the plaintiff? This plaintiff would have been lucky prior to suing and unlucky in court. The plaintiff would not have established a prima facie case in battery. In this example the plaintiff would not have introduced proof adequate to support a jury's conclusion that two of the elements of the prima facie case had ever existed (a harmful or offensive touching of the plaintiff, and causation of that touching by an action of the defendant).

3. Judgment as a Matter of Law or Based on a Jury Verdict

In any lawsuit the plaintiff's preference is to have the judge grant the plaintiff judgment as a matter of law (sometimes called a directed verdict). This means that the jury would not deliberate or decide the case. The defendant's preference also is to win judgment as a matter of law. In deciding whether a party is entitled to curtail the usual process of a jury trial by having the judge order a result, courts use burden-of-proof concepts known as the burden of production and the burden of persuasion.

a. **Burden of proof.** The expression "burden of proof" refers to two related concepts: the burden of production and the burden of persuasion.

b. **Burden of production.** The burden of production is the obligation to produce evidence on an aspect of a claim. At the start of a trial, the plaintiff bears this burden.

c. **Burden of persuasion.** The burden of persuasion, also known as the risk of nonpersuasion, determines who will win a case if the jury is exactly in equipoise after both parties have presented their evidence. If the jury is not persuaded by either side in the case, then whichever party bears the persuasion burden (or the risk of nonpersuasion) loses the case.

4. Allocation of Burdens

The burden of production rests on the plaintiff at the start of a case. It may shift to the defendant, depending on the type and quantity of evidence the plaintiff introduces in meeting the initial production burden. The burden of persuasion usually remains on the plaintiff throughout a case.

5. Opportunities for Judgment as a Matter of Law

A trial can be conceptualized as a tug of war between the plaintiff and the defendant. At each party's end of the tug-of-war rope is a zone that could be called judgment as a matter of law for the other party. The middle zone is the jury's area, where a case cannot be decided as a matter of law for either the plaintiff or the defendant.

a. **Plaintiff fails to meet production burden.** A plaintiff may fail to introduce evidence that a reasonable juror could use as a basis for finding that each required element of the plaintiff's case actually did exist. In the battery example above the plaintiff might fail to meet the production burden if the plaintiff's case has no proof about the defendant's actually having caused a contact with the plaintiff. In that situation the plaintiff will have failed to meet the production burden. The defendant will be entitled to judgment as a matter of law.

b. **Plaintiff meets production burden and defendant makes no response.** If some evidence is introduced on each required aspect of the plaintiff's case, the defendant may or may not respond. If the defendant chooses not to respond, the plaintiff can seek judgment as a matter of law. That motion will require the judge to evaluate the strength of the plaintiff's evidence. The judge must characterize the plaintiff's case as fitting into one of two categories: leading to judgment as a matter of law for the plaintiff, or leading to a decision to allow the jury to deliberate and reach a verdict.

i. **Judgment as a matter of law for the plaintiff.** If the judge believes that the plaintiff's evidence is so strong that there is no legally sufficient evidentiary basis for a reasonable jury to find for the defendant, then the plaintiff is entitled to judgment as a matter of law.

   In the battery example above, the plaintiff might introduce substantial proof showing the defendant's volitional act and the defendant's intention to cause a harmful or offensive contact, and the plaintiff might have eyewitnesses testify that they saw the defendant stab the plaintiff. This would probably be a legitimate case for a plaintiff's judgment as a matter of law.

   If the only evidence that contact happened is testimony by the plaintiff such as, "I think he touched me, because I noticed some dust on my coat after he walked by," then it would be wrong to grant the plaintiff judgment as a matter of law, since a reasonable juror might be unpersuaded that contact really did happen.

ii. **Judgment based on jury verdict.** The judge may believe that, while the plaintiff's evidence is adequate to satisfy the production burden, meaning that it is strong enough that a reasonable juror could agree with it, it is not so strong that there is no legally sufficient evidentiary basis for a reasonable jury to find for the defendant. In this situation the case would go to the jury for resolution.

   A battery case in which the only proof of contact is testimony that the plaintiff thought contact had happened because the defendant had moved quickly toward the plaintiff and after that movement the plaintiff had a bruise and a ripped coat would probably be allowed to go to the jury.

c. **Plaintiff meets production burden and defendant responds.** In most torts cases the plaintiff does meet the production burden, and the defendant responds with evidence contradicting the plaintiff's. After all of the evidence has been produced, either party may move for a directed verdict. Considering such a motion, the judge will view all the evidence in the light most favorable to the nonmoving party (the party who would lose if the case were taken from the jury and judgment as a matter of law were granted to the moving party).

i. **Judgment as a matter of law for the plaintiff.** If the judge believes that the plaintiff's evidence is so strong that there is no legally sufficient evidentiary basis for a reasonable jury to find for the defendant, then the plaintiff is entitled to judgment as a matter of law.

Judgment as a matter of law could result for the plaintiff in a battery case if the plaintiff introduced persuasive evidence on all the required elements of the tort and the defendant's only response was that he believed stabbing to be neither harmful nor offensive.

ii. **Judgment as a matter of law for the defendant.** If the judge believes that there is no legally sufficient evidentiary basis for a reasonable jury to find for the plaintiff, then the defendant is entitled to judgment as a matter of law.

iii. **Judgment based on jury verdict.** The judge may believe that neither the plaintiff's nor the defendant's evidence is so strong that all reasonable jurors would have to agree with it. In this situation the case would go to the jury for resolution.

6. **Burden of Persuasion**

The burden of persuasion concept is important for cases that are submitted to the jury or that do not qualify for judgment as a matter of law for any party. To win a judgment the party assigned this burden must persuade the jury by a preponderance of the evidence that the required elements of that party's cause of action actually did exist. If the jury is unpersuaded about an element in a torts case, believing that arguments for and against the existence of the element are in equal balance, then the jury will decide that question against the party who had the burden of persuasion on that issue.

Review Questions and Answers

Question: Sam Storeman operated a store. He did not pay adequate attention to keeping the floor clean, and Stan Shopper, a customer, slipped and fell because the floor had become too slippery. Tort law allows Shopper to win damages for his injury from Storeman. Is this consistent with tort law's goals of compensation, deterrence, and setting of societal standards?

Answer: Yes. This serves the compensation goal because Shopper gets money to pay for medical costs and any additional costs of the injury, such as past and future lost wages if the injury prevents Shopper from working. Shopper's damages can also include an amount of money for "pain and suffering," although the relationship of this category of damages to compensation is sometimes hard to justify. The deterrence goal is served because Storeman will try harder in the future to avoid causing situations that could lead to injuries and additional lawsuits requiring him to pay money to plaintiffs. The deterrence goal is further served because other business operators will know that they risk having to pay customers for negligently inflicted harms and will try to protect themselves from that liability by acting carefully. Finally, the goal of setting societal standards is served by representing a societal consensus that store operators should act reasonably to protect their customers from injuries.

Question: Sally Stabber stabbed Victoria Victim. She was prosecuted criminally for that crime and was convicted. Can tort law play any additional role in dealing with Stabber's conduct?

Answer: Yes. Victim can sue Stabber for monetary damages. (Many criminals do not have much money and are therefore not worth suing, but some may have assets that would enable them to pay tort judgments.) A criminal prosecution is initiated by a public official such as a district attorney, and the penalties that can result from criminal prosecution are inflicted by the state on the criminal. Tort law is different from criminal law. In a case like the one in this question, a tort suit would be initiated by the victim, and the monetary liability that the tort suit might establish would be a debt owed by the criminal to the victim. A convicted criminal might be sentenced to jail or sentenced to pay a fine. The fine would be paid to the state. A tort defendant would be ordered to pay money to the individual plaintiff.

Question: When a plaintiff suffers an injury from a defendant's actions, depending on the nature of the defendant's activity, tort law will apply either negligence or strict liability theories. How does the choice between negligence and strict liability matter to plaintiffs and defendants?

Answer: If negligence theories govern the case, the plaintiff has to prove that the defendant acted unreasonably in a way that caused the plaintiff's injury. If strict liability theories apply, the plaintiff has to prove only that the defendant carried out an activity that tort law treats with strict liability and that this activity caused the plaintiff's injury. Negligence doctrines require the plaintiff to show some flaw in how the defendant acted, while strict liability doctrines require the plaintiff to show only that the defendant acted. It is easier for plaintiffs to win strict liability cases than negligence cases.

Question: Are the three types of damages—nominal, compensatory, and punitive—all available in all types of torts cases?

Answer: No. Compensatory and punitive damages are available in all types of torts cases, but nominal damages are allowed only in intentional tort cases.

Question: When tort law considers how many consequences of a defendant's act the defendant should be required to pay for, does it matter whether the defendant was an intentional wrongdoer or was only negligent?

Answer: Yes, this distinction matters. Since there is more moral blame associated with intentional wrongdoing than with negligent conduct, tort law doctrines impose liability for more consequences on an actor whose conduct was intentionally tortious than on an actor whose conduct was merely unreasonable and therefore negligent.

Question: To win damages in a lawsuit based on negligence, a plaintiff must prove, among other things, that the defendant caused the injury by acting in a way that was less careful than a reasonably prudent person would have acted. Suppose that a plaintiff, having slipped and fallen in a store, sought damages on the theory that the store owner had negligently failed to keep the floor free from slippery debris. If the plaintiff introduced no evidence about the store's procedures for inspecting and cleaning the floor, and the defendant introduced evidence showing that workers inspected every part of every floor at least once every five minutes, would the defendant have a good chance of winning judgment as a matter of law?

Answer: Yes. Judgment as a matter of law is available to a defendant if the judge believes that the plaintiff has failed to produce evidence on some required element of the cause of action or if there is no legally sufficient evidentiary basis for a reasonable jury to find for the plaintiff. On the facts of this question, there are two reasons why the defendant is entitled to judgment as a matter of law. First, the plaintiff failed to satisfy the production burden with regard to evidence of the defendant's failure to act reasonably. Second, considering all the evidence in the case on the subject of the defendant's conduct, it would be virtually impossible for a reasonable jury to conclude that the defendant's conduct was less careful than the conduct of a reasonably prudent person. The evidence shows that the defendant's conduct was extraordinarily careful.

Exam Tips

- Bear in mind the three goals of tort law. If an exam question asks about rights and liabilities of parties involved in an injury, after you have answered the question based on the specific doctrines that apply, you can refer to the goals of compensation, deterrence, and setting of societal norms to explain whether the result from applying the doctrines meets those goals. This can support a brief discussion of whether the doctrines seem to work well.

- If a question asks specifically whether some doctrine is sensible or just, using the goals of tort law is an excellent way to organize your answer.
- Remember that contracts, criminal law, and torts are separate ways in which the legal system reacts to people's conduct and to injuries from conduct. Tort law and its causes of action are independent of these other fields of law. A person who has been convicted of a crime can be sued by the victim under various tort doctrines.
- Sometimes it is difficult to classify a defendant's conduct as intentional misconduct, negligent conduct, or conduct subject to strict liability. If you think a case is hard to classify, say so and explain why. Then discuss how choosing one category or another would affect the outcome of the problem.
- Always know the elements that define a particular tort cause of action and discuss them in terms of whether the plaintiff has established a prima facie case.

2 INTENTIONAL TORTS: BACKGROUND CONCEPTS

CHAPTER OVERVIEW

- This chapter explains the intent concept that is fundamental for understanding intentional torts.
- To be liable for an intentional tort, the defendant must have done some volitional act. A person who moves unconsciously or who is moved by another person has not acted with volition.
- A volitional act is intentional, for the purpose of establishing the actor's liability for an intentional tort, if the actor desired to cause the consequences of the act or if the actor believed it was substantially certain that the consequences would result from the act.
- An actor who has no desire to harm another person will still be liable for an intentional tort if he or she intends the consequences that tort law defines as tortious.
- Under the transferred intent doctrine an actor's intent to commit an intentional tort against someone is adequate to support an action against the actor even if: 1. the actor inflicted a different intentional tort on that person; 2. the actor inflicted the same intentional tort on a different person; or 3. the actor inflicted a different intentional tort on a different person.

A. ELEMENTS OF INTENTION

For every intentional tort a plaintiff must show that the defendant did some volitional act and that the defendant intended consequences of that act of a type that tort law prohibits.

1. Defendant's Volitional Act

To establish that an intentional tort defendant acted with the required intent, a plaintiff must show that the defendant's act was volitional. The defendant must have moved in some way as a result of a conscious decision to move. This means that bodily movements when a person is unconscious are not intentional. Also, movements of a person's body that happen without control are not intentional.

2. Defendant's Mental State with Regard to Consequences of Volitional Act

To establish that an intentional tort defendant acted with the required intent, the plaintiff must make an important showing in addition to proof that the defendant acted volitionally. The plaintiff must show that the defendant intended that his or her action would have a consequence that tort law prohibits. This aspect of intent is usually defined in two alternative ways: willful purpose and substantial certainty.

a. **Willful purpose.** The defendant must have desired to cause some physical or mental effect on the plaintiff.

Example: Battery is an intentional tort that involves touching someone in an unlawful way. A defendant will be liable for battery if he or she desired to touch the plaintiff and did actually touch the plaintiff.

EXAMPLE AND ANALYSIS

Carl Collector ran in a field, trying to capture a rare butterfly with his bare hands. He lunged for a butterfly and hit Barbara Bystander with one of his arms. He did not see Bystander before he hit her, and he did not know anyone was in the field. Could Collector be described as having had a willful purpose to hit Bystander?

Absolutely not. Collector could not have had a willful purpose to hit Bystander. Two reasons support this conclusion. Collector was trying to capture a butterfly, not to make any contact with any human being. Also, Collector had no knowledge that any human being was in the field. It is therefore doubtful that he had a desire to touch any person when he moved his arms.

b. **Substantial certainty.** Sometimes a plaintiff may have difficulty finding proof that a defendant really desired a tortious act to take place. A doctrine known as "substantial certainty" can substitute for proof of willful purpose by the defendant. A plaintiff can satisfy the requirement of proving a defendant's intent with evidence that shows that the defendant knew with substantial certainty that the tortious event would flow from his or her conduct.

E&A

EXAMPLE AND ANALYSIS

Penny Peoplehater drove her car into a crowd of people waiting at a bus stop. Could she properly be described as having acted with substantial certainty of coming into contact with at least one of those people?

Absolutely yes. It is a matter of common sense that anyone who drives a car that way has to anticipate driving into at least one person.

B. RECURRING INTENT ISSUES

That the intent requirement for intentional torts is subtle often leads to misunderstandings. A person intends an intentional tort if he or she commits a volitional act wanting to cause a prohibited consequence or being substantially certain that the consequence will occur. This definition can be satisfied even for the defendant who did not mean to hurt the plaintiff, who was not aware that the law forbids certain conduct, or who was mentally ill.

1. Desire to Hurt Not Required

In an intentional tort case the plaintiff need not show that the defendant intended to hurt the plaintiff. Even if the defendant did not want to hurt the plaintiff or wanted to help the plaintiff, so long as the defendant did mean to affect the plaintiff, the intent element of the tort is established. Most intentional torts involve conduct that does actually hurt the defendant's victim, but the plaintiff is not required to establish the defendant's intent to hurt the plaintiff.

Illustration: Garratt v. Dailey, 46 Wash.2d 197, 279 P.2d 1091 (1955). A five-year-old child pulled a chair from under the plaintiff as she was about to sit on it. The trial court acting as trier of fact found for the defendant, stating that the child had not meant to hurt the plaintiff. The supreme court remanded for additional factual findings. It stated that the child would be liable for battery if he meant to make the plaintiff fall or if he knew with substantial certainty that she would fall. The supreme court made it clear that a defendant's desire to harm someone is different from a defendant's desire to cause a prohibited contact (contact of the plaintiff with the ground) or from a defendant's substantial certainty that a prohibited contact will occur.

2. Ignorance of Legal Standards Is No Defense

A defendant who intentionally acts in a way that the law prohibits will be liable for an intentional tort, regardless of whether he or she was aware of the legal rule. Ignorance of the law is no excuse in the typical intentional tort case.

E&A EXAMPLE AND ANALYSIS

A visitor to New York City grabbed a person on the street and threw him over his shoulder, because in his small village in a technologically simple, nonindustrialized society that is the way people introduce themselves to each other. Would he be liable for battery to the person he tossed?

Yes. His ignorance of our laws against mayhem and his subjective desire to be friendly (not aggressive or mean) have no relevance to tort law's evaluation of his conduct.

---

3. Mental Illness Does Not Preclude Mental State of Intent

A mentally ill person may have an intent to commit the types of actions that are the basis for intentional tort claims.

Illustration: McGuire v. Almy, 297 Mass. 323, 8 N.E.2d 760 (1937). The mentally ill defendant hit the plaintiff with a leg from a piece of furniture. The trial court denied the defendant's motion for a directed verdict. On appeal it was held that the defendant's insanity was not a factor that prevented a jury conclusion that the defendant had intended to hit the plaintiff.

C. TRANSFERRED INTENT

A doctrine known as "transferred intent" applies to five of the most common intentional torts: assault, battery, false imprisonment, trespass to land, and trespass to chattels. The transferred intent doctrine takes an actor's intent to commit any one of those intentional torts against a particular person and treats that intent as equivalent to an intent: 1. to commit the same tort against a different person; 2. to commit a different one of those five torts against the same person; or 3. to commit a different one of those five torts against a different person.

1. Intent to Commit a Different Tort

A defendant will be treated as having had the intent required for one type of intentional tort if the plaintiff shows that the defendant acted with the intent required for some other type of intentional tort.

2. Intent to Commit a Tort on a Different Person

The doctrine of transferred intent holds that a defendant acting with the intent required to establish liability for an intentional tort to one person will be liable to some other person with whom the defendant did not mean to be involved if the defendant's actions affect that other person.

Illustration: Talmage v. Smith, 101 Mich. 370, 59 N.W. 656 (1894). The defendant threw a stick at a boy who was among a group on the roof of the defendant's shed. The stick hit a boy the defendant had not seen and had not intended to hit. The appellate court held that an intention to hit "somebody" is adequate to satisfy the intent requirement of the tort of battery. Modern courts would expand this holding to rule that an intent to hit someone or an intent to commit assault, false imprisonment, trespass to property, or trespass to a chattel would be adequate to satisfy the intent requirement of battery.

3. Intent to Commit a Different Tort on a Different Person

The doctrines governing transferred intent and allowing the intent required for one intentional tort to be treated as the intent required for another intentional tort can both apply in a single case. Thus, if a person means to threaten someone with imminent harm (which would establish the intent element of assault) but acts in a way that leads to an unpermitted physical contact with some other person (which is the conduct required for the tort of battery), the person who actually became the victim of the defendant's conduct will have a cause of action for battery.

D. DISTINCTION BETWEEN INTENTIONAL AND UNINTENTIONAL CONDUCT

There can be no liability for intentional tort in cases where there is proof only that the defendant was careless, was reckless, or knew it was very likely (but not substantially certain) that prohibited consequences would follow his or her actions. In any of these situations, a plaintiff may still be able to seek damages on a negligence theory.

REVIEW QUESTIONS AND ANSWERS

Question: Fran Faller fell down a flight of stairs and collided with Barbara Backstop, who was standing at the bottom of the stairs. Does Faller's conduct satisfy the intent requirement for the tort of battery?

Answer: No. Faller's conduct was involuntary, or nonvolitional. Also, she had no willful purpose to collide with Backstop.

Question: Bob Bigfan thought he saw a famous movie star crossing a crowded city street. Vilma Viewblocker happened to be standing between Bigfan and the person Bigfan wanted to see. To improve his view of that person, Bigfan pushed Viewblocker down. Bigfan had no desire to harm Viewblocker. Did Bigfan have the intent required for the tort of battery?

Answer: Yes. Bigfan committed a volitional act to accomplish the result of pushing Viewblocker down. The fact that Bigfan had no interest in hurting Viewblocker does not matter, since Bigfan did have a willful purpose to knock her down.

Question: Thinking that Paul Plaintiff was an alien invader, Wendy Weakmind hit him with a rock. Can Plaintiff show that Weakmind's conduct satisfied the intent requirement for the tort of battery?

Answer: Yes. If Weakmind moved her arm volitionally and did that with the purpose of causing a contact between the rock and Plaintiff, then Weakmind's conduct satisfies the definition of intent. Weakmind's motivation was founded on a misperception of reality, but this does not matter. An actor's motive or fundamental reason for desiring some consequence is not relevant in analyzing the intention element in intentional torts.

Question: Mike Misser hid in a car near the house of his enemy, Ed Enemy. Misser saw Enemy approach the house and tried to shoot him with a high-powered rifle. Misser's shot missed Enemy but hit William Wrongplace, a person Misser did not see and did not intend to shoot. If Wrongplace sues Misser for battery, can Wrongplace show the required intent on the part of Misser?

Answer: Yes. The transferred intent doctrine treats Misser's intent to shoot Enemy as equivalent to an intent to shoot Wrongplace.

Exam Tips

- For an actor to have the intent required for liability for an intentional tort, the actor must have undertaken a volitional act. If the actor is picked up and thrown by another person or moves some muscles because of an involuntary seizure, the actor has not committed a volitional act and cannot be found to have had the intent required for intentional tort liability.
- A frequent issue in intentional tort questions involves a person who means to touch another person but does not mean to hurt that person. For most

intentional torts liability is based on the actor's intent to accomplish a prohibited result, no matter whether the actor thinks that result will be good or bad from anyone's point of view.

- Remember the transferred intent doctrine: It applies when a defendant intends to commit any one of five intentional torts (assault, battery, false imprisonment, trespass to land, and trespass to chattels) against a particular person but inflicts that tort on someone else, or inflicts a different tort on the intended victim, or even inflicts a different tort on a different victim. The original intent is adequate to supply the required intent element in any of the transfer situations.

3 Intentional Torts Against People

Chapter Overview

- Battery, assault, false imprisonment, and intentional infliction of emotional distress are the main intentional torts that a defendant can inflict against a person.
- One commits a battery by committing a volitional act with the intent to cause a contact with another person if the act causes such a contact and the contact is harmful or offensive.
- One commits an assault by committing a volitional act with the intent to cause a person to expect an imminent battery if the act causes such apprehension.
- One commits the tort of false imprisonment by committing a volitional act with the intent to confine a person within boundaries set by the actor if the person is confined within those boundaries and is aware of the confinement.
- One commits the tort of infliction of emotional distress by intentionally or recklessly committing a volitional act that is extreme and outrageous and that causes a person to feel severe emotional or mental distress.
- Under the transferred intent doctrine a plaintiff can satisfy the required showing of intent for battery, assault, false imprisonment, trespass to chattels, or trespass to property by showing that the defendant acted with whatever intent is required for any one of those torts.
- A plaintiff may not use the transferred intent doctrine to satisfy the required showing of intent for the tort of intentional infliction of emotional distress.

A. BATTERY

Battery is one of the best-known intentional torts. Generations of torts students have concluded that it may be hard to understand false imprisonment or proximate cause, but everybody can understand a punch in the nose.

1. Definition

One commits a battery if one: 1. commits a volitional act; 2. with the intent to cause a contact with another person; and 3. causes such a contact either directly or indirectly; if 4. the contact is either harmful or offensive. See Restatement (Second) of Torts §§13, 18 (1979). Harmful or offensive contacts are sometimes called "unpermitted" contacts.

E&A

EXAMPLE AND ANALYSIS

You punch someone in the nose on purpose. You have committed a battery. You punch someone in the nose to stop a fly from biting him on the nose. You have committed a battery. You punch someone in the nose because he has just punched you in the nose. You have committed a battery, but it might be privileged. Privileges are covered in Chapter 5, Defenses to Intentional Tort Liability.

2. Intent in the Context of Battery

The plaintiff must show that the defendant committed a volitional act and that the defendant intended that act to cause a contact with the plaintiff. The plaintiff must also establish that the contact was harmful or offensive, but the plaintiff need not show that the defendant meant it to be harmful or offensive. Battery requires an intention to touch, not an intention to cause harm.

If someone means to act in a way that satisfies the intent requirement for an intentional tort other than battery but actually commits a harmful or offensive contacting of the plaintiff, the actor's conduct satisfies the intent requirement for battery. For example, the intentional tort of assault requires a showing that the defendant meant to cause the plaintiff to fear an imminent battery. If a defendant means only to act in a way that constitutes an assault but then actually touches the plaintiff, the intent to commit an assault is treated as the intent to commit a battery.

Illustration: Vosburg v. Putney, 80 Wis. 523, 50 N.W. 403 (1891). One schoolboy playfully kicked another in the shin during a class. The kick happened to cause a serious injury because the victim had an unusual susceptibility. Battery damages were allowed, since the defendant's lack of desire to cause a harm had no relevance to the defendant's intention to cause the contact.

3. Types of Touching That Constitute Battery

To be a battery a touching has to be harmful or offensive. A harmful contact is a contact that actually causes physical harm. An offensive contact is a contact that is contrary to a reasonable sense of dignity.

a. **Unconsented.** If someone consents to have another person touch him or her, no battery action is allowed. Thus, a contact must have been unpermitted to be a basis for a battery action.

   i. **Express consent.** Sometimes people expressly consent to being contacted by others. Consent to surgery is an example.

   Illustration: Mohr v. Williams, 95 Minn. 261 104 N.W. 12 (1905). The defendant surgeon operated on the plaintiff's left ear, although the plaintiff had given permission only for an operation on her right ear. Since there had been no consent, the surgeon's conduct was a battery. Modern doctors avoid this result by having patients sign consent forms prior to surgery. These forms usually anticipate that the doctor may vary the type of operation when that is medically reasonable.

   ii. **Implied consent.** People ordinarily expect and tolerate some types of touching in our society. Examples are gently touching someone while passing by in a crowded hallway or bus, and gently touching a person on the shoulder to get his or her attention. Doctrinally, courts hold that people impliedly consent to such contacts. For that reason they cannot be bases for battery actions. To be a battery a contact must be outside the scope of these generally accepted contacts.

b. **Objective standard for offensiveness.** Rather than a subjective standard based on the particular sensitivities of the person who is touched, an objective societal standard applies to the issue of whether a touching is offensive. Thus, one person who slides past another on a bus is protected from liability for battery, even if the latter had an unusual sensitivity to being touched. Tort law allows us to act on the assumption that the people with whom we come into contact have standard ideas about acceptable behavior.

   i. **Defendant with special knowledge.** The objective standard may not apply if the battery defendant knew or had reason to know about the special sensitivity of the battery plaintiff.

c. **Touching something other than the plaintiff's body.** Cases have held that touching the plaintiff's horse while the plaintiff is riding it can be equivalent to touching the plaintiff. Also, a defendant can commit a battery by touching a plaintiff with an object or a person or by causing the plaintiff to come into contact with something (like an object or the ground).

Illustration: Fisher v. Carousel Motor Hotel, Inc., 424 S.W.2d 627 (Tex. 1986). The defendant's employee grabbed a plate from the plaintiff's hand while the plaintiff was in line to participate in a buffet lunch. The employee took the plaintiff's plate away because he did not want a person of the plaintiff's race to eat in the restaurant. The trial court entered judgment as a matter of law for the defendant (judgment n.o.v.), after the jury had found for the plaintiff. The supreme court reversed. It held that touching something intimately associated with the plaintiff is an adequate touching for battery.

d. **Touching unknown to the plaintiff.** In a famous Restatement example it is stated that a person commits the tort of battery by kissing a woman while she is asleep, even though she has no knowledge of the unpermitted contact.

E&A EXAMPLE AND ANALYSIS

For fun Jack Joker sneaked up behind Frank Friend and squeezed Friend's neck as if to choke him. Joker had no intention to hurt or injure Friend in any way. Unfortunately, when Joker touched him, Friend snapped his head around quickly and suffered a neck injury. Would Friend have a cause of action against Joker for battery?

Probably yes. Joker committed a volitional act, Joker intended to cause the squeezing contact with Friend's neck, and Joker did cause a harmful contact. These are the required elements for battery liability. There would be no liability for battery, however, if Friend had expressly consented to Joker's playing this type of practical joke on him. Neither would there be liability for battery if a jury were to find that people in our society in a relationship such as Joker's and Friend's expect and therefore give implied consent to contacts of the type Joker inflicted on Friend. Without consent, Joker would not be protected from liability by showing that he had no intent to harm Friend. The fact that the contact actually did harm Friend satisfies the requirement of a harmful or offensive contact. Joker's good intentions are no defense so long as he actually intended to touch Friend.

4. Unusual Results of a Defendant's Action

A defendant who acts in a way that supports liability for battery is liable for all the consequences of that conduct, regardless of whether the defendant intended them to happen or whether a reasonable person would have expected them to occur.

5. Damages

Battery plaintiffs can win three types of damages: actual (or compensatory) damages, nominal damages, and punitive damages.

a. **Actual damages.** A battery plaintiff is entitled to an award of money equal to the jury's valuation of the plaintiff's past and predicted future medical expenses, lost wages, and pain and suffering due to the battery. The award for pain and suffering can be based on emotional consequences the plaintiff suffers, whether or not the plaintiff suffers any physical harm from the battery.

b. **Nominal damages.** In a case where the plaintiff has no way to establish actual damages, nominal damages are available. They are a symbolic award of a small sum, such as one dollar, to show that the legal system has evaluated the defendant's conduct and found it to have been objectionable.

c. **Punitive damages.** Where the battery involves particularly outrageous conduct, the defendant may be liable for punitive damages in addition to the other types of allowable damages. Only some batteries are considered so outrageous that they justify the imposition of punitive damages.

B. ASSAULT

Assault is an intentional tort. Students and some courts sometimes use an unhelpful phrase *assault and battery* that confuses two separate torts, assault and battery.

1. Definition

One commits an assault by: 1. committing a volitional act; 2. with the intent to cause a person to expect an imminent battery; and 3. causes such apprehension directly or indirectly. See Restatement §§21, 32. This tort is different from the tort of battery. Assault requires proof that the defendant did something that caused the plaintiff to anticipate a harmful or offensive touching, but it does not require proof that a touching ever happened.

2. Intent in the Context of Assault

A number of rules govern recurring problems related to the intent element of assault.

a. **Intent to cause expectation of contact, not harm.** The intent required for the tort of assault is the intent to make the plaintiff feel fear, expectation, or apprehension of an unpermitted touching. This is different from an intent to touch the plaintiff. It is also different from an intent to inflict physical harm on the plaintiff.

b. **Jokes and friendly acts.** Conduct that a defendant means to be a joke or an act of friendship can be an assault if its effect is to make the plaintiff believe an unpermitted touching is about to happen.

c. **Transferred intent.** Intent to commit certain different intentional torts against the plaintiff is equivalent to intent to commit an assault in some circumstances. Also, intent to commit an assault against one person is sometimes equivalent to intent to commit it against another.

   i. **Intent to commit other intentional torts.** If a defendant means to commit certain other torts against the plaintiff—specifically, battery, false imprisonment, trespass to chattels, or trespass to land—but his or her actions lead only to the plaintiff's suffering an expectation of an imminent unpermitted touching, the defendant's conduct satisfies the intent requirement for the tort of assault. The intent to do one of the specified intentional torts is equivalent to the intent to do a different one.

   ii. **Intent directed at a different person.** Sometimes a defendant means to act in a way that would be a battery, assault, trespass to chattels, or trespass to property against a particular person, but the defendant's conduct leads somebody else to anticipate an imminent unpermitted touching by the defendant. In such a case the other person, whom the defendant did not intend to touch or to scare, has a valid cause of action against the defendant for assault.

   iii. **Unintended victim must fear actual contact.** Note that the transferred intent doctrine allows an assault cause of action by a person who actually fears imminent unpermitted touching by the defendant, even though that person is not the one the defendant means to threaten. If a defendant threatens someone and that action upsets a third person, the third person may have a cause of action for intentional infliction of emotional distress, but he or she does not have a cause of action for assault, since he or she does not feel personally threatened with an unpermitted contact.

E&A Example and Analysis

Jill Jerk ran toward a table in a cafeteria, intending to hit Ollie Oneman in the head with a baseball bat. When Jerk swung the bat in the direction of Oneman, the bat nearly hit Tommy Twoman. Twoman saw this and feared contact. Twoman has a valid assault claim against Jerk. Jerk's intent was to commit battery against Oneman, but Twoman nearly was hit and did fear contact by the bat. This is an example of transferred intent, taking an intent to commit one tort against one person and treating that intent as adequate to support an intentional tort cause of action by a different person for a different intentional tort.

---

3. Apprehension of Imminent Contact

A number of rules apply to recurring problems in defining "apprehension of immediate contact."

a. **Threat must be of immediate contact.** To be an assault a threat must convey the meaning that the defendant will commit a battery in the very near future. A defendant's statement to the plaintiff, "I would hit you if it were not springtime," is not an assault because it does not suggest an imminent physical contact.

Illustration: Tuberville v. Savage, 86 Eng. Rep. 684 (K.B. 1669). The statement, "If it were not assize-time, I would not take such language from you," was ruled not to constitute an assault.

b. **Possible overt act requirement.** It is unclear whether a plaintiff must allege that the defendant committed some threatening overt act in addition to communicating a threat.

i. **Traditional view.** In many courts, to avoid dismissal a plaintiff must allege that the defendant did some overt act (other than speaking words) that contributed to the plaintiff's impression that an unpermitted touching was about to happen. These jurisdictions hold that mere words cannot constitute an assault.

ii. **Restatement view.** The Restatement takes the position that communication of words alone may sometimes constitute an assault, if surrounding circumstances make it reasonable for the plaintiff to believe that an imminent unpermitted touching has been threatened.

c. **Defendant's capability.** The defendant must seem capable of fulfilling the threat. The plaintiff must have a reasonable belief that the defendant is capable of carrying out the conduct that he or she has threatened. A defendant who makes a credible threat is liable for assault even if the defendant is actually unable to carry out the threat, if the plaintiff reasonably believes that the defendant can do it.

Illustration: Western Union Telegraph Co. v. Hill, 25 Ala. App. 540, 150 So. 709 (1933). The defendant's employee reached across a counter toward the plaintiff, after saying he wanted to "pet" her. A jury question was presented as to whether the employee could reasonably have been seen as capable of touching her, given the width of the counter and the height of the employee. If touching had been plausible, that aspect of the assault cause of action would have been satisfied.

d. **Plaintiff's awareness.** The plaintiff must be aware of the defendant's threat. The tort of assault involves the feeling of expecting an imminent unpermitted touching. Since people who are asleep or otherwise unaware of a threat cannot in any way perceive that a touching is about to occur, a plaintiff must be aware of the defendant's conduct in order to recover for assault.

e. **Objective standard for perception of threat.** Usually, in deciding whether a defendant's conduct can be treated as having caused apprehension of imminent contact, a court will apply an objective standard, assessing whether a typical person would have perceived the defendant's conduct as threatening. The Restatement departs from this position for some cases involving plaintiffs who are unusually susceptible to fear. If a defendant knows that a person has that trait and acts in a way that could cause that person apprehension of an unlawful contact, the defendant will be liable for assault even though the act would not have caused a typical person to fear an unlawful contact.

f. **Extortionate threats can be assaults.** If a defendant makes a threat like "your money or your life," tort law treats it as a threat to kill and therefore as an assault. One of tort law's fundamental principles is that each individual has freedom to act within legal boundaries without intrusions by others. The right to keep one's own money is fundamental, so a demand that a plaintiff give it up to avoid being hurt must be treated as an assault.

g. **Terminated assault is an assault.** If a defendant acts in a way that satisfies the definition of assault, the defendant has committed an assault, whether or not the defendant then uses words or actions to indicate that the threat is terminated. Once the defendant's conduct, intent, and the consequences of the conduct are consistent with the required elements of the tort, the defendant has committed an assault, regardless of whether the defendant changes his or her mind and abandons the conduct.

h. **Expectation, not fear, is required for assault.** Because assault is sometimes defined as the apprehension of an unpermitted touching, students may think that a plaintiff must be put in fear, or must be afraid, in order for the defendant's conduct to be treated as an assault. This impression is wrong. *Apprehension* is synonymous in this context with *expectation* or *belief.* If a defendant gives a plaintiff the reasonable expectation that the defendant is about to hit the plaintiff, the defendant has committed an assault even if the plaintiff is much stronger than the defendant and was never in any fear about the anticipated contact.

Example and Analysis

Sam Stupid, a 145-pound, five-foot-tall man, ran to Barry Bigman and waved a stick at him, moving closer and closer until he nearly hit Bigman in the head with the stick. Bigman is more than six feet tall and weighs almost 300 pounds. If Stupid did that conduct intentionally, meaning to cause Bigman to anticipate that he was about to be hit, Stupid would be liable for assault. This is true even if Bigman could not reasonably have expected to be harmed by Stupid. The assault cause of action merely requires an anticipation of being touched in a harmful or offensive way.

4. Attempted Battery

It would be wrong to state that every assault is an attempted battery. Some attempted batteries involve conduct that satisfies the definition of assault, and some do not. It is also true that conduct which does not meet the definition of attempted battery can satisfy the definition of assault.

a. **Attempted battery that is an assault.** Sometimes an attempt to commit a battery constitutes an assault. For example, there is attempted battery if a defendant points a loaded gun at a plaintiff, fires it, and misses the plaintiff. This conduct is also an assault only if the plaintiff is aware of it as it is happening.

b. **Attempted battery that is not an assault.** Some conduct by a defendant might be intended as a battery, might fail to satisfy all the elements of the tort of battery, and might also fail to meet the definition of assault. For example, if a defendant fires a weapon at a plaintiff from a hidden location and misses, there is no assault cause of action if the plaintiff is unaware of the effort to harm him or her.

c. **Conduct other than attempted battery that is an assault.** If a defendant does something to cause a plaintiff to have a reasonable fear of unpermitted contact, the definition of assault is satisfied even if the defendant has no intention to complete the threatened act. Thus, a defendant commits an assault by swinging a baseball bat at a plaintiff's body whether or not the defendant means to hit the plaintiff and whether or not the defendant actually does hit the plaintiff.

5. Damages

Assault plaintiffs can win the same three types of damages as battery plaintiffs: actual (or compensatory) damages, nominal damages, and punitive damages.

a. **Actual damages.** An assault plaintiff is entitled to an award of money equal to the jury's valuation of the plaintiff's past and predicted future medical expenses, lost wages, and pain and suffering due to the assault. The award for pain and suffering is based on emotional consequences the plaintiff suffers from the fear of being the victim of an unlawful touching.

b. **Nominal damages.** In cases where the plaintiff has no way to establish actual damages, nominal damages are available.

c. **Punitive damages.** If the defendant's assault involves conduct that is particularly outrageous, the defendant may be liable for punitive damages in addition to the other types of allowable damages.

C. FALSE IMPRISONMENT

False imprisonment is an intentional tort that involves a defendant's restricting a plaintiff's freedom of movement. It does not necessarily involve a prison.

1. Definition

One commits the tort of false imprisonment if one: 1. commits a volitional act; 2. with the intent to confine a person within boundaries set by the actor; 3. the person is confined within those boundaries; and 4. the person is aware of his or her confinement. (Note that these elements constitute the prima facie case for false imprisonment. Chapter 5, Defenses to Intentional Tort Liability, explains the many defenses that may prevent a plaintiff who establishes the prima facie case from being entitled to damages.)

2. Intent in the Context of False Imprisonment

To be liable for false imprisonment the defendant must act with the intent to limit someone's ability to leave a place.

a. **Transferred intent.** The transferred intent doctrine applies in false imprisonment cases. If the defendant has the required intention with regard to one person but inadvertently limits another person's freedom to leave a particular place, the defendant is liable to that other person for false imprisonment, under the doctrine of transferred intent. For example, if a defendant turns off the power to an elevator, meaning to trap a particular person in it, but a different person happens to be in the elevator at the time, the intent requirement for the tort of false imprisonment will be met in a suit brought by the person who was trapped in the elevator.

3. Place of Imprisonment or Confinement

The plaintiff must show that the confinement was real. This involves consideration of the area of confinement, whether escape was possible, whether the plaintiff knew about the confinement, and various methods of restraint.

a. **Area of confinement.** The plaintiff must be confined in a defined place. This can be a room or a place outdoors. However, blocking someone's path does not constitute false imprisonment if the person still retains the ability to move freely and select another route to his or her destination. A person whom the defendant excludes or keeps out of a particular place does not have a false imprisonment action for being "imprisoned" or "confined" in the rest of the world.

b. **Reasonable escape.** There can be no false imprisonment if the plaintiff has a way out of the place of confinement. The method must be known to the plaintiff. If a means of escape is dangerous or involves conduct that is offensive to the plaintiff's dignity, then the availability of that method of escape will be ignored in deciding whether he or she was confined.

c. **Plaintiff must be aware of confinement.** A plaintiff who is unaware of being confined does not suffer the tort of false imprisonment. Note that the Restatement takes the position, somewhat contradictory, that a false imprisonment cause of action should be available to someone who is confined, is unaware of the confinement, and suffers some physical harm from the confinement.

Illustration: Big Town Nursing Home, Inc. v. Newman, 461 S.W.2d 195 (Tex. 1970). The plaintiff's nephew took him to the defendant nursing home and signed papers for the plaintiff's admission. The plaintiff asked to leave, but the defendant's employees would not let him use the telephone to call a taxi. They also locked his clothes away from him. When he left the premises, the defendant's employees caught him and brought him back against his will. These facts supported a judgment against the defendant for false imprisonment.

E&A EXAMPLE AND ANALYSIS

Sally Studier, a serious student, worked all night long at a table in the rare book room of a large library. She was unaware that from midnight until seven o'clock in the morning, the building was locked and she would have been unable to leave if she had wanted to stop studying and go home. On these facts Studier would not be able to establish one of the required elements of false imprisonment: knowledge of being confined. (Whether she could establish the other elements would depend on whether the person who locked the library intended to lock in Studier.)

4. Method of Restraint

Defendants can restrain plaintiffs in many ways; most will support a cause of action in false imprisonment.

a. **Physical barriers.** A plaintiff is treated as having been restrained if he or she is locked in a room, or if the defendant uses other physical means to prevent the plaintiff from leaving a place.

b. **Force.** Threatening to use or actually using physical force against the plaintiff is another way a defendant may restrain a plaintiff.

Illustration: Hardy v. LaBelle's Distributing Co., 203 Mont. 263, 661 P.2d 35 (1983). The plaintiff's employer asked her to go to an office in a store where she was asked to take a lie detector test in connection with a suspicion that she had stolen merchandise. Since she had not been physically restrained and could have left the room at any time, a jury verdict for the defendant was affirmed. Moral persuasion is different from force and cannot constitute a restraint for the purpose of false imprisonment.

c. **Denial of escape method.** Any time a plaintiff wants to leave a place, if the defendant is in control of the methods for leaving and denies the plaintiff access to those methods, defendant's conduct is treated as a restraint. Even if the plaintiff originally was willing to be in that location, the defendant's refusal to facilitate the plaintiff's departure equals a restraint of the plaintiff.

Illustration: Whittaker v. Sandford, 110 Me. 77, 85 A.2d 399 (1912). After the defendant had promised the plaintiff that she would be allowed to leave the defendant's yacht when it reached a port, the defendant refused to give the plaintiff access to a boat to go from the yacht to the shore. This conduct satisfied the confinement element of the false imprisonment tort.

d. **Threats.** A defendant may restrain a plaintiff with threats. One such threat is that unless the plaintiff remains in a certain place, the defendant will use physical force against someone the plaintiff wants to protect. Another threat is that the defendant will take or harm the plaintiff's property unless the plaintiff stays in a place. A third type of threat is the threat of arrest.

   i. **Future threats.** To constitute a restraint for the purpose of false imprisonment, a threat must seem to involve the risk of imminent conduct by the person making it. Statements about what someone will do in the future are not restraints, regardless of how the recipient of the threat treats them. This is parallel to the treatment of this issue for the tort of assault.

   ii. **Commands.** A request or a command unaccompanied by an explicit or implied threat does not constitute the type of restraint required for false imprisonment.

iii. **Merchants and shoplifters.** In many states statutes authorize store personnel to impose reasonable restraints on a person they suspect is a shoplifter. Absent such a statute if personnel threaten a suspect with arrest in order to keep the suspect on the store premises, this conduct is a restraint adequate to support a false imprisonment claim. If personnel do not threaten arrest, however, and the customer decides to spend time in the store to explain what happened and to persuade the personnel not to take action against him or her, the customer will be unable to claim that he or she was restrained.

e. **Arrest.** If the defendant tells the plaintiff that the plaintiff is under arrest, and the plaintiff then limits his or her movements according to the defendant's instructions, the restraint element of false imprisonment is satisfied.

i. **Validity of the arrest.** Whether or not the defendant actually has the right to arrest the plaintiff, the defendant's assertion of that right is treated as restraint if the plaintiff believes the defendant has that right or if the plaintiff is in doubt about whether or not the defendant has that right.

ii. **Non-compliance with asserted arrest.** If the defendant tells the plaintiff that he or she is under arrest, but the plaintiff ignores the defendant's subsequent instructions, there is no false imprisonment claim, because the plaintiff's freedom to move is not curtailed.

f. **Instigating arrest.** An individual is liable for false imprisonment if: 1. he or she furnishes information to police that leads the police to make an improper arrest; and 2. he or she does something additional in connection with an arrest, such as urging that the police carry it out.

5. Damages

False imprisonment plaintiffs can win the same three types of damages as battery and assault plaintiffs: actual (or compensatory) damages, nominal damages, and punitive damages.

a. **Actual damages.** A false imprisonment plaintiff is entitled to an award of money equal to the jury's valuation of the plaintiff's past and predicted future pain and suffering due to the false imprisonment. If the plaintiff suffered any nonemotional harm, damages for that are also available.

b. **Nominal damages.** If the plaintiff has no way to establish actual damages, nominal damages are available.

c. **Punitive damages.** If the defendant's conduct is particularly outrageous, the defendant may also be liable for punitive damages.

D. INFLICTION OF EMOTIONAL DISTRESS

Tort law seeks to deter people from intentionally causing others to suffer emotional distress. As one would expect, this tort action has a number of doctrinal limitations reflecting the tension between protecting emotional well-being and avoiding judicial evaluation of private relations.

1. Definition

A defendant commits the tort of infliction of emotional distress by: 1. intentionally or recklessly; 2. doing something extreme and outrageous that 3. causes; 4. the plaintiff to feel severe emotional or mental distress.

2. Defendant's Mental State

While infliction of emotional distress is usually classified as an intentional tort, liability may be based on recklessness as well as on actual intent to cause the harm.

a. **Recklessness defined.** Reckless conduct is done with deliberate disregard of a high degree of probability that an injury will result. It is different, therefore, from intentional conduct and from negligent conduct. As Chapter 6 explains, negligent conduct creates risks of harm greater than a reasonable person would create. Negligent conduct is what most people call careless conduct. Obviously, reckless acts are much less common than negligent acts.

Recklessness is a mental state other than those that can support liability in battery or assault. For battery or assault the plaintiff must show that the defendant either intended the result that occurred or was substantially certain the result would occur. Either of these mental states can be a basis for intentional infliction of emotional distress liability; in addition infliction of emotional distress liability can be based on a showing that the defendant was reckless with regard to the risk of inflicting such distress on the plaintiff.

b. **Recovery by plaintiffs other than the defendant's intended victim.** The general doctrine of transferred intent—treating an actor who intends to commit an intentional tort against one person but who in fact acts against another as having intended to commit an intentional tort against that other person—does not apply to the tort of intentional infliction of emotional distress. Courts are reluctant to expose defendants to the risk of litigation by vast numbers of people (for example, where a criminal commits a horrifying crime in view of hundreds of people on a crowded city street). There are, however, a few specific situations in which certain rules produce for the tort of intentional infliction of emotional distress the type of result ordinarily created by the transferred intent doctrine.

i. **Family member present, with presence known to defendant.** In many states a plaintiff has a cause of action for intentional infliction of emotional distress against a defendant who commits an outrageous act against a member of the plaintiff's family if the defendant does the act in the presence of the plaintiff and knows that the plaintiff is present.

ii. **Restatement view: Relative of intended victim.** The Restatement recognizes a cause of action by a relative of the defendant's intended victim if the relative is present when the defendant commits an outrageous act against the defendant's intended victim.

iii. **Restatement view: Anyone who witnesses act against intended victim.** The Restatement recognizes a cause of action by anyone present when the defendant commits an outrageous act against an intended victim if the plaintiff suffers bodily harm from the emotional distress caused by witnessing the defendant's act.

iv. **Analysis of Restatement provisions.** The difference between the Restatement position for a relative of the intended victim and its position for anyone other than a relative who is present when the defendant acts against an intended victim is that a relative is not required to show bodily harm, while any other person is required to show bodily harm as a result of the emotional distress. The Restatement does not require that the defendant be aware of the presence of either a relative or another person for those individuals to have causes of action.

E&A EXAMPLE AND ANALYSIS

Nathan Nofun found out that Charles Checkup had just had an annual physical examination. Nofun went to Checkup's house, saying that he was a representative from Checkup's health care provider and that he had information about Checkup's health. Checkup invited Nofun in. In the presence of Checkup's wife and one of Checkup's friends, Nofun said, "This is really bad news. You have a rare tropical disease that's going to make things fall off your body, starting with your limbs and ending with your head." Everything Nofun said was false. Checkup, Checkup's wife, and Checkup's friend all became extremely upset and suffered physical symptoms of their upset. Checkup would have a cause of action against Nofun for intentional infliction of emotional distress in virtually every jurisdiction. The Restatement would allow a cause of action for Checkup's wife since she was present when Nofun did his outrageous act. The Restatement would also allow a cause of action for Checkup's friend, since the friend was present during the outrageous act and suffered bodily harm from being upset.

---

c. **Defendant's intent to commit a different intentional tort.** For assault, battery, false imprisonment, and trespass against chattels or property, if the defendant means to commit one of these torts but actually inflicts another one, the intent requirement is satisfied. This treatment of intent for one tort as equivalent to the required intent for another does not apply to intentional infliction of emotional distress.

   i. **Example.** A person who attempts to arrest someone in a situation where he or she has no legal right to make the arrest is liable for false imprisonment if he or she is successful in detaining the person. If the person avoids being detained but is humiliated by the experience, there is no cause of action for intentional infliction of emotional distress, because the defendant's only purpose was to commit the tort of false imprisonment.

   ii. **Actionable emotional harms related to other intentional torts.** If a defendant attempts to commit any intentional tort and does something that gives the plaintiff an apprehension of imminent unpermitted contact, the defendant is liable for assault and therefore is liable for emotional harms that the assault may cause. Also, if emotional distress is a consequence of battery or false imprisonment, recovery for that emotional distress is permitted.

3. Types of Conduct That Constitute Infliction of Emotional Distress

To constitute infliction of emotional distress a defendant's conduct must be extreme and outrageous. This terminology is from the Restatement and is frequently used by courts. Restatement §46, comment *d*, defines conduct that can make an actor liable for intentional infliction of emotional distress as that which is "utterly intolerable in a civilized community" and which, when explained to a typical member of the community, would arouse "resentment against the actor" and would lead a typical community member "to exclaim, 'Outrageous!' "

a. **Policy issues related to mental effects.** The types of conduct that can cause mental distress are more numerous and less predictable than those that can constitute an assault or a battery. Thus, the Restatement definition of the cause of action is unavoidably vague, but its use of the expression "Outrageous!" reflects judicial concern that this tort might, unless carefully limited, allow too many interpersonal interactions to become the subject of litigation. A concept difficult to define, emotional distress is also a subject about which it is easy for plaintiffs to give false or misleading testimony. This factor, too, has influenced the development of this cause of action, with some jurisdictions imposing requirements meant to weed out cases in which plaintiffs are exaggerating their responses to defendants' conduct.

b. **Type of distress victim must suffer.** Where a plaintiff's cause of action is based on intentional infliction of emotional distress, and no other tort is involved, some rules apply to protect defendants against false claims.

   i. **Evidence required.** A plaintiff's claim of mental harm must be supported by evidence. In most cases this evidence is proof of medical treatment for the emotional harm.

   ii. **Physical harm.** In some states the plaintiff must show physical harm, like an ulcer or a rash, in addition to emotional distress. This doctrine is based on a belief that, unless there is tangible evidence of the distress, plaintiffs too easily lie about how they were affected by a defendant's conduct.

   iii. **Restatement position.** The Restatement does not require the plaintiff to show any physical consequences of the emotional distress allegedly caused by the defendant. It states, however, that in a case where a plaintiff does not show physical signs of harm a court may give greater emphasis to the requirement that the defendant's conduct be outrageous in order to increase the likelihood that the plaintiff's claimed emotional harm is real.

   iv. **Reasonable, not idiosyncratic, reaction.** A defendant's conduct is defined as outrageous, and therefore a possible basis for liability for intentional infliction of emotional distress, if it would cause serious distress to a typical member of the community. If it would cause distress only to an unusual or idiosyncratic member of the community, there is usually no liability for the act or its consequences to such a rare person. In a case where the defendant knows about the plaintiff's unusual sensitivity, however, the defendant is liable for intentional infliction of emotional distress for acting in a way that causes the harm to which the defendant knows the plaintiff is atypically susceptible.

c. **Effect of plaintiff's characteristics.** Courts recognize that a plaintiff's social or legal status may have a significant effect on a plaintiff's response to actions by a defendant.

   i. **Plaintiff's social or legal status.** If the plaintiff is in some way subservient to the defendant, that relationship may affect how a court treats conduct by the defendant. Examples include a defendant who in the role of school principal makes very embarrassing accusations against a student, and a defendant who under the guise of being a police officer does things that frighten the plaintiff severely.

ii. **Debtor.** Many cases have involved efforts by debt collectors to make debtors so uncomfortable that they pay the debt to halt the collector's conduct. Now, federal legislation controls extremely harassing conduct by debt collectors in many instances.

Conduct that is a straightforward presentation of a legal claim cannot be a basis for recovery for intentional infliction of emotional distress. A debt collector may be liable for the tort, however, for conduct that involves threats that the collector will get the plaintiff fired from a job or will do things to make it impossible for the plaintiff to live an ordinary day-to-day life.

d. **Wide range of facts.** The facts of cases involving this tort can involve a wide range of conduct. This tort ordinarily involves an objective test of the quality of the defendant's conduct. To be a basis for liability the conduct must be outrageous to typical people in the community. The only exception to this objective test is for cases where the plaintiff has an unusual reaction to the defendant's conduct but the defendant is aware of the likelihood of that rare reaction.

Illustrations: Wilkinson v. Downton, 2 Q.B. 57 (1897). The defendant made a false statement to the plaintiff that her husband had been badly hurt in an accident and had suffered two broken legs. Recovery was permitted for the plaintiff's resultant nervous reaction and related physical illness.

State Rubbish Collectors Assn. v. Siliznoff, 38 Cal. 2d 330, 240 P.2d 282 (1952). The president of an association of garbage collectors told the plaintiff that if he did not give the association part of the revenue from his own garbage collection business, members of the association would attack him personally and would destroy his garbage truck. This was not an assault because it involved threats of harm that might take place in the future. The court held, however, that the plaintiff was entitled to recover for intentional infliction of emotional distress.

Slocum v. Food Fair Stores of Florida, 100 So. 2d 396 (Fla. 1958). A store's employee told a customer, "You stink." The trial court dismissed a claim for intentional infliction of emotional distress, and the supreme court affirmed the dismissal. Holding that this statement would not lead a typical person to suffer severe emotional distress, it declined to use the case as an occasion to recognize the tort of intentional infliction of emotional distress.

4. **Duty of Hotels, Common Carriers, and Public Utilities**

There is a special doctrine for employees of hotels, common carriers, and public utilities. If they direct a gross insult toward a patron, and the patron reasonably suffers emotional distress, the employer is liable for intentional infliction of emotional distress.

a. **Gross insult standard.** This liability can be based on gross insults, which are considered outrageous in view of the common law's treatment of innkeepers, common carriers, and public utilities as entities with special obligations of care toward their patrons.

b. **Scope of employment.** The employee who communicates the insult or acts in an insulting way must do it while acting (in other ways) within the scope of employment in order for the hotel, common carrier, or public utility to be liable.

5. **Damages**

Intentional infliction of emotional distress plaintiffs can win the same three types of damages as other intentional tort plaintiffs: actual (or compensatory) damages, nominal damages, and punitive damages.

a. **Actual damages.** These are an award of money equal to the jury's valuation of the plaintiff's past and predicted future medical expenses, lost wages, and pain and suffering due to the emotional distress.

b. **Nominal damages.** In cases where the plaintiff has no way to establish actual damages, nominal damages are available.

c. **Punitive damages.** Where the defendant's conduct is particularly outrageous, the defendant may also be liable for punitive damages.

6. **First Amendment Restrictions**

Constitutional considerations under the First Amendment restrict the right of states to permit individuals to recover for defamation if they are public figures. Similar restrictions apply to a public figure's effort to use state intentional infliction of emotional distress doctrines to recover for harms caused by a publication.

Illustration: Hustler Magazine, Inc. v. Falwell, 485 U.S. 46, 108 S. Ct. 876, 99 L. Ed.2d 41 (1988), involved a suit against Hustler magazine by the famous minister Jerry Falwell. He sought damages for distress caused by the magazine's publication of an advertisement parody that ascribed revolting conduct to the plaintiff and his mother. The court ruled that no recovery was constitutionally permissible unless the publication contained a false statement of fact made with knowledge that the statement was false or with reckless disregard of its truth or falsity.

Review Questions and Answers

Question: At a professional football game the home team scored a touchdown. One of the people in the stadium jumped up and down with excitement and hugged a stranger who was standing in the next row. If the stranger suffered a strained back from being hugged, would the stranger have a cause of action in battery against the fan who did the hugging?

Answer: Maybe. Intending to touch the plaintiff, the defendant committed a volitional act, did touch the plaintiff, and did cause a harm. This would constitute battery, unless our legal system were to describe this incident as one in which there was implied consent. A jury could decide whether fans in a football stadium ordinarily treat each other this way; if it were to find that this type of contact was part of the normal pattern at football games, then there could be no cause of action in battery.

Question: On a crowded city street a pedestrian dashed from between two parked cars and tried to cross a lane of traffic. The cars in the lane were moving slowly. One driver shouted to the pedestrian, "You have to cross at the corner—I'll show you what happens when you dart out into the street." He then drove his car suddenly toward the pedestrian. The pedestrian jumped aside; the driver then stopped his car. Could the pedestrian have a cause of action against the driver for assault?

Answer: Yes. These facts support a conclusion that the defendant acted volitionally to make the pedestrian fear an imminent battery and that the pedestrian did in fact have that fear. That no battery occurred is not significant; assault requires only that the plaintiff have had a reasonable fear of battery.

Question: Veronica Violent got angry at Tina Target in a bar. Violent lurched toward Target and tried to punch her in the jaw. Target ducked, and Violent hit Nathan Nextman, a person who had been standing behind Target when Target ducked. Violent did not see Nextman until she hit him. Could Nextman have a successful cause of action against Violent for battery?

Answer: Yes. Violent did not intend to touch Nextman, but her actions would have satisfied the intent requirement if she had touched Target. Since Target could have established the intent element of battery, Nextman is allowed under the transferred intent doctrine to treat the intent toward Target as equivalent to an intent directed at him.

Question: Edward Evil, who collected debts on behalf of a famous criminal, approached Gary Gambler and said, "Give me the money you owe my boss right now, or I'll make you sorry you were ever born." Would this make Evil liable for assault?

Answer: Yes or no, depending on whether a jurisidiction adopts the majority view or the Restatement view on the issue of whether a mere statement, with no accompanying physical act, can be a basis for an assault claim. Traditional common law principles hold that there can be no assault cause of action in a situation where the defendant uses words alone and takes no physical action. Some modern courts and the Restatement hold that an assault action should be allowed where a combination of the defendant's words and other circumstances makes it reasonable for the plaintiff to believe that an unpermitted touching is imminent. Under common law doctrines there is no cause of action here for assault. Under the Restatement view an action is allowed, since Mr. Evil's job as a debt collector for a criminal and his association with that criminal make it reasonable for a person he threatens to believe that genuine physical consequences are likely to follow the threat immediately.

Question: At closing time the librarian in charge of locking up a college library failed to notice a student studying in an obscure corner of the reading room and locked the student in. If the student sought damages for false imprisonment, would the student be able to satisfy the tort's element of intent to confine?

Answer: The person who locked the student in at closing time did not know the student was there and had no intention to confine him or her. Therefore, there was no false imprisonment action.

Question: A librarian noticed a student sleeping at a library table at closing time. To "teach the student a lesson," the librarian intentionally locked the library without waking the student to give the student a chance to leave. The student awoke the next morning when a library worker opened the library for the next day's hours of operation. Would the student have a successful cause of action against the librarian for false imprisonment?

Answer: No. The librarian's purposeful action satisfies the intent requirement, but there would be a fatal flaw in the student's claim. The student had no awareness of his or her confinement; generally this would preclude recovery for false imprisonment.

Question: A famous college rejected a high school senior's application for admission. This made the student extremely upset. Could the student assert a successful claim for damages for intentional infliction of emotional distress?

Answer: No. The college's action would not seem extreme or outrageous to a typical community member. The tort of intentional infliction of emotional distress does not prevent people in society from disappointing each other.

Exam Tips

- Each intentional tort requires a volitional act by the defendant. Be sure to identify the act or to notice if the actor in an exam question did not commit a volitional act.
- A defendant who has no desire to hurt a plaintiff can still be liable for battery if the defendant means to touch the plaintiff and the touching is either harmful or offensive.
- For battery and assault a plaintiff's idiosyncratic nature is usually not relevant. A touching that virtually all people would consider a normal part of life in a particular setting does not support a battery claim even if the person who is touched has an unusual fear of being touched or has an unusual sense of personal privacy and decorum.
- The rule that battery and assault causes of action apply without regard to the special sensitivities of plaintiffs is withdrawn in cases where the defendant knows about the special sensitivity of the plaintiff before the defendant acts.
- Words and actions that would not make a typical person fear an imminent battery do not support a claim for assault, even if the person at whom they are directed has a strong reaction of fear in response to them.
- For intentional infliction of emotional distress questions, pay attention to the type of harm the plaintiff suffers. In many states a plaintiff must have physical manifestations of emotional distress to be entitled to recover. In some other states emotional distress without external physical symptoms may be enough to support recovery, but courts are likely to require significant proof of the bad quality of the defendant's conduct to permit recovery in the absence of physical symptoms of harm.

4 INTENTIONAL TORTS AGAINST PROPERTY

CHAPTER OVERVIEW

- Trespass to land is the intentional entering of another's land.
- At early common law trespass was a strict liability tort with no requirement that the plaintiff show the defendant's intent. Now a plaintiff must show that the defendant undertook a volitional act intended to result in an invasion of the plaintiff's land.
- The defendant's intent to enter the land is crucial for trespass. There is no requirement that the plaintiff show that the defendant intended to harm the land or to violate the owner's property rights.
- Various types of entries on land can be trespasses: a person on the land, an object on the land, vibrations, dust and gas, and some intrusions under and above the surface of the land.
- Conversion and trespass to chattels are the intentional interference with another's tangible property.
- If an interference with the plaintiff's property is relatively slight, the appropriate cause of action is trespass to chattels.
- For serious interference with a plaintiff's property, the appropriate cause of action is conversion.

A. TRESPASS TO LAND

Trespass to land is one type of intentional tort against property. The other types are conversion and trespass to chattels (chattels are objects or things a person can own, including documents that are equivalent to property).

1. Definition

One commits a trespass to land if one: 1. commits a volitional act; 2. with the intent to cause a physical invasion of another's land; and 3. causes such an invasion directly or indirectly. The invasion can occur when a defendant enters a plaintiff's land or when a defendant causes an object or another person to enter a plaintiff's land. The term *trespass* usually refers to a situation where a defendant causes an entry intentionally; it is important to remember, however, that there are three ways an entry to land can happen:

- intentionally, with the defendant's moving himself or herself or some object onto the plaintiff's land; or
- with the defendant's accidental conduct; or
- with no willful act by the defendant.

Some consequences of these characterizations are explained in the section on intent.

2. Intent

There was no intent requirement for trespass actions at early common law. In modern times a plaintiff must show that a defendant's entry on the plaintiff's land involved intentional conduct. Negligence concepts apply to entries that do not involve intentional conduct but that do cause injury.

a. **Unintentional entry actionable at common law.** At early common law a defendant who entered another's land was liable for trespass regardless of whether the entry was because of negligence or intentional conduct. This was strict liability, where the plaintiff had no obligation to prove anything about the defendant's mental state or style of conduct.

   i. **Involuntary acts.** Even at common law there was no trespass action against a person who was put on the plaintiff's land by others and thus had done no voluntary act related to his or her presence on the land.

b. **Modern intent requirement.** The plaintiff must show, under modern doctrines, that the defendant had some intent to make the entry that is the subject of the suit. Strict liability continues to apply, however, to one category of contemporary trespass actions: actions based on the consequences of a defendant's abnormally dangerous activity.

   i. **Intent to cause harm not required.** The plaintiff must show that the defendant meant to enter or put someone or something on the plaintiff's property, but plaintiff need not show that the defendant meant to cause any harm.

ii. **Intent to trespass not required.** If a defendant intentionally enters a place or puts something there, the defendant has committed a trespass if the place is in someone else's possession. The defendant's intentional act is adequate for the intent element of trespass, even if the defendant mistakenly believes that he or she has permission to be there or to put something there, and even if that mistake is a reasonable one.

E&A EXAMPLE AND ANALYSIS

Bob Busrider walked across a field, using it as a shortcut to a bus stop. Busrider had no desire to break any law that he knew about, and he had no knowledge about who might own the field. Linda Landowner, who owned the field, had a valid trespass cause of action against Busrider, because Busrider intentionally used her land.

iii. **Intent not required if defendant's conduct is abnormally dangerous.** Sometimes a defendant will cause an entry onto a plaintiff's land through some activity the defendant carries out near that land. If the activity is abnormally dangerous, strict liability will apply in a damages action brought by the land occupier against the defendant.

3. Types of Entries

Trespass law deals with the presence of people or things on a plaintiff's property. As might be expected, there are many ways a person or a thing can come to be on someone's land. The physical invasion that a plaintiff must show has occurred does not require proof of any damage to the land. Note that invasion, for trespass law, does not mean tangible harm to the land.

Illustration: Dougherty v. Stepp, 18 N.C. 371 (1835). The law infers damage, even if it is just an assumed trampling of grass or herbage, when a defendant commits an act of trespass.

a. **Human being on land without permission.** The classic trespass situation involves a person who enters another's land. A person on someone else's land is a trespasser unless that person has permission to be there.

b. **Human being enters land with permission but stays after permission is revoked.** A person who enters land with permission becomes a trespasser by staying on the land after being asked to leave. The permission a person receives to enter and stay on someone else's land is not permanent. If the permission is withdrawn, the person becomes a trespasser unless he or she leaves the land.

c. **Human being put on land by someone else.** It is theoretically possible—and occasionally actually happens—that one person can put another person in a certain location. The person who is put on someone else's land is not a trespasser.

d. **Object put on land without permission.** Anyone who puts something on someone else's land without permission has committed the tort of trespass. Someone who puts another person on someone else's land is a trespasser (analytically, the person he or she put on the land is an object).

e. **Object put on land with permission but not removed after permission is revoked.** A person who puts something on someone else's land is liable for trespass if he or she fails to remove it when asked to do so by the land occupant.

f. **Vibrations (blasting).** If a person does something like blasting that affects someone else's land through vibration or concussion, has the person committed a trespass? Common law and modern doctrines approach this problem differently.

   i. **Common law: no trespass.** The common law's answer to this question was "no trespass," since the blaster did not go personally onto someone else's land and did not put anything on it. Because the blaster only shook the land, there was no trespass. In the absence of any direct injury, a plaintiff was required to seek damages for trespass on the case rather than trespass. The significance to plaintiffs was that liability for trespass was strict, but liability for trespass on the case required a showing of intent, negligence, or the conducting of an abnormally dangerous activity.

   ii. **Modern doctrines: trespass.** Modern doctrines treat a vibration or a concussion that affects another's land as a trespass.

   iii. **Significance of classification.** Under early, common law doctrines it was very helpful to a plaintiff for a defendant to be characterized as having committed a trespass in a case involving concussion or vibration from blasting, because there was strict liability for trespass. This meant that the plaintiff would recover damages without having to show that the blaster had been negligent. Under modern law there is no strict liability for an accidental trespass. Strict liability is usually available for damages from blasting, however, under a theory different from trespass (conduct of abnormally dangerous activity).

g. **Dust and gas.** A defendant's actions may put dust or gas on a plaintiff's land. Liability for trespass may depend on the actual amount of material that intrudes on the land.

i. **Accumulation required.** Some jurisdictions permit a trespass action for a defendant's placing dust or gas on a plaintiff's land only if an accumulation of the material occurs.

Illustration: Bradley v. American Smelting and Refining Co., 104 Wash. 2d 677, 709 P.2d 782 (1985). Transitory and airborne particles that dissipate quickly do not interfere with a landowner's possessory rights and cannot be a basis for a trespass claim. If invisible particles accumulate, however, a trespass action is permitted if there is actual damage to the land.

ii. **Microscopic entry recognized.** A minority view allows an action for trespass when a defendant's conduct places only microscopic amounts of dust or gas on a plaintiff's land.

iii. **Relationship to nuisance.** Other theories of liability, such as nuisance, may be available for invasions of dust or gas, but the statute of limitations for trespass may have a longer period than that for nuisance.

h. **Above the land's surface.** Courts at one time referred to a Latin maxim *cujus est solum, ejus est usque ad coelum et ad inferos,* meaning: the one who has the soil also has possession from the depths to the sky. This idea has been restricted significantly under modern decisions. If a flight over someone's land is made at or above the minimum height authorized by federal regulations, federal law preempts any common law action seeking damages for the flight. If a flight is below the height recognized in the federal regulations, a plaintiff landowner is usually required to show some harm from the flight, and the law of nuisance will apply. Under nuisance law the reasonableness of the defendant's conduct will be examined.

i. **Restatement position.** Restatement §159(2) allows recovery for a flight over a plaintiff's land if the flight goes through the **immediate reaches** of the land's airspace and if the flight substantially interferes with the **use and enjoyment** of the land. This is similar to general nuisance law, except that it assumes the defendant's conduct is not justifiable.

Illustration: City of Newark v. Eastern Airlines, 159 F. Supp. 750 (D.N.J. 1958). The public has a right to the airspace ordinarily used for aviation. A landowner's trespass claim would be recognized only if it showed that the defendant's flight was in the immediate reaches of the plaintiff's land.

i. **Below the land's surface.** Entry under a plaintiff's land is usually a trespass; however, some entries incidental to a defendant's use of his or her own land may be excluded from the definition of trespass. For example, nuisance rather than trespass doctrines may apply if a landowner injects water into oil wells on his or her land to increase the production of oil, and a consequence of that action is the introduction of water under a neighbor's land.

j. **Continuous entry.** When a trespass involves a defendant's placing something on a plaintiff's land, it may be defined as a "continuing trespass." Courts examine the details of the entry to decide whether the plaintiff must seek past and future damages in a single lawsuit or must sue for only past damages (and sue again in the future if the defendant continues the trespass).

4. Plaintiff Must Be Land Possessor

The plaintiff in a trespass case must be the possessor of the land on which the defendant has allegedly trespassed. This is not necessarily the same as being the owner of the land. An owner not in possession of his or her land is prohibited from seeking damages for trespass. Such an owner may have other causes of action to establish damage to his or her right of reversion (the interest retained when an owner leases or otherwise allows another person to occupy his or her land).

a. **Lessee may sue.** A lessee may sue in trespass even though a lessee is not an owner. The trespass suit seeks damages for the harm inflicted on the lessee's right to occupy the land for a specific period of time.

b. **No trespass claim against wrongful possessor.** A wrongful possessor who has a plausible claim to ownership may not be sued for trespass by an allegedly rightful owner. The allegedly rightful owner must bring an ejection action or some other action to determine ownership rights in real property.

5. Damages

Trespass damages may be nominal or actual. Nominal damages are less readily available at present than at early common law.

a. **Nominal damages.** Nominal damages are a token payment ordered to be made by the defendant to the plaintiff.

i. **Common law.** Nominal damages were available at early common law in any case of trespass, regardless of whether the defendant had acted intentionally, carelessly, or reasonably.

ii. **Modern doctrine.** Nominal damages are available in modern times only in cases of intentional trespass.

b. Actual damages. Actual damages are available under both common law and modern doctrines. Courts hold the defendant responsible for all the direct consequences of his or her act, such as damage to property or personal injury to someone on the land.

i. Unusual victim or unusual extent of harm. If a defendant's conduct causes unpredictable harms or affects individuals whose injury was unlikely, that defendant is ordinarily responsible for such remote or unforeseeable harms.

B. CONVERSION AND TRESPASS TO CHATTELS

The two other intentional torts against property are conversion and trespass to chattels. For each of these torts, a defendant intentionally interferes with a rightful possessor's possession or use of the property. The degree of interference distinguishes trespass and conversion actions.

1. Definitions

Conversion and trespass to chattels are common law actions a plaintiff can bring against a defendant who takes something or impedes the plaintiff's use of something that belongs to the plaintiff.

One commits a trespass to a chattel when one: 1. commits a volitional act; 2. with the intent to cause an interference with the plaintiff's chattel; and 3. causes such an interference directly or indirectly.

One commits a conversion when one: 1. commits a volitional act; 2. with the intent to cause an interference with the plaintiff's chattel; and 3. causes destruction of the chattel or serious interference with it directly or indirectly.

a. Difference between trespass to chattels and conversion. The primary difference between the two torts is the actual effect of the defendant's conduct on the plaintiff's property. Trespass to chattels is the older of the two actions. It applies when the defendant's conduct imposes a minor interference with the plaintiff's possession or use of his or her property. Conversion applies when a defendant inflicts a significant harm to a plaintiff's interest in his or her property.

b. Different remedies. Since trespass to chattels involves only a small invasion of a plaintiff's interest, the damage award involved is likely to be small. The plaintiff is ordinarily entitled to compensation only for harm done to the thing. In contrast, the remedy for conversion is a judgment for the market value of the item the defendant has taken or used. Because the conversion cause of action involves more serious wrongs and permits larger recoveries, it is more important at present than the trespass to chattels cause of action.

2. Intent

To commit a trespass to chattels or a conversion of a chattel a defendant must act intentionally. Careless or negligent conduct that deprives a plaintiff of some use or possession of property can be a basis for a cause of action in negligence; it is not treated as trespass or conversion. The intent required for trespass to chattels or conversion need not be an intent to cause a harm or to deprive the plaintiff of a property right. It need only be an intent to do something to the chattel.

3. Characterization of Conduct as Trespass or Conversion

Courts use a variety of factors to decide whether a defendant's taking or controlling a plaintiff's property should be treated as a trespass or a conversion. These factors include:

- the amount of the defendant's control over the thing or the defendant's interference with the plaintiff's right to have it or to use it;
- the amount of any additional consequential interference with the plaintiff's right to control the thing;
- the defendant's intention to assert a right inconsistent with the plaintiff's right to control the thing;
- the defendant's good faith;
- harm to the thing;
- expense and inconvenience suffered by the plaintiff. In evaluating the impact of the defendant's conduct, courts consider two aspects of the defendant's relationship with the plaintiff's property: the extent of the contact and the duration of the contact.

E&A EXAMPLE AND ANALYSIS

Ralph Reader took a walk early one morning and picked up a newspaper that had been delivered to the front lawn of a neighbor's house. Reader read the newspaper during his morning walk and then returned it to the neighbor's lawn. Reader committed a trespass, not a conversion. If Reader had kept the newspaper, he would have committed a conversion.

4. Damages

In a trespass to chattels case the plaintiff is entitled to compensation for whatever actual harm was done to his or her property, or for whatever actual harm the plaintiff suffered by being briefly deprived of use of his or her property. Nominal damages, which are available in trespass to land cases, are not allowed in trespass to chattels cases.

In conversion cases the plaintiff is entitled to be paid the full value of the thing that the defendant either took from the plaintiff or prevented the plaintiff from using.

a. **Return of the item.** In trespass to chattels cases a defendant who returns the item is entitled to have its value used as a mitigating factor to reduce the judgment against the defendant. In conversion cases title to the item is said to have been transferred from the plaintiff to the defendant, and the defendant is ordinarily not entitled to have a judgment reduced by the act of giving that property (now the defendant's but formerly the plaintiff's) to the plaintiff.

   i. **Minority view.** A minority view permits the defendant to return the thing and thus reduce the damages award if: the defendant committed the conversion in good faith, the item has suffered no damage, and the plaintiff has not suffered related additional damages due to the interference with his or her property.

5. Possible Plaintiffs

When a defendant takes or interferes with the use of property, other individuals affected can be those who were in possession of it when the defendant acted, those who were entitled to immediate possession of it, and those who were entitled to future possession of it.

a. **Liability to person in possession.** For both trespass to chattels and conversion—a suit may be brought by an individual who was in possession of the item at the time the defendant took some action that affected it.

   i. ***Jus Tertii* defense rejected.** A doctrine known as *jus tertii* held that if a person owned property, a second person who happened to have the property in his or her possession was forbidden to sue a third person for trespass. Modern courts reject this doctrine on the theory that it helps preserve the peace to allow possessors to vindicate whatever rights they may have in property.

b. **Liability to a person entitled to immediate possession.** For both trespass to chattels and conversion suit may be brought by an individual who was entitled to immediate possession of the item at the time the defendant took some action that affected it.

c. **Liability to a person entitled to future possession.** Common law did not recognize liability for trespass to chattels or conversion to an individual whose only interest in the property was a right to future possession.

Modern decisions and the Restatement recognize a cause of action in this situation to allow recovery of the full value of the future interest impaired by the defendant's conduct.

d. **No liability without some ownership interest. Illustration:** Moore v. Regents of the University of California, 793 P.2d 479 (Cal. 1990). The plaintiff was treated for leukemia at a hospital operated by the defendant. Employees discovered that his cells were unique and used some of them to develop products with a market potential estimated at $3 billion. The plaintiff sought damages for conversion of the cell material obtained from him during his cancer therapy. No cause of action was permitted, because the plaintiff had no ownership interest in the cells removed from his body for therapeutic purposes. He had no expectation to retain possession of them, the court held.

6. Methods of Committing a Trespass Against a Chattel

A person can commit a trespass against a chattel by dispossessing someone of it, by using it, or by meddling with it. These types of conduct overlap with the types of conduct that can constitute a conversion. It is important to remember that conversion is a tort that allows a greater remedy than trespass to chattels, so that a plaintiff will seek to have a defendant's conduct characterized as conversion rather than as trespass to a chattel.

a. **Dispossession.** A person can dispossess another of a chattel by taking it from him or her without consent; by obtaining it by fraud or duress; by preventing the other's access to it; by destroying it while someone else has it; or by taking it into the custody of the law.

b. **Use or meddling.** Meddling is defined as intentionally causing a contact with something that belongs to another.

7. Methods of Committing a Conversion

Many recurring situations are recognized in the common law as constituting conversion.

a. **Gaining possession.** The most obvious method of committing a conversion is by gaining possession of something that belongs to another by stealing it, by using fraud to get it, or by using apparent legal authority.

i. **Belief in right to possession.** Whether a person believes he or she has a right to the thing taken has no bearing on the definition of conversion. It may be relevant, however, to a defense of privilege.

ii. **Bona fide purchasers.** A bona fide purchaser (a buyer in good faith) who "buys" something that did not belong to the seller commits the tort of conversion.

(a) **Restatement modification.** The Restatement modifies the strictness of the common law position by stating that a bona fide purchaser may return the item and thereby reduce the damages that would otherwise be owed to the rightful possessor.

(b) **Bona fide purchaser from fraudulent possessor.** If someone obtains an item from its owner by fraud, that person is subject to liability for conversion. If the person who obtained something by fraud then transfers it to a bona fide purchaser, however, that bona fide purchaser has no liability to the owner for conversion. If the owner asks that bona fide purchaser for the return of the item, the bona fide purchaser may ultimately become liable for conversion if he or she refuses to give it to the owner.

(c) **Bona fide purchasers of negotiable instruments.** A negotiable instrument is a document that entitles its owner to be paid a sum of money or to receive certain specific property. A person who obtains a negotiable instrument in good faith is treated specially: There is no conversion in this circumstance because of the public policy of supporting the negotiability and reliability of negotiable instruments.

b. **Destruction or alteration.** Conversion can be done by destroying or altering a chattel. To constitute a conversion an alteration must significantly change the item.

Illustration: Pearson v. Dodd, 410 F.2d 701 (D.C. App. 1969). A journalist's employees took documents from the plaintiff's office, made copies of them, and returned them to the office. The appellate court held that this conduct was not a conversion of the documents. It stressed the fact that there had been no significant deprivation of the plaintiff's possessory rights, because the papers were removed at night and returned in the morning in time for their use in the office. The court also stated that the information in the papers had no commercial value.

c. **Use.** A person can commit a conversion by using something in a way that seriously violates another's right to control its use.

d. **Use exceeding permission.** A person who has permission to use something can commit a conversion by using the thing in a way that exceeds the permission received.

i. **Proof of excessive use.** To establish that a defendant has exceeded his or her permission to use an owner's item, the owner must ask for its return and show that the defendant declined to give it back. The defendant is entitled, however, to make a reasonable effort to determine whether the plaintiff is really entitled to have it.

E&A EXAMPLE AND ANALYSIS

The owner of a car might give it to a dealer to evaluate for a trade-in offer. If the dealer refused to return the car to the owner after a reasonable time, the owner would have a conversion action against the dealer.

e. **Storing or transporting.** A person who agrees to keep something or to transport it can be liable for conversion, but only if he or she had reason to know that a third person was entitled to immediate possession of the item. This is another instance in which good faith prevents the imposition of liability for conversion.

   i. **Unpermitted moving.** Moving something without permission can constitute a conversion if the defendant's conduct places a significant burden on the plaintiff.

f. **Agent or employee's possession.** Someone's agent or employee may obtain possession of something either by negotiating on behalf of the principal or employer or by accepting it, without negotiations, on behalf of the principal or employer. If the agent or employee negotiates a transaction, the agent or employee will be liable for conversion if ultimately the transaction cannot transfer the ownership interest it purports to transfer (as when the seller or purported transferor did not have a property interest in the item). If the agent or employee accepts something for the principal or employer without having negotiated about it, the agent or employee is free from liability for conversion if he or she was reasonably unaware that the transferor did not have a right to transfer it.

g. **Misdelivery by agent, employee, or bailee.** An agent, employee, or bailee commits a conversion if he or she makes an unauthorized delivery of the owner's item to someone to whom the owner did not instruct the agent, employee, or bailee to deliver it.

   i. **Unauthorized delivery to rightful possessor.** An unauthorized delivery to the rightful immediate possessor of an item, however, is not a conversion.

   ii. **Bailed stolen property.** A bailee ordinarily has no conversion liability if a thief has bailed an item and the bailee returns it to the thief. Liability for conversion can occur, however, if the real owner asks for return of the item and the bailee fails to give it to the owner.

Review Questions and Answers

Question: Mary Maniac grabbed a stranger, Francine Flyer, and threw Flyer over a fence into Oscar Owner's backyard. Flyer landed in Owner's backyard. Is Flyer liable for trespass?

Answer: No. Trespass is an intentional tort requiring a volitional act on the part of the defendant. Flyer committed no volitional act in connection with her presence on Owner's land.

Question: Walter Wrongway took a shortcut across some land that he thought was part of a public park. In fact the land belonged to Olivia Owner. Did Wrongway commit a trespass?

Answer: Yes. Wrongway committed an act (walking) that was intended to cause a physical invasion of Owner's land and that did cause that invasion. The invasion occurred and the tort of trespass was committed, even though Wrongway believed he was on public land and had no intention of using land that belonged to Owner.

Question: Susan Shopper entered a large shopping mall during its regular business hours and bought some things. She refused to leave at the close of the business day, even after a security guard told her the mall was closed. Was Shopper a trespasser?

Answer: Yes. Shopper had permission to enter the land and therefore was not a trespasser while she was on the land within the scope of the permission the owner had granted to her. When permission to be present was revoked, or when the time for which permission had been granted expired, Shopper committed a trespass by staying on the land.

Question: Nathan Neater saw a stack of magazines on a table in a school cafeteria. He took them away and left them in a nearby student lounge. In theory, did the owner of those magazines have a tort cause of action against Neater because of this conduct?

Answer: Yes. Neater acted volitionally with an intent to interfere with the magazines (by moving them from one place to another), and he actually did accomplish that result. His conduct constitutes the tort of trespass against chattels. If Neater believed that the magazines had been abandoned but was wrong about that, the owner of the magazines has a valid cause of action against Neater for trespass against chattels.

Question: Tina Tricker saw Greta Gullible using an expensive camera in a park. Tricker told Gullible that type of camera had been recalled by the government because its viewfinder could injure the eye of anyone who used it. Tricker offered to take it to a camera store for Gullible to exchange it. Gullible gave Tricker the camera. Tricker kept it and refused to give it back. She had been lying about the hazard and the recall. Did Tricker commit the tort of conversion?

Answer: Yes. Even though Gullible gave Tricker the camera voluntarily, Tricker committed some volitional acts to obtain possession of the camera and actually did obtain it. Because her interference with Gullible's use of the camera was total, a cause of action in conversion is proper.

Exam Tips

- Remember that trespass to land is an intentional tort. A person who enters another's land without taking any volitional action to do so cannot be liable for trespass.
- A defendant's belief that he or she had a right to enter land or take a chattel has no relevance to possible liability for trespass to land, trespass to a chattel, or conversion. Interference with the plaintiff's right to use or possession is the key idea, regardless of whether the defendant acted reasonably.
- Recall that the main difference between trespass to chattels and conversion is that the interference with the plaintiff's property is relatively slight in trespass to chattels cases and large in conversion cases.

5 DEFENSES TO INTENTIONAL TORT LIABILITY

CHAPTER OVERVIEW

- Even if a plaintiff establishes the prima facie case for an intentional tort, a defendant can avoid liability by successfully asserting a privilege or by proving that the plaintiff consented to the defendant's act.
- A plaintiff who consents to a defendant's conduct is usually barred from recovering damages for it.
- Certain types of consent are not valid, such as consents obtained by duress, consents to criminal conduct, or consents made by people not entitled to make binding legal commitments.
- Self-defense is a privilege that allows a person to use force to protect himself or herself from physical injury.
- The force a self-defender uses must be proportional to the injury it is meant to prevent.
- Protection of property is another basis for a privilege to use force against others. Deadly force is not permitted merely to defend property but may be used to stop a felony.
- A privilege called "necessity" entitles a person to use another's property, but a parallel doctrine requires that the person give compensation for the effects that use may have on the property.
- The state may take property under a necessity rationale without paying compensation.

A. INTRODUCTION

Many plaintiffs who establish prima facie cases for intentional torts are not entitled to judgments in their favor. This is because many defendants have adequate defenses. This chapter explains the most important defenses to intentional torts and explains their procedural effects.

Defendants are protected from liability for intentional torts in two main circumstances: when the plaintiff has consented to the defendant's conduct or when legal doctrines give the defendant a privilege to act in a way that would otherwise constitute an intentional tort. Consent usually involves an agreement between the parties. Privileges arise as a matter of law, without regard to any agreement between plaintiff and defendant.

B. CONSENT

Ordinarily, a plaintiff who consents to conduct by a defendant is not permitted to win a suit against that defendant based on the authorized action. For a number of recurring situations, specific rules apply so that consent is sometimes effective and sometimes not effective.

1. Express Consent

Express consent is an explicit agreement between a plaintiff and a defendant in which the plaintiff grants the defendant permission to do certain conduct, including conduct that might harm the plaintiff. Express consent can be oral or written. It is relatively rare in intentional tort cases.

E&A EXAMPLE AND ANALYSIS

A student might say to someone, "Please lock me in my room until tonight, so I'll be sure to study." That statement authorizes the other person to lock the student up and prevents the student from suing for false imprisonment.

2. Implied Consent

In a variety of recurring situations, the law treats a person as having consented to conduct that would otherwise be an intentional tort. This type of consent is known as implied consent.

a. **Defendant's reasonable belief.** If the defendant has a reasonable belief that the plaintiff consents to the defendant's conduct, that belief is a complete defense to an intentional tort cause of action.

i. **Belief based on objective manifestations.** Often, a plaintiff acts in a way that makes it reasonable for the defendant to believe the plaintiff consents to the defendant's conduct. The defendant may base his or her belief on anything the plaintiff does that can reasonably be understood as a manifestation of consent. Note that the plaintiff's personal and unexpressed feelings are not relevant, since the law evaluates the situation based on the objective and external conduct observed by the defendant.

Illustration: O'Brien v. Cunard S.S. Co., 154 Mass. 272, 28 N.E. 266 (1891). The defendant's employee physician gave the plaintiff a smallpox vaccination as part of the procedure followed when steerage passengers were about to disembark in the United States. The plaintiff claimed she had not consented to the procedure, but evidence showed she had held up her arm without making an objection. Consent could be implied from that conduct.

ii. **Belief based on custom.** A defendant is entitled to assume that the plaintiff consents to an action by the defendant if people in the plaintiff's position ordinarily consent to actions like the one taken by the defendant.

iii. **Belief based on plaintiff's failure to object.** A defendant may form a reasonable belief that a plaintiff consents to his or her conduct if the plaintiff is aware of the defendant's conduct and does not make an objection that most people would make if they were unwilling to have the defendant act in the anticipated way.

b. **Plaintiff's uncommunicated grant of permission.** An individual who has expressed a willingness for the defendant to act in a certain way may not recover for an intentional tort based on that type of conduct, even if the defendant never knows that the plaintiff has consented to that type of conduct.

3. Consent Based on a Mistake

If a plaintiff consents to conduct that would otherwise be an intentional tort, the consent is valid even if the plaintiff based the decision to consent on a mistake he or she made about some significant circumstance.

a. **Mistake induced by the defendant.** The general rule that mistaken consents are effective is changed for cases where the defendant induces the plaintiff's mistake. A consent based on fraud perpetrated by the defendant has no validity.

b. **Mistake on a collateral topic.** If a defendant's fraud involves a topic that is collateral, then a plaintiff's consent induced by the fraud is valid.

EXAMPLE AND ANALYSIS

Jan Jacobs consented to sexual relations with Pat Patterson. If Jacobs based that consent in part on a personal but mistaken belief that a person of Patterson's age could not have a sexually transmitted disease, Jacobs's consent would be an effective defense in a battery suit by Jacobs against Patterson seeking damages for having contracted the disease from Patterson. If Jacobs consented because Patterson persuaded Jacobs falsely that a person of Patterson's age could not have a sexually transmitted disease, consent by Jacobs would not be a defense in that battery suit. If Jacobs consented because Patterson falsely claimed to have a serious interest in classical music of the fifteenth century, Patterson's fraud on that topic likely would be called collateral and would therefore not prevent Patterson from relying on Jacobs's consent as a defense.

4. Consent Under Duress

A plaintiff's consent has no effect if it is induced by threats of violence or force, or by a false statement of legal right by a defendant. In general, however, the threat must be of immediate harm. If a plaintiff gives consent in response to a defendant's threat of some future reprisal for a failure to consent, then that consent is valid.

5. Consent to Criminal Acts

The majority rule provides that a person cannot make an effective consent to an illegal act. This means that participants in an illegal boxing match, for example, may sue each other for battery. A minority position, reflected in the Restatement, allows consent to illegal acts except where the statute making the conduct illegal was adopted to protect a class of individuals especially in need of protection.

a. **Statutory rape.** An adult who has sexual contacts with a minor below the age of consent may not defend a battery cause of action with a defense that the minor consented. Jurisdictions that follow the majority rule reach this result because consent is never a defense to an illegal act. Jurisdictions that follow the minority rule also reach this result, since their recognition of consent to illegal acts does not apply to acts made illegal to protect a class in need of special protection, such as minors.

6. People Incapable of Consenting

Minors, people with certain disabilities, and individuals who are very sick do not have the capacity to grant permission for conduct that would otherwise be an intentional tort. Consent may be implied by the law in some situations, may be given by a person's parent or guardian, or may be ordered explicitly by a court.

a. **Person in need of treatment.** Legal doctrines allow health care practitioners to treat a patient without that patient's actual consent when:

- the patient is incapacitated; and
- is in an emergency situation; and
- has not shown an unwillingness to consent; and
- a reasonable person would consent in that situation.

i. **Parents and other relatives.** If parents or close relatives of a minor or an incapacitated adult are available, they can provide consent to medical procedures on behalf of that person. Some jurisdictions require a physician to seek consent from parents or relatives if they can be contacted, even if the emergency conditions listed above are present.

ii. **Permission from a court.** If a minor's parents refuse to consent to a medical procedure needed to save the child's life, a court may grant permission in an action brought by the doctor or a hospital.

b. **Procedure to benefit another person.** There are situations where a medical procedure on a person incapable of giving consent can benefit another person. A kidney transplant is an example. Courts are divided on whether consent to such a procedure can be given by people who act on behalf of the incapacitated person. It is ordinarily required that the incapacitated person receive a benefit from any authorized procedure. One view is that there is no benefit to being a transplant donor, so no consent may properly be given to such a procedure. Another view allows consent on the theory that being a transplant donor to assist a relative does benefit the donor, because it lengthens the life of a relative who might care for or otherwise help the donor.

7. Scope of Consent

Any consent is valid only for the acts it authorizes. If a defendant acts in a way that exceeds the scope of consent, the consent is unavailable as a defense to an intentional tort action. For example, if a group of people agreed to play a game of touch football, any of them who actually tackled another player could be found to have committed a battery.

a. **Consent covers conduct regardless of the result.** A plaintiff's consent authorizes a defendant to act in a certain way. Regardless of the consequences of the defendant's action, consent is a valid defense if the defendant's actions are ordinarily understood to be of the type to which the plaintiff agreed.

b. **Medical cases.** A plaintiff's consent to a surgical operation is usually treated as consent to a specific operation and to treatment of other problems discovered during the surgery if they constitute an emergency or relate to the purpose of the treatment.

   i. **Operation on different part of body.** If a patient consents to an operation on a particular part of the body, and a surgeon operates on some significantly different part of the patient's body, the surgeon is treated as having acted outside the scope of the patient's consent.

   Illustration: Mohr v. Williams, 95 Minn. 261, 104 N.W. 12 (1905). The plaintiff consented to surgery on one of her ears, but while she was unconscious for the operation the doctor operated on the other ear. The plaintiff was entitled to recover for battery, even though the operation was a benefit to her.

   ii. **Misrepresentation.** Consent that a patient bases on false information from a physician has no effect as a defense to a battery claim.

   iii. **Written consent forms.** Doctors and hospitals usually require patients to sign consent forms. If the consent form is extremely broad in its language, a court might treat it as invalid. More usually, courts give effect to consent forms that provide very general permission for treatment within professional judgment.

   iv. **Informed consent.** For operations and other medical procedures physicians must obtain the patient's informed consent. This requires the professional to provide adequate information to the patient about the proposed treatment. In theory, a physician who touches a patient without first satisfying the informed consent requirement commits a battery. Most courts, however, use a negligence analysis to treat shortcomings in the category of informed consent disclosures.

c. **Professional athletes.** The rules governing consent have been applied in a number of cases involving injuries to professional athletes. Thus, even a professional football player has been permitted to seek intentional tort damages from an opposing player who intentionally hit him in a way that was clearly outside the rules of the game.

   i. **Distinction between intentional misconduct and other misconduct.** A professional athlete is probably precluded from recovering for injuries caused by another player's negligence or recklessness, since courts are likely to treat those types of injuries as ordinarily expected elements of a sport. In contrast, intentional misconduct is viewed as so clearly outside the rules of sport that it would be unrealistic to treat a professional athlete as having consented to it. (Negligence and recklessness as causes of action for sports-related injuries are covered in the sections on negligence and assumption of risk.)

Illustration: Hackbart v. Cincinnati Bengals, Inc., 601 F.2d 516 (10th Cir. 1979). During a professional football game a player employed by the defendant team hit the plaintiff "out of frustration" in a way that was prohibited by the football league's rules. The trial court dismissed the plaintiff's battery claim, but on appeal it was held that the plaintiff's consent was only to conduct within the rules.

C. DEFENSE OF HUMAN BEINGS

Conduct that would otherwise subject a defendant to liability for many intentional torts is often permitted if the defendant does it for self-defense or for the defense of others. The privileges for self-defense and defense of others are essentially identical. This chapter is written in terms of self-defense, but its concepts also apply to defense of others.

1. Self-Defense

Tort law recognizes privileges meant to protect human life and personal physical integrity. The self-defense privilege allows one person to use force against another when the former reasonably believes that the latter is committing or is about to commit an intentional tort against him or her. The person who uses force bears the burden of proving that it was justified. This burden involves two related ideas: that the circumstances justified the use of force and that the amount of force used was reasonable.

2. Defense of Others

In addition to self-defense, the privilege to defend human beings includes a privilege to act to protect another person from harm. A person is justified in using force to prevent an attack on someone else if the person would be justified in using that force to respond to the same attack if it were directed against him or her.

3. Circumstances Justifying Use of Force

The privilege to use force is based on the belief that human beings confronted with serious threats to their physical integrity should have the right to meet those threats with force. It has certain doctrinal limits related to the underlying notion that everyone's physical safety is of paramount societal value.

a. **Reasonable belief that force is necessary.** A person is privileged to use force against another when he or she has a reasonable belief that the other person is about to harm or is in the act of harming him or her.

i. **Reasonable mistake and self-defense.** A self-defender's perception that the circumstances justify the use of force need not be accurate to legitimize the use of force. It need only be reasonable.

E&A Example and Analysis

Ralph Rational was hiking on a deserted trail in a lonely forest. He was startled to see Sam Scary rushing toward him, waving a butcher knife, and shouting obscenities. Rational shot Scary with a small pistol he happened to be carrying. Rational was entitled to use deadly force to respond to his reasonable belief that his life was threatened. If Scary was only trying to tease Rational or was participating in a fraternity initiation that did not include acts of violence, Rational would still be entitled to the self-defense privilege.

ii. **Reasonable mistake and defense of others.** Authority is split on how to treat mistakes in connection with an actor's defense of someone other than himself or herself. The majority view is: If one person seeking to protect a third person is mistaken about whether that third person is really being threatened, the first person does not have a privilege to use force. A minority of courts and the Restatement hold: A privilege is in effect if the person who seeks to aid a third person has a reasonable belief that the third person is being threatened.

iii. **Comparison with mistake in trespass or intentional infliction of emotional distress.** A reasonable but mistaken belief that a person presents a danger can be an adequate basis for the self-defense privilege, even though incorrect but reasonable beliefs are sometimes irrelevant in other aspects of intentional tort law, such as trespass or intentional infliction of emotional distress.

b. **Origin of threatening conduct.** The threatening conduct that provides a basis for a privileged act of self-defense may be intentional, reckless, or negligent conduct. It also may be felonious conduct.

4. Future Harm

The self-defense privilege does not allow force intended to stop future harm, unless the future harm is imminent.

E&A EXAMPLE AND ANALYSIS

Gertrude Gangster told Wanda Worried that she would have Worried killed in a month if Worried failed to pay a large sum of money to Gangster. That threat does not give Worried a privilege to use force against Gangster in self-defense.

5. Amount of Force Allowed

The amount of force allowed by the self-defense privilege is roughly equal to the force put into motion against the person who ultimately claims the privilege.

a. **Punishment.** The self-defense privilege has no application where an actor uses force to punish another person for some wrong after the threat presented by that wrong has been eliminated.

b. **No physical response to threatening words.** Use of physical force in response to another's threatening words is usually not justified. Words may, however, be part of a series of events including some physical actions that do in totality justify a physical response.

c. **Approximate equivalence of offensive and defensive actions.** Usually, the self-defense privilege protects a response to an offensive act that is roughly equivalent in force to that act. Thus, a person who attacks another with fists has no cause of action for a response that includes wrestling or punching but would probably have a cause of action if the claimed self-defense involved resort to firearms or other weapons.

   i. **Cross-claims.** It is possible for two participants in a fight to have causes of action against each other: the attacked person against the instigator for damages from the instigator's harmful or offensive contacts; and the instigator against the attacked person for damages from an excessively forceful self-defense effort.

   ii. **Helpless attacker.** There is no privilege to use physical force against a person who has stopped an attack or who has become disarmed or helpless.

d. **Deadly force.** Deadly force is the use of deadly weapons or any means of self-defense that, in the hands of the one who employs it, can potentially cause death. A general rule about deadly force is that it may only be used to defend against threats of death or serious bodily harm. A sexual assault is considered a threat of serious bodily harm.

   i. **Retreat.** There are three positions on the question of whether the use of deadly force can be considered a necessary response to a threat if a reasonable method of retreat is available to the threatened person.

(a) **Traditional view.** The traditional view is that no retreat is necessary prior to a threatened person's use of deadly force to meet deadly force.

(b) **Alternative view.** An alternative view is that outside one's home an individual must use an available safe retreat instead of deadly force to meet deadly force. This view does not require retreat if an attack is made in the individual's home.

(c) **Restatement view.** The Restatement analyzes the relationship of deadly force and retreat in three situations: outside one's home, the use of deadly force is not privileged if a safe method of retreat is available; inside one's home the use of deadly force against someone else who lives in the home is not privileged if a safe method of retreat is available; and inside one's home the use of deadly force against someone who does not live in the home is privileged whether or not a safe method of retreat is available.

E&A EXAMPLE AND ANALYSIS

Harry Homeowner and his wife Harriet Homeowner got into an argument at home. If Harry threatened Harriet with deadly force, under the Restatement analysis she would have no privilege to use deadly force against Harry if a safe retreat was available. If a stranger had attacked her with deadly force in the home, she would have been privileged to use deadly force whether or not a retreat was available. The Restatement provision requires greater restraint when force is used among people who live under the same roof than when it is used between strangers or people in any less intimate relationship.

ii. **Anti-felony privilege.** A privilege to use deadly force to stop a felony is separate from and overlaps the common law justifications for the use of deadly force in life-threatening situations. This privilege does not require retreat, and it applies whether or not the one using force is personally in danger of physical harm.

6. Harm to Third Parties

If a self-defender is free from negligence in the use of a privileged method of self-defense, a third person who suffers an injury from the self-defender's action has no cause of action to recover for that injury.

D. DEFENSE OF PROPERTY

When an individual uses force in defense of property, two different privileges may be involved: privileges for protection of property and for prevention of felony. The common law recognizes a privilege for individuals to use force to defend property, conditioned on a requirement that the amount of force be reasonable (in this context reasonable means nondeadly). A separate privilege covers the use of force to prevent a felony. This antifelony privilege traditionally allows the use of deadly force. In many situations where defense of property is concerned, the aggressor's conduct is both a threat to property and a felony such as burglary or grand larceny. If the aggressor is committing a felony, the rule allowing use of deadly force to counter a felony supersedes the common law's general structure of rules about force and defense of property.

1. Mistakes

Mistakes related to the defense of property privilege can involve two main topics: whether a person's threat to another's property is itself privileged, and what amount of force is appropriate in response to a threat to property. The common law excuses only a mistake about the amount of force.

a. **Type of threat to property.** Sometimes conduct that harms another's property is permitted by a privilege (see discussion of necessity). There is no privilege for the use of force to defend property against a person who has a privilege to use that property. If a person defends property because of a mistaken belief that the one against whom he or she is defending it has no privilege in connection with the property, then the mistaken defender is liable for whatever harm he or she inflicts on the one attempting to use the property. Thus, the common law does not excuse a mistake about whether any force at all is permitted. Even a reasonable error that leads someone to use force when no force is allowed blocks the operation of a privilege.

b. **Appropriate amount of force.** Someone who defends property with force ultimately deemed excessive is protected by the privilege if the force is appropriate in terms of the threat as reasonably perceived by the defender. A reasonable error about the amount of force appropriate in a situation where some force is permissible allows the operation of the privilege.

2. Type of Force

The general rule allows only the type of force that is reasonably needed to protect the threatened property.

a. **Words instead of force.** Where it is reasonable to believe that mere words might work to stop a threat, a person is obligated to try that method prior to using force.

i. **Warnings.** Many courts require that a property owner post warnings or otherwise alert potential entrants on land about the use of dangerous methods of protection, such as barbed wire, unless a warning would be superfluous due to local customs.

b. **Deadly force.** Deadly force is never allowed under the privilege to protect property, but other privileges do legitimize its use.

i. **Response to felonious conduct that does not threaten serious bodily harm or death.** The privilege to stop a felony allows the use of deadly force in situations such as burglary, where the aggressor's conduct is simultaneously a threat to property and a felony. It should be noted that trespassing is not a felony, so the antifelony privilege has no application in the case of a trespasser.

ii. **Response to conduct that threatens serious bodily harm or death.** The privilege to use deadly force to protect a person from death or serious bodily injury sometimes overlaps the privilege to protect property, since in many situations an aggressor simultaneously threatens to take or harm property and to kill or seriously injure the property's owner.

c. **Nonhuman force.** Many people protect property with guard dogs, mechanical devices, or barriers such as barbed wire. Where these have the capacity to harm an intruder, the general rule is that the harm they inflict is privileged only if the property owner would have been privileged to inflict the same type of harm in person, had he or she been present. It is important to distinguish between things that can cause death or serious bodily harm and things that do not threaten death or serious bodily harm.

Illustration: Katko v. Briney, 183 N.W.2d 657 (Iowa 1971). The plaintiff was injured when a spring gun set by the defendant in the defendant's vacant house went off and shot the plaintiff in the leg. It was acknowledged that the plaintiff had entered the building to steal things from it. Liability to the plaintiff was affirmed, with the court holding that the plaintiff's attempted felony was not a felony of violence, so the use of deadly force was not privileged.

E&A Example and Analysis

A property owner is liable for injuries inflicted if an automatic weapon or even an electrified fence that could cause a fatal injury actually does injure a person who is not attempting to commit a felony or who is privileged to enter the property. Since the property owner would not have been privileged to use deadly force had he or she been there in person, neither is the application of that force by mechanical means privileged.

---

i. **Deadly force privilege: Limited version.** Katko v. Briney illustrates the variety of detailed differences among jurisdictions with regard to privileges. For the Iowa court, unless a felony involved violence, there was no privilege to attempt to stop it with deadly force.

ii. **Deadly force privilege: All felonies version.** In some jurisdictions there is a privilege to use deadly force to respond to any felony regardless of whether the felony involves violence.

iii. **Warnings.** The privilege to use nondeadly devices is subject usually to a requirement that the user provide a warning. In contrast, a warning is not prerequisite to the privilege to use deadly force.

(a) **Reason for warning requirement with nondeadly devices.** The Restatement §84, comment *f*, justifies the requirement of a warning by stating that nondeadly devices such as barbed wire are effective primarily because of their deterrent effect. Thus, a warning is consistent with the rationale for their use.

(b) **Reason for omitting warning requirement for deadly devices.** The Restatement explains the lack of a warning requirement for deadly devices by stating that mechanical devices are unable to give a warning prior to inflicting harm. That rationale is obviously false for some deadly devices and does not explain why, for all deadly devices, there is no requirement of a general warning such as a sign. That people who use deadly devices are subject to a very high risk of liability may have led the Restatement drafters to conclude that adding a warning requirement was not necessary to protect people from the risk of injury from such devices.

E. RECAPTURE OF PROPERTY

A property owner has a fresh-pursuit right to use reasonable force to regain possession of his or her property wrongfully taken by another person, as long as the force is reasonable and as long as the property owner tries to get the property back quickly.

1. Fresh Pursuit

The fresh pursuit requirement means that if a property owner does not act quickly, the owner loses the right of self-help and must resort to methods involving the police or the legal system to recover the property. Special rules cover storekeepers and their rights to deal with people whom they suspect of shoplifting.

2. Amount of Force

Reasonable force is allowed for the recapture of property, but deadly force is never justified. A recapture-of-property situation, however, can sometimes become a self-defense situation. The possessor of the disputed property may attack the recapturer, making self-defense legitimate; deadly force may become appropriate, depending on the amount of force the possessor uses.

3. Entry on Another's Land

Just as there is a privilege to use force to regain possession of property, there is a privilege to enter another's land for that purpose. A person who claims the protection of this privilege must show that he or she acted reasonably with respect to the time of day and type of entry used.

a. **Landowner not responsible for the presence of item on land.** If the landowner is not responsible for the presence of someone else's item on the land, the item's owner is privileged to enter the land to recapture it but must pay damages to the landowner for any actual damage he or she causes to the land.

b. **Item owner responsible for presence of item on landowner's land.** If an item is on someone's land through fault of the item's owner, its owner has no privilege to enter that land to recapture the item. The legal system provides a cause of action known as replevin for situations like this. Self-help is not allowed, and the item's owner is required to use the legal system if he or she wants to regain possession of the item.

4. Wrongful or Fraudulent Possession

The recapture privilege applies only to property that a person has taken wrongfully from its owner. Wrongful takings include theft and fraud. If a person obtains property legitimately but then loses the right to keep it, there is no privilege of recapture. The rightful owner must use methods other than self-help to get the property back.

5. Mistake

Mistakes related to the recapture-of-property privilege can involve two main topics: whether the target of the recapture attempt really does possess goods that belong to the person attempting the recapture; and whether the person attempting the recapture has used an amount of force that is appropriate and not excessive. Under the common law either type of mistake destroys the privilege. Note that with regard to defending property, a privilege can continue to operate even if a person makes a mistake about the amount of force.

6. Storekeepers

Under the Restatement and in a number of jurisdictions, a storekeeper has a privilege to detain a person suspected of shoplifting. The detention must be relatively brief, and there must be reasonable grounds for suspecting the person of the crime.

a. **Limitations on merchant's privilege.** The privilege is intended to allow the merchant to investigate. If there are other purposes to the detention, the privilege may not protect the merchant against liability for false imprisonment or false arrest. These other purposes might include: coercing payment, arresting the suspected thief, or extracting a confession from him or her.

b. **Privilege in store or beyond store.** Courts are split on whether this privilege is available to a storekeeper only within the store premises or whether it should also apply in the area outside but near the store.

Illustration: Bonkowski v. Arlan's Department Store, 12 Mich. App. 88, 162 N.W.2d 347 (1968). A store security guard suspected the plaintiff of having stolen some merchandise. He confronted her in a parking lot about 30 feet from the store. On a step in front of the store, she allowed him to examine the contents of her purse. She had not stolen anything. She sought damages from the store for false arrest. Judgment was entered for the plaintiff, but on appeal the case was remanded. The trial court should have applied a merchant's privilege, allowing detention of the customer in a reasonable manner if there were reasonable grounds to suspect her of stealing.

7. Real Estate

A tenant who fails to move out of leased premises when the lease expires is similar to a person who takes possession of another's property without a right to possess it. At common law and in a minority of states at present, an owner is privileged to use reasonable force to eject a former tenant or other person who is wrongfully in possession of land. Most states now prohibit this type of conduct, since nonforceful, legal means are readily available to property owners to deal with persons wrongfully in possession of land or premises.

a. **Peaceful entry.** The modern denial of a privilege to use force to regain possession of real property has no bearing on a landowner's right to enter the land peacefully (without force). It also may have no effect in a case where a lease itself specifies that the landlord may use force after the lease expiration to regain possession of the premises.

F. NECESSITY

In certain rare situations the law gives the state or an individual a privilege to take property of another. The privilege is called "public necessity" when the taker is the government and "necessity" when the taker is an individual. The privilege exists when use of the property protects an individual or society from a harm greater than that inflicted on the property. Ordinarily an act justified by public necessity is performed by public officials or employees, but it is possible for an individual to perform an act that qualifies for the public necessity privilege.

1. Inflicts Harm on Blameless Individuals

Most privileges involve some wrongdoing by the person against whom another person asserts the privilege. For example, a person asserts the self-defense privilege against another person who has attacked him or her. The necessity privilege is different. Those who are harmed by individuals acting under the privilege are generally free from blameworthy conduct.

2. Compensation for the Privileged Use

An individual who takes advantage of the private necessity privilege to use another's property must pay damages for any harm he or she causes. When the government takes property under the public necessity privilege, the common law does not require any payment of damages.

Illustration: Surocco v. Geary, 3 Cal. 69, 58 Am. Dec. 385 (1852). On orders from the mayor, the plaintiff's building was blown up to prevent the further spread of a fire. This action denied the plaintiff the opportunity to remove belongings from the building. No damages could be recovered for that loss, because the common law privilege of necessity entitled the public authority to take the property without compensation.

a. **Statutes.** In some states there are statutes that provide for payment in cases of takings accomplished under the public necessity privilege.

E&A EXAMPLES AND ANALYSIS

The classic example of public necessity is a fire department's destruction of a building or an area of woods to prevent the spread of a fire that otherwise would destroy things of greater value than the building or woods that the fire department intentionally destroys.

Someone sailing on a lake and encountering a sudden emergency is entitled, under the private necessity privilege, to use a stranger's dock in order to save the boat and protect human life as well.

3. Rules for Private Necessity

Private necessity is governed by specific doctrines for certain recurring situations. A property owner has no right to use force to repel a person who seeks to use property in a situation where the private necessity privilege applies.

Illustration: Vincent v. Lake Erie Transp. Co., 109 Minn. 456, 124 N.W. 221 (1910). The defendant's steamship was at the plaintiff's dock to unload cargo. After the unloading was finished, the steamship crew tried to have the ship moved from the dock. No tugboats were available because a severe storm was in progress. The crew kept the steamship tied to the dock to prevent it from drifting away. When the lines chafed or broke, the crew replaced them. The ship was saved from harm, but the dock was damaged. The dock owner sued to recover for this injury and won a judgment. On appeal the judgment was affirmed. Even though the defendant acted reasonably, it was required to pay for the harm suffered by the dock owner.

a. **Inflict harm to avoid greater harm.** The danger that an actor seeks to avoid by invoking the private necessity privilege to make use of a stranger's property must be greater than the risk the actor imposes on the stranger's property.

b. **Privilege claimant is responsible for actual harm inflicted.** The privilege is not a defense to a suit seeking compensation for any damage the actor actually inflicts on that property.

c. **No responsibility for technical torts.** The privilege is a complete defense to an action brought against a person who acted under the privilege if the action does not seek actual damages, such as a suit for trespass where no actual harm was inflicted on the plaintiff's property.

G. ARREST

Acting under authority of law provides a privilege for actions that would otherwise constitute intentional torts. The arrest privilege is the most important instance of privilege for acting under authority of law. Its common law details are complex, and the common law doctrines have been replaced or supplemented in most places by statutes.

1. Warrant

Under common law an arrest warrant justifies an arrest, so long as the warrant has no obvious flaws.

a. **Arrest of wrong person.** A warrant does not give an officer the authority to arrest anyone other than the person named in the warrant. Mistaken identity, even if reasonable, eliminates the privilege.

b. **Trespass *ab initio.*** A strongly criticized doctrine known as trespass *ab initio* provides that if an officer makes an error in any part of the arrest process (such as failing to bring the arrested person before a magistrate promptly), then all parts of the arrest process lose the protection of the arrest privilege. In the jurisdictions that continue to follow this doctrine, even proper conduct by an officer early in the arrest process can be a basis for a false arrest cause of action, if it is followed by an error in a later stage of the process.

2. Absence of a Warrant

In certain circumstances the common law provides a privilege for arrests made without warrants.

a. **Present or imminent felony.** Officers and anyone else may arrest a person who has committed a felony or is about to commit a felony in the presence of the person making the arrest.

b. **Past felony.** An officer has a privilege to arrest someone in connection with a past felony, if the officer reasonably believes the felony did occur and the person arrested is the one who committed it.

   i. **Mistake about occurrence.** Anyone other than an officer who makes an arrest in connection with a past felony is privileged only if the past felony actually did take place. Mistake about the occurrence of the past felony precludes application of the privilege. The privilege will continue to operate, however, if the individual has made a reasonable mistake about the identity of the person arrested (or identity of the person who committed the felony).

   ii. **Past crimes less than felonious.** A warrantless arrest is justified only where the officer or other person who makes an arrest makes it in fresh pursuit of the person arrested. This rule applied originally only to breaches of the peace but is now sometimes applied to misdemeanors as well.

3. Force

The only force justified by the arrest privilege is reasonable force. Different rules govern arrests to stop or prevent a felony and arrests to capture someone who has already committed a felony.

a. **Stopping a felony.** Deadly force is permitted only where the felony itself threatens death or serious injury.

b. **Arrest for past felony.** Under federal constitutional law if a crime has already been committed, deadly force is allowed only if the target of the arrest attempt presents a significant threat of death or serious physical injury to others. This doctrine precludes any state common law doctrines allowing greater freedom to use deadly force.

H. DISCIPLINE

A person who acts in a role that gives him or her authority over another person has a privilege to use force for the purpose of discipline. This privilege requires that the force be limited to whatever is appropriate for discipline. Individuals who typically benefit from this privilege are parents, teachers, and military officers.

I. JUSTIFICATION

In cases where imposing liability on a defendant for an intentional tort seems highly inappropriate for public policy reasons, a court may refer to justification as a general and overriding privilege.

Illustration: Sindle v. New York City Transit Auth., 307 N.E.2d 245 (N.Y. 1973). Justification protected the defendant in this case from liability for false imprisonment. The defendant, a school bus driver, drove his bus with its passengers to a police station, effectively imprisoning his passengers during that trip, because they were engaging in dangerous and rowdy behavior on the bus.

J. PROCEDURAL TREATMENT OF CONSENT AND PRIVILEGES

In all intentional torts a defendant who seeks to justify his or her conduct with a privilege is responsible for pleading that privilege and supporting it with proof. Consent is treated differently. For most intentional torts other than trespass to land, the plaintiff is required to plead and prove the absence of consent.

1. Battery Example

In a battery case a defendant might admit having touched the plaintiff but the plaintiff might lose the case because he or she consented to the touching or because the defendant had a privilege such as self-defense that permitted the touching. The issue of consent is treated as part of the plaintiff's burden, meaning that the plaintiff is required to prove that there was no consent. The self-defense privilege is treated as the defendant's burden, meaning that the defendant must prove that self-defense was proper.

2. Trespass to Property Example

In a trespass to property case the existence of privileges and the existence of consent are both the burden of the defendant. A defendant who believes he or she has no liability for trespass because the owner granted permission for the entry has to persuade the jury that the plaintiff gave consent. (In other cases a plaintiff must persuade the jury that the plaintiff did not give consent.)

REVIEW QUESTIONS AND ANSWERS

Question: Betty Buyer, shopping for a new car, was in the office of Sam Seller, a salesman. Seller asked, "Is it all right if I lock the office door while I'm out talking to the owner about the deal we're making?" Buyer agreed to that, thinking that the office had another door she could use to leave. Actually the other door was only a closet door, and Buyer was unable to leave the office. Did Buyer consent to conduct that might otherwise have been false imprisonment?

Answer: Yes. Buyer was motivated to consent because she had a mistaken idea about an alternate way to leave the office, but Buyer did agree to be locked in. A plaintiff's own mistake does not destroy the validity of the plaintiff's consent.

Question: Largestore, a large department store, employed Dinah Demo to demonstrate a back massage appliance. After Demo finished demonstrating it to a shopper, she said "Next," looking out into the group of shoppers who had been watching. Tom Tryer walked up to Demo and leaned over. Demo demonstrated the machine on Tryer, and Tryer's back started to hurt immediately. Would a consent defense be helpful to the store, if Tryer sought damages for battery?

Answer: Yes. A reasonable person would interpret Tryer's conduct as indicating his consent to being touched. That consent prevents recovery in battery.

Question: Gary Greedy asked Carrie Casual if it would be all right to park a "camper" in Casual's driveway for a few days. Casual granted permission. Greedy then drove a two-story structure on a large flatbed truck onto Casual's driveway. Casual asked Greedy to remove the camper after one day and Greedy refused to move it. Would Casual's permission prevent Casual from seeking damages for trespass?

Answer: No. The permission would not prevent Casual from seeking trespass damages, since Greedy's action far exceeded the scope of any reasonable interpretation of the permission Casual granted.

Question: Louise Lexus was walking toward her car in a large parking lot. About 30 feet away, Yancy Yeller started to yell at Lexus and wave a baseball bat toward her. Lexus got into her car while Yeller was still about 20 feet away. Lexus started the car and drove it directly over Yeller. Yeller was injured and sued Lexus for damages. Would a self-defense privilege likely be available to Lexus?

Answer: No. Yeller was no longer a threat to Lexus when Lexus ran over him. No amount of force would be covered by a privilege, since Lexus was not in danger when she injured Yeller. If some force were determined to be legitimate, the fact that the force Lexus used was disproportionate to the force Yeller had employed would probably prevent application of a privilege. It seems as though Lexus was using her vehicle to punish Yeller. That type of conduct is never protected by a privilege.

Question: Harry Helper saw a man and a woman quarreling in a hotel lobby. The man started to shove the woman. Helper picked up a table lamp and hit the man with it to stop the attack. Unbeknownst to Helper, the man and woman were sociology graduate students, pretending to have a fight to see if people in the hotel would call for assistance. If the man sued Helper for battery, could Helper invoke the privilege for defense of a third person?

Answer: No, in most jurisdictions; yes, in some jurisdictions and under the Restatement view. The majority position on defense of third parties requires that the third party actually be in danger, not that the defender have a reasonable perception that the third party is in danger.

Question: Three months after someone had stolen Bonnie Biker's distinctive and expensive motorcycle, Biker saw Rhonda Rider riding it slowly down a city street. Biker pushed Rider off the motorcycle and rode it away. Would Rider be entitled to damages for battery?

Answer: Yes. Biker's conduct satisfies the elements of battery, so there would be liability unless the activity was consented to or was privileged. There was no consent. The only relevant privilege is the one for defense of property. That privilege allows force to be used only when there is fresh pursuit. Biker was not in fresh pursuit of anyone when she used force to get back something that had been taken three months earlier.

Question: Harry Hiker was caught on a mountain in a sudden snowstorm. To save his life he broke into a deserted cabin. He used the cabin for shelter and ate some canned goods he found there. Would Hiker be liable for trespass or any other damages?

Answer: The defense of necessity would be available to Hiker. He would have no liability for trespass unless he inflicted actual harm on the property. He would have the responsibility of paying for the food he used.

Exam Tips

- Exam questions frequently combine issues about the existence of the basic elements of an intentional tort with issues about the existence of consent or privilege. Be sure to explore the prima facie case as well as defenses.
- When you think the prima facie case is not present, it might be logical to ignore defenses, but if you are wrong about the presence of the prima facie case, you will have lost your chance to show what you know about defenses. Therefore, it is a good idea to discuss the defenses anyway.

- Questions about the degree of force that a self-defender can use are common. Be alert to problems where the threat has ended; in these situations no force is allowed.
- Where a mechanical device (like an electrified fence) has inflicted harm, the person who set it up is liable for the resultant injury unless he or she would have been protected by a privilege had he or she been present. If a device causes harm to a burglar, the owner is likely to be free from liability. If a device harms an innocent trespasser, however, the owner is denied access to the privilege defense.

6 NEGLIGENCE

CHAPTER OVERVIEW

- A plaintiff who is injured by a defendant's negligent conduct is entitled to damages. This chapter explains how tort law characterizes conduct as negligent or not negligent.
- The finder of fact must compare the defendant's conduct to conduct that would be required by an applicable standard of care.
- If a defendant's conduct is less careful than the conduct required by the standard of care, the defendant is negligent.
- The reasonable prudent person test is the standard of care used in many cases.
- The reasonable prudent person test is objective, but it takes into account certain special circumstances, such as physical disabilities and emergencies.
- The reasonable prudent person test ignores a person's mental weaknesses.
- The reasonable prudent person in a commercial setting usually follows the industry's customs. Proof of compliance with custom is never an absolute defense; similarly, proof of violation of custom is always relevant but never conclusive to establish negligence.
- A child is judged by a special standard of care, defined as the care a child of similar age, intelligence, and experience would exercise.
- A professional is judged by a special standard of care, defined by the custom of professionals in either the defendant's locality or the entire country.

- Statutes intended to promote safety also provide standards of care for tort law. A person who violates a statute intended to promote safety is usually defined as negligent.
- The *res ipsa loquitur* doctrine allows juries to infer negligence in cases with circumstances strongly consistent with the likelihood that the defendant was negligent.

A. INTRODUCTION

Negligence is the name of a tort cause of action that allows a plaintiff to recover damages for injuries caused by conduct that is called negligence or negligent conduct. The word *negligence* describes both a cause of action and the conduct that the cause of action scrutinizes.

1. General Definition

Negligent conduct is conduct less careful than an applicable standard of care requires to protect people from unreasonable risks of harm. In most cases the applicable standard of care requires a person to act as carefully as a reasonable prudent person would act.

2. Distinction from Intentional Torts

Negligence is not an intentional tort. The plaintiff does not have to show that a defendant did something on purpose with an intent to inflict an unpermitted consequence on the plaintiff. The plaintiff is only required to show that the defendant's conduct fell below a required degree of care. Negligently inflicted injuries are accidental injuries, in the sense that the plaintiff does not prove that the defendant intended to cause any injury.

B. BASIC ELEMENTS OF NEGLIGENCE

The negligence cause of action has four elements: duty, breach, causation, and damages.

1. Duty

To be entitled to damages from another person or enterprise, a plaintiff must show that the potential defendant owed the plaintiff a duty to act or refrain from acting in a certain way. If a defendant owed no duty to a plaintiff, the defendant is entitled to judgment as a matter of law regardless of how dangerously the defendant acted. In most cases the issue of duty is so clear that litigants and judges pay almost no attention to it. For example, drivers have a duty of care toward pedestrians and other drivers. An opposite example is a person's lack of duty to aid a stranger in need of help.

a. **Specific requirements of duty.** The quality of conduct that tort law requires varies according to the type of actor and type of conduct. Section C., Standards of Care, explains this.

b. **Limited-duty rules.** In certain types of recurring cases, limited duty rules (described in Chapter 10) apply to control the obligations of certain classes of potential defendants to certain classes of potential plaintiffs. For example, in many states a landowner owes a general duty to refrain from negligence to people who enter the land for the owner's business purpose. Most states modify this general doctrine with a limited duty rule, holding that a landowner has no duty to refrain from negligence in connection with dangers that are open and obvious.

c. **No-duty rules.** In some aspects of modern life, one person's conduct might be thought to be injurious to another, but because of principles related to individual freedom and personal responsibility, the legal system does not make the injurer pay the person who is harmed. (These rules are described in Chapter 10.) For example, a medical researcher's carelessness might delay the discovery of a cure for a disease, but someone who suffers from the disease has no cause of action against the researcher. The researcher owes no duty of reasonable care to the patient.

2. Breach

The plaintiff must show that the defendant breached a duty. This means that the defendant's conduct failed to conform to a specific level of quality or of care that tort law imposed on the defendant.

3. Causation

The plaintiff must show that the defendant's conduct, which violated a duty owed by the defendant to the plaintiff, caused an injury to the plaintiff.

a. **Cause in fact.** The plaintiff must show that the defendant's conduct was a cause in fact of the plaintiff's injury. This usually requires evidence to support a jury's finding that the plaintiff's injury would not have occurred in the absence of the defendant's conduct. (Chapter 7 covers cause in fact.)

b. **Proximate cause.** Proximate cause, sometimes called "legal cause," is another aspect of the causation element. In addition to showing that the defendant's conduct was a factual cause of the plaintiff's injury, the plaintiff must show that the link between the defendant's conduct and the plaintiff's injury was adequately close to permit recovery. A defendant's conduct is likely to be a cause in fact of nearly infinite consequences; the proximate cause element defines some consequences as closely enough related to the defendant's conduct to make it fair to require the defendant to pay for them. (Chapter 8 covers proximate cause.)

4. Damages

The plaintiff must show actual damages to recover in a negligence suit. Punitive damages may also be available in special circumstances. (Damages are explained in Chapter 12.)

C. STANDARDS OF CARE

Every negligence case involves a comparison of the defendant's actual conduct to some standard of care that defines how the defendant should have acted. This standard is a control on the jury's decision-making process. A jury does not evaluate the defendant's conduct according to whatever standard of behavior that the jury thinks is sensible; instead, the jury is asked to compare the defendant's conduct to a specific standard. Usually this standard is the conduct the jury thinks a reasonable prudent person would have done. The jurors' conclusion about what a reasonable prudent person would have done can be different, theoretically, from a conclusion about what they personally would have done or about what would have been desirable for the defendant to have done on the occasion that led to the plaintiff's injury.

1. Reasonable Prudent Person

The usual standard for negligence cases is the reasonable prudent person standard. With this standard a jury is told to decide how a reasonable prudent person would have acted in the situation that caused the plaintiff's injury. It must then compare the defendant's conduct with its conclusion about how a reasonable prudent person would have acted. The jury must find the defendant negligent if it believes the defendant's conduct was less careful than a reasonable prudent person's conduct would have been.

a. **Objective test.** This is an objective test, in which the standard of comparison is the hypothetical typically reasonable person. A subjective test, rarely used, evaluates the actor against his or her own individual capabilities, asking whether the actor did the best he or she could have done.

i. **Easy to apply.** The jury can apply an objective test with more accuracy and confidence than a test requiring estimation of each actor's own particular level of skill.

ii. **Reciprocal fairness.** The objective test also represents a kind of reciprocal social contract: Each of us knows that others will act as well as a typically prudent person would act, and that if others fail to act that well, they will pay us for harms they cause. This enables us to use only normal caution in going about the aspects of our lives that expose us to the risk of injury from other people's actions.

EXAMPLE AND ANALYSIS

If a jury were to evaluate the conduct of a storekeeper to decide whether the storekeeper was negligent in setting up a tall display of boxes that toppled over and hurt someone, the jury would decide how a reasonable and prudent person would have set up such a display; then the jury would compare that to the way the storekeeper actually did it. The jury would not decide whether the storekeeper did the best job that particular storekeeper was capable of doing; and the jury would not decide whether the storekeeper's conduct was the safest possible conduct. The jury would just decide what a hypothetical reasonable and prudent person would have done.

b. **Knowledge.** The reasonable prudent person is assumed to have knowledge typical of people in his or her community.

Illustrations: Delair v. McAdoo, 324 Pa. 392, 188 A. 181 (1936). The defendant drove a car with defective tires, and the plaintiff was injured when one of the tires blew out and caused the defendant's car to swerve into the plaintiff's car. The plaintiff sought damages on a negligence theory, claiming that the defendant had been negligent to drive with obviously bad tires. The plaintiff won a jury verdict, and the trial court denied the defendant's motion for judgment notwithstanding the verdict (judgment as a matter of law). On appeal it was held that anyone who drives is assumed to know that obviously bad tires can be very dangerous. This idea supported the trial court's denial of the defendant's motion, since a reasonable person who knows that driving with obviously bad tires is dangerous would repair the tire or choose not to drive.

Blyth v. Birmingham Waterworks Co., 11 Ex. 781, 156 Eng. Rep. 1047 (1856). The defendant installed water mains and fire plugs in a city, and the plaintiff's house was harmed when one of the fire plugs sprung a leak due to unusually severe, freezing weather. The defendant was entitled to judgment because the weather that made the fire plug leak was far worse than anyone would have expected in that city. A person is expected to act reasonably in connection with circumstances that one would reasonably expect, not in connection with circumstances that are extraordinarily unusual.

i. **Superior knowledge.** There is debate about cases where the person whose conduct a jury must evaluate has special skills or unusually extensive knowledge. The Restatement §298, comment *d*, requires an actor to use the qualities and facilities of a reasonable person and any "superior qualities that the actor happens to possess." In

Fredericks v. Castora, 241 Pa. Super. 211, 360 A.2d 696 (1976), however, the court refused to charge a jury that a professional truck driver's conduct should be judged by a standard different than the standard used for an ordinary driver.

c. **Physical disabilities.** The reasonable prudent person test acknowledges physical disabilities. The jury is instructed to consider whether the actor's conduct met the standard of care that a reasonable prudent person with the actor's disability would have exercised in the situation under examination.

Illustration: Roberts v. State of Louisiana, 396 So. 2d 566 (La. 1981). A blind man who was walking across a post office lobby bumped into the plaintiff. The plaintiff fell and was injured. The plaintiff alleged that the blind man should have been using a cane and that had he used his cane, he would not have bumped into the plaintiff. The trial court dismissed the plaintiff's claim and was affirmed on appeal. The reasonable prudent person test applies to a person with a physical disability in a special way: The actor's conduct is compared with how a reasonable prudent person with that disability would have acted.

d. **Mental illness.** A person with a mental illness generally is required to act as reasonably as a person with ordinary mental health would act. This doctrine is hard to reconcile with the common law's willingness to take physical disabilities into account.

Illustration: Breunig v. American Family Ins. Co., 45 Wis. 2d 536, 173 N.W.2d 619 (1970). The defendant's insured drove her car onto the wrong side of a road and injured the plaintiff. Proof showed that the insured was under an insane delusion at the time and believed that God was directing her car. A jury verdict for the plaintiff was upheld on appeal. The supreme court approved the common law rule that mentally ill people must act as reasonably as people of ordinary mental health. It recognized an exception for a sudden mental incapacity that might be similar to a heart attack or stroke but did not apply that exception to the insured's mental illness.

e. **Low intelligence.** Traditional common law applications of the reasonable person test deny any special consideration to people who claimed to have mental disabilities or mental weakness. In contrast to the person with a physical disability, the person of low intelligence must act like a reasonable prudent person or must pay for the consequences of not acting that way.

Illustration: Vaughn v. Menlove, 3 Bing. (N.C.) 467, 132 Eng. Rep. 490 (C.P. 1837). The defendant constructed a hay rick in a way that led to its catching fire through spontaneous combustion. The fire spread to the plaintiff's cottages. The defendant claimed that he should be free from liability if he acted according to the best of his judgment, arguing that he should not be responsible for the misfortune of not possessing the highest order of intelligence. The Court of Common Pleas ruled that a jury must not be permitted to take an actor's mental weakness into consideration. It stated that to do so would make tort standards as "variable as the length of the foot of each individual."

i. **Rationale for ignoring mental weakness.** The common law rationale for ignoring a person's mental weakness is based on a belief that uniform standards are better for society. Other factors may support the result. Degrees of mental power are difficult to identify. Thus, it would be hard for a judge to decide when to reject the usual reasonable prudent person test in favor of a different charge dealing with mental weakness. Also, it is unlikely that jurors would be familiar with different degrees of mental weakness, so an instruction requiring their evaluation would be difficult to apply. Finally, although imposing liability for conduct that falls below a reasonable prudent person standard cannot serve to encourage a mentally weak person to act better in the future—since by hypothesis he or she does not have the power to act that well no matter how strongly motivated—using that standard may encourage those with influence over the mentally weak person to help him or her to restrict or avoid activities that present a high risk of causing injuries to others.

f. **Intoxication.** A person who is intoxicated is expected to act as well as a person who is sober. While this is obviously unrealistic, it is a doctrinal choice that may discourage intoxicated people or those who can control them from mixing intoxication with potentially dangerous conduct.

E&A Example and Analysis

Dan Drinker, while he was intoxicated, walked across a street without looking for moving vehicles. He was hit by a car. If he sought damages, claiming that the car's driver had been negligent, Drinker's own conduct would also be scrutinized in the lawsuit. The jury would decide how a reasonable and prudent person would have walked across the street; it would then compare that with the way it believed Drinker had walked across the street. Drinker's intoxication would have no relevance to the jury's analytical process.

g. **Custom.** For some kinds of activities, it is possible to show how most people act when they do them. This kind of proof is known as proof of custom. A defendant's conduct may be as good as the custom for that activity, or it may be riskier than the custom. Proof about the relationship between a defendant's conduct and customary practices for the activity is almost always relevant in negligence cases. It is important to remember, though, that proof that a defendant's conduct complied with custom is a complete defense only in professional standard cases (see Section C.3. of this chapter). Particularly in cases involving businesses, a defendant may seek to prove that its conduct was typical for companies in its line of business. That evidence is admissible, but the jury is instructed that compliance with an industry custom is not necessarily a defense.

Illustrations: Trimarco v. Klein, 56 N.Y.2d 98, 451 N.Y.S.2d 52 (1982), 436 N.E. 2d 502. The plaintiff was injured when a glass tub-enclosure door in his apartment shattered. He sought damages from the landlord, claiming that safety glass rather than ordinary glass should have been installed. The plaintiff introduced evidence that after the glass in his apartment had been installed, there developed an industry custom which rejected the use of that type of glass. The trial court charged the jury that it could consider the custom in connection with the reasonableness of the defendant's actions under all the circumstances, and that deviation from the custom is not conclusive proof of negligence. The court of appeals approved this instruction. It pointed out that custom is relevant because it shows the feasibility of the customary practice and because it represents the judgment and experience of many individuals.

The T.J. Hooper, 60 F.2d 737 (2nd Cir. 1932). A tugboat was not equipped with a radio that would have received weather information. Partly due to this omission, it was involved in an accident. The defendant showed that lack of a radio was customary. Affirming a judgment for the plaintiff, Judge Learned Hand wrote, "Courts must in the end say what is required; there are precautions so imperative that even their universal disregard will not excuse their omission."

h. **Emergencies.** A reasonable prudent person may act differently in an emergency than he or she would act in normal circumstances. In applying the reasonable prudent person test, a jury is entitled to consider all the circumstances in which a person's challenged conduct took place. In some jurisdictions a sudden-emergency instruction is given, emphasizing to jurors that people in emergency situations may not be able to act as carefully as they would in normal situations. A defendant who created an emergency situation is never allowed to use the emergency he or she created as a basis for a sudden-emergency instruction.

Illustration: Cordas v. Peerless Transp. Co., 27 N.Y.S.2d 198 (City C. N.Y. County 1941). A thief forced a taxi driver at gun point to drive him away from the scene of a crime. The driver jumped out of the taxi, and the taxi ran onto a sidewalk and hit the plaintiffs. The trial court dismissed the plaintiffs' suit, reasoning that a person in an emergency need only live up to a reasonable-person-in-an-emergency standard of care.

i. **Learned Hand test:** United States v. Carroll Towing Co., 159 F.2d 169 (2nd Cir. 1947). In a very famous opinion Judge Learned Hand suggested that an algebraic equation can help determine how a reasonable prudent person would act in any situation. He believed that a reasonable prudent person will use precautions or be careful in every instance where the cost of the precautions or of being careful is less than the cost of injuries the person can anticipate occurring in the absence of the precautions or the careful way of acting. Judge Hand referred to precautions or carefulness as a "burden." He treated anticipated losses with two concepts: the expected cost of an injury ("loss") and the expected likelihood of the loss happening ("probability"). His formula multiplies the loss times the probability to calculate the likely social cost of injuries that might be caused by certain conduct. In Judge Hand's opinion it is negligent to act without a precaution if the burden is less than the expected loss. In algebraic terms he expressed this as $B < PL$. Under this formula a person's conduct is negligent if the injuries it is likely to cause are more costly than some precautions or avoidance behavior that could have prevented them.

   i. **Not used by juries.** This test is never used explicitly by juries, but some appellate courts use it in deciding whether a jury's finding of negligence or no negligence is supported adequately by the evidence at trial.

   ii. **Not precise.** The test cannot be applied with precision because it involves guesses about the odds of an injury happening and the likely harms of different ways of acting. Furthermore, in cases where loss of life might be involved, it is difficult to apply the formula. Courts are usually reluctant to assign a dollar value to the importance of avoiding deaths, even though once deaths occur our legal system does require juries to estimate the economic losses they cause.

2. Child's Standard

The method used in most jurisdictions for evaluating the conduct of a child in tort litigation is a comparison of that child's conduct with the conduct the jury believes would have been done by a child of similar age, experience, and intelligence.

a. **Rationale.** The common law developed this standard in the era when the nearly universal contributory negligence doctrine held that any negligence by a plaintiff was a complete bar to recovery. In many cases this doctrine prevented recoveries by children whose negligence seemed slight in comparison to the negligence of the adults or enterprises that had harmed them. The child's standard of care may have developed to decrease the number of cases in which child plaintiffs would be found to be negligent.

   Other ideas also support use of the standard. Society wants to encourage children to be active, since activity helps their normal development. The injuries children inflict are likely to be small, since they do not have great strength or access to dangerous things. Judges are able to decide readily whether a particular person's conduct should be governed by the standard, since it is easy to determine people's ages. Jurors are likely to apply the standard well, since all people have experience with children.

b. **Age limits.** The child's standard of care is never used for conduct by people who have reached the age of majority. Some states also follow a rule that a child younger than seven may not be found negligent and that a child between the ages of seven and fourteen is presumed to be free from negligence.

c. **No application to adult activities.** The child's standard is available only when the child is engaging in conduct typical of children. If the child engages in primarily adult activities that require special skill or training, such as driving a motor vehicle, the child is judged by the reasonable prudent person standard.

   Illustration: Robinson v. Lindsay, 92 Wash. 2d 410, 598 P.2d 392 (1979). A 13-year-old boy drove a snowmobile in a way that caused an injury to the plaintiff. The trial judge instructed the jury on the child's standard of care, then granted a new trial when the jury found for the plaintiff. On appeal the supreme court agreed that despite the widespread use of a child's standard for evaluating how a child does activities that are typical for children, the adult standard should be used when a child does something that is inherently dangerous or involves a motorized vehicle. On that basis it concluded that the adult standard applies to a child who drives a snowmobile.

E&A EXAMPLE AND ANALYSIS

Assume that a plaintiff, injured by a 12-year-old engaged in each of the following activities, sued the youngster seeking damages for the injury. Would a child's standard of care be used to evaluate the defendant's conduct in each case?

- Bicycling. Yes.
- Skateboarding. Yes, unless a court were to find that activity to be inherently dangerous because of the speeds skateboards achieve and the difficulty riders have in controlling them.
- Big game hunting. No, this is definitely an activity primarily for adults and inherently dangerous.
- Playing with matches. No, this is something children do more than adults, but because of the dangers it presents, it is an activity to which a court would probably apply an adult standard of care.

3. Professional Standard

When it is necessary for the tort system to evaluate the conduct of a professional person, such as a doctor or a lawyer, a professional standard of care is used instead of the reasonable prudent person standard. The jury does not decide what conduct it thinks a reasonable person would have used in the situation under review. Instead, the jury must determine the level of conduct employed by typical professionals in that situation. If the person whose conduct is being evaluated acted in conformity with typical professional performance, the person acted without negligence. If the person did not conform with what typical professionals would have done, then he or she must be found to have been negligent. Note that the jury does not use its own judgment about what type of conduct is reasonable. It only compares what it thinks someone did to what it learns is the typical practice of professionals in the relevant field.

Illustration: Hodges v. Carter, 239 N.C. 517, 80 S.E.2d 144 (1954), illustrates the power of the professional standard in the context of a malpractice case against a lawyer. It was alleged that the lawyer had been negligent in representing the plaintiff in a suit against some insurance companies by failing to serve process in a way that would withstand legal challenge. The defendant was entitled to judgment as a matter of law (nonsuit at the close of the plaintiff's case), because evidence showed that the defendant had acted in the same way that attorneys throughout the state generally acted to serve process. The jury would not be allowed to characterize those actions as negligent.

E&A Example and Analysis

In a medical malpractice case in which a plaintiff claims a surgeon did not use enough knots to attach a part of a transplanted vein, who will win on that issue if the jury concludes that the defendant doctor used as many knots as most doctors would have used for that procedure? The doctor will win, even if the jurors also conclude that more knots would have been better.

---

a. **Jury instructions.** A typical jury instruction incorporating the professional standard states that "a doctor must use that degree of skill and learning which is normally possessed and used by doctors in good standing in a similar practice in similar communities and under like circumstances." Kalsbeck v. Westview Clinic, P.A., 375 N.W.2d 861, 868 (Minn. App. 1985). Another typical instruction states that a "physician who undertakes a mode or form of treatment which a reasonable and prudent member of the medical profession would undertake under the same or similar circumstances shall not be subject to liability for harm thereby caused to the patient." Hood v. Phillips, 554 S.W.2d 160, 165 (Tex. 1977).

b. **Professions covered.** All jurisdictions apply the professional standard of care to conduct by doctors and lawyers. For other types of workers, jurisdictions decide whether to apply a professional standard by considering factors such as the degree of independence the individual has in his or her work, the need for specialized knowledge, and whether organizations within the field seek to maintain high standards.

c. **Expert testimony.** Courts usually require any party expected to show deviation from or compliance with a professional standard of care to introduce expert testimony from which the jury can determine exactly what that standard is.

Illustration: Boyce v. Brown, 51 Ariz. 416, 77 P.2d 455 (1938). The defendant doctor used a metal screw to repair the plaintiff's broken ankle. When she complained to him about pain in the ankle a number of years later, he did not have an X-ray taken. Another doctor did order an X-ray, discovered dead tissue around the screw, and treated the problem. The plaintiff did not provide expert testimony to describe whether doctors generally would have had an X-ray taken in a case like hers. For that reason the trial court was correct in ordering judgment as a matter of law (directed verdict) for the defendant.

i. **Lay knowledge exception.** If the claimed negligence of a professional involves something well within common knowledge, no expert testimony is required to establish a standard of care.

Example: If a surgeon failed to wash his or her hands prior to operating on a patient, a jury would be allowed to evaluate that conduct without expert testimony on the standard of care for surgeons.

d. **National or locality standard.** Most professional standard of care cases involve doctors. Under the locality rule the majority of states once required that expert testimony demonstrate the professional practice in the precise locality of the professional whose conduct was being evaluated in a lawsuit. This rule has been liberalized in a variety of ways.

i. **Traditional locality rule.** Some states continue to enforce the locality rule, despite the obvious difficulty it presents to plaintiffs, who must find expert witnesses to testify against professionals who work in the same locality as the experts. Some locality rule states have broadened the definition of "locality" from the actual community in which the professional works to "the same or similar community."

ii. **National standard.** Some jurisdictions have abandoned the locality rule, on the theory that the practice of medicine is national in terms of training and accreditation of medical schools. They require all medical personnel to conform to a national professional standard, so that expert witnesses may be drawn from any location to testify about the details of a standard.

iii. **Standard related to type of practice.** Some jurisdictions apply a national standard of care to work by specialists but continue to apply a locality standard to work by general practitioners.

Illustration: Morrison v. MacNamara, 407 A.2d 555 (D.C. Ct. App. 1979). A medical laboratory that was nationally certified was charged with having administered a test to the plaintiff in a negligent manner. Testimony about the customary practice in the District of Columbia supported the defendant, but testimony about customary practice nationally supported the plaintiff. Judgment for the defendant was reversed, with the court holding that a national standard should apply to any health care provider with a national certification.

iv. **Local circumstances.** In applying a national standard, jurisdictions take local circumstances into account.

Example: If a national professional standard of care called for prompt CAT scans of vehicular accident victims, a doctor who began treatment without having such scans would be free from negligence if no CAT scan machine had been available in the area or at the time of the incident.

v. **Statutes.** Many jurisdictions have statutes that specify whether the locality rule or a national standard applies in medical malpractice cases. Some of these statutes additionally state that a person may not be an expert witness if more than a specified percentage of his or her ordinary work is the giving of testimony rather than the practice of medicine.

e. **Informed consent.** Physicians are required to obtain informed consent from patients prior to examining them or treating them. This means a physician must give a patient relevant facts about risks and alternatives that will allow the patient to make a rational choice about whether to be examined or treated. A patient may bring a cause of action based on lack of informed consent if the patient undergoes treatment and suffers some injury as a result of the treatment.

i. **Professional or lay standard.** A physician who has given limited or no information to a patient may have two defenses. One is that the physician did not know about the risk that he or she failed to communicate to the patient. The other defense is that the physician did know about the risk but did not believe that it was necessary to tell the patient about it. The majority of jurisdictions apply a professional standard of care to both of these aspects of the case. A minority view applies a professional standard of care to the issue of whether the doctor's state of knowledge was adequate but applies a lay standard to the issue of whether the doctor's choice about how much to tell the patient was appropriate. The minority position is based on the idea that a lay jury can evaluate how much information a lay person (the patient) would have wanted to have and how much information would have been material to the patient's decision making process.

Illustration: Scott v. Bradford, 606 P.2d 554 (Okla. 1979). The court held that a physician must disclose "all material risks." This is different from a duty to disclose what typical physicians ordinarily disclose. The court rejected use of the professional standard because "a patient's right to make up his mind whether to undergo treatment should not be delegated to the local medical group." A risk is material if it would likely affect the patient's decision.

ii. **Causation.** The plaintiff in an informed consent case is required to establish a causal link between the physician's failure to provide adequate information and the patient's ultimate injury. This link is evidence on which a jury can find that with better information the patient would not have undergone the procedure that caused injury.

Illustrations: Canterbury v. Spence, 464 F.2d 772 (D.C. Cir. 1972). On the issue of causation, this decision held that an objective test applies, with the jury being asked to determine whether a reasonable prudent person would have rejected the procedure if more complete information had been given. This is the majority view on causation.

Scott v. Bradford, 606 P.2d 554 (Okla. 1979), represents a minority approach to the causation issue in formed consent cases. This allows the jury to consider the causation element satisfied if it believes that the patient personally would have rejected the procedure had he or she been given more complete information. The subjective standard may involve testimony by the injured person stating that he or she would have avoided the procedure had he or she known about its risks; the reliability of such testimony, given after the procedure and the injury have occurred, may be subject to question.

D. STANDARDS FROM STATUTES (NEGLIGENCE PER SE)

In most cases when an actor's conduct violates a safety statute, the statute is used to define the standard of care, and violation of that standard is called negligence per se. This is different from cases that do not involve statutory violations. In those cases a jury decides what a reasonable person would have done and then compares that concept with what it believes the actor did. In statutory violation cases the jury is told to decide only whether the actor violated a statute. If the actor violated a statute, the conduct is defined as negligent regardless of how reasonable it might seem to the jury. Use of the fact of a statutory violation moves the evaluative part of the tort law process from the jury to the legislature. Our system borrows the wisdom of the legislature and uses it to replace the wisdom of the jury.

Illustration: Osborne v. McMasters, 40 Minn. 103, 41 N.W. 543 (1889). A druggist sold the plaintiff's decedent a poison and, in violation of a statute, failed to label it as poison. Judgment for the plaintiff was affirmed on the ground that violation of this statute was conclusive evidence of negligence (or negligence per se).

1. Majority Rule

Either a plaintiff or a defendant may violate a statute in a situation giving rise to injury. For convenience this discussion assumes that the party seeking to introduce evidence is the plaintiff and the party alleged to have violated a statute is the defendant. The plaintiff must establish that his or her injury is of the type the statute was adopted to prevent and that he or she is a member of the class the legislature intended to protect. When the plaintiff makes these showings, the jury is instructed to find that the defendant was negligent, unless the defendant has an excuse for violating the statute.

Illustration: Martin v. Herzog, 228 N.Y. 164, 126 N.E. 814 (1920). The plaintiff's decedent in a vehicular accident case violated a statute that required his buggy to have lights. At trial the jury found that the decedent had not been negligent (This allowed recovery, while a finding of negligence would have precluded recovery under the doctrine of contributory negligence). On appeal it was held that the unexcused violation of the statute was equivalent to proof of negligence.

2. Minority Rules

A minority of jurisdictions treat statutory violations as evidence of negligence. The plaintiff is entitled to introduce evidence showing the violation, but the jury is not required to decide that the defendant was negligent, even if it believes the defendant did violate the statute. In some jurisdictions a plaintiff who introduces evidence showing violation of a statute receives the benefit of a presumption that the defendant was negligent. This procedural device gives the plaintiff a benefit greater than that in an evidence-of-negligence jurisdiction but weaker than that in a negligence-per-se jurisdiction.

3. Types of Statutes

All jurisdictions apply their violation-of-statute rules to instances in which the defendants violate state statutes. Jurisdictions vary in their approaches to violations of local statutes and local ordinances. The most common approach is to treat such violations as evidence of negligence.

4. Reason for Statutory Purpose Inquiry

No jurisdiction gives effect to proof of a statutory violation unless the plaintiff shows that the injury suffered is the kind of injury the legislature meant to avert and that the plaintiff is the type of person the legislature meant to benefit. The reason for these restrictions relates to the basic theory of the negligence per se doctrine. The doctrine displaces the jury's social role of evaluating conduct. It relies on the legislature's judgment about how people should act. If the legislature has not paid attention to a situation like the one in which the plaintiff was injured, then there is no legislative "wisdom" available to import into the tort litigation process.

Illustrations: Stachniewicz v. Mar-Cam Corp., 259 Or. 583, 488 P.2d 436 (1971), illustrates the inquiry into the purpose of the statute or regulation sought to be used as a standard of care. The plaintiff was injured in a fight in a bar and sought damages from the operator of the bar. The plaintiff showed that the defendant had violated a statute prohibiting the sale of liquor to intoxicated persons and had violated administrative regulations forbidding a bar operator to allow boisterous conduct in a bar. The trial court excluded evidence of both violations, and the jury found for the defendant. On appeal the supreme court examined the purposes of the statute and regulation. It found that the statute was meant to protect drinkers, not people who might be injured by drinkers, but that the regulation was meant to protect against barroom brawls. Thus, the statute was not meant to protect people like the plaintiff from injuries like those the plaintiff suffered, but the regulations were. For this reason the statute was properly excluded, but the plaintiff should have been allowed to introduce evidence of violation of the regulation.

Brown v. Shyne, 242 N.Y. 176, 151 N.E. 197 (1926). The plaintiff sought damages from a chiropractor and used the chiropractor's failure to comply with a licensing statute as evidence of negligence. On appeal judgment for the plaintiff was reversed, with the court holding that the licensing statute was not intended to establish a standard of skill for the practice of medicine. This is the majority position on the question of whether violation of licensing statutes—including statutes requiring the driver of a vehicle to have a driver's license—can be used as proof of negligence.

E&A EXAMPLE AND ANALYSIS

Suppose a statute requires that an emergency exit door at a theater be equipped with a "panic bar," a flat metal lever that opens the door when a person pushes against it. The purpose of this statute is to insure that such a door opens quickly in an emergency. A regular doorknob is not allowed under this statute. If a defendant were to install an ordinary door knob on such a door and a person were to be hurt by banging against the protruding door knob, the statutory violation would have no effect on a negligence claim by the injured person. The statute's purpose is to make it likely that people escape the building easily in an emergency. Its purpose has nothing to do with protecting someone from being hurt by the shape of the door's opening device.

5. Causation

The negligence per se doctrine can satisfy the plaintiff's obligation to show that the defendant's conduct was substandard. It does not necessarily satisfy the plaintiff's obligation to show that the defendant's negligent conduct was an actual cause of the plaintiff's harm. The plaintiff must establish causation, in the two important senses of cause in fact and proximate cause, even in a case where the plaintiff can show a defendant's violation of a statute.

6. Excused Violations

In many situations a defendant may admit to having violated a statute but may offer an excuse to show that the violation was justified. Jurisdictions have varied approaches to the relationship of excuses and negligence per se.

a. **Statutory violations for which no excuses are allowed.** A small number of statutes are adopted to protect specially weak classes of individuals or to protect all people against particularly significant dangers. Violations of statutes in these categories are not subject to excuses but will always be treated as negligence per se. One example of such a statute is a child labor law restricting the ways children may be employed. Other examples are acts that prohibit the sale of food with dangerous impurities, statutes that require workplaces to be safe, and statutes prohibiting the sale of firearms to minors.

b. **Procedural treatment of excuses.** For statutes not meant to protect a particularly weak class of individuals, there are two main ways jurisdictions respond to defendants' claims that their violations should be excused.

   i. **Excuse considered equally with evidence of statutory violation.** In many jurisdictions, when a defendant introduces evidence of an excuse, the jury evaluates all the evidence, including the statutory violation and the excuse, and decides whether the defendant was negligent exactly as it would in a case that did not involve a statute. The plaintiff receives virtually no special benefit from showing that the defendant's conduct was in violation of a statute. The Restatement takes this position but limits the types of excuse on which a defendant may rely.

   ii. **Excuse considered to rebut presumption.** In some jurisdictions a plaintiff who shows that a defendant violated an applicable statute gains the benefit of a presumption that the defendant was negligent. This means the defendant will lose unless the defendant persuades the jury that he or she was free from negligence (This is different from ordinary cases in which the plaintiff must persuade the jury that the defendant was negligent). The jury is allowed to consider the excuse as evidence that can rebut the presumption of negligence.

c. **Types of excuses.** The Restatement catalogs typical excuses in §288A. In jurisdictions that follow the Restatement, judges allow defendants to introduce evidence only about excuses that fit those general descriptions. In other states judges are free to admit evidence of additional types of excuses. Following are the primary Restatement categories of allowable excuses:

i. **Reasonable ignorance.**

ii. **Reasonable attempt to obey the statute.**

iii. **Emergency that is not the fault or responsibility of defendant.**

iv. **Greater risk of harm would be incurred by obeying than by disobeying statute.**

Illustration: Zeni v. Anderson, 397 Mich. 117, 243 N.W.2d 270 (1976). On a snowy day the pedestrian plaintiff was walking on a path, in violation of a statute that required pedestrians to walk on available sidewalks, when she was hit by a vehicle. The plaintiff's negligence was an issue in her suit against the vehicle's driver. She was properly allowed to introduce evidence that most people used the path instead of the sidewalk under snowy conditions because it was far less slippery than the sidewalk. This evidence could be used to excuse her violation of the statute.

E. STANDARDS FROM JUDICIAL PRECEDENTS

Courts sometimes attempt to develop precedents that detail exactly what would be careful behavior in specific situations. This effort is likely to be unsuccessful because of the wide variety of circumstances involved in actual instances of injury. A famous example is Baltimore & Ohio v. Goodman, 275 U.S. 66 (1927). In that case Justice Holmes sought to establish exact rules of conduct for people who are about to cross railroad tracks (stop, look, and get out to see better if necessary). Seven years later the Supreme Court essentially rejected his effort. In Pokora v. Wabash Ry. Co., 292 U.S. 98 (1934), the Court refused to characterize a driver as negligent for failing to leave his vehicle to inspect a railroad crossing. It affirmed a result based on a jury verdict that absolved the driver of negligence, stating that unusual situations should not be governed by "tests or regulations that are fitting for the commonplace or normal."

F. INFERRED NEGLIGENCE: *RES IPSA LOQUITUR*

Res ipsa loquitur (the thing speaks for itself) is a procedural device that applies to cases where: 1. the occurrence that caused the plaintiff's injury is ordinarily caused by someone's negligence; and 2. the defendant is likely to be the one who was negligent. The doctrine prevents a defendant from winning dismissal of the plaintiff's claim on the ground that the plaintiff does not have adequate evidence to support a finding in the plaintiff's favor. Some courts allow a plaintiff the benefit of this doctrine only if the plaintiff shows that the instrumentality that caused the harm was under the exclusive control of the defendant. Some also limit the doctrine to cases where the plaintiff does not have direct proof of the details of the defendant's negligence. Regardless of variation among jurisdictions in the specific articulation of what a plaintiff must show, in every jurisdiction the *res ipsa loquitur* doctrine can be used only in a case in which the judge believes that the type of incident that injured the plaintiff usually involves negligence.

The judge must also believe that the defendant identified by the plaintiff is likely to have been the one who actually caused the injury.

1. Byrne v. Boadle: The Original Example

The clearest example of a *res ipsa loquitur* case is the one in which the term was first used: Byrne v. Boadle, 2 H. & C. 722, 159 Eng. Rep. 299 (Ex. 1863). The plaintiff was injured when a barrel came from a second-story window and hit him as he walked past. The plaintiff had no evidence about how the barrel happened to fall out the window but was protected from dismissal of his case on the theory that the accident "speaks for itself."

2. Elements of *Res Ipsa Loquitur*

To obtain the benefit of the doctrine the plaintiff must persuade the judge that the plaintiff's injurious experience had certain attributes. Not all jurisdictions require all of the attributes to be shown.

a. **Incident usually involves negligence.** The plaintiff must show that the type of event that hurt the plaintiff usually occurs due to negligence.

i. **Logical analysis of likely negligence.** The answer to the question of whether a particular type of injury was the result of an incident that usually involves negligence is sometimes controlled by precedents in a particular jurisdiction. For example, the *res ipsa loquitur* doctrine ordinarily applies to airplane crashes and elevator accidents. If there are no precedents, a court must hypothesize what all the probable causes for the incident could be; it then must guess whether most of those probable causes involve negligence. If the bulk of the probable causes are usually associated with negligence, the court applies the *res ipsa loquitur* doctrine.

E&A EXAMPLE AND ANALYSIS

A barrel falling from a second-story window is a good example of an incident that usually involves negligence. An example of an incident that does not satisfy this element is a vehicular collision caused by a sudden flat tire. Because there are many explanations for a tire blowing out that do not involve anyone's negligence, a judge would not rule that it is the type of incident that usually involves negligence.

b. **Defendant's exclusive control or likely responsibility.** The traditional statement of the *res ipsa loquitur* doctrine includes a requirement that the plaintiff show that the "instrumentality" or thing that caused the plaintiff's injury was under the defendant's control at the time.

Modern courts apply this element with some flexibility. For example, a plaintiff, sitting in a chair at a store is injured when the chair collapses. A literal interpretation of the exclusive-control element supports the conclusion that the chair is not under the exclusive control of the defendant store operator at the time of the injury, since the plaintiff is sitting in it at the time. Most courts interpret the element as requiring a decision about who was in control of the chair at the times when negligence, if any, probably happened. In that analysis they hypothesize that negligence could have happened in the store's selection of the chair, in its maintenance of the chair, or in its way of positioning the chair. When these activities occurred, the store was in exclusive control of the chair.

c. **Plaintiff's freedom from responsibility.** Most courts state that the plaintiff must show that he or she did not personally cause the injury. This element of the doctrine may be interpreted in two ways, one related to contributory negligence and the other related to the *res ipsa loquitur* doctrine's focus on identifying the actual wrongdoer.

   i. **Contributory negligence analysis.** The plaintiff's-freedom-from-responsibility element may be a remnant of the contributory negligence era, when any negligence at all by a plaintiff was a complete bar to recovery. From that point of view, a plaintiff who was in part to blame for his or her own injury was not entitled to any recovery from the defendant and therefore was not entitled to the benefit of the *res ipsa loquitur* doctrine. This rationale is significantly weakened by the general replacement of contributory negligence with comparative negligence doctrines (Chapter 13, Defenses, explains comparative negligence).

   ii. **Identifying actual wrongdoer analysis.** Some courts treat the plaintiff's-freedom-from-responsibility element as a factor aimed at increasing the likelihood that the named defendant actually was the wrongdoer who caused the plaintiff's injury. The plaintiff is obligated to provide a basis for the conclusion that the injury was caused by the defendant and not by anyone else. Since the plaintiff is someone who might have caused the injury in many cases, requiring the plaintiff to show that he or she did not personally cause the injury may just be a specific application of the general idea that the plaintiff must show that it is likely that the defendant is the one who harmed him or her.

d. **Plaintiff's ignorance of defendant's actual conduct.** Some courts require the plaintiff to show that he or she does not have information about the details of the defendant's conduct that caused the plaintiff's injury. This information gap was present in the original *res ipsa loquitur* case, *Byrne v. Boadle,* since the plaintiff did not know what had caused the defendant's barrel to fall from the defendant's second-story window. A majority of courts do not require this showing of plaintiff's ignorance.

3. Specific Proof of Defendant's Negligent Acts

Some plaintiffs seek to rely on the *res ipsa loquitur* doctrine to support an inference of the defendant's negligence but also introduce proof that provides some details about the defendant's actions. Courts are divided on whether such plaintiffs should continue to have access to the *res ipsa loquitur* doctrine. Some courts take the position that such plaintiffs must lose the benefit of the doctrine. They reason that the doctrine is meant to assist plaintiffs who do not know how the defendant really acted, and that it therefore should be withdrawn from a case where the plaintiff does attempt to use proof about the details of the defendant's conduct. Other courts hold that the introduction of some specific evidence does not change the underlying thesis of the *res ipsa loquitur* doctrine, namely that the type of injury the plaintiff suffered usually is caused by negligence. They therefore allow the plaintiff to benefit both from the *res ipsa loquitur* doctrine and any conclusions that the plaintiff's specific evidence may lead the jury to reach.

4. Multiple-Defendant Cases

Where more than one defendant may be responsible for the plaintiff's injury, the plaintiff cannot literally satisfy the required showing that the defendant was the cause of the injury; the injury might have been caused by any one of the defendants. In many cases this fact deprives the plaintiff of access to the *res ipsa loquitur* doctrine. A minority approach grants plaintiffs the benefit of the doctrine in cases of this type but offers each defendant individually an opportunity to avoid liability.

Illustration: Ybarra v. Spangard, 25 Cal. 2d 486, 154 P.2d 687 (1944), is the leading case for the pro-plaintiff treatment of this situation. In the case a plaintiff was injured while under anesthesia required for an operation. The court allowed the plaintiff to assert a negligence claim against a variety of doctors and nurses involved in his treatment, using the rationale that they all, as a group, had knowledge of who among them had caused the injury. The court ruled that each of the defendants could be found negligent, unless each individually persuaded the jury that he or she was not to blame.

a. **Significance of medical context.** The court in *Ybarra* was strongly influenced by the medical setting of the case. Acknowledging that its resolution stretched the boundaries of the *res ipsa loquitur* doctrine, the court stated that the only fair alternative would be to impose strict liability for medical injuries. That choice, it implied, would be even more problematic for health care defendants.

5. Procedural Effect of *Res Ipsa Loquitur*

The main significance of the res ipsa loquitur doctrine is its procedural benefit to the plaintiff. The doctrine always protects the plaintiff from a defendant's motion for directed verdict on the basis of inadequate evidence of negligence. Some courts give the doctrine greater power.

a. **Establishes prima facie case.** The basic benefit all courts give to a plaintiff whose case qualifies for the *res ipsa loquitur* doctrine is protection from dismissal on the basis of failure to establish a prima facie case. The doctrine is treated as equivalent to evidence on which a jury can conclude that the defendant was negligent.

b. **Shifts production burden.** A minority of courts give more power to the doctrine. In these courts a plaintiff whose case qualifies for the *res ipsa loquitur* doctrine is entitled to judgment as a matter of law unless the defendant introduces evidence to rebut the conclusion that the defendant was negligent.

c. **Shifts persuasion burden.** In a few jurisdictions, when the plaintiff establishes that his or her case meets the requirements for the *res ipsa loquitur* doctrine, the burden of persuasion shifts to the defendant. This means that the jury is instructed to find for the plaintiff unless it is persuaded that the defendant was free from negligence. Note that this shift in the persuasion burden is unusual. In the vast majority of cases, a jury is told that it must find for the plaintiff only when the plaintiff persuades the jury that the defendant was negligent.

6. Impact of Defendant's Case on Procedural Effect

A defendant may introduce evidence to defeat the plaintiff's efforts to establish the foundation elements of the *res ipsa loquitur* doctrine. A defendant may also introduce evidence that contradicts the inference of negligence that the plaintiff's foundation evidence seeks to support. In the majority of jurisdictions where the *res ipsa loquitur* doctrine satisfies the plaintiff's obligation to present a prima facie case, the defendant's rebuttal evidence has the following impact. The defendant is entitled to judgment as a matter of law if his or her evidence is so strong that no reasonable juror could believe that the foundation requirements were met or that there actually was negligence by the defendant. If the defendant's evidence is not that strong but could support a jury finding that the plaintiff failed to meet the foundation requirements or failed to establish that there actually was negligence by the defendant, then the defendant is protected from judgment as a matter of law.

7. Procedural Example

Figure 6-1, p. 104, shows the procedural consequences of the *res ipsa loquitur* doctrine, using the barrel-falling-from-the-window case as an example. If

FIGURE 6-1

PROCEDURAL EFFECTS OF *RES IPSA LOQUITUR* DOCTRINE

Defendant's Proof	*Prima Facie Jurisdiction*	*Production Burden Jurisdiction*	*Persuasion Burden Jurisdiction*
Defendant introduces no evidence.	Plaintiff is protected from judgment as a matter of law for the defendant. Jury will be instructed that plaintiff must establish case by preponderance of evidence and that jury may infer negligence from the fact of the barrel's falling.	Jury will be instructed that if it believes the barrel fell, it must find for the plaintiff.	Jury will be instructed that if it believes the barrel fell, it must find for the plaintiff.
Defendant introduces evidence that the barrel did not fall.	Plaintiff is protected from judgment as a matter of law for the defendant. Jury will be instructed that plaintiff must establish case by preponderance of evidence and that jury may infer negligence from the fact of the barrel's falling.	Jury will be instructed that if it believes the barrel fell, it must find for the plaintiff.	Jury will be instructed that if it believes the barrel fell, it must find for the plaintiff.
Defendant introduces evidence of having handled the barrel carefully.	Plaintiff is protected from judgment as a matter of law for the defendant. Jury will be instructed that plaintiff must establish case by preponderance of evidence and that jury may infer negligence from the fact of the barrel's falling.	Defendant has met its production burden. Therefore, the *res ipsa loquitur* device may have no further effect in the case. Jury will be instructed that plaintiff must establish case by preponderance of evidence. In some states jury will be told it may infer negligence from the fact of the barrel's falling.	Jury will be instructed that if it believes the barrel fell, it must find for the plaintiff unless it believes the defendant has shown freedom from negligence by a preponderance of the evidence.

the plaintiff must establish that the defendant was negligent but can offer proof only that the defendant's barrel came from a high window and hit the plaintiff, proof of the barrel's falling may be treated as: 1. adequate to establish a prima facie case; 2. adequate to shift the production burden to the defendant; or 3. adequate to shift the persuasion burden to the defendant. The table shows the result required by each of these possible treatments of the *res ipsa loquitur* doctrine in a case where the injured plaintiff introduces evidence sufficient to support a finding of the basic fact (barrel falling) and the defendant makes each of the three responses specified in the first column.

Review Questions and Answers

Question: Max Manager, the manager of a grocery store, made a large display of heavy cans of fruit juice. The cans were stacked in a pyramid, six feet wide at the bottom and about eight feet tall. Yancy Yanker, a customer, yanked a can from the middle of the display, and the pyramid collapsed. Some of the cans hit other customers who were nearby. If they sue Manager and Yanker, how would tort law determine if either defendant had been negligent?

Answer: The reasonable prudent person test would apply to each defendant's conduct. Would a reasonable prudent person who worked as a grocery store manager know that tall displays of heavy objects are dangerous? A jury would have to determine this. It would decide whether the risk that the cans would fall or that the display would be disturbed was so significant that Manager should have avoided it by choosing to build a different type of display or choosing not to build any display at all. Yanker also would be evaluated in terms of the reasonable prudent person. A jury would determine whether the risks connected with taking a can from the middle of this type of display were clear enough that a reasonable prudent person would have been aware of them. The jury would also have to decide whether a reasonable prudent person would have taken that risk.

Question: A public transit system operated buses with special lifts to accommodate people in wheelchairs. Hilda Hasty, who used a wheelchair, attempted to place her chair on the lift of one of these buses at a bus stop. She wheeled her chair very quickly and collided with a protective metal guard on the lift. That made the chair veer at a sharp angle and hit Rona Rider, who was waiting at the bus stop for another bus. Rider fell and was injured. If Rider sues Hasty, claiming that Hasty was negligent in the way she attempted to board the bus, and that Hasty's negligence caused Rider's injuries, how would a jury evaluate Hasty's conduct?

Answer: The jury would evaluate Hasty's conduct under the reasonable prudent person test, modified to reflect Hasty's physical disability. It would decide how a reasonable prudent person with Hasty's disability would have operated the wheelchair; it then would compare that concept with what it thought Hasty actually did. If Hasty acted less carefully than the jury thought a reasonable prudent person with Hasty's disability would have acted, it would find that Hasty was negligent.

Question: Paul Patient sued David Doctor for negligence, claiming that Doctor had harmed him by reporting him to a credit rating bureau as owing Doctor money, even though Patient had paid his bill in full. Patient claimed this had injured his credit rating and sought damages for that harm. Should the professional standard of care apply to Doctor's conduct, and should Patient be required to introduce expert testimony?

Answer: The professional standard should not be used, and Patient should not be required to introduce expert testimony. Doctor's conduct should be evaluated under the reasonable prudent person test, not the professional standard, because it is identical to conduct employed by all types of business people in our society, not just by professionals such as doctors and lawyers. Patient should not be required to introduce expert testimony, since lay people can understand billing procedures and can decide on the basis of their own experience whether Doctor's efforts to be accurate in billing and credit reporting were reasonable.

Question: Sarah Speeder drove her car at 80 miles per hour on a road with a posted speed limit of 55 miles per hour. She hit Cora Careful and injured her. In Careful's suit against Speeder, Careful showed that Speeder violated the speed limit (a violation of statute). Speeder testified that she violated the speed limit because she believed the United States Constitution guaranteed freedom to travel and that speed limits were an infringement on that right. What role would the statutory violation have in the lawsuit?

Answer: In most places the statutory violation would be conclusive proof of negligence, unless it were excused. In a minority of states, the statutory violation would be evidence of negligence unless it were excused. This is because the statute was adopted for safety reasons related to appropriate driving speeds and because it was meant in part to protect people like Careful from being hit by drivers. No court would allow a jury to consider Speeder's excuse for violation, since it merely rejected the right of the legislature to adopt its position. Allowable excuses deal with issues like greater safety through disobeying the statute or impossibility of complying with the statute but Speeder's excuse was essentially a rejection of the negligence per se concept.

Question: A large pane of glass fell from the tenth story of a building under construction and hit Willy Walker, a pedestrian who was passing by the building site. The glass broke into many pieces. Walker was injured. If he sued the construction company, could Walker have the benefit of the *res ipsa loquitur* doctrine?

Answer: Yes. If all workers involved in a construction project are acting as reasonable prudent people should act, nothing will fall from the work area onto a street where a pedestrian could be injured. Clearly, Walker had nothing to do with the cause of his harm, highlighting the likelihood that the defendant construction company was responsible.

EXAM TIPS

- When a question asks you whether someone was negligent, remember that you must specify what standard of care the legal system would apply to evaluate that person's conduct. Then you can sensibly give an opinion as to whether the conduct met or failed to meet that standard.

- Sometimes the best response to a question that asks whether conduct was reasonable will admit that the question is too close to call, so that a reasonable jury could find either negligence or freedom from negligence.

- Be aware that traditional tort principles may be inconsistent because they apply the usual, objective, reasonable-person standard to conduct of a mentally weak person but apply a modified version of that standard to conduct of a physically disabled person.

- Remember that the child's standard of care is used only when a child is engaged in nonadult activities.

- Compliance with custom is always relevant, but it is a conclusive defense only where the professional standard of care applies.

- In cases that would ordinarily be controlled by the professional standard of care, the lay-person exception is very important. Where the professional's alleged misconduct is easy to understand, a plaintiff is not required to have expert testimony to establish the standard of care.

- In violation-of-statute cases always pay attention to the purpose for which the legislature adopted the statute, the classes of individuals whose conduct the legislature wanted to control, and whose safety the legislature wanted to protect. When there is a discrepancy between the circumstances of a case and these attributes of the statute, applying the statute may be wrong.

- The *res ipsa loquitur* doctrine is a common-sense doctrine of circumstantial evidence. When you are asked to explain whether it should apply in a particular situation, say more than "yes, because this type of injurious incident usually involves negligence." Explain why you think that type of injurious incident really does usually involve negligence.

- Remember that the *res ipsa loquitur* doctrine requires a showing that any negligent act was probably done by the defendant. This is sometimes called the "exclusive control" element and is sometimes approached by stating the the plaintiff must have been free from responsibility. Both of these ideas are aimed at the same issue, requiring the plaintiff to give the court a basis for believing that negligent conduct, if any, was probably done by the defendant. Explaining this in common sense terms is better than merely stating terms like *exclusive control* without showing that you understand the reason that some jurisdictions use them.

7 CAUSATION IN FACT

CHAPTER OVERVIEW

- To recover damages, besides showing that a defendant acted unreasonably, a plaintiff must show that the defendant's conduct actually caused some harm to the plaintiff.
- *Cause in fact* is a term that defines the actual or factual cause element of a plaintiff's case. Cause in fact can be established with either a but-for test or a substantial factor test.
- Scientific evidence sometimes establishes the cause-in-fact element of a plaintiff's case. Courts limit the use of such evidence by requiring that it conform to generally accepted methodologies or by requiring that it meet standards such as peer review and replicability of results.
- In medical malpractice cases where a defendant's negligent conduct has harmed a patient but the patient's disease was the predominant factor in the harm, traditional doctrines absolve the doctor of any responsibility. Some courts now allow proportional damage awards for loss of a chance of recovery.
- In some rare cases with multiple but indistinguishable wrongdoers, any one of which might have caused the plaintiff's harm, some states treat cause in fact as having been established against each wrongdoer, even though it is clear that the harm was not inflicted by each of them.

A. BASIC PROBLEM

A fundamental principle of tort law is that it never serves only to impose a sanction on a wrongdoer. It always operates to do justice between a wrongdoer and an injured victim. Another basic principle, for reasons that are both practical and philosophical, is that wrongdoers should not have to pay for all of the potentially infinite consequences of their conduct. The causation requirement in tort law serves both of these concepts. It pairs up wrongdoers and victims, and it limits the amount of liability that is imposed on any single wrongdoer.

The causation inquiry is usually straightforward. In a simple case, a driver might drive into a pedestrian and the pedestrian might suffer physical injuries from being hit. It is easy to see that the driver's conduct was a cause of the pedestrian's injuries. Nothing in this chapter's detailed exploration of causation would matter in a case of that type.

Causation issues, however, can sometimes be complex. For example, when a pedestrian is hit by a car, the driver is not the only cause of the incident. Logically, the pedestrian is also a cause of his or her injury since he or she had to be at that location in order for the injury to occur. Thus, tort law has to recognize that events have multiple causes.

Causation is also complicated because multiple results can follow from a person's single act. Some of the consequences may seem strange, because they happen far away from the actor's conduct, because much time passes between the conduct and the consequence, or because the type of consequence is different from what one would have expected from the conduct. Sometimes the results are not strange at all but seem so remote that it would not be fair to make the actor pay for them. Tort law has methods of dealing with consequences that are remote in space or time, that are weird, or that a sense of justice prevents blaming on a particular actor.

B. CATEGORIES OF ANALYSIS

Most courts and scholars treat causation with separate analyses of cause in fact and legal cause. Cause in fact is considered a historical question in any case: Was the defendant's conduct a cause of the plaintiff's injury? Legal cause is a second level of inquiry: Even though the defendant's conduct was a cause of the plaintiff's injury, is there a reason why the legal system should protect the defendant from having to pay for the plaintiff's injury? Legal cause is often called "proximate cause." Some courts do not analyze the causation problem in its two components of cause in fact and legal cause. They simply refer to the whole issue as proximate cause.

C. BASIC CAUSE-IN-FACT TEST

The most common test used for cause in fact is called the "but-for" test. The test asks the jury to decide whether the defendant's conduct was an essential factor in the sequence of events that caused the plaintiff's injury. The jury decides, in other words, whether the plaintiff would have been all right except for the fact that the defendant did what he or she did. Except for and but for are synonymous terms. They convey the idea that the jury must believe that things would have been better for the plaintiff if the defendant's act had never happened. The Latin expression sine qua non is also used for this idea.

1. **Examples**

The but for test is inclusive, since it can lead to a finding of causation where the defendant's conduct does not have a close relationship to the plaintiff's harm. It can, however, sometimes support a finding of no cause in fact.

a. **Cause in fact established.** A defendant drives at a speed over the limit for twenty city blocks and slows to a safe speed for another twenty blocks. If the defendant then hits a pedestrian, the defendant's speeding is a cause in fact of the collision. If the defendant had not driven too fast for the first twenty blocks, the defendant would have arrived at the place where the pedestrian was hit at a later time, and thus would not have hit the pedestrian.

b. **Cause in fact not established.** During a bad storm a person drowns after falling from a ship that the owner failed to equip with lifeboats. If the jury concludes that a lifeboat would not have saved the victim's life because of the severity of the storm, the failure to provide a lifeboat is not a cause in fact of the victim's death.

2. **Not Completely Factual**

When a jury uses the cause-in-fact test, it compares what it believes really happened with what it believes would have happened if the defendant's conduct had been different or had not occurred. Obviously, this requires thinking about a hypothetical or imaginary state of affairs. Thus, the jury's "factual" finding about cause in fact really involves judgment about how things usually work in the world as well as about what actually happened in the particular event that hurt the plaintiff. A defendant's conduct can be a cause in fact of the plaintiff's injury even if there is a chance that the injury would have happened in the absence of the defendant's conduct. The plaintiff is required to prove the but-for test only by a preponderance of the evidence.

E&A Example and Analysis

Tick-tock Clock Repair Company negligently attempted to repair Sarah Scientist's alarm clock. Because of Tick-tock's negligence, the clock failed to wake Scientist up one morning. This made Scientist arrive at her laboratory later that day than she had planned. Unfortunately, this meant that Scientist was unable to stop a chain reaction that caused a big explosion. The explosion caused whatever additional events you would like to add to this example. Tick-tock's negligence is a cause in fact of everything.

Legal cause (or proximate cause) principles, however, will limit the range of consequences that Tick-tock will have to pay for.

---

3. Substantial Factor Test: Twin Fires and Other Concurrent Causes

The substantial factor test has been developed for certain cases where the but for test produces an unsatisfactory answer. Primarily, these are cases where two events combine to produce an injury. The classic example of this is when two fires, started by different people, merge just prior to burning up the plaintiff's property. The but for test would not treat either fire as a cause of the plaintiff's loss, since neither individually was a necessary preceding event in relation to the plaintiff's loss. Applying the but for test to one of the twin fires, a jury would have to conclude that it was not a cause in fact of the plaintiff's loss, since the loss would have occurred even without that fire. The jury would then follow the same reasoning with respect to the other fire.

The substantial factor test asks whether an event that happened to coincide with another event was a substantial factor in causing the plaintiff's injury. This allows a jury finding of causation in fact in twin fires and other concurrent cause cases.

a. **California replaces but-for test with substantial factor test.** The California Supreme Court has rejected use of the but-for test on the ground that it can confuse juries. California requires use of the substantial factor test for the issue of cause in fact in all cases, not just concurrent cause cases.

b. **Critique of reliance on substantial factor test.** One criticism of relying on the substantial factor test in all cases is that the test may lead a jury to decide the cause-in-fact question against a plaintiff even when it might have concluded that the defendant's conduct was a but for cause. A jury might believe that the defendant's conduct was actually a necessary antecedent of the plaintiff's injury (a but for cause) but might conclude that the conduct's contribution to the injury was slight. Thinking that a slight cause cannot be a substantial factor, the jury might decide the cause-in-fact question against the plaintiff in this situation.

D. PROOF OF CAUSE IN FACT

As is true for most issues, a plaintiff is free to select any method of proof he or she thinks will be convincing. Sometimes cause in fact is established with eyewitness testimony; more often circumstantial evidence supports an inference that the defendant's conduct was a but-for cause.

Illustration: Reynolds v. Texas & Pacific Ry. Co., 37 La. Ann. 694 (1885). Evidence that the victim fell down an unlighted flight of stairs was adequate to support a finding that the lack of light was a cause in fact of the plaintiff's fall. The court emphasized that the plaintiff was not required to negate possibilities that other causes were responsible, since the defendant's negligence had increased the risk of falls like the plaintiff's.

E. SCIENTIFIC EVIDENCE

Expert testimony linking a plaintiff's injury to some conduct by a defendant often provides an adequate basis for a finding of cause in fact.

1. Physician's Expert Testimony

Physicians who have treated an injury victim or examined the victim for the purpose of testifying may express opinions about the causation of a plaintiff's injury. Testimony must support a conclusion that the causation claimed by the plaintiff is more likely than not to be true, to justify a verdict for the plaintiff.

Illustration: Kramer Serv., Inc. v. Wilkins, 184 Miss. 483, 186 So. 2d 625 (1939). The plaintiff suffered a cut on the head when a piece of glass from the transom above a hotel room door fell on him. He then developed skin cancer at the spot that had been cut. He sought damages from the hotel. A jury verdict for the plaintiff included damages for cancer but was supported only by a doctor's testimony that it was "possible" that the injury had caused the cancer. On that basis recovery for cancer-related damages was improper.

2. Experiments and Scientific Analyses

When a party seeks to introduce scientific evidence, particularly if it is based on experiments or scientific analyses, courts apply certain evidentiary rules. These rules vary in the degree to which they restrict the jury's access to information.

a. ***Frye* test.** In many states scientific testimony is admitted only if its proponent can show that the methodology on which it is based has received general acceptance in some relevant scientific community. This test excludes evidence based on new theories or methods, making it likely that an opponent will have a fairly easy time locating a rival expert who can evaluate evidence that is admitted.

b. **Modern relevancy tests.** States that have adopted codes of evidence based on the Federal Rules of Evidence may treat scientific evidence with a stance skewed in favor of admissibility. They may require only a showing that the information could be helpful to the jury. This position relies on the jury's ability to give unusual theories and "junk science" only as much effect as they deserve.

c. ***Daubert* test.** In Daubert v. Merrel Dow Pharmaceuticals, Inc., 113 S. Ct. 2786, 125 L. Ed.2d 469 (1993), the United States Supreme Court announced a new method for deciding admissibility of scientific evidence in federal trials. Under this test the proponent need not show general acceptance, as the *Frye* test requires. The proponent must establish, however, that the evidence meets certain scientific standards. Compliance with standards including peer review, publication, general acceptance in a scientific community, and the replicability of the results is to be evaluated by the trial judge. The *Daubert* decision does not control the weight the judge must give to any one of these factors. A number of states have adopted the *Daubert* analysis.

E&A EXAMPLE AND ANALYSIS

Nat Nasal claims that impurities in the air in the large office building where he works have harmed his health. If his only evidence of causation is a study by a single scientist about the effects of the building's air on the behavior of a chicken exposed to the air for several days, would the *Frye* or *Daubert* analysis be more helpful to Nasal?

If the scientist's method represented a generally accepted methodology, the evidence of the test would be admissible under the *Frye* analysis. The method's general acceptance would also support its admissibility under the *Daubert* test. If the method were unusual, the evidence would be excluded under *Frye;* it would have a chance of admissibility under *Daubert* if Nasal could show that the scientist's work was done in accordance with scientific principles.

d. **Distinction between admissibility and sufficiency.** A plaintiff must do more than introduce admissible evidence in support of a scientific theory of causation. The plaintiff must have enough evidence to support a jury verdict in his or her favor. Judges have a fair amount of discretion in interpreting this other requirement, sufficiency of evidence. In the field of toxic torts or in product liability actions seeking damages for drug side effects that are not widely known, judges may use the sufficiency of evidence requirement to keep from the jury cases where the scientific bases of plaintiffs' cases are unusually weak.

F. LOSS OF A CHANCE

A number of states have recently dealt with the problem posed by a case where a defendant's conduct contributed to an injury that would likely have occurred even without the defendant's conduct. The typical problem occurs with a delayed or erroneous diagnosis by a doctor and the subsequent death of the patient. The plaintiff claims that the defendant's conduct caused the decedent to suffer the loss of a chance of survival.

1. Traditional Treatment

If the plaintiff's testimony shows that the medical error more likely than not caused the death, under traditional doctrines the plaintiff is entitled to full recovery. If testimony cannot support a conclusion that the error more likely than not caused the death, no recovery is allowed. The rationale for the latter result is that the error was not a cause of the death, since the death would have occurred anyway.

2. Proportional Recovery

Some states have avoided this causation problem by changing the inquiry. Rather than seeking to determine a cause of death, they seek to determine a cause of a lost chance of survival. If there is testimony in support of a finding that the defendant's conduct more likely than not deprived the decedent of a chance of survival, these states allow recovery for the value of that lost chance. The recovery is less than the recovery allowed in standard wrongful death actions, since the value of a lost chance is not as great as the value of a lost life. The consensus among jurisdictions that recognize this theory is to multiply standard wrongful death damages by the percentage of decedent's chance for survival that the defendant's conduct eliminated.

Illustration: Herskovits v. Group Health Coop. of Puget Sound, 99 Wash. 2d 609, 664 P.2d 474 (1983). The plaintiff's decedent had a 39-percent chance of survival when the defendant doctor allegedly failed to diagnose an illness that was eventually fatal. By the time the disease was diagnosed, the chance of survival was only 25 percent. The trial court granted summary judgment to the defendant doctor on the theory that wrongful death damages may not be recovered without proof that proper treatment would likely have allowed the decedent to have a normal life expectancy. The supreme court reversed, holding that the claimed decrease in survival chances could support a finding by a jury that the defendant's conduct was a proximate cause of the decedent's death. Damages, the court held, would have to be less than the ordinary wrongful death damages.

E&A Example and Analysis

Under the loss of a chance doctrine, if a plaintiff's evidence showed that there was a 30-percent chance of survival when medical negligence deprived the patient of that chance, the plaintiff would be required to provide evidence about the damages that would be legitimate in a standard wrongful death case. The plaintiff's award would be 30 percent of that amount. If standard wrongful death damages would be $1,000,000, the plaintiff would be awarded $300,000.

G. INCREASED RISK OF FUTURE HARM

Somewhat similar to the loss of a chance problem is the situation where the defendant's conduct allegedly has imposed on the plaintiff an increased risk of some future adverse consequence. For example, medical errors during an operation might make it somewhat likely that the patient will suffer a dangerous internal condition some time in the future.

1. Traditional Treatment

If the plaintiff's proof about likelihood of additional harm related to the defendant's medical error supports a conclusion that the future harm more likely than not will occur, the majority of jurisdictions permit full recovery for that harm. If the plaintiff's evidence supports only a conclusion that there is less than a 50-percent chance that the consequence will occur, the majority of jurisdictions deny all recovery for that consequence. Plaintiffs are thus in a difficult position, since most jurisdictions require all damages relating to a defendant's conduct to be sought in a single action, and since the statute of limitations for tort suits would likely run out prior to occurrence of slightly likely future consequence.

a. **Precautionary future medical expenses.** Most courts allow recovery for medical monitoring that would reasonably be due to a chance of future medical complications caused by the defendant's conduct, even if the chance of those complications is 50 percent or less.

2. Proportional Recovery

A few jurisdictions have dealt with this problem by allowing proportional recovery. If by a preponderance of the evidence the plaintiff's evidence supports a conclusion that there is less than a 50-percent likelihood that some future consequence of the defendant's wrongful act will occur, damages are allowed for that likelihood. The court takes the percentage of likelihood that the injury will occur and uses it (by multiplying) to reduce the standard damages that would have been awarded had the future consequence been more likely than not to occur.

EXAMPLE AND ANALYSIS

If a plaintiff's evidence shows a 30-percent chance that a harmful consequence of the defendant's conduct will occur in the future, the plaintiff is required to provide evidence about the likely financial cost of that consequence. The plaintiff's award would be 30 percent of that amount. If the monetary value of the possible future injury is $100,000, the plaintiff would be awarded $30,000.

---

3. Full Application of Proportional Recovery

A jurisdiction that applies proportional recovery to predicted future consequences when the plaintiff's evidence suggests that the odds of their occurrence are 50 percent or less might logically change its rule for injuries with odds of occurrence greater than 50 percent. The standard treatment of such predicted injuries is to allow full recovery for them. If a defendant were able to produce evidence on which a jury could base a conclusion that the chance of an admittedly likely future injury was something less than 100 percent, a court could use that figure to reduce damages.

H. DIFFICULTY IN IDENTIFYING THE DEFENDANT

A plaintiff usually has to prove what happened and who did it. Sometimes, however, a plaintiff is allowed to sue a group of defendants on the theory that at least one of them caused the plaintiff's injury, and there are public policy reasons to expose all members of the group of defendants to liability.

1. Double Fault and Alternative Liability: *Summers v. Tice*

In Summers v. Tice, 33 Cal. 2d 80, 199 P.2d 1 (1948), two hunters discharged shotguns in the direction of the plaintiff, who was wounded by a single shot. The plaintiff was allowed to obtain a judgment against both shooters, even though there was no way the plaintiff could prove which one's shot had hit him. The court reasoned that each of the defendants had contributed to a circumstance that deprived the plaintiff of the ability to identify the hunter who shot him. It also noted that applying the usual proof requirements would prevent the plaintiff from gaining any recovery. Faced with an information gap, the court decided that the parties who should appropriately suffer the consequences of that lack of information were the defendants, rather than the blameless plaintiff.

2. Allocation Between Tortfeasors

In the alternative liability circumstance it is theoretically possible for one of the defendants to attempt to prove that his shot was not the one that hit the plaintiff. That proof could be a basis for shifting all responsibility to the defendant who had actually harmed the plaintiff. On the facts of *Summers v. Tice,* however, that type of proof would likely have been impossible.

3. DES and Market Share Liability

In cases involving injuries from the drug DES (diethylstilbestrol, a synthetic hormone prescribed to reduce the risk of miscarriage), courts have developed a market share theory to direct compensation to injured plaintiffs. DES caused some daughters of women who had taken the drug during their pregnancies to suffer serious health consequences after they reached puberty. It was virtually impossible for any victim to identify the company that had made the pills her mother had taken. The drug had been manufactured by more than two hundred companies, many years had passed between the time the mother took the drug and the daughter suffered the consequences, and druggists usually did not keep records showing which producer's drug they supplied to any particular customer. A victim is permitted to recover damages from any company that manufactured the drug in proportion to its past share of the market for the drug.

a. **Sindell v. Abbott Laboratories,** 26 Cal. 3d 588, 163 Cal. Rptr. 132, 607 P.2d 924 (1980). California's supreme court decided the first DES case and applied market share liability. It allowed a plaintiff to sue numerous manufacturers and excused her from having to show which particular manufacturer made the drug supplied to her mother. Each manufacturer's liability was limited to a percentage of the plaintiff's damages that equaled the market share (percentage of sales) of that manufacturer during the relevant time period. The court reached this conclusion on public policy grounds, acknowledging that the individual defendants had acted alone (not in concert). Among courts that have considered this issue, market share liability is the majority result.

   i. **Joint and several or individual liability.** Courts applying the market share theory tend to reject joint and several liability, in which any defendant may be required to pay the plaintiff's entire judgment. They impose individual (several) liability, holding each defendant responsible for a share of damages equal to its percentage of market share.

   ii. **National or local market share.** Principally because of problems with availability of data, courts tend to require market share to be calculated on a national rather than a local basis.

   iii. **Exculpatory evidence.** If a particular defendant can show that it did not produce the pills given to the plaintiff's mother, that defendant is free from liability in all jurisdictions except New York. In Hymowitz v. Eli Lilly & Co., 73 N.Y.2d 487, 541 N.Y.S.2d 941, 539 N.E.2d 1069 (1989), New York's highest court stated that participation in the overall creation of the risk would be the basis for a company's liability. That theory made it logical to compel payments by any manufacturer to any victim, even if the manufacturer were able to prove in a particular case that it had definitely not produced the doses of drug that the victim's mother had taken. In New York a company can avoid liability only by showing that its drug was never marketed for use in pregnancies.

b. **Narrow applicability of market share theory.** Plaintiffs seeking to use the market share theory in cases involving injuries other than DES-related injuries face significant resistance. Courts require strong showings that the inability to identify a particular defendant is not the fault of the plaintiff and that the defendants against whom recovery is sought all made identical products that affected victims identically. Suits for injuries from lead-based paints may meet these requirements, but no state supreme court has yet approved such a use of the market share theory.

Illustration: Shackil v. Lederle Laboratories, 116 N.J. 155, 561 A.2d 511 (1989). In a case with facts very similar to those in DES cases, New Jersey's supreme court refused to apply the market share doctrine to a vaccine-related injury—influenced perhaps by federal legislation creating an alternative method of compensation for those injuries.

I. DIFFICULTY IN IDENTIFYING THE PLAINTIFF

People exposed to a defendant's toxic product may suffer consequences that the product is known to cause. That any particular person's injury was caused by the product, however, may be impossible to prove, since the same consequences may be the result of influences other than the defendant's product. In a case involving the herbicide Agent Orange, a federal district court approved a settlement providing for payments to anyone who was exposed to the product and who suffered the consequences that the product may cause. See In Re "Agent Orange" Product Liability Litigation, 611 F. Supp. 1223 (E.D.N.Y. 1985).

REVIEW QUESTIONS AND ANSWERS

Question: Wally Watcher bought a ticket for a movie from Sarah Seller, the theater's ticket seller. He asked her how long the movie lasted, and she mistakenly told him it was 105 minutes long. Its length was actually 180 minutes. While Watcher was walking to his seat, he slipped and fell. Was Seller's conduct a cause in fact of Watcher's injury?

Answer: No. Watcher would have fallen even if Seller had bcen accurate about the length of the movie. The only connection between Seller's conduct and Watcher's fall is that both happened in the same movie theater. That connection is not adequate to establish cause in fact.

Question: Fred Foot had an infection in one of his feet. He sought treatment from a doctor, Marilyn Mild. Dr. Mild prescribed strong doses of vitamins but did not prescribe any antibiotics. The infection continued to be serious while Foot was under Dr. Mild's care. Foot's injury eventually became permanent. Foot sought damages from Dr. Mild based on a showing that the professional standard of care required treatment of his injury with antibiotics, not vitamins. If Foot established through expert testimony that proper treatment would have given him a 35-percent chance of full recovery, would he be entitled to damages from Dr. Mild?

Answer: Yes or no, depending on the jurisdiction. In many jurisdictions Foot would be barred from recovery against Dr. Mild, because he failed to show by a preponderance of the evidence that Dr. Mild's conduct was a cause in fact of the ultimate harm. This is because the ultimate harm was highly likely to have occurred no matter what type of treatment Foot had received.

A number of jurisdictions would treat this situation differently, allowing a plaintiff to receive damages for the loss of a chance. The damages allowed would be a portion of the usual damages for the injury. In this case the damages would be 35 percent of whatever amount would ordinarily have been awarded had there been proof to support a contention that the defendant's conduct actually caused the injury more probably than not.

Question: Wally Weird sought damages from a department store, on a claim that he became ill after inhaling fumes from a cleaning chemical that the store had used on the carpeting in a dressing room. He supported the claim with testimony by a person who had been a self-employed psychic for many years. The psychic testifed that he had killed a chicken, asked its entrails how Weird had become sick, and learned from the entrails that the store's fumes had harmed Weird. Was Weird's evidence adequate to present a jury question on the causation of his illness?

Answer: No. This testimony would be rejected under either the *Frye* or *Daubert* standards. The witness's scientific method was not generally accepted, as *Frye* requires, nor could it be replicated or meet other characteristics that the *Daubert* test imposes.

Question: Carla Crosser attempted to cross a street behind a car that was moving in a lane of traffic. Unfortunately, Crosser hit the back of that vehicle when its driver stopped suddenly. At the same time, another vehicle banged into Crosser and the first car, because its driver had been using a speed considerably faster than was reasonable. Would the but for test of causation allow recovery by Crosser against the two drivers? How would the substantial factor test apply?

Answer: The but for test might excuse each driver, since Crosser would likely have been hit by one of the vehicles even if the other had been operated without negligence. The substantial factor test would treat each driver's conduct as a cause in fact of Crosser's injury.

EXAM TIPS

- Always discuss cause in fact in a question that involves an accidental injury. Do not assume that it is clear. Work through how a plaintiff would attempt to establish causation with either the but for test or the substantial factor test.
- Remember that circumstantial evidence can support the plaintiff's required cause-in-fact showing.
- Where scientific evidence is involved, as in environmental injuries or injuries alleged to have been caused by drugs or toxic substances, apply both the *Frye* and *Daubert* tests.
- Market share liability has been limited to injuries from the drug DES, but plaintiffs have attempted to use the theory for other injuries, including those from asbestos and lead additives in gasoline. Be prepared to discuss how the theory might work in non-DES contexts and to discuss whether the fairness arguments that support its use in DES cases apply to other situations.
- The two-hunters situation in *Summers v. Tice* can be analogized to other situations in which more than one person has acted unreasonably and may have injured the plaintiff but clearly only one actually caused the specific injury the plaintiff suffered. For example, a question might involve a hit-and-run injury connected to a drag race.

8 PROXIMATE CAUSE

CHAPTER OVERVIEW

- To recover damages a plaintiff must show that the defendant's negligent conduct was a proximate cause of the plaintiff's injury.
- Proximate cause is usually treated as a question of fact for the jury, unless the issue in a particular case is so one-sided that it can properly be taken from the jury.
- One test for proximate cause is directness. A defendant is held responsible for all the consequences of his or her conduct that the conduct directly causes.
- Another test for proximate cause is foreseeability. A defendant is held responsible for all the consequences of his or her conduct that were reasonably foreseeable to the defendant when he or she acted negligently.
- The Restatement adopts a foreseeability test for proximate cause but applies it in a retrospective way, so that proximate causation is established if, after an injury, a person would not think it highly extraordinary that the defendant's conduct had led to the plaintiff's injury.
- An event that occurs after the defendant's conduct and that contributes to the plaintiff's harm prevents the imposition of liability on the defendant if it is characterized as a superseding event. Generally, an event is superseding if it was not foreseeable.

A. BASIC ISSUE

Even if a plaintiff establishes that a defendant's conduct was a cause in fact of an injury to the plaintiff, all jurisdictions require the plaintiff to satisfy another causation requirement: proximate cause (or legal cause). This concept enables the legal system to insulate some defendants from paying for some of the harm they inflict. Justice seems to require such protection for defendants in some circumstances.

Illustration: In Enright v. Eli Lilly & Co., 77 N.Y.2d 377, 568 N.Y.S.2d 550, 570 N.E.2d 198 (1991), the plaintiff sought damages from the defendant drug company, alleging that she had suffered physical harm because her grandmother had taken the drug DES during the pregnancy that resulted in the birth of her mother. Noting that "the rippling effects of DES exposure may extend for generations," the court held that no cause of action could be maintained. It stated, "It is our duty to confine liability within manageable limits."

There are two main doctrinal positions on proximate cause. One emphasizes the directness of a consequence; the other emphasizes the foreseeability of a consequence. In many cases doctrines about intervening causes will also be significant.

B. USUALLY A JURY QUESTION

The issue of proximate cause is usually a question for the jury. This means that the judge gives the jury an instruction that reflects the jurisdiction's proximate cause doctrines. The jury then analyzes the case itself and decides whether a proximate cause problem should prevent the plaintiff's recovery. When a case goes to the jury, the doctrinal differences among various proximate cause theories lose most of their significance, because the jury is likely to use a common-sense approach to reflect the community's sense of justice.

The proximate cause issue can be taken from the jury and decided by the court in any circumstance where the question is so clear that only one jury decision on it would be supported by the evidence.

C. DIRECTNESS TEST

One main approach to proximate cause is the directness test. Under this analysis a defendant's conduct is a proximate cause of a plaintiff's injury if the injury followed directly from the defendant's conduct. The only case in which a plaintiff's injury does not directly follow from the defendant's conduct is one in which a superseding cause occurs between the defendant's conduct and the plaintiff's injury.

1. Example: Risk a Dent, Pay for a Fire

In re Arbitration Between Polemis and Furness, Withy & Co., Ltd., 3 K.B. 560 (Court of Appeal 1921), is the leading case for the directness test. In *Polemis,* the defendant's employee carelessly dropped a plank into the hold of a ship. This conduct was negligent because it could have caused some physical harm to the ship, such as a dent. In a way that no one could have predicted, the dropping of the plank caused a spark that ignited inflammable vapors. The ship was destroyed. The court reasoned that conduct that risks harm of one type should logically be a basis for liability when the same conduct causes some different type of harm.

2. Natural and Probable Consequence Test

Many American jurisdictions use a jury instruction that includes the words *natural and probable consequence.* If a result is a natural and probable consequence of the defendant's actions, then the defendant's actions are a proximate cause of the result. This test is similar to the direct causation test, although some juries may rely on the word *probable* to add some element of foreseeability to it.

3. Policy Analysis of Directness Test

There are reasonable arguments opposed to and in support of the directness test. While the weight of scholarly opinion rejects the test, it continues to be the explicit rule in many jurisdictions. In other jurisdictions different tests may be used, but they often produce results that the directness test itself would have produced.

a. **Criticism.** Opponents of the direct causation test argue that it does not allow any reasonable limit on the scope of a defendant's liability. If a defendant's careless conduct starts a fire, for example, the defendant may be liable for the ultimate destruction of a whole city. Another problem with the test is that it may lead to overdeterrence. The deterrence goal of tort law uses the threat of liability to encourage people to take precautions against known risks. If an actor has to pay for unknown or unforeseeable risks, the actor's decisions about expenditures for safety may become inefficient.

b. **Support.** Supporters of the direct causation test argue that it is a fair response to a situation involving a blameworthy defendant and a blameless plaintiff who has suffered an unexpected loss. Moving the loss from the innocent victim and placing it on an actor whose conduct was substandard makes sense. In connection with the deterrence goal of tort law, it can be argued that extra deterrence is desirable, since the exact amount of deterrence can never really be measured. It may also be true that many defendants whose conduct causes numerous consequences are large enterprises with the ability to spread the loss.

E&A Example and Analysis

Florence Foolhardy handed a loaded gun to Lisa Little, a three-year-old child. Little dropped the gun on her foot and suffered a broken toe. Under the directness test

Foolhardy would be responsible for Little's damages, since it was negligent to give a toddler a loaded gun, and Little's injury was a direct result of Foolhardy's conduct.

D. FORESEEABILITY TEST

The other main approach to proximate cause is the foreseeability test. Using this analysis, a defendant is responsible for all the consequences of his or her actions that can be characterized as foreseeable. This test ordinarily overlaps with the basic test for negligence, since it is the existence of foreseeable risks of harm that makes conduct negligent. The scope of the risk analysis is another version of the general foreseeability test: A defendant is responsible for any consequences of his or her actions that involve the type of risk that is the basis for characterizing the defendant's conduct as negligent

1. Example: Risk a Smudge, Cause a Fire for Free

One of the leading cases for the foreseeability test is Overseas Tankship (U.K.) Ltd. v. Morts Dock & Engineering Co., Ltd., 1961 A.C. 388 (1961), known as "Wagon Mound No. 1." It is an Australian case involving the defendant's spill of furnace oil into the Sydney harbor. Proof in the case showed that the spill was negligent, because it exposed operators of businesses in the harbor to the risk that their equipment would be smudged or fouled with oil and would be impaired somewhat in its effectiveness. Unexpectedly, the oil caught fire and burned the plaintiff's dock. The appellate court held that it would be wrong to make the defendant pay for the fire damage, since (on the facts as proved in the case) no one would have anticipated that a fire would result from the spill.

2. *Palsgraf* and the Unforeseeable Plaintiff

Just as an unforeseeable type of harm is an important factor for the foreseeability test, the unforeseeability of a plaintiff is also significant. The most famous case in tort law, Palsgraf v. Long Island R.R. Co., 248 N.Y. 339, 162 N.E. 99 (1928), involved this problem. The defendant railroad's employees jostled a passenger they were trying to push onto a train, causing a package he was carrying to drop to the platform floor. The package exploded, and the plaintiff was injured at a distant point on the station platform, when a scale fell on her.

a. ***Palsgraf* majority.** Writing for the majority of a divided New York Court of Appeals, Judge Cardozo held that there could be no liability since the defendant railroad owed no duty to a person unless its employees could have foreseen that their conduct might injure that person. Negligence toward someone else (the passenger) could not be a basis for recovery by the plaintiff. In Cardozo's terms the defendant had no duty to the plaintiff.

Judge Cardozo also noted that the railroad's workers had been negligent with respect to a risk of injury to property (the passenger's package), while the plaintiff's harm was injury to a person (the plaintiff). That the defendant's negligence was defined in terms of an interest different from the interest harmed was a reinforcing argument for Cardozo's position.

b. ***Palsgraf* dissent.** Judge Andrews dissented, arguing that once a defendant has been negligent, the legal system should hold that person responsible for most of the consequences of that negligence. He recommended a foreseeability inquiry that assumes the immediate results of the negligence and then uses a variety of techniques to decide whether any further consequences are the defendant's responsibility.

   i. **Limiting factors.** Judge Andrews referred to hints that could help a judge or jury decide whether some consequences of a defendant's conduct are too remote for the defendant to have to pay for them. He suggested that useful concepts include natural and continuous sequence, directness, existence of intervening actions, and remoteness in time and space.

c. **Contemporary understanding of *Palsgraf*.** The *Palsgraf* decision is the most cited case in tort law and consequently has been used as a basis for a wide variety of positions. The majority's reasoning, although expressed in terms of duty, is consistent with the usual foreseeability approach to proximate cause. The dissent's reasoning is consistent with the direct causation approach, although it limits that approach with considerations of foreseeability and other factors.

d. **Similarity of unforeseeable plaintiff and unforeseeable injury issues.** From the viewpoint of the foreseeability approach to proximate cause, it is unfair to impose costs on a defendant for an unforeseeable result of the defendant's actions. This conclusion is the same regardless of whether the unforeseeable aspect is the type of injury suffered or the identity of the sufferer.

E. FLEXIBILITY OF THE FORESEEABILITY APPROACH

The foreseeability approach compares a characterization of what the defendant risked with a characterization of what the plaintiff suffered. If these two characterizations are phrased in very general terms, they likely seem similar and the foreseeability test is satisfied. If either of the characterizations is made in highly specific terms, there is usually a discrepancy between descriptions of what the defendant risked and what the plaintiff suffered, and the foreseeability test produces a finding of no proximate cause. Advocates (and jurors) have great freedom in this process.

1. Illustration of General Descriptions

In Hughes v. Lord Advocate, [1963] A.C. 837, a well-known case, the defendant was careless in leaving lanterns near the manhole at a work site. Young boys playing at the site went into the manhole. One of the lanterns fell into the manhole and caused a fire. As he tried to escape, the plaintiff suffered burns on his hands because the fire had heated the metal rungs of the manhole ladder. The appellate court held that the plaintiff had satisfied the proximate cause requirement since the defendant had created a risk of burns, and the plaintiff had suffered burns.

2. Illustration of Specific Descriptions

In Doughty v. Turner Mfg. Co., [1964] 1 Q.B. 518, another well-known case, the defendant's factory had a vat containing extremely hot, molten cyanide, covered with an asbestos lid. A worker dropped the lid into the vat; shortly thereafter it exploded. Prior to the accident no one had suspected that the lid could explode. The explosion sent some of the molten material into the plaintiff. The plaintiff was held to have failed to satisfy the proximate cause requirement. The risk of poorly handling the lid was that it might drop and splash the molten material onto a worker. This was significantly different, in the court's analysis, from the type of injury that occurred (molten material directed onto a worker by an explosion).

E&A EXAMPLE AND ANALYSIS

Florence Foolhardy handed a loaded gun to Lisa Little, a three-year-old child. Little dropped the gun on her foot and suffered a broken toe. Under the foreseeability test Foolhardy would probably be free from responsibility for Little's damages. The foreseeable type of harm from giving a toddler a loaded gun is an injury from a bullet (either because the toddler shoots the gun or because someone else is shot while taking the gun away from the toddler). Little's harm, a broken toe, has almost no relationship to the risks that make it wrong to give a child a gun. Therefore, under the foreseeability test Foolhardy would probably have no responsibility for Little's injury.

A court that wanted to impose liability on Foolhardy could justify a finding of proximate cause by reasoning that the harm risked in giving a child a gun is bodily harm to a person. In that analysis the harm risked is exactly equivalent to the harm that occurred.

3. Very Slight Foreseeability

The Wagon Mound incident led to another trial, with a different plaintiff, in which the evidence showed that there was very small foreseeability of fire risk from the spilled furnace oil. In Overseas Tankship (U.K.) Ltd., v. Miller Steamship Co., [1967] 1 A.C. 617 (1966), known as "Wagon Mound No. 2," the plaintiff was the owner of ships damaged in the fire. While perhaps not severe enough to have made the spilling of the oil negligent, the small risk of fire nonetheless justified imposing liability for fire losses on the oil spiller. This result would have been reached under the direct causation analysis as well, suggesting that some applications of foreseeability may be as pro-plaintiff as direct causation.

F. CONVENTIONAL APPLICATIONS OF FORESEEABILITY ANALYSIS

For a number of recurring situations, precedents control whether proximate cause does or does not exist under the foreseeability analysis.

1. Eggshell-Skull Plaintiff

A plaintiff may have a particular weakness or susceptibility to injury, such as a thin or "eggshell" skull. If this unusual trait makes the defendant's conduct hurt the plaintiff more than it would have hurt a typical person, the cost of the unforeseeably severe injury is borne by the defendant. This violates the logic of the foreseeability principle, but it is the uniform result in foreseeability jurisdictions. Courts often say that "the defendant takes the plaintiff as he finds him."

Illustration: Bartolone v. Jeckovich, 103 A.D.2d 632, 481 N.Y.S.2d 545 (1984). The defendant's negligent driving caused the plaintiff to suffer relatively minor injuries, including back strain. Prior to the accident the plaintiff had exhibited an unusually strong psychological need for regular exercise. The collision injuries led him to believe that he could no longer exercise. This belief aggravated a pre-existing psychotic illness, leading him to become withdrawn and delusional, "a life lost." A jury verdict awarding damages for all these consequences of the accident was sustained on appeal. The defendant was liable for the plaintiff's mental illness even though it was in part caused by a pre-existing weakness and was an unusually severe reaction to the traffic accident.

2. Rescuers

If a defendant's conduct puts a person in peril, rescuers' presence and rescuers' conduct are treated as foreseeable consequences of the defendant's conduct.

Illustration: Wagner v. International Ry. Co., 232 N.Y. 176, 133 N.E. 437 (1921). This opinion contains Judge Cardozo's famous sentence: "Danger invites rescue." The plaintiff suffered a serious fall while he was attempting to rescue someone (his cousin) who had fallen from an interurban railway car. Judgment for the railroad in the rescuer's suit was reversed, because the trial court's jury instruction improperly defined the duty owed to a rescuer.

a. **Injury to rescuer or person being rescued.** Conduct by a rescuer is deemed foreseeable as a consequence of negligence that creates the need for a rescue. For this reason the original tortfeasor may be liable to a rescuer or a person being rescued, for injuries related to a rescue attempt.

b. **Gross negligence not foreseeable.** A rescuer's gross negligence is usually considered unforeseeable and therefore is treated as a superseding event.

3. Same Class of Harm

Foreseeability jurisdictions may impose liability on a defendant for unforeseeable injuries if they happen to involve the same risks or forces that were the basis of defining the defendant's conduct as negligent.

Illustration: Petition of Kinsman Transport Co., 338 F.2d 708 (2nd Cir. 1964). Bad handling of two barges and a drawbridge caused flood damage to land on the banks of a river. The court approved liability to the landowners since the forces involved—bad weather, the flow of water, icy conditions, and the masses of the barges—were the same forces with respect to which the defendants had been negligent.

G. RESTATEMENT POSITION ON FORESEEABILITY

The Restatement recommends a kind of hindsight-foreseeability analysis. For unforeseeability to block liability under the Restatement, a person looking back from the harm to the defendant's conduct must consider it highly extraordinary that the conduct caused the harm. This analysis does not depend on the defendant's awareness of circumstances that may have been unknown to the defendant. The pro-plaintiff result in thin-skulled plaintiff cases is logically supported under the Restatement position.

H. INTERVENING EVENTS: GENERAL RULE

Sometimes a defendant's act inflicts an injury on a plaintiff immediately, as in a vehicular collision. There may be scenarios, however, in which natural forces or acts by other people take place between the defendant's conduct and the plaintiff's injury. When there are contributing events such as these, the defendant continues to be liable if the events are merely intervening. The defendant is absolved of responsibility if the events are characterized as "superseding." The general rule is that only unforeseeable subsequent events can be superseding causes; even those events will not insulate the defendant from liability if they lead to a type of harm that could have been foreseen.

Illustration: Derdiarian v. Felix Contracting Co., 51 N.Y.2d 308, 434 N.Y.S.2d 166, 414 N.E.2d 666 (1980). The defendant contracting company was negligent in protecting a work site. The plaintiff was injured while working there, when another defendant drove his car into the work area, hitting the plaintiff and throwing him into the air. The plaintiff fell into a kettle filled with hot enamel and was severely burned. The trial court entered judgment for the plaintiff based on a jury verdict, which was affirmed on appeal. The unusual way the actual injury occurred did not block the imposition of liability on the defendant who was responsible for the work site's negligent protection. The jury was entitled to find, as a matter of fact, that the plaintiff's injury was a natural and foreseeable result of the risk created by that defendant.

E&A Example and Analysis

ParkWorld, the operator of a parking lot, carelessly marked an exit with a sign that said "Right Turn Only," even though a person who turned right would be headed the wrong way on a one-way street. Vince Victim drove out of the lot, turned right, and was hit by a vehicle driven 35 miles over the speed limit by a driver who, after robbing a bank, was being chased by police. Victim would be able to recover from ParkWorld for bodily harm and damage to his car, since the intervening event (bad driving by another person) was foreseeable.

If Victim had turned right and been hit by a large air-conditioning unit that installers accidentally dropped from a crane high above the street, ParkWorld would still have been responsible for Victim's damages, since the intervening act was unforeseeable but the resultant injuries were exactly what ParkWorld's conduct would have been expected to cause.

ParkWorld would have been free from liability if Victim had been robbed by thieves who were able to stop his car when he turned right, and who would have been unable to stop it had he turned left. These events would have been unforeseeable and would have led to a harm different from the type of harm to be expected from ParkWorld's negligent conduct.

The following table summarizes the combinations of types of subsequent events and resultant harms, showing which combination can exculpate the defendant.

Type of Subsequent Event	*Type of Resultant Harm*	*Is the Combination Superseding or Nonsuperseding?*
Foreseeable	Foreseeable	Nonsuperseding
Foreseeable	Unforeseeable	Nonsuperseding
Unforeseeable	Foreseeable	Nonsuperseding
Unforeseeable	Unforeseeable	Superseding

I. RISK OF INTERVENING EVENT WAS PART OF THE DEFINITION OF DEFENDANT'S NEGLIGENCE

If the reason the defendant's conduct was negligent is that it made the subsequent injurious event possible or more likely, that subsequent event is treated as foreseeable. It is not a superseding cause of the plaintiff's injury.

E&A EXAMPLE AND ANALYSIS

Felicity First drove badly and blocked a road with her immobilized vehicle. Sabrina Second, who had been driving on that road, stopped to avoid hitting First's vehicle. Second was then hit by a vehicle driven by Thelma Third.

First is responsible for Second's injury. Neither Second's conduct nor Third's conduct is a superseding cause of Second's injury since one of the reasons First's conduct was negligent is that it created the risk of subsequent collisions on the road.

1. Third-Party Negligence

The likelihood that others may be negligent is sometimes a factor in characterizing a defendant's conduct as negligent. It may be negligent, for example, to locate a telephone booth close to a highway because of the risk that a careless driver may hit it and injure someone who is using it. The driver's negligence in such a case does not insulate the owner of the telephone booth from responsibility for the injury suffered by the person who is hit by the car.

J. STANDARD INTERVENING-CAUSE SITUATIONS

Certain types of intervening events are common in accidental injury cases. These situations are all treated as foreseeable. They are not superseding causes.

1. Bad Medical Treatment

Medical malpractice inflicted on someone who needed medical care because of the defendant's initial, injurious conduct is not a superseding cause of the victim's ultimate injury.

2. Extraordinarily Bad Medical Treatment

Gross negligence by a health care provider is treated as a superseding cause of injuries if the jury can divide the victim's injuries into two categories: original injury caused by the defendant and enhanced injury caused by the health care worker's gross negligence.

3. Injuries During Evasion of Initial Threat

If a plaintiff is injured while trying to avoid a risk of injury posed by the defendant's conduct, the defendant is responsible for the resulting injury.

4. Additional Injury Due to Original Harm

When a defendant's conduct makes the plaintiff weak or susceptible to future injuries, consequences of that weakness or susceptibility are the responsibility of the defendant.

5. Suicide

If the victim of the defendant's accidental, injurious behavior suffers psychological consequences due to the injury and then commits suicide, the defendant is responsible for the death. Note that the defendant is free from responsibility if the victim chooses to commit suicide while his or her mental state is not impaired due to the injury.

6. Injuries Due to Drunkenness

In many cases a defendant negligently serves liquor to a minor or to an adult who is already intoxicated, and the drunken person then injures someone else (usually by driving while drunk). The traditional common law response to these cases was to place all responsibility on the drinker. Modern decisions tend to reject the idea that the intoxicated individual is the sole cause of the ultimate harm.

a. **Commercial liquor providers.** Bars, restaurants, and stores that sell alcoholic beverages are liable in most states to the victim of a person whose drunkenness they caused by improper sales. Dram shop acts in many states require this result, and states without such statutes have reached it under a standard common law duty analysis.

b. **Social hosts.** A minority of jurisdictions impose liability on social hosts who serve liquor to a minor or to someone they should know will drive while drunk, refusing to treat the minor's or driver's conduct as a superseding cause.

Illustrations: Kelly v. Gwinnell, 96 N.J. 538, 476 A.2d 1219 (1984). This decision is the most pro-plaintiff case on this topic. Its holding has been modified by a subsequent statute. The defendant social host served liquor to an adult guest, who became intoxicated and then caused a traffic accident that injured the plaintiff. The trial court dismissed the complaint on the theory that the defendant could have no liability for the consequences of serving liquor to an adult. The supreme court remanded for trial, holding that the consequences to the plaintiff could be found to have been foreseeable if the defendant's guest was obviously intoxiated and if the defendant knew the guest would be driving.

c. **Injury to drinker.** Jurisdictions are divided on whether recovery should be permitted against the liquor provider for injuries suffered personally by the drinker.

K. THIRD-PARTY CRIMINAL CONDUCT

Many decisions hold that criminal conduct by a third party is a superseding cause because it is not foreseeable. In a number of instances, however, third parties' criminal acts are not treated as superseding because they are characterized as foreseeable.

Illustration: Watson v. Kentucky & Indiana Bridge & R.R. Co., 137 Ky. 619, 126 S.W. 146 (1910). The defendant railroad company negligently spilled gasoline into a street. A third party struck a match and caused the gasoline to ignite, injuring the plaintiff. A directed verdict for the defendant railroad was reversed; a jury should have been allowed to decide whether the third party's conduct was intentional or careless. If it had been intentional (and therefore criminal), it would properly have insulated the railroad from liability for the plaintiff's injury. If it had been negligent, the act would not have insulated the railroad from liability.

1. Theft

A defendant whose negligent conduct immobilizes a vehicle containing valuable freight may be liable for the loss of the freight to thieves, depending on the total circumstances. In some cities theft in such a situation is readily foreseeable.

Illustration: Brower v. New York Central & H.R.R., 103 A. 166 (N.J. 1918). The "natural and probable result of [the driver's abandonment of his freight because of a collision at a grade crossing] in the street of a large city was its disappearance."

2. Negligent Driving of Stolen Vehicle

Most states have decided keys-in-the-car cases. In these cases the defendant leaves a motor vehicle with its keys in the ignition, a thief steals the car, and then the thief injures the plaintiff while driving the car (sometimes while avoiding apprehension).

a. **Foreseeable, not superseding.** Some jurisdictions hold that one of the foreseeable risks of facilitating theft of a vehicle is that the thief will injure someone by driving carelessly.

b. **Superseding.** Other jurisdictions hold that the risk involved in leaving an ignition key in a vehicle is loss of the vehicle, not bad driving by a thief, and that an instance of bad driving by a thief is unforeseeable and therefore superseding.

c. **Jury decides foreseeability.** In some states the jury must decide in any particular case whether the likelihood of theft was significant enough to have made an injury by a thief foreseeable.

d. **Negligence per se.** If a statute prohibits leaving an ignition key in a vehicle, the court's interpretation of the purpose of the statute controls whether conduct by a thief is treated as superseding. If the statute's purpose is to prevent thefts, the conduct of the thief is an intervening cause that is not superseding.

L. THIRD PERSON'S FAILURE TO PREVENT HARM: USUALLY NOT SUPERSEDING

If an actor negligently creates a situation that presents a danger to the plaintiff, a third person's failure to correct what the first actor has done may be negligent but is not usually a superseding cause of some eventual harm. If the third person's failure to eliminate or decrease the risk is negligent, in a typical case both the original actor and the third person are responsible for the ultimate harm.

1. Responsibility Shifts in Rare Cases

The original wrongdoer may be protected from liability if a contract or other agreement that is not against public policy transfers full responsibility from that wrongdoer to another person. In the absence of a contract or agreement, there may still be situations in which the third person's conduct is characterized as a superseding cause. Factors that may support this characterization include the degree of danger, the degree of risk, the character and position of the third person, and the lapse of time.

a. **Conduct that is not superseding.** Most subsequent conduct is not superseding. For example, Driver One negligently hits a pedestrian and leaves him or her on the street, seriously injured. Driver Two passes by and ignores the pedestrian. The pedestrian then dies. Even if Driver Two is a person who has a duty to render aid in this type of situation, Driver Two's conduct is not treated as a superseding cause of the pedestrian's death.

b. **Responsibility shift by agreement.** Agreements can provide for shifts in responsibility. For example, a landlord leases a building with dangerous defects to a business operator who plans to use it as a theater. The lease obligates the lessee to repair the building before admitting members of the public. The lessee fails to make the repairs, and a member of the public is injured. The landlord has no liability, since the agreement placed responsibility for the repairs on the theater operator.

c. **Responsibility shift reflecting degrees of fault and status of third person.** Courts sometimes treat subsequent conduct as superseding because of the degree of fault it represents and the relationship of the subsequent actor to the victim. For example, a construction company's worker carelessly leaves an explosive blasting cap near a construction site. A child picks it up and carries it home. The child's parent sees it and takes it away from the child, knowing that it is extremely dangerous. The parent puts it on a table. The child takes it from the table to play with it and is injured when it explodes. Some courts would likely hold that the parent's conduct was a superseding cause of the child's injury, basing that holding on the passage of time between the worker's carelessness and on the parent's carelessness and the appropriateness of recognizing parents' obligations to take care of their children.

REVIEW QUESTIONS AND ANSWERS

Question: Dan Driver drove a truck carrying a shipment of tranquilizer capsules and was involved in a collision due to his negligence. Many cartons of drugs fell from the truck and were run over by various vehicles in the aftermath of the accident. A large number of the capsules fell onto the street and were crushed. Sam Sweeper, a city sanitation worker was ordered to clean up debris at the site. He became ill from inhaling an overdose of the drug. If Sweeper sought damages from the trucking company that employed Driver, how would courts analyze the proximate cause element of his case?

Answer: In a jurisdiction that uses the directness test, a jury would probably be permitted to find that Driver's bad driving was a proximate cause of Sweeper's injury. In a jurisdiction that uses the foreseeability test, it is also possible that a jury would be permitted to find that physical injury to someone who works in the street was a foreseeable consequence of Driver's bad driving. An opposite result could be sustained, if a jury concluded that drug overdoses were not a foreseeable consequence of bad driving. Sweeper would not likely be treated as an unforeseeable plaintiff, since he was similar to a rescuer whose presence would be treated as foreseeable in the aftermath of an accident.

Question: On the same facts, how would courts analyze the proximate cause element of a suit by Sweeper against the drug manufacturer, if Sweeper were to show that it had packed the capsules in containers that were not properly child-proofed?

Answer: In a jurisdiction that uses the directness test, a jury would probably be prohibited from finding that the drug company's packaging was a proximate cause of Sweeper's injury, since Sweeper was hurt long after the drug company had done its packaging, Sweeper was hurt far from the scene of the drug company's packaging, and bad driving by Driver might be treated as a factor that interrupted any direct link between the drug company's conduct and Sweeper's injury. In a jurisdiction that uses the foreseeability test, it is unlikely that a jury would be permitted to find that physical injury to someone who works in the street was a foreseeable consequence of bad packaging. Foreseeable victims of bad drug packaging were drug users and people with access to the drugs in users' homes. Sweeper is a plaintiff far outside these categories. Sweeper would probably be treated as an unforeseeable plaintiff, since his interaction with the drug company's product came about in a highly unusual way, and he was not in the class of intended users of the product.

Question: Helen Hasty ran through a crowd in the lobby of a theater and accidentally knocked down Vanessa Vulnerable. Hasty's conduct was unreasonable, since it created the risk that a person in the lobby could be knocked down. Unbeknownst to Hasty, Vulnerable suffered from a disease that made her bones brittle. Vulnerable was permanently disabled as a consequence of Hasty's collision with her. Would Hasty's conduct be treated as a proximate cause of Vulnerable's serious injury?

Answer: Yes. Hasty must take the plaintiff as she finds her. Vulnerable's unusual weakness became the responsibility of the tortfeasor who wrongly created a circumstance in which that weakness led to an unusually severe consequence.

Question: About a foot away from Wilma Weak, Stuart Slob sneezed without covering his mouth. Weak had very low resistance to infections and suffered a severe illness as a consequence of having been sneezed at. Would the eggshell-skull-plaintiff doctrine allow Weak to recover damages from Slob?

Answer: No. The rule that a defendant takes the plaintiff as the defendant finds him or her controls the types of consequences for which a defendant is responsible in a case where the defendant has been negligent. In deciding whether Slob was negligent, his conduct would be evaluated with a reasonable prudent person test. While it might be disgusting to sneeze as Slob did, a jury would be very unlikely to characterize his conduct as negligent. Since the conduct would not be negligent, it could not be a basis for imposing liability on Slob for any consequences of the conduct, regardless of what proximate cause rules a jurisdiction might use in cases where a defendant has acted negligently.

Question: The owner of a gas station violated a statute by selling gasoline to a customer who put it in a can that was not a properly vented container designed for carrying and storing gasoline. The customer used the gasoline to set fire to a small store, causing a loss of property and injuring some people. Would the gas station's conduct be a proximate cause of those harms?

Answer: No. The customer's intentional criminal conduct was not foreseeable, even though loss of property and some personal injuries could have been foreseeable consequences of selling gasoline in a container that was unsafe. A criminal's intentional criminal conduct usually blocks imposition of liability for its results on another actor who may have been negligent in some other way that is related to the plaintiff's harm.

EXAM TIPS

- Remember to treat proximate cause separately from legal cause.
- Proximate cause is almost always a jury question. Therefore, your analysis should not announce your own conclusion about whether a case can satisfy the proximate cause requirement. You should write your answer in terms of whether a jury could find proximate cause under the standards that control it.
- The main concept in modern proximate cause analysis is the foreseeability of harm. Be aware that you can describe harms with varying degrees of specificity. If you describe with narrow detail the harm that a defendant's conduct risked, it may look like a resulting injury to the plaintiff was unusual and not foreseeable. If you describe the harm risked very broadly (like "injury to a person"), the apparent foreseeability of the plaintiff's injury will be greater.
- Intervening events that occur between the defendant's negligent act and the plaintiff's injury sometimes protect the defendant from responsibility. The crucial element is foreseeability of a criminal act. Be alert for facts in an exam question that increase or decrease the likelihood of the criminal act.
- Remember the conventional recurring situations for which common law has standard proximate-cause answers. Bad medical care following an accident is usually treated as foreseeable. Intentional criminal conduct is usually treated as not foreseeable.

9 Multiple Party Cases

Chapter Overview

- Joint and several liability determines each defendant's responsibility for a judgment in a multiple defendant case. When two or more defendants cause a plaintiff's injury, if there is no factual way to assign responsibility for particular parts of the injury to particular defendants, each defendant is individually responsible for the entire judgment.
- Contribution is a cause of action available to a defendant who has paid more than his or her fair share of a judgment under the joint and several liability doctrine. A contribution action allows the defendant to be reimbursed by other defendants who are responsible for the plaintiff's injury.
- A number of states have restricted or eliminated joint and several liability.
- Where joint and several liability does not exist, no defendant can seek contribution because no defendant pays more than his or her share of the plaintiff's damages.
- When a party with potential liability settles with the plaintiff, the settling party is protected from contribution liability to any other party which eventually loses the litigation and pays a judgment to the plaintiff.
- When a plaintiff who was injured by the actions of more than one party settles a claim against one party but wins a judgment against another party, the judgment is reduced in some way to reflect the value of the plaintiff's settlement.

- Some jurisdictions reduce a plaintiff's judgment by the exact dollar amount of any settlements the plaintiff has received. Other jurisdictions reduce the judgment by an amount that reflects the percentage responsibility of the settling party.
- Indemnity is losing defendant's right to complete reimbursement of any damages paid, enforceable against some other actor whose responsibility for the plaintiff's harm is significantly greater than the defendant's responsibility.

A. ISSUES IN MULTIPLE PARTY CASES

When two or more defendants have been involved in causing a plaintiff's injury, contemporary tort law recognizes several important issues and treats them in a variety of ways.

Traditionally, each defendant was subject to liability for the entire amount of a plaintiff's indivisible damages under the doctrine of joint and several liability. At present, some states have abolished that doctrine and others have modified it.

Where joint and several liability applies, each jurisdiction has rules about how much financial responsibility each defendant ultimately bears. If a defendant pays the plaintiff more than that amount, the defendant is entitled to bring a contribution action against any other defendant with whom he or she is jointly and severally liable. In the contribution action the overpaying defendant seeks reimbursement from any underpaying defendant.

Plaintiffs often accept settlement payments from one or more of the defendants in a multiple defendant case. Jurisdictions differ on how the settlement is reflected in the judgment, if any, the plaintiff obtains against any nonsettling defendant.

B. INDIVISIBLE INJURIES

Joint and several liability is a traditional doctrine for multiple defendant cases that means each defendant is subject to joint liability or joint plus individual liability. It applies to damages for a plaintiff's indivisible injuries and makes each defendant subject to a judgment for the whole amount of the damages.

1. Divisibility of Injuries in General

Because joint and several liability applies only to indivisible injuries, defining an injury as either divisible or indivisible can be highly significant.

a. **Indivisible injury definition.** An injury is indivisible if more than one defendant caused the injury and no one can prove by a preponderance of the evidence that a particular defendant is responsible individually for a particular part of the injury.

b. **Divisible injury definition.** A plaintiff's injuries are divisible if there is a way to show by a preponderance of the evidence that a particular defendant is responsible individually for a particular part of the injuries.

E&A Example and Analysis

If two drivers collide with someone, the victim's damages are likely to be indivisible, since there is no way to ascertain which car's impact caused which parts of the injuries.

If two drivers hit the victim, but one runs over the victim's arm and the other runs over the victim's feet, the victim's injuries will likely be divisible, since proof can show that one driver harmed the arm and the other driver harmed the feet.

---

c. **Action in concert.** People who agree to carry out a particular type of conduct or to work to achieve a particular result are described as acting in concert. Each person is responsible for any harms that the joint effort may cause. Drag racing is a typical example of action in concert.

d. **Environmental harms.** Nuisance cases and other environmental harm cases may involve conduct by more than one defendant that impairs someone's land or affects some natural resource. Scientific evidence may allow apportionment, or division, of harm that seems at first to be indivisible.

e. **Death.** Death is classically considered an indivisible injury.

f. **Fire loss.** The loss of property due to fire is also considered an indivisible injury.

g. **Burden of proof on divisibility.** In cases where it is theoretically possible to divide the plaintiff's harm into categories or amounts caused by each of two or more defendants, the burden of proof on divisibility of damages is usually on the defendant who seeks to avoid responsibility for the entire injury.

C. VARIED TREATMENTS OF JOINT AND SEVERAL LIABILITY

Where two or more defendants contribute to an indivisible injury, the majority of jurisdictions apply some form of the joint and several liability doctrine.

1. Traditional Rule

When two or more defendants contribute to a plaintiff's injury, each is subject to a judgment for the entire amount. The plaintiff is allowed to enforce the judgment against any one or more of the defendants and can collect all or a part of the amount from any one of them. Note, however, that the plaintiff is allowed only to collect a total of money equal to the total judgment.

Illustration: Coney v. J.L.G. Industries, Inc., 97 Ill. 2d 104, 73 Ill. Dec. 337, 454 N.E.2d 197 (1983). The court rejected the argument that adoption of comparative negligence required it to abrogate the traditional joint and several liability rule. It justified the rule on a number of theories, including the ideas that a plaintiff's injury is still indivisible even though various defendant's shares of blame for it can be identified, and that a blameless plaintiff deserves the greatest possible chance to recover full damages. (An Illinois statute subsequently rejected the application of joint and several liability to any defendant whose share of responsibility is less than 25 percent.)

E&A Example and Analysis

Harry Hurt was injured during medical treatment. He sought damages from Susanna Surgeon, a surgeon, and Scalpelco, a manufacturer of scalpels. The jury found both Surgeon and Scalpelco reponsible for Hurt's harm, and set Hurt's damages at $100,000. Under traditional joint and several liability principles, the judge would award Hurt a judgment for $100,000 against Surgeon and Scalpelco. Hurt could collect all of the $100,000 or any part of it from either defendant. Hurt would not be allowed to collect a total greater than $100,000.

2. **Applied to Economic Damages, Not to Noneconomic Damages**

   Some jurisdictions now require the jury to identify separate amounts of damages for economic and noneconomic damages. Economic damages are amounts for categories such as past and future medical expenses and lost income. Noneconomic damages are typically amounts awarded for pain and suffering. In these jurisdictions joint and several liability applies to economic damages. There is no joint and several liability for non-economic damages.

3. **Particular Limitations**

   Tort reform legislation in many states has led to a wide array of treatments of joint and several liability.

   a. **Applies to small cases.** The doctrine applies only to economic damages for most cases but applies to all damages for cases where the total judgment is a statutorily specified amount, such as $25,000 or less.

   b. **Ceiling for defendants with small responsibility.** The doctrine may apply in general, but a party whose percentage of responsibility (established under comparative fault principles) is less than a statutorily specified percent is subject to joint and several liability only up to a share of the judgment equal to a specified multiple of his or her percentage of responsibility.

c. **Limited to 51-percent-responsible defendant.** Some jurisdictions apply the doctrine only to a defendant whose responsibility (set under comparative negligence principles) is 51 percent or more.

d. **Environmental torts.** Some jurisdictions have abolished the doctrine generally but have retained it for environmental torts.

e. **Acts in concert.** Some jurisdictions have abolished the doctrine generally but have retained it for cases in which the plaintiff can establish that the defendants acted in concert.

4. Abolished

About ten states have completely eliminated joint and several liability. In these states a factual finding is made assigning a percentage of responsibility to each defendant. Each defendant is liable for a judgment equal to the plaintiff's total damages multiplied by his or her percentage share of responsibility.

Illustration: Bartlett v. New Mexico Welding Supply Co., 98 N.M. 152, 646 P.2d 579 (N.M. Ct. App. 1982). The court rejected the joint and several liability doctrine, holding that the adoption of comparative negligence made the concept of indivisible injury obsolete. It also rejected the suggestion that plaintiffs deserved protection against the possible insolvency of defendants. The court stated that no such protection was available to a plaintiff in a case involving only a single defendant and that there was no reason to alter that concept because a case happened to involve two or more defendants.

D. CONTRIBUTION

Under the doctrine of joint and several liability, a plaintiff chooses to enforce a judgment against any one or more of the defendants. A plaintiff ordinarily enforces as much of the judgment as possible against whichever defendant has assets that are easiest to reach. Contribution is the process through which a defendant can sue other defendants to be reimbursed if he or she has paid "too much" of the joint and several judgment to the plaintiff. Contribution suits may also be maintained against defendants who could have been named in the plaintiff's original suit but who are not parties to that action.

Illustration: Knell v. Feltman, 85 U.S. App. D.C. 22, 174 F.2d 662 (1949). The plaintiffs were passengers in a car driven by Knell and were injured when Knell's car collided with a taxi owned by Feltman. A judgment was entered for the plaintiffs against Feltman, based on findings that the driver of Feltman's taxi and Knell were both negligent. The court also entered a judgment in favor of Feltman against Knell for contribution, requiring Knell to reimburse Feltman for a one-half share of the judgment if Feltman paid it. The appellate court affirmed this judgment, noting that Knell should not escape responsibility for the incident merely because his passengers declined to sue him.

E. DOCTRINAL RESTRICTIONS ON CONTRIBUTION

Certain threshold requirements may limit the availability of contribution.

1. Not Available to Intentional Tortfeasors

In most states a defendant whose liability is based on intentional misconduct is forbidden to seek contribution.

2. Not Available from Actors with No Liability to Original Plaintiff

A defendant may bring a contribution action only against other actors who are liable or who could have been liable to the original plaintiff.

a. **Immune actors.** An injured worker ordinarily has no tort cause of action against his or her employer because of workers' compensation statutes. If a worker is injured in an accident that involves both a defective machine and careless conduct by the employer, the worker can seek damages from the manufacturer of the machine. That manufacturer has no contribution action against the employer, because the employer has no liability to the worker.

Intrafamilial immunity provides another instance in which a defendant who has liability to the plaintiff may be barred from seeking contribution from another participant in the plaintiff's injury. This is the result if, for example, the defendant is a stranger to the plaintiff but the other participant in causing the injury is the plaintiff's parent.

F. AMOUNT OF CONTRIBUTION PERMITTED

Jurisdictions differ in defining a defendant's proper share of the judgment. This definition controls the amount of contribution to which a defendant may be entitled, since a defendant is entitled to reimbursement only for the amount a defendant has paid the plaintiff in excess of the defendant's "proper" share of the judgment.

1. Common Law Rule: No Contribution

At common law contribution was prohibited.

2. Statutory and Judicial Developments

Most states that permit joint and several liability now allow contribution, as a result of either statutory enactments or judicial decisions.

a. **Equal shares.** Prior to the adoption of comparative negligence, joint and several liability was universally imposed and jurisdictions that allowed contribution defined each defendant's proper share of liability by dividing the total judgment equally among all the defendants.

b. **Percent-of-responsibility shares.** In many comparative negligence jurisdictions that have retained joint and several liability, any defendant who has paid an amount larger than his or her percentage share of the judgment is entitled to seek reimbursement from other defendants for the extra amount paid.

E&A EXAMPLE AND ANALYSIS

In a two-defendant case prior to adoption of comparative negligence, each defendant was responsible for half the judgment. A defendant who paid more than half was entitled to seek reimbursement of the extra amount from the other defendant. If a plaintiff won a judgment of $100,000 against two defendants and collected $80,000 from one and $20,000 from the other, the one who paid $80,000 was entitled to contribution from the other in the amount of $30,000. If the one who paid $80,000 actually collected the $30,000 in contribution from the other, each defendant's outlay to satisfy the judgment equaled $50,000 (half the total judgment).

In a two-defendant case under comparative negligence, where Defendant One was 60 percent responsible, Defendant Two was 40 percent responsible, and the plaintiff's judgment was for $100,000, the plaintiff could collect the entire judgment from Defendant One. If that happened, Defendant One would be entitled to contribution from Defendant Two. The amount of contribution would be $40,000, since Defendant One's percentage share of responsibility required Defendant One to pay $60,000, but the plaintiff (under joint and several liability) actually collected $100,000 from Defendant One.

c. **No contribution where joint and several liability is abolished.** Many jurisdictions have eliminated or restricted joint and several liability. Since contribution is only possible where joint and several liability has led to a defendant's paying more than his or her share to a plaintiff, there can never be contribution in a situation where joint and several liability does not apply.

G. SETTLEMENTS

The plaintiff may reach a settlement with one of the parties that caused an injury and accept a payment in exchange for releasing that party from liability. This process involves two conflicting goals of tort law. First, tort law seeks to encourage settlements, which resolve cases more quickly and cost the state and the parties less than litigation does. Second, tort law protects the nonsettling defendant from bearing an unfair amount of responsibility for the injury. Common law approaches did not do a good job of balancing these goals. Modern statutes take many approaches to the problems.

1. Common Law

A party who settled with the plaintiff was still liable for contribution in a lawsuit brought by some other party who ultimately paid a judgment to the plaintiff. Note that under this rule, there was very little incentive to settle, since a party who made a settlement was subject to additional liability.

A party who settled was also entitled to contribution from other parties if he or she could prove that those defendants could have been liable to the plaintiff and that the settlement amount paid to the plaintiff was reasonable.

2. Modern Statutes

Most states now control contribution by statute, in many cases with versions of Model Acts.

a. **1955 Uniform Contribution Among Tortfeasors Act.** This act provides that a release or covenant not to sue does not release any other tortfeasor from liability. It provides that any judgment ultimately won by the plaintiff must be reduced by the amount of any good-faith settlement. It also provides that a settling party has no liability for contribution to any other tortfeasor involved in the case.

   i. **California interpretation.** California decisions have interpreted the good-faith provision of this act to allow a nonsettling defendant to show that a settlement was not reached in good faith. A trial court may find that a settlement was not in good faith if it is significantly outside the normal range of settlements for similar suits. A finding of bad faith makes the settling defendant liable for contribution.

b. **1977 Uniform Comparative Fault Act.** This act is similar to the 1955 act, except that the amount by which any plaintiff's judgment must be reduced is not the amount of the settlement payment. The plaintiff's judgment is reduced by an amount equal to the released party's share of responsibility. Under the act a factual finding establishes the share of responsibility for each actor involved in the plaintiff's injury, regardless of whether the actor has settled with the plaintiff.

   The act also contains a complicated method of determining the amount of contribution to which an overpaying defendant is entitled. The act's goal is to have each defendant pay a sum equal to the plaintiff's damages multiplied by that defendant's share of responsibility. If the plaintiff enforces the total judgment against a single defendant, that defendant is entitled to contribution from any other defendant who has paid less than his or her share. If any defendant is insolvent or otherwise judgment-proof, that defendant's share is deemed uncollectible. The burden of the uncollectible share is required, under the act, to be spread among all the other parties in the case, including the plaintiff. Each of those parties bears a part of the uncollectible share based on his or her fraction of the shares of responsibility assigned by the jury to the plaintiff and all solvent defendants. In this situation a defendant is entitled to contribution only if that defendant has made a payment exceeding the total of his or her original responsibility plus his or her share of any uncollectible amount.

E&A EXAMPLE AND ANALYSIS

Under the 1977 act a jury that finds the plaintiff has damages of $120,000 might assign responsibility for the injuries among the plaintiff and three defendants as follows:

Plaintiff	25 percent
Defendant One	25 percent
Defendant Two	25 percent
Defendant Three	25 percent

The plaintiff is entitled to recover $90,000 ($120,000 reduced by 25 percent to reflect the plaintiff's own share of responsibility). If the plaintiff collects the full $90,000 from Defendant One, Defendant One becomes entitled to contribution from Defendants Two and Three: Each would owe $30,000 to Defendant One.

If Defendant Three is insolvent, his or her share of the judgment is treated as uncollectible. Responsibility for that amount is divided among all remaining parties to whom the jury assigned shares of responsibility. The Plaintiff, Defendant One, and Defendant Two are the remaining parties. The uncollectible share is assigned according to the ratio of each remaining party's individual share to the total of all the remaining parties' shares. In this example, the total shares of the remaining parties equal 75 percent. Plaintiff's proportion of that amount is one-third (plaintiff's 25 percent is one-third of 75 percent), Defendant One's share is one-third, and Defendant Two's share is one-third. Plaintiff is responsible for one-third of the uncollectible $30,000; Defendant One is also responsible for one-third, as is Defendant Two. One third of $30,000 is $10,000. Thus, Plaintiff is entitled to recover only $80,000. Defendant One is required to pay $40,000, and Defendant Two is required to pay $40,000. If Defendant One pays the full $90,000 to Plaintiff, Defendant One becomes entitled to reimbursement of $10,000 from Plaintiff and $40,000 from Defendant Two.

3. Mary Carter Settlements

Mary Carter settlement agreements take their name from the first case in which one was used, Booth v. Mary Carter Paint Co., 202 So. 2d 8 (Fla. Dist. Ct. App. 1967). In this type of agreement, the settling defendant continues to be a party and to litigate in an effort to reduce or avoid a share of liability. The agreement requires the settling defendant to pay the plaintiff a certain amount of money unless the plaintiff's ultimate recovery from the nonsettling defendant reaches or exceeds a specified amount. The settling defendant has incentive to introduce evidence and cross-examine witnesses with two goals: to make the nonsettling defendant seem bad and to make the plaintiff seem good. These goals make it more likely that the plaintiff's recovery against the nonsettling defendant will be large enough to cancel the settling defendant's obligation to pay a settlement amount.

a. **Disclosure.** Most jurisdictions require that the parties involved in a Mary Carter settlement reveal it to the court, and some permit its existence to be disclosed to the jury. These restrictions are meant to minimize the effects of the settling defendant's unusual motives.

b. **Prohibition.** Some jurisdictions prohibit these agreements on the theory that they distort the ordinary judicial process.

   Illustration: Elbaor v. Smith, 845 S.W.2d 240 (Tex. 1992). The court stated that a Mary Carter agreement encourages the settling defendant to help the plaintiff with discovery material, challenges to jurors, witness examination, and other trial tactics. These consequences are not outweighed by the benefit to the judicial system of encouraging settlements. For this reason the Texas court prohibited such agreements.

H. INDEMNITY: GENERAL RULE

Indemnity is a complete transfer of the entire burden of a judgment that one party has paid. It transfers the cost from that party to another party. This process seems fair in situations where a defendant has been liable to the plaintiff even though the defendant was completely free from fault. It is also allowed, sometimes, where two defendants have been at fault but the fault of one defendant was drastically less than the fault of the other.

I. INDEMNITY AND COMPARATIVE FAULT

As jurisdictions have adopted comparative negligence and become more familiar with assigning percentage shares of responsibility to various actors involved in a plaintiff's injury, some jurisdictions have developed comparative or proportional indemnity principles. Under these doctrines a defendant is able to shift some but not all of his or her liability to another defendant. The amount to be shifted is calculated with reference to the comparative responsibility of each defendant.

1. Gross Negligence as a Basis for Indemnity

A minority view, developed prior to the adoption of comparative fault, allows a defendant whose negligence was relatively slight to obtain full indemnity from another defendant whose negligence was gross or whose misconduct was intentional.

J. CONTRACTUAL AND JUDICIALLY IMPOSED INDEMNITY

In some business arrangements the parties provide for indemnity in their contract. This is common in construction contracts between contractors and their subcontractors, for example. The following examples illustrate common instances of judicially imposed indemnity.

1. Vicarious Liability

An employer is completely responsible for torts committed against a plaintiff by an employee if the injury occurs within the scope of the worker's employment. This liability is imposed without regard to fault by the employer, even if the employer selected and supervised the employee perfectly. When an employer pays a judgment in this situation, the worker is liable to the employer for the full amount.

2. Failure to Discover Contractor's Hazard

If a contractor acts negligently and creates a dangerous condition on someone's land, in many jurisdictions the landowner is entitled to indemnity from the contractor if the landowner pays a judgment to someone who was injured due to the dangerous condition. Indemnity is available whether or not a reasonable landowner should have discovered the hazard.

3. Failure to Discover Manufacturer's Hazard

Under traditional doctrines indemnity is available if a customer obtains damages from a retailer because the customer was injured by a flaw in something the retailer sold. The retailer is entitled to indemnity from the manufacturer, whether or not the retailer could have discovered the flaw with a reasonable inspection. A modern view in these circumstances allows indemnity only if the retailer was free from fault.

4. Liability for Subsequent Tortfeasor's Conduct

Partial indemnity is sometimes available where a defendant's conduct harms a plaintiff but the damages are increased by another party's subsequent negligence. This scenario is exemplified when a first defendant's bad driving is followed by a second defendant's medical malpractice. Some jurisdictions allow partial indemnity paid by the second defendant to the first if it is possible to evaluate the proportion of the plaintiff's damages that (although paid by the first defendant) were caused by the second defendant's conduct.

Review Questions and Answers

Question: Walter Walker slipped and fell as he was walking across a busy street. Frank First negligently drove his car over Walker's right arm. At the same time Sandra Second drove her car over Walker's left foot. Walker's arm and foot were injured. Would traditional joint and several liability doctrines make First and Second each responsible for the full amount of Walker's injuries?

Answer: No. The injuries are separate, and each defendant can be associated with the particular injury he or she inflicted. Therefore, joint and several liability would not apply.

Question: If Frank First and Sandra Second had run over Walter Walker at the same time, causing injuries that led to Walker's death, would traditional joint and several liability doctrines make First and Second each responsible for the full wrongful death damages for Walker's death?

Answer: Yes. Death is an indivisible injury, and jurisdictions that recognize joint and several liability would apply it to make First and Second each responsible for the full amount of damages for Walker's death.

Question: Consider a case in a comparative negligence jurisdiction where a plaintiff was found to have no responsibility for his injury, one defendant was found to have been 60 percent at fault, and a second defendant was found to have been 40 percent at fault. Damages were set at $100,000. If the plaintiff enforced the entire judgment against the first defendant, would that defendant be entitled to contribution from the other defendant?

Answer: Yes. The first defendant would be entitled to a payment from the second defendant to reduce the first defendant's total outlay to $60,000 (representing the 60 percent of the injury the jury assigned to that defendant).

Question: Assume that: 1. a plaintiff was harmed by the negligent conduct of two individuals; 2. the plaintiff settled a negligence claim against one of them for $100,000; 3. the plaintiff sued the other negligent actor; 4. the jury found that the nonsettling defendant was liable to the plaintiff; and 5. the jury set the plaintiff's damages at $600,000. How would the court calculate the amount of judgment to award to the plaintiff?

Answer: The court would take account of the amount the plaintiff had received in settlement. In most places the plaintiff's award would be reduced by the actual amount the plaintiff had received in settlement. This would lead to a judgment of $500,000. In some places the plaintiff's recovery against the nonsettling defendant would be reduced by whatever share of responsibility the jury assigned to the settling defendant. In that type of jurisdiction, if the percentage of responsibility the jury had assigned to the settling defendant was, for example, 30 percent, the court would subtract 30 percent from the damages found by the jury and award the remaining amount to the plaintiff in judgment against the nonsettling defendant. That would lead to a judgment for the plaintiff of $420,000 ($600,000 minus 30 percent of $600,000).

EXAM TIPS

- The distinction between divisible and indivisible injuries is important. No joint and several liability concerns arise in connection with divisible injuries, since each defendant is required to pay only for the precise identifiable harm he or she committed.
- Be prepared to argue for and against the retention of traditional joint and several liability. Support for the doctrine usually emphasizes the plaintiff's need for full recovery; the opposition usually emphasizes the unfairness of requiring a defendant to bear a cost that was inflicted by someone else (the same unfairness that a plaintiff suffers by failing to collect part of a judgment).
- Among jurisdictions that have limited or rejected the doctrine of joint and several liability in general, it usually remains effective for defendants who act in concert and for some other types of actions as well, such as environmental and toxic torts.
- Be aware that jurisdictions differ in how they treat settlements. Some subtract the actual amount of the settlement from damages that would otherwise be awarded to the plaintiff from a nonsettling defendant. Others subtract whatever amount is represented by the settling defendant's percentage of responsibility.

10 DUTY AND LIMITED-DUTY RULES

CHAPTER OVERVIEW

- In most injury cases courts find that the defendant owed the plaintiff a duty of reasonable care.
- Limited duty rules are important exceptions to the general obligation people have to protect others from foreseeable harms.
- Liability for negligent infliction of emotional distress is controlled by a variety of limited duty rules.
- In many situations a person who could help another avoid injury has no duty to furnish that help. Where there is a special relationship, one person may be obligated to act reasonably in a situation where assistance could be beneficial.
- Liability for negligent conduct that inflicts only economic losses on a plaintiff is imposed only in rare circumstances.
- Common law doctrines protected negligent actors from responsibility for harms their conduct inflicted on a fetus, unless the fetus was born alive.
- Modern doctrines recognize several causes of action for prenatal injuries and for wrongful conception, wrongful birth, and wrongful life.

A. FUNCTION OF DUTY IN TORT LAW

To recover damages for an injury a plaintiff must show that the defendant had a duty to avoid inflicting that type of harm on the plaintiff or a person like the plaintiff. The duty concept is primarily important as a limitation on defendants' obligations in certain cases. For some types of cases, there are no-duty or limited-duty rules.

1. Typical Definition

Courts typically state that one has a duty to avoid creating risks of foreseeable harm to foreseeable individuals. The duty concept is usually expressed in terms of general classes of plaintiffs, defendants, and injuries. The plaintiff must establish that the relationship between the plaintiff and defendant is one in which the legal system requires the defendant to protect the plaintiff from the type of injury suffered.

2. Duty Usually Present

In most cases where a defendant's conduct causes a noticeable harm to a plaintiff, the defendant is under a duty to avoid inflicting that harm. In the vast majority of vehicular accident and medical malpractice cases, for example, the duty of the defendants is clear.

3. Duty as a Limitation on Liability

A no-duty rule establishes that a defendant had no duty to avoid inflicting injury on a particular plaintiff or that a defendant had no duty to avoid inflicting a particular type of injury on anyone. In addition to no-duty rules, there are limited-duty rules that minimize the care particular types of defendants must take with respect to possible injuries that some types of plaintiffs might suffer.

a. **Rationale and effect of no-duty and limited-duty rules.** These rules are supported by many of the same social factors that led to the development of proximate cause doctrines. They can protect defendants whose conduct causes harm from having to pay for the harm. Courts make these rules in situations where making defendants pay for the consequences of their conduct seems unfair, for example, where damages are very difficult to prove or are so attenuated from the defendants' conduct that leaving their costs with the victims seems fairer than transfering them to the defendants.

b. **Overlap between duty and proximate cause.** Courts can use duty and proximate cause concepts for the same purpose: to limit the consequences of a defendant's actions for which the defendant is required to pay. *Palsgraf* is a famous example (See Chapter 8, section D). The majority used a duty analysis, holding that the railroad had no duty to the plaintiff, who had been so far away from the railroad's employees that they could not have foreseen their conduct causing her any harm. The dissenting opinion would have used proximate cause theories to determine whether the remote plaintiff was entitled to damages.

B. COURT AND JURY ROLES

In theory the issue of duty is a legal question to be decided by a court. Where factual questions are related to the duty inquiry, the trial judge frames jury instructions based on the jurisdiction's legal doctrines about duty.

E&A EXAMPLE AND ANALYSIS

A typical limited-duty rule states that a defendant has no obligation to protect a plaintiff from "mere" economic harm due to a defendant's negligence. In other words, unless the defendant's negligence causes physical harm to the plaintiff in addition to the economic harm, the defendant has no liability. In a case involving an economic injury suffered by a business allegedly because of negligence by a defendant, if a jurisdiction follows that limited-duty rule, the judge instructs the jury to decide whether the defendant's conduct caused any physical harm to the plaintiff. Note that the judge does not ask the jury to decide whether defendants should be obligated to use reasonable care to protect plaintiffs from mere economic harm. That is a duty question, controlled by the jurisdiction's common law precedents.

C. EMOTIONAL DISTRESS

Human beings can suffer emotional distress from many causes. If someone's negligent conduct causes a person to suffer merely emotional distress, the victim may have no cause of action, because there is no duty to avoid negligent conduct that leads another person to suffer only emotional consequences. This general limitation on duty applies to many cases, but in a number of circumstances the limitation is withdrawn and defendants are exposed to liability.

1. Intentional Misconduct

Courts recognize a cause of action for intentional infliction of emotional distress. That cause of action is not restricted by the limited-duty rules for negligent infliction of emotional distress.

2. "Parasitic" Damages

When a defendant's conduct is negligent because it involves an improper risk of harm other than emotional distress and the plaintiff suffers physical injuries as a result of that conduct, the plaintiff is entitled to recover for emotional distress associated with the injury. These emotional distress damages are sometimes called "parasitic" damages since they are allowed only in combination with other damages for nonemotional harms.

3. Initial Physical Impact

Under traditional common law principles recovery for emotional distress was allowed only if the plaintiff could show an impact as part of the allegedly tortious conduct by the defendant. This doctrine led to many strange decisions, considering whether the impact requirement was satisfied by dust, spit, vibrations, or other types of contact inflicted on a plaintiff by a defendant.

4. Zone of Danger (Near-Miss Cases)

Recovery for emotional distress is now allowed in some cases where the plaintiff suffers no initial physical impact or harm but where the defendant's conduct does cause the plaintiff to have a harmful emotional reaction. The plaintiff is entitled to damages for this negligently inflicted emotional distress if the plaintiff was in a zone of danger created by the defendant's conduct. "Zone of danger" means an area in which the plaintiff might have suffered actual physical harm from the defendant's conduct. Zone of danger cases can be thought of as near-miss cases.

Illustration: Daley v. LaCroix, 384 Mich. 4, 179 N.W.2d 390 (1970). The defendant snapped some electric lines, causing an explosion that damaged the plaintiff's house. The issue on appeal was the trial court's dismissal of the plaintiff's claim for emotional disturbance damages. The trial court held that no recovery was allowed for emotional distress in the absence of proof that the defendant's conduct had caused a physical impact on the plaintiff. The supreme court reversed, holding that no impact need be shown where the plaintiff can prove a "definite and objective physical injury is produced as a result of emotional distress" caused by the defendant's conduct.

E&A EXAMPLE AND ANALYSIS

A defendant might negligently drive a car onto a sidewalk and narrowly miss hitting the plaintiff. If the plaintiff suffered emotional distress from this event, the plaintiff could be entitled to damages, since the plaintiff was in the zone of danger created by the defendant.

---

a. **Fear of fraud.** A person can lie about feelings more easily than about a physical condition (like a broken arm). This fact is the main justification for limiting the plaintiffs' ability to recover for emotional distress in the absence of other injuries. Courts apparently believe that the likely truthfulness of a claim of emotional distress increases when accompanied by a claim of physical harm.

b. **Ultimate physical consequences or manifestation usually required.** In addition to initial physical impact, traditional common law doctrines about emotional distress damages required that the plaintiff suffer some physical consequence or manifestation of the claimed emotional distress. As an additional effort to combat false claims, the majority of jurisdictions continue to require this physical manifestation, even under the zone of danger approach.

   i. **Exceptions to physical consequences requirement.** Some jurisdictions do not impose the physical consequences requirement in two types of cases in which the likelihood of emotional upset is extremely high. These cases are based on negligent transmission of a telegram about a relative's death and on mishandling of a corpse.

   ii. **Minority rejection of physical consequences requirement.** A number of jurisdictions have rejected the requirement of physical manifestations of plaintiffs' upset. They allow juries to decide whether plaintiffs' emotional distress really exists and was caused by defendants' conduct.

E&A EXAMPLE AND ANALYSIS

A plaintiff who was in a zone of danger created by a defendant's negligent conduct and who suffered an emotional reaction to the experience is required in most jurisdictions to prove physical signs of the emotional distress in order to recover damages. Physical manifestations of emotional distress can include a rash, insomnia, stomach upset, and other symptoms.

5. Bystander Recovery

In a minority of jurisdictions, a bystander outside the zone of danger may recover for emotional distress caused by a defendant's conduct under certain specific circumstances.

a. **Original victim must be relative of emotional distress plaintiff.** Cases recognizing bystander recovery have so far allowed damages only to a parent, sibling, spouse, grandparent, and child of the original victim whose injury they see.

b. **Presence at scene.** The emotional distress plaintiff must see the injury directly. Recovery is not allowed to a plaintiff who learns about the loved one's injury and rushes to the scene or who suffers severe distress from learning about the event in some other way.

c. **Awareness of injury.** The plaintiff must also establish that he or she was aware of the injury to a loved one at the time the plaintiff witnessed the defendant's conduct.

Illustrations: Dillon v. Legg, 441 P.2d 912 (Cal. 1968). The mother and sister of a child struck and killed by an automobile while all three individuals had been crossing a street were entitled to recovery for emotional distress they suffered from seeing the death. The mother clearly had been out of the zone of physical danger, and the sister may have been out of that zone. The court required the plaintiffs to show that they were near the scene of the accident, that their shock resulted from contemporaneous observation of the accident, and that they and the victim were closely related.

Thing v. LaChusa, 771 P.2d 814 (Cal. 1989). The plaintiff learned that her young son had been struck by the defendant's car. She reached the scene of the accident and saw her son, who was bloody and seemed to be dead. The trial court's denial of her claim for emotional distress was affirmed. Distress must come from direct observation of a defendant inflicting a serious injury on one of the plaintiff's close relatives, the court held. This limited the holding in *Dillon,* which had led to some expansive definitions of "contemporaneous" observation.

D. FAILURE TO ACT

People have no duty to help other people under general principles of tort law. A failure to help a person who would benefit from that help is usually not actionable. In applying this doctrine courts distinguish nonfeasance (inaction) from misfeasance (bad action), although some commentators find that distinction illogical. In many recurring situations tort law deviates from the basic rule of no duty to render aid and imposes a duty to be helpful to others.

1. Special Relationship with Plaintiff

A major category of exceptions to the rule that individuals have no duty to assist others is based on special relationships recognized by courts. Special relationships support duties to render aid and provide reasonable protection against harms that might be inflicted by third parties or forces of nature.

a. **Common carriers, innkeepers, and other businesses.** Under traditional common law doctrines common carriers and innkeepers are obligated to act with care in all that they do to provide transportation or lodging to their passengers and guests. They also are obligated to act reasonably to protect their passengers and guests from hazards created by third parties or by forces of nature. A modern trend extends the common carrier's and innkeeper's duty to other types of businesses. See Restatement §314A.

b. **Employers.** An employer has a duty to act reasonably in response to a worker's injury, if the injury occurs in the course of the worker's employment.

c. **Schools.** Schools have a duty to protect their students. At the university level this duty does not extend to a requirement that the school supervise the private lives of students.

Illustration: Hegel v. Langsam, 29 Ohio Misc. 147, 55 Ohio Ops. 2d 476, 273 N.E.2d 351 (Court of Common Pleas 1971). A university had no duty to protect its student from becoming associated with criminals, being seduced, and being a drug user.

d. **Coventurers.** People who embark on an activity together, such as camping or even a social activity like an evening of bar-hopping, may be obligated to each other to act reasonably in the event that one of them needs assistance.

2. Defendant Caused Plaintiff's Peril

If a defendant's conduct has caused the plaintiff to need assistance, the defendant is often under a duty to act reasonably in response to that need for help.

a. **Negligent defendant.** All jurisdictions apply this duty in a case where the defendant's conduct is negligent. If the defendant, for example, drives negligently and injures the plaintiff, the defendant is obligated to take reasonable steps to assist the plaintiff.

i. **Hit-and-run drivers.** Statutes in some states require a driver to assist anyone who has been injured by the driver's vehicle. Violation of such a statute supports a negligence per se claim by the victim for whom the driver fails to obtain help.

b. **Non-negligent defendant.** In many jurisdictions and under the Restatement, one whose non-negligent conduct puts another person in a position of peril is obligated to act reasonably in response to that other person's needs.

Illustration: L.S. Ayres & Co. v. Hicks, 220 Ind. 86, 40 N.E.2d 334, 41 N.E.2d 195 (1942). After a child's fingers became caught in the defendant department store's escalator, the store had a duty to act reasonably in response to the situation. The court based this duty on the child's status as an invitee and on the defendant's ownership of the thing that caused his harm.

E&A Example and Analysis

A defendant's car might stop and block a road through no fault of the defendant, and the defendant might act reasonably in trying to warn other drivers about the danger. If another driver collided with the defendant's car, the defendant would be obligated to use reasonable care to assist that other driver, even though the defendant was free from negligence in every aspect of the incident.

---

3. Assumed Duty

A defendant who could have ignored a plaintiff's need for help without incurring any liability owes a duty to act reasonably once he or she begins to offer help. The defendant is characterized as having assumed a duty of care.

a. **Begin assistance.** A defendant who begins helping an imperiled plaintiff must use reasonable care in his or her actions. This is usually interpreted to mean that he or she must keep the plaintiff safe. The defendant is free to stop giving assistance unless that would put the plaintiff in a position worse than when the defendant intervened. See Restatement §324. A rationale courts sometimes use for imposing this duty is that the defendant's efforts may prevent the plaintiff from obtaining help in other ways.

   i. **Customary conduct.** A defendant who customarily provides a helpful service may be liable for injuries that occur because the defendant has failed to continue to provide the service. Cases of this type usually involve guards at railroad or school crossings. If the plaintiff has been aware of the service, the case for imposing a duty is stronger than if the plaintiff was not aware of the defendant's custom.

b. **Promise to help.** Traditional doctrine has held that a mere promise to offer assistance cannot be a basis for imposing a duty. This pro-defendant doctrine has been subject to considerable erosion.

   i. **Promise plus defendant's action.** Courts may impose a duty where a promise is combined with some small act. For example, a hospital's advice to a prospective patient that he return a day later to see a doctor was a basis for imposing a duty of care in O'Neill v. Montefiore Hospital, 202 N.Y.S.2d 436 (N.Y. 1960).

   ii. **Promise plus plaintiff's reliance.** Some tort cases have adopted an estoppel argument to allow a plaintiff's cause of action where the plaintiff has relied on a defendant's promise of assistance. In Marsalis v. La Salle, 94 So. 2d 120 (La. 1957), a mere promise to keep a pet animal under observation so that someone the animal had bitten would know whether to have rabies shots was a basis for liability when the promisor failed to fulfill the promise.

c. **Inspections and examinations.** Insurance companies often inspect factories and other facilities to determine how safe they are. Courts are divided on whether an insurance company that conducts such an inspection has a duty to individuals who are employed in the inspected location to perform the inspection with due care. If it is found that an insurance company had motives other than its own financial interests, a duty is usually imposed.

   Doctors sometimes examine people in connection with applications for employment or welfare benefits. As is true for an insurance company inspection, courts are divided on whether a doctor in this circumstance owes a duty of care to the examined individual.

4. Special Relationship with Third Party

In a few circumstances an individual has a duty to protect another from potential injury by a third party. That duty is owed to an individual who is a foreseeable victim of misconduct by the potential injurer.

a. **Psychotherapist and patient.** In some jurisdictions a psychotherapist owes a duty to potential victims of a patient's injurious acts, if the therapist has a basis for predicting those acts.

   Illustration: Tarasoff v. Regents of University of California, 529 P.2d 553 (Cal. 1974). The defendant mental health care providers believed that a patient was likely to harm the plaintiffs' daughter. The patient did, in fact, kill her. The plaintiffs sought damages for the defendants' failure to take reasonable steps to protect their daughter. The California supreme court held on these facts that such a duty does exist. The value that confidentiality may add to psychotherapy does not outweigh the social good in requiring breaches of confidentiality where there is a high likelihood of preventing serious harm.

b. **Vehicle owner and vehicle driver.** The owner of a vehicle has a duty to use reasonable care in controlling the conduct of a person who operates the vehicle in the owner's presence. This duty is owed to people who might be injured through use of the vehicle.

c. **Health care.** In some health care situations a person in charge of treatment, such as a surgeon, may be responsible for negligence by others under his or her supervision.

5. Legislation to Encourage Helpfulness

There are two types of legislation relevant to the general problem of encouraging individuals to help others.

a. **Good Samaritan statutes.** Good Samaritan statutes have been adopted in most states. They vary in their coverage, but their general effect is to immunize health care professionals from liability for negligent acts they commit while rendering aid in emergency situations without payment.

   i. **Definition of emergency.** Varying degrees of danger characterize situations that qualify as emergencies under different good Samaritan statutes. A decision at one extreme treated a person's fainting in a hospital as an emergency covered by the state's statute. Other courts exclude events in a hospital from statutory immunity and require a more significant emergency than an episode of fainting.

b. **Vermont duty-to-aid statute.** A Vermont statute requires people to aid others in grave physical danger where those who give aid can do so without being personally imperiled. The statute immunizes one who gives aid from liability for negligence.

E. MERE ECONOMIC LOSS

Special rules govern a situation where a defendant's conduct causes the plaintiff to lose money, but the plaintiff does not suffer any bodily harm or property damage from the defendant's conduct. These cases are referred to as cases of "mere" or "pure" economic harm.

1. Economic Harm Without Other Harm: Traditional Rule

A traditional common law rule denies recovery of economic loss in a case where the defendant's conduct causes only economic losses and does not cause damage to the plaintiff's property or person. This rule is meant to prevent exposing wrongdoers to infinite liability.

Illustration: State of Louisiana ex rel. Guste v. M/V Testbank, 752 F.2d 1019 (5th Cir. 1985). The defendant negligently spilled twelve tons of a toxic chemical in the Mississippi River Gulf outlet. This spill caused a temporary suspension of commercial fishing in the area. The court affirmed dismissal of the majority of claims made by various businesses that had lost income because of the spill, although it treated certain claims by commercial fishermen as eligible for redress. The court examined the history of the rule prohibiting recovery of pure economic loss and declined to reject that rule.

E&A EXAMPLE AND ANALYSIS

A public utility might negligently cut a factory's supply of electricity. Although the factory workers would lose wages for the time they could not work, the utility would have no liability for the workers' economic loss. Similarly, a vehicular accident might cause a road to be closed for a time. The operator of a business located on that road could suffer losses because customers would be prevented from reaching the store. The driver whose negligence caused the accident would have no liability for the economic loss the business suffered.

2. Economic Harm Plus Additional Harm, Distinguished

In many cases a defendant's conduct causes a plaintiff to suffer economic harm in combination with harm to property or personal injury. In this type of case, the plaintiff may recover damages for the economic harm, subject to whatever limits the jurisdiction's proximate cause doctrines impose.

a. **Impact rule parallel.** Note that this approach is parallel to the way the now-discredited impact rule worked in emotional distress cases. Under that rule emotional distress damages were allowed only if there had been an initial touching. For mere economic harm cases, most jurisdictions require that the plaintiff suffer property damage or personal injury (similar to impact) to be permitted recovery for consequential economic harms.

3. Economic Harm Without Other Harm: Modern View

Two notable decisions have abandoned the traditional rule and allowed recovery in situations where the plaintiffs' economic losses were highly foreseeable.

a. **Particular foreseeability.** A minority approach allows recovery for pure economic harms if the plaintiff can establish the particular foreseeability of the harm.

Illustration: People Express Airlines, Inc. v. Consolidated Rail Corp., 495 A.2d 107 (N.J. 1985). The defendant handled some toxic freight negligently and the plaintiff was forced to shut down its nearby telephone reservations office. Recovery was allowed for the resultant economic losses on the theory that the plaintiff and the plaintiff's type of loss both were particularly foreseeable. The court required a high degree of foreseeability. On the facts of the case, the defendant was aware of the location of the plaintiff's enterprise and was aware that its carelessness would require evacuation of that specific plaintiff's employees.

b. **Special relationship.** A special relationship between the plaintiff and defendant may also support recovery of damages for pure economic harm.

Illustration: J'Aire Corp. v. Gregory, 598 P.2d 60 (Cal. 1979). A general contractor performed work carelessly for the plaintiff's landlord. The shortcomings in the contractor's performance caused the plaintiff's restaurant to be shut down for a time. The court allowed a cause of action by the restaurant's operator against the contractor, citing the foreseeability of harm, the blameworthiness of the defendant's conduct, and the defendant's awareness that its work was meant to have an effect on the plaintiff's restaurant.

F. PRECONCEPTION AND PRENATAL INJURIES

A variety of causes of action are now available in connection with harms to fetuses and the birth of children after negligent sterilization procedures or negligent genetic counseling. No-duty or limited-duty rules related to these actions have undergone significant changes in recent years.

An unborn child can suffer injury or death because of a doctor's negligence during the child's gestation or because of an injury negligently inflicted on the mother prior to the child's conception. Where a child's parents would have aborted the pregnancy or where the pregnancy occurred in part because of a failed sterilization procedure, the birth of a child with birth defects is now usually characterized as an injury. The birth of a child free from birth defects is also treated as an injury in some jurisdictions, when it was caused in part because of a failed sterilization procedure.

1. Abrogation of Common Law No-Duty Rule

At common law no cause of action was allowed by or on behalf of a child allegedly injured prior to birth. Virtually all jurisdictions now allow such lawsuits, having abrogated this common law no-duty rule. Defendants in such cases are usually individuals who have injured a fetus in a vehicular accident or physicians who have allegedly committed malpractice that harmed the fetus.

a. **Viable at time of injury.** Some jurisdictions require proof that the fetus was viable at the time the defendant's conduct occurred, but the majority rule rejects that limitation. Proof of causation, however, may be difficult for a plaintiff to establish.

b. **Born alive.** Another requirement in some jurisdictions is that the allegedly injured fetus be born alive, rather than stillborn. Application of this requirement depends on interpreting the definition of "person" under a jurisdiction's wrongful death statute.

Illustration: Endresz v. Friedberg, 24 N.Y.2d 478, 301 N.Y.S.2d 65, 248 N.E.2d 901 (1969). Under the state's wrongful death statute, a defendant who injured a pregnant woman had no liability for wrongful death when she delivered twins stillborn as a consequence of the injuries. Unless a child had been delivered alive, there could be no wrongful death action.

2. Duty to Child for Preconception Conduct

A child may suffer harm because of a doctor's or a drug company's conduct in connection with the child's mother prior to the time the child was conceived. Courts are divided on whether children are entitled to causes of action in these circumstances.

a. **Drug company's duty.** In cases involving harm to children of mothers who took the drug DES during their pregnancies, the majority of courts allow the children to seek relief against the drug makers. A minority reject the cause of action. In a jurisdiction that allows the action, a similar claim brought by a DES grandchild was rejected. See Enright v. Eli Lilly & Co., 570 N.E.2d 198 (N.Y. 1991).

b. **Doctor's duty.** A doctor's failure to deal properly with a woman's RH-negative status may lead to harm to a later-born child. On such facts, one jurisdiction allowed a cause of action by the child against the allegedly negligent physician. See Renslow v. Mennonite Hosp., 367 N.E.2d 1250 (Ill. 1977).

3. Wrongful Conception

The term *wrongful conception* applies to a cause of action for the parents of a child born free from birth defects to parents who had not wanted to have a child. The alleged negligence of the defendant is usually malpractice in performing a sterilization procedure.

a. **Costs of pregnancy.** All courts allow damages for the economic costs and pain and suffering associated with the pregnancy and childbirth.

b. **Costs of child rearing.** Some courts also allow damages for child-rearing costs, which include all the normal costs of supporting the child until he or she reaches the age of majority.

i. **Offset of benefits.** Any benefits the parents receive from the child's existence are offset from the damage award. Some courts have held as a matter of law that the benefits are so great as to be immeasurable; they have relied on that concept to preclude any award for child-rearing expenses.

4. Wrongful Birth

The term *wrongful birth* applies to a parents' cause of action where a child is born with birth defects, and the parents allege that the child would not have been conceived or would have been aborted if the defendant had provided proper genetic counseling or other prenatal health care.

a. **Costs of pregnancy.** All courts allow damages for the economic costs and pain and suffering associated with the pregnancy and childbirth.

b. **Extraordinary costs of child rearing.** The majority of courts allow parents to recover the expected costs of providing whatever unusual care is needed due to the child's birth defects. The issue of recovery of the usual costs of raising a child is identical to that in the case of an unwanted child born free from birth defects.

   Illustration: Procanik by Procanik v. Cillo, 97 N.J. 339, 478 A.2d 755 (1984). The defendant doctor allegedly failed to diagnose that the plaintiff's mother had contracted German measles early in her pregnancy. The plaintiff was born with significant birth defects and sought damages on the theory that his mother would have aborted her pregnancy if the defendant doctor had made the proper diagnosis. The court recognized that the defendant had denied the plaintiff an opportunity never to have existed and treated that as a tort injury. Damages could include the extraordinary costs of living related to the plaintiff's health problems during his childhood and his adult life.

c. **Damages for child's adult life.** In a state that recognizes damages for extraordinary child-rearing costs, and where parents are obligated to provide care for a disabled adult child, the parents' damages are calculated to reflect that obligation. In the *Procanik* case, damages for the plaintiff's adult expenses were allowed.

5. Wrongful Life

The term *wrongful life* applies to a child's cause of action for the injury of being born with birth defects as compared with not being born at all. Most jurisdictions reject this theory, reasoning that having a life in any condition is better than not having a life. A minority allow damages for expenses not covered in the child's parents' wrongful birth suit. These might include damages for the child's expenses as an adult, if those damages are not allowed in the parents' cause of action.

EXAMPLE AND ANALYSIS

Cases involving a prenatal injury or a failed sterilization and subsequent birth involve a variety of factors: identity of the plaintiff (parent or child); condition of child (born with or without birth defects); and damages sought (costs and effects of pregnancy, extraordinary costs of child rearing associated with child's special health problems, or regular costs of child rearing). A case in which courts are most likely to recognize a cause of action involves a parent suing for the extraordinary costs associated with raising a child with birth defects. The type of claim least likely to be recognized is one where a parent seeks damages for the costs of raising a child born with no defects (after a failed sterilization procedure).

G. PROMISE AS A BASIS FOR TORT DUTY

Promises or contracts sometimes become bases for tort duties owed to promisees or even to third parties. A starting point for analysis, however, is a traditional common law rule that one who makes a gratuitous promise is never liable in tort for consequences of the failure to fulfill the promise. Similarly, no tort duty is imposed on a person who breaches a contractual obligation by failing to take actions that he or she is obligated to perform under the contract.

1. Nonfeasance

Failure to act, in the context of either a gratuitous promise or a contract, is usually not a basis for tort liability. Thus, there is ordinarily no liability for a person's nonfeasance, even where it can be predicted that the nonfeasance will cause an injury.

Illustration: Thorne v. Deas, 4 Johns. Cas. 84 (N.Y. 1809). A person who promised to obtain insurance for a ship but failed to do so had no responsibility for economic losses that resulted from the ship's lack of insurance.

H. MISFEASANCE AS A BASIS FOR TORT DUTY

The careless performance of an act, in the context of a gratuitous promise, a contract, or even in the absence of either a promise or a contract, is often the basis for tort liability.

1. Significance of Contract Context

If an actor's misfeasance involves a contractual obligation, a plaintiff who was a beneficiary of the contract may have a choice of suing in contract or tort. A plaintiff usually prefers a tort cause of action, since damages are free from the strict foreseeability rules of contract damages. However, the statute of limitations is usually longer for contract actions than for tort actions.

a. **Election or gravamen.** In some jurisdictions a plaintiff is allowed to choose to pursue an action as based on tort, contract, or tort and contract. In others a court characterizes the action's gravamen, its main characteristics, and requires it to be litigated in the doctrinal context, contract or tort, that is closest to its main features.

2. Standard Negligence Analysis

Once someone begins to act in accordance with a contract's requirements, standard negligence doctrines apply to evaluate possible liability to anyone who suffers an injury related to the person's actions.

I. TORT REMEDY FOR CONTRACTING PARTY'S LACK OF GOOD FAITH AND FAIR DEALING

A contract law principle requires that contracting parties act in good faith and deal fairly. This duty of good faith and fair dealing is sometimes enforceable by a contracting party under tort doctrines.

1. Insurance Bad-Faith Litigation

In many states insurance companies are subject to tort remedies in favor of their insureds if they act in bad faith, given opportunities to settle claims against their insureds. This is significant because an insurer's failure to settle a case can leave the insured party subject to liability for an ultimate tort judgment. That liability might exceed the limits of the insured's insurance policy.

2. Unlawful Discharge

An at-will employee is subject to firing at any time for any reason. Tort actions for unlawful discharge, however, are available in many jurisdictions under particular circumstances.

a. **Retaliatory firing.** An at-will employee is entitled to tort damages for wrongful discharge if the discharge was motivated by the employer's interest in retaliating against the employee for obtaining workers' compensation benefits.

b. **Other public-policy exceptions to at-will employment doctrine.** Wrongful discharge suits are allowed in many jurisdictions to redress firings done in response to employees' disclosure of their employers' illegal acts or in response to employees' refusal to commit illegal acts.

REVIEW QUESTIONS AND ANSWERS

Question: The defendant, Giant Gas Company, negligently caused a hideous explosion that injured many people who were standing at a street corner waiting for a bus. Larry Looker saw this carnage from a window high in a nearby office building and became very upset. Since that time he has suffered from serious indigestion and insomnia. Can Looker recover damages from Giant Gas?

Answer: No. The defendant's conduct had no physical impact on Looker, and Looker was not in a zone of danger that might have exposed him to physical contact. The defendant had no duty to him, despite the fact that he suffered physical consequences of his emotional distress.

Question: As in the question above, the defendant, Giant Gas Company, negligently caused an explosion that injured people who were standing at a street corner. Mary Mother saw the incident from a window high in a nearby office building and saw that one of the victims was her young child. Since that time she has suffered physical problems due to the shock and upset she suffered from seeing her child injured. Can Mother recover damages from Giant Gas?

Answer: Yes (in many jurisdictions). Although Mother was outside the zone of danger and suffered no physical touching from the defendant's conduct, in many jurisdictions she is entitled to recover damages for the consequences of the emotional distress she suffered because: 1. she and the immediate victim have a close familial relationship; 2. she was a direct and contemporaneous observer of the injury to her daughter; and 3. there is clear evidence of the consequences of her emotional distress.

Question: Sam Shopper tripped and fell in a department store and banged his knee on an unusually shaped display case. He asked a salesperson to call a doctor, but the salesperson refused. Shopper limped out of the store. Walking with the injury made it much worse than it would have been had Shopper received medical attention at the site of the fall. He seeks damages from the store, claiming that it was unreasonable in failing to help him when he was hurt. Can Shopper's claim withstand a motion for summary judgment?

Answer: Yes. Shopper does not claim that the defendant was negligent in causing his fall or in having a display case that he hit with his knee. To have a duty to respond reasonably once an injury has occurred, however, the store need not have been negligent in connection with the cause of the injury. Since the injury did involve the store's own equipment (the display case), the store had an obligation to act with reasonable care. A jury could decide whether refusing to call for help was or was not reasonable.

Question: Several college students heard Victoria Violent, a classmate, mumbling in the back of a room, "Got to kill the cafeteria manager, got to kill the cafeteria manager." None of them warned the manager, and unfortunately Violent did kill the manager. Is any of the students who overheard Violent's statement liable for the wrongful death of the manager?

Answer: No. The usual tort rule in cases like this is a no-duty rule. A mental health worker might have a duty to warn an identifiable victim if the worker had reason to believe that the threat was genuine. In this case the fellow-student relationship is not likely to be treated as being as significant as the therapist-patient relationship. Also, the likelihood that the students had the ability to identify the threat as genuine is low. It is doubtful that a court would make an exception to the usual no-duty rule for this case.

Question: Because of the driver's negligence, a truck collided with a telephone pole in an industrial neighborhood. Debris from the accident fell onto the roof of One Corporation's factory, causing some small damage to the roof. Traffic was stopped in the area for two days while repairs were made to the street and to overhead wires. One Corporation was required to stop its production work for two days, losing a large volume of sales. The accident also required Two Corporation, the owner of another factory in the area, to stop its manufacturing work for the two-day period, losing a similarly large volume of sales. One Corporation and Two Corporation each seek damages for lost profits from the truck driver. Does either plaintiff have a valid cause of action?

Answer: Yes, for One, but no, for Two. One Corporation suffered physical harm to its property; it also suffered economic losses. Most jurisdictions would therefore allow it to recover for both categories of loss from the defendant driver. Two Corporation would be described as having suffered mere economic harm, since it suffered no physical impact from the defendant's negligence. In most places a plaintiff with only economic harm has no tort cause of action.

Exam Tips

- Duty in most cases is not a significant issue. It is worth mentioning, however. Usually a duty exists because a defendant's conduct exposed a foreseeable plaintiff to a foreseeable risk of physical harm.
- If a plaintiff suffers emotional distress in addition to some physical harm from a defendant's conduct, recovery for the emotional distress is always allowed.
- Where the only consequence of a defendant's actions is emotional distress suffered by a plaintiff, limited-duty rules apply. Be alert to facts that place a plaintiff in or out of the zone of danger.
- For bystander recovery remember that plaintiffs must establish the truthfulness of their claims to emotional harm. In many jurisdictions they do this through rules that require physical manifestations of the distress.
- Freedom to refrain from helping a person in peril or a person whose condition could be improved by help is fundamental in our society. Questions often

involve situations where tort law takes away this freedom of nonaction: they involve special relationships; situations where the defendant caused the plaintiff's need for help; or situations where the defendant, having begun some action, is then required to do it reasonably.

- When a plaintiff has suffered only economic losses, the general rule prohibits recovery. Some modern decisions reject this rule and allow recovery on particular showings of strong foreseeability.
- Be prepared to distinguish between wrongful conception, wrongful birth, and wrongful life causes of action.

11 LAND OCCUPIERS' DUTIES

CHAPTER OVERVIEW

- A landowner's duty with regard to injuries caused by conditions on the land is traditionally related to the identity of the victim as a person off the land, a trespasser, a licensee, or an invitee.
- A trespasser traditionally is owed the least duty. A landowner is prohibited from harming a trespasser through intentional or wanton actions.
- A child trespasser is sometimes entitled to a greater duty of care in accordance with the attractive nuisance doctrine.
- A licensee is usually a social guest. A licensee is entitled to a warning from a landowner about hidden risks if the landowner knows about the risks and the licensee does not.
- An invitee is an entrant for the landowner's business purposes or for purposes for which the landowner keeps the land open to the public. An invitee is owed a duty of reasonable care.
- There are two modern views on the duty of landowners to entrants on land. One view imposes a duty of reasonable care without regard to the classification of the plaintiff. The other modern view retains the traditional limited duty owed to trespassers but requires reasonable care for all nontrespassers.
- If an injury occurs on property that the owner has leased to someone, special landlord-tenant rules apply.
- Landlords in many jurisdictions have only limited duties with regard to conditions on land. They must act reasonably with regard to common areas, for

example, but not with regard to conditions in places limited to individual tenants' access.

- Some jurisdictions have rejected the limited-duty rules for landlords and replaced them with a general duty of reasonable care.

A. SPECIAL RULES FOR LANDOWNERS AND LAND OCCUPIERS

Special rules control the liability of landowners and land occupiers for injuries related to conditions on the land or to ways in which people use the land. In many circumstances the landowner or land occupier has only a limited duty. In some situations, however, a landowner or land occupier has the typical duty to use reasonable care to prevent foreseeable injuries. Jurisdictions differ about how much limited-duty rules should protect landowners and land occupiers.

1. Equivalence of Landowners and Land Occupiers

Landowners and land occupiers are treated identically for most of the special-duty rules related to injuries on or adjacent to land. In this chapter the term *landowner* is equivalent to *landowner and land occupier.*

B. INJURIES OUTSIDE THE LAND

Landowners ordinarily have a duty to use reasonable care to prevent injuries to people outside their land from risks related to the condition of the land or to activities on the land.

1. Natural Conditions

An exception to the general duty applies to hazards that nature creates on land. There is usually no duty to remove or otherwise control such a hazard. For example, a snow drift on the defendant's land might pose a peril to people on an abutting road, but the defendant has no obligation to remove it.

a. **Human-nature interaction.** Human beings sometimes act in ways that combine with natural phenomena. Hazards created in this way are not considered natural conditions.

b. **Urban-rural distinction.** Some courts have withdrawn the no-duty rule for natural conditions where the defendant's land is in an urban area.

Illustration: Taylor v. Olsen, 282 Or. 343, 578 P.2d 779 (1978). A tree fell from the defendant's land onto a public road and injured the plaintiff there. Alleging negligence, the plaintiff sought damages from the defendant. A directed verdict for the defendant was upheld on appeal. There was no evidence to support a finding that reasonable inspection of the tree would have shown that it was likely to fall. Had such evidence been available, a duty might have existed due to a balance of factors such as the location of the tree and whether the road on which it fell was busy or seldom-traveled.

EXAMPLES AND ANALYSIS

A landowner might dig a trench or build a structure that funnels water onto neighboring land in a way that can cause a dangerous patch of ice. That situation is outside the immunity for hazards created by natural conditions, since human intervention is significant in creating it.

An urban landowner might have a duty to trim trees that pose a hazard to people on an adjacent road, while a rural landowner has no duty to do so.

2. Conduct by People on the Land

A landowner also has a duty to protect people off the land from foreseeable injuries that might be caused by the conduct of people on the land. This rule can impose liability on the landowner for the actions, for example, of hotel guests, people playing a sport on the defendant's land, and contractors or other employees of the landowner.

C. INJURIES ON THE LAND: DUTY RELATED TO PLAINTIFF'S STATUS

When a plaintiff seeks damages for an injury suffered on a defendant's land, many jurisdictions relate the degree of the defendant's duty to the plaintiff's status at the time of the injury. A plaintiff can be characterized as a trespasser, a licensee (social visitor), or an invitee (business visitor).

1. Traditional Three-Category Jurisdictions

Traditional common law jurisdictions use all three of the status categories.

2. Modern Two-Category Jurisdictions

Some jurisdictions recognize only two categories. These are trespasser and nontrespasser. Another way to describe these two categories is: 1. trespasser, and 2. the categories formerly defined as licensee and invitee.

3. Modern One-Category Jurisdictions

Some jurisdictions reject the method of defining a landowner or land occupier's duty according to the status of the injured entrant on land. These jurisdictions can be described as including all entrants in a single category called "all entrants"; alternatively, these jurisdictions can be described as using no categories.

D. DUTY TO TRESPASSERS

A landowner has almost no duty for the safety of a trespasser. A landowner must refrain from committing an intentional tort against a trespasser. In many jurisdictions a landowner must also refrain from willful, wanton, or reckless conduct that could harm a trespasser. In general there is no duty to make the land safe, to warn a trespasser of dangers, or to control hazardous activities that might harm a trespasser.

1. Discovered Trespassers

A discovered trespasser is one the landowner learns is on the land. For a discovered trespasser the general no-duty rule for trespassers is replaced by a rule that requires more care by the landowner. A landowner must use reasonable care for the safety of a discovered trespasser. This reasonable-care duty applies with respect to conduct by a landowner or to artificial conditions on the land. If a hazard is a natural condition of the land, applicability of the reasonable-care duty is unclear.

Illustration: Sheehan v. St. Paul & Duluth Ry. Co., 76 Fed. 201 (1896). The plaintiff was injured by a train while he was trespassing on the railroad's track. The trial court held that the railroad had done no wrong and directed a verdict for the defendant. On appeal it was held that there was generally no duty of reasonable care owed to a trespasser but that once a trespasser was discovered, there was a duty to act reasonably. In the circumstances of this case, no evidence supported a conclusion that the railroad crew failed to act reasonably once they were aware of the plaintiff's presence.

2. Frequent or Tolerated Trespassers

Sometimes a landowner knows or has reason to know that people often trespass on a limited part of the land. That landowner has a duty to make the premises safe or to provide a warning of dangers that such frequent or tolerated trespassers will not likely discover themselves.

E&A EXAMPLE AND ANALYSIS

A sloppy landowner keeps a huge pile of junk near his house. The junk heap contains broken glass, barbed wire, sharp sticks, and a random collection of partly empty containers of industrial chemicals. If a trespasser falls into the pile and is cut, scratched, stabbed, and poisoned, the trespasser has no cause of action against the landowner. The landowner is required only to refrain from harming the trespasser by willful, wanton, reckless, or intentional conduct.

3. Child Trespassers

The attractive nuisance doctrine increases the duty a landowner owes a trespassing child to a duty of reasonable care with respect to artificial conditions on the land. Without the attractive nuisance doctrine a landowner owes a trespassing child only the duty to refrain from intentional torts and reckless or wanton conduct.

a. **Elements of attractive nuisance doctrine.** Most jurisdictions apply the doctrine when the child trespasser establishes the following required elements.

   i. **Likelihood of child's trespassing.** The place of injury must be a place to which the landowner knows or should know children are likely to go.

      (a) **Place not necessarily attractive.** In its earliest versions the doctrine applied only to locations on the defendant's land that the trespassing child could see from outside the land. This idea, that the location must attract the child onto the land, has been rejected in modern versions of the doctrine.

   ii. **Danger.** The landowner knows or should know that the place is unreasonably dangerous to children.

   iii. **Child's ignorance.** The child must be unaware of the danger because of his or her youth.

   iv. **Utility of condition or activity.** The utility of the condition or activity must be less than the risk it imposes on children.

   v. **Landowner's unreasonable conduct.** The landowner's failure to reduce the risk must be unreasonable.

b. **Age limits for attractive nuisance doctrine.** Early decisions applied strict rules that denied a child over a particular age the benefit of the attractive nuisance doctrine. Modern decisions usually compare the child's degree of knowledge to the type of risk that harmed the child, so that a child close to the age of majority can still be entitled to application of the doctrine if the risk was unknown to him or her.

c. **Natural conditions.** The Restatement takes no position on whether the doctrine can apply to natural conditions. Some case law limits the doctrine to artificial conditions on the land.

   i. **Bodies of water.** In some jurisdictions the attractive nuisance doctrine can never apply to a body of water such as a pond or swimming pool. These decisions may be based primarily on the idea that virtually all children capable of trespassing know that bodies of water are dangerous.

d. **Conduct by landowner.** The attractive nuisance doctrine applies only to conditions on land, not to conduct by a landowner. For injuries related to active operations, a trespassing child is treated in the same way as a trespassing adult.

E&A EXAMPLE AND ANALYSIS

A child trespasser is hurt climbing on a landowner's junk heap that contains broken glass, barbed wire, sharp sticks, and a random collection of partly empty containers of industrial chemicals. To recover from the landowner the child has to show that the landowner should have anticipated his or her presence, that the child did not comprehend the risks presented (was the glass easy to see?), that keeping the junk pile had low utility compared with the risks to children, and that the landowner's overall conduct with regard to the pile was unreasonable. Note that the child has a significantly stronger chance of recovery than traditional doctrines give to an adult trespasser.

E. DEFINITION OF LICENSEE

A licensee is one invited or allowed on the land by the landowner for social purposes that have no economic value to the landowner. (Note that being invited socially does not make a person an invitee. The invitee category is defined below.)

1. Mixed Business and Social Purposes

When an entrant on land has a combination of social and other purposes, most decisions incline toward defining the entrant as a licensee. Typical cases involve people who attend scout meetings or fraternal organization meetings, or those who enter land to borrow things even if there is an implied willingness to lend things at other times to the landowner.

Illustration: Barmore v. Elmore, 83 Ill. App.3d 1056, 38 Ill. Dec. 751, 403 N.E.2d 1355 (1980). The plaintiff entered the defendants' home to discuss business affairs of a fraternal organization. The plaintiff and one of the defendants were both officers of the organization. While the discussion was going on, the other defendant (who had a mental illness) stabbed the plaintiff. The plaintiff's action was based on violation of duties owed to an entrant on land. The trial court granted a directed verdict for the defendants. On appeal the directed veredict was affirmed. Discussion of lodge business did not make the plaintiff an invitee rather than a social guest (licensee). The duty owed to a licensee is only to warn of hidden dangers that the defendant knows and that the plaintiff does not know. The facts did not support a finding that this duty had been violated.

2. Automobile Passenger

In some jurisdictions the licensee category includes a person who accepts a free ride in another person's vehicle.

3. Firefighters and Police Officers

Firefighters and police officers are usually characterized as licensees if they enter a landowner's premises in emergency situations.

F. DUTY TO LICENSEE

A landowner owes only limited duties to a licensee, with slightly more obligations than are owed to a trespasser. Under common law a guest must tolerate whatever conditions and whatever level of safety the host ordinarily employs for the host's own safety. The limited-duty rules attempt to protect a host from having to do more for a guest than the host is accustomed to doing for his or her own safety.

1. Warn of Known-Dangerous Conditions

A host must warn a licensee about any dangerous condition that the host knows is on the land if the host knows or should know that the guest may not discover it.

2. Natural Conditions

The duty to warn covers natural conditions. This is consistent with the rationale of duties to licensees, since a licensee is entitled to as much safety as the host has, and a host's knowledge of dangerous natural conditions is a significant component of his or her own safety on the land.

3. No Duty to Repair

The host has no duty to make the land or premises safe.

4. No Duty to Inspect

The host has no duty to inspect the land or premises. The duty to warn applies only to conditions that the host knows and that the host knows or should know the licensee will not observe.

5. Distinction Between Conditions and Activities

The limited-duty rules for licensees originally applied to conditions and activities on a landowner's land or premises. In many jurisdictions that continue to use the licensee category for land entrant cases, the licensee limited-duty rules now apply only to conditions on the land. In these jurisdictions, a landowner owes a duty of reasonable care to licensees for risks related to activities on the land.

6. Recreational-Use Immunity Statutes

Almost every state has adopted a recreational-use immunity statute. These statutes provide that a person who enters another's land for recreational purposes does not have the status of licensee or invitee. The landowner owes the person only the duties owed to an undiscovered trespasser. In some states the landowner must allow the recreational use without requiring payment in order to be entitled to the statutory immunity.

E&A EXAMPLE AND ANALYSIS

Sally Socialguest, a licensee, had three injuries while visiting Howard Host at his house. She slipped on a huge patch of ice Host had allowed to accumulate at the front door of the house; in a remote part of the backyard she fell into a hole that Host had never known about; and she got burned when Host spilled a tureen of soup onto her while serving dinner. Poor Socialguest. Recovery against Host is barred for the ice, since Host could reasonably have expected her to see it. Recovery against Host is barred for the hole injury, since Host did not know about the hole. Sally can recover in most jurisdictions for Host's spilling soup on her, since that injury resulted from conduct, not a condition of the land.

G. DEFINITION OF INVITEE

A person a landowner invites onto land to transact business with the landowner is an invitee under the traditional definition. In addition the majority of jurisdictions define "invitee" to include a public invitee. A "public invitee" is someone who enters land for a purpose for which the land is held open to the public.

1. Customer

A customer in a store is an invitee.

2. Bathroom User

Someone who uses a bathroom in a store is an invitee, either under the public invitee definition or under an expanded view of business purpose for the traditional invitee definition.

Illustration: Campbell v. Weathers, 153 Kan. 316, 111 P.2d 72 (1941). The plaintiff browsed at the defendant's lunch counter and cigar stand but did not buy anything. He then fell in an open trap door as he walked toward a toilet in the back of the building. He sought damages from the defendant. A demurrer granted to the defendant was reversed on appeal. The plaintiff could be classed as an invitee, because the public was generally permitted to use that toilet and because his presence at the counter and on the way to the toilet had an adequate relationship with the business purpose of the defendant's enterprise.

3. Door-to-Door Salesperson

An uninvited salesperson on the porch of a landowner's house is not an invitee. If the landowner invites the salesperson to enter the house, the salesperson becomes an invitee.

4. Public Employees

Public employees whose work is not related to emergencies are often characterized as invitees. Examples are letter carriers, building inspectors, and garbage collectors.

a. **Emergency workers' routine entries.** In some jurisdictions firefighters and police officers are treated as invitees if they enter premises for a routine, nonemergency purpose.

5. Time and Space Limits on Invitation

The time and space limits on the landowner's invitation are usually determined by the entrant's reasonable beliefs about the invitation.

a. **Private areas.** If an invitee receives permission to enter a private area of a landowner's premises, his or her status will change to licensee while in that private area.

H. DUTY TO INVITEE

A landowner owes a duty of reasonable care to an invitee. This obligation is the one owed in most torts cases by most potential defendants to most potential plaintiffs. A jury determines whether the defendant acted as a reasonably prudent person would have acted.

1. Duty to Inspect

A reasonable prudent landowner is expected to inspect his or her land or premises. A perfect inspection is not required, but the landowner must conduct a reasonable inspection.

2. Warnings

Sometimes reasonable care requires only that a landowner give a warning to an invitee. Whether a warning (instead of removing the danger) is adequate depends on the circumstances of a case. Some jurisdictions apply a distraction doctrine in commercial settings. This doctrine recognizes that the operators of stores try to direct customers' attention to merchandise. In such a situation giving a warning of a hazard is not exercising reasonable care, since it is likely that a customer will be distracted and will forget the warning.

Illustration: Wilk v. Georges, 267 Or. 19, 514 P.2d 877 (1973). The plaintiff sought damages from the defendant nursery in a slip-and-fall case. Judgment for the defendant was reversed, since the jury instruction might have suggested that warning signs at the defendant's nursery were adequate as a matter of law. Whether warnings were adequate depended on a variety of factors. If the defendant should have realized that the conditions were risky even to a person who had been warned about them, the defendant owed an invitee a duty to obviate the dangers.

3. Open and Obvious Dangers

If a danger is open and obvious, traditional common law doctrine excuses a landowner from any obligation to remove or warn about it. A small number of modern decisions reject the idea that the landowner should have a complete defense if a danger is open and obvious. These decisions use the comparative negligence doctrine to deal with the open and obvious nature of the hazard. The plaintiff is entitled to a cause of action, but the jury can reduce the plaintiff's recovery to reflect the plaintiff's carelessness in being hurt by something that is open and obvious.

E&A Example and Analysis

If Paul Plumber, a plumber, were called to Hilda Host's house to work on a leaky pipe, what would be his chances of recovery if he were hurt by slipping on ice Host had allowed to collect at the front door, if he fell into a hole Host did not know about in the backyard, or if Host spilled hot coffee on him? Plumber could recover for Host's negligent handling of the coffee, could recover for falling into the hole if a reasonable landowner would have discovered it and warned an entrant about it, and might or might not recover for slipping on the ice. Recovery for the ice-related injury would be prohibited in jurisdictions that do not give landowners a duty to warn about or correct open and obvious dangers. In a small number of states, landowners do have such a duty and Plumber might recover.

4. Protection from Criminal Conduct

Landowners may owe invitees a duty to protect them from foreseeable criminal conduct by third persons on the land. This situation ordinarily arises when a customer in a store or restaurant is injured by someone attempting to rob the business or the customer.

a. **No-duty position.** Some jurisdictions treat the criminal conduct as a superseding cause and refuse to expose the business to liability. Others follow a no-duty rule based on other public policy reasons.

Illustration: Williams v. Cunningham Drug Stores, Inc., 429 Mich. 495, 418 N.W.2d 381 (1988). The plaintiff was injured during an armed robbery at the defendant's store. The defendant was granted a directed verdict. On appeal the supreme court held that police protection was generally a public function, so it imposed no duty on a store owner to provide essentially the equivalent of that service, armed guards. The opinion took no position on a duty to provide a response to the risk of criminal conduct that might cost less than providing armed guards.

b. **Foreseeability analysis.** Other jurisdictions base liability on foreseeability, holding that past crimes at the location can subject the landowner to liability for failing to take reasonable precautions to prevent future crimes.

   i. **Same location rule.** To determine whether past crimes are a basis for imposing a duty due to foreseeability of a future crime some jurisdictions require the plaintiff to show that there were previously a significant number of past crimes at the specific establishment where the plaintiff's injury occurred.

   ii. **Totality of circumstances rule.** Other jurisdictions allow a plaintiff to show that an attack was foreseeable at the defendant's location by showing evidence of past crimes at that location and in the surrounding locality. This is known as the "totality of circumstances rule."

5. Danger Known to Invitee

If an invitee knows about a danger, traditional common law doctrine excuses a landowner from any obligation to remove or warn about it. Some modern decisions treat the invitee's knowledge as relevant to the invitee's comparative negligence, not as a complete defense for the landowner.

a. **Necessity.** Under common law an invitee who confronted a risk that he or she had learned about might be permitted to recover if confronting the risk was a necessity, as in a case where a railroad passenger saw ice on a platform but had to cross that area in order to reach a train.

I. DUTY IN MODERN TWO-CATEGORY JURISDICTIONS

Some jurisdictions now place entrants in two categories: trespassers and all other entrants. The duty owed to a trespasser is the same as the traditional common law duty to a trespasser. The duty owed to all other entrants is reasonable care.

Illustration: Jones v. Hansen, 867 P.2d 303 (Kan. 1994). Licensees and invitees should be treated equally, but a limited-duty rule with respect to trespassers continues to apply.

J. DUTY IN MODERN ONE-CATEGORY JURISDICTIONS

In jurisdictions that have abolished the three categories of trespasser, licensee, and invitee, a landowner owes a duty of reasonable care to all entrants on the land.

Illustration: Rowland v. Christian, 69 Cal. 2d 108, 70 Cal. Rptr. 97, 443 P.2d 561 (1968). The court rejected use of the three categories because cases applying them had reached inconsistent conclusions, suggesting that policies underlying definition of the categories were no longer consistent with modern understanding of landowners' and entrants' expectations. The court also placed great significance on the social goal of protecting people from injuries.

1. Factual Significance of Entrant's Status

In jurisdictions that have eliminated clear-cut rules about limited duty to particular types of entrants, an entrant's status continues to be significant in a factual sense. If the presence of a trespasser, for example, is difficult for a landowner to anticipate, a jury applies the reasonable person test with that fact in mind.

E&A EXAMPLE AND ANALYSIS

Tom Thief stole some office equipment and then was hurt trying to escape by running down poorly lighted emergency stairs in an office building owned by Officeco. In a one-category jurisdiction Thief would have a cause of action against Officeco if he claimed that maintenance of the stairs had been less careful than the reasonable prudent person standard required. In a two-category jurisdiction Thief would be a trespasser and would be owed virtually no duty of care. Thief might not win in the one-category jurisdiction, because a jury might find that his manner of using the stairs was unforeseeable; nonetheless, his opportunity to reach the jury would be a clear consequence of the abrogation of categories.

K. SUMMARY OF GENERAL LAND ENTRANT DOCTRINES

See Figure 11-1, p. 185.

L. LANDLORDS' OBLIGATIONS TO TENANTS AND OTHER ENTRANTS

When someone is injured on leased property, most jurisdictions use special rules for the landlord's liability (the terms *landlord* and *lessor* are equivalent). The rules protect landlords from liability in many situations. They are based on the feudal concepts that a tenant has great independence from the owner and lessor and that the tenant usually is the exclusive source of inspection and repair work on

FIGURE 11-1

SUMMARY OF GENERAL LAND ENTRANT DOCTRINES

Type of Entrant	*Type of Hazard: Intentional or Reckless Conduct*	*Type of Hazard: Active Operations*	*Type of Hazard: Latent Conditions*
Trespasser	DUTY TO REFRAIN FROM CONDUCT	NO DUTY	NO DUTY
Discovered Trespasser	DUTY TO REFRAIN FROM CONDUCT	DUTY OF REASONABLE CARE	Restatement: DUTY OF REASONABLE CARE Decided Cases: DUTY OF REASONABLE CARE/NO DUTY
Licensee	DUTY TO REFRAIN FROM CONDUCT	Traditional common law: DUTY OF REASONABLE CARE if: 1. defendant should expect that licensee will not realize the danger; and 2. licensee actually does not know or have reason to know the danger Modern view: DUTY OF REASONABLE CARE	DUTY TO MAKE CONDITION SAFE OR GIVE WARNING if: 1. defendant should expect that licensee will not realize the danger; 2. licensee actually does not know or have reason to know the danger; and 3. defendant knows or has reason to know of the danger
Invitee	DUTY TO REFRAIN FROM CONDUCT	DUTY OF REASONABLE CARE	DUTY OF REASONABLE CARE

the leased premises or land. The general rule gives landlords a no-duty defense. Exceptions to the rule impose a duty of reasonable care owed to tenants and to licensees and invitees of tenants.

Illustration: Borders v. Roseberry, 216 Kan. 486, 532 P.2d 1366 (1975). The social guest of the lessee of a single-family house slipped on an icy step. He sought damages from the landlord, claiming that the roof had been maintained badly, allowing water to drip onto the step to create the condition that caused his harm. The trial court held that the landlord owed no duty in this circumstance. On appeal the supreme court affirmed. It reasoned that landlords had only limited duties, none of which covered the current case.

In some jurisdictions a landlord owes a general duty of due care to all entrants on the land. This position is parallel to the reform in some jurisdictions abolishing use of the trespasser, licensee, and invitee categories.

1. General Rule: No Duty

Landlords or lessors have no duty to protect anyone from hazards in leased premises. The rule is subject to many exceptions.

2. Exception: Dangers Known to Lessor at Start of Lease

A landlord has a duty of reasonable care with respect to dangers that are present on the premises at the start of the lease if the danger meets two definitional elements. The injured tenant must prove that the landlord knew or should have known about the risk and that the tenant was reasonably unaware of the risk. If these two conditions are met, the landlord is liable to a tenant or the tenant's licensee or invitee for injuries related to the danger.

3. Exception: Common Areas

A landlord owes a duty of reasonable care for conditions in common areas. A common area is a place that remains in the landlord's control even though some of the premises have been leased. Examples are stairways, elevators, and lobbies. This duty is owed to tenants and to the invitees and licensees of tenants. Jurisdictions split on whether hazards caused by natural conditions are within the scope of this duty.

4. Exception: Premises Leased for Public Use

If a landlord knows that a tenant will use the premises for a function to which the public is invited, under certain circumstances a landlord is liable to a member of the public who is injured by a dangerous condition on the premises. To impose liability the injured member of the public must show that the landlord knew the premises would be open to the public and knew the premises might be open before the dangerous condition was repaired.

a. **Lease provisions about repairs.** A general statement in a lease that the tenant will keep the premises in good repair does not protect a landlord from liability under this exception to the usual no-duty rule. A landlord will be protected, however, by a provision in which the tenant promises to keep the public out until he or she makes repairs.

5. Exception: Landlord's Repair Promises and Repair Efforts

If a lease obligates the landlord to maintain the leased premises, most courts impose a duty of reasonable care on that landlord as a basis for liability to a tenant or a tenant's licensee or invitee injured due to a condition that the landlord should reasonably have repaired. Regardless of lease provisions, when a landlord makes efforts to repair something, the landlord is liable if repair work is done badly or is left unfinished in a way that is hazardous to the tenant or the tenant's licensees or invitees.

a. **No extra danger from repair.** If a landlord's carelessly performed repair does not make conditions worse than they were prior to the repair, some courts impose liability for an injury related to the condition, and some courts excuse the landlord's carelessness.

b. **Tenant's knowledge of hazard.** The majority of jurisdictions impose liability on landlords for inept or partial repairs only if the tenant is ignorant of the danger presented by the landlord's conduct. If a tenant does know about the danger, ordinarily no cause of action for an injury is allowed. Where a social guest or invitee of the tenant is injured, that person's action against the landlord is allowed if the tenant was ignorant of the hazard. If the tenant did know about the hazard, that knowledge defeats an action by an injured licensee or invitee regardless of whether the licensee or invitee actually learned of the hazard from the tenant.

6. Modern Full-Duty Rule

Some states impose a general duty of reasonable care on landlords with respect to all hazards and all entrants on leased premises. The factual settings that supported the common law categories have effect in these states only as part of the world view that jurors use in deciding whether the landlord's conduct was reasonable.

Illustration: Pagelsdorf v. Safeco Ins. Co. of America, 91 Wis. 2d 734, 284 N.W.2d 55 (1979). The court rejected the general no-duty rule for landlords and replaced it with a duty of reasonable care in maintenance of premises.

E&A EXAMPLE AND ANALYSIS

Tina Tenant touched a light switch in an apartment she rented from Lance Landlord. The switch was defective and Tenant suffered an electric shock. In most jurisdictions Tenant would have no cause of action against Landlord to recover for her injuries. The switch was not in a common area of Landlord's premises, there was no reason to believe Landlord knew about this risk prior to the beginning of the lease, the apartment was not leased for public occupancy, and Landlord had not attempted nor promised to repair the switch. In a jurisdiction that abrogated the general no-duty rule, Tenant would be able to recover from Landlord if a jury were to find that Landlord had in some way failed to act as a reasonable and prudent landlord in relation to the switch.

7. Protection from Third-Party Criminal Acts

In some jurisidctions a landlord has a duty to take reasonable care to protect tenants from foreseeable criminal acts by third parties.

Illustration: Kline v. 1500 Massachusetts Ave. Apartment Corp., 141 U.S. App. D.C. 370, 439 F.2d 477 (1970). The tenant plaintiff sought damages from the defendant landlord for injuries she had suffered when she was assaulted in a common area of an apartment house. The trial court dismissed the claim on the theory that the defendant owed no duty. The appellate court reversed, stating that a landlord owed tenants a duty to take reasonable measures to protect tenants from the risks of third-party criminal conduct. The court analogized landlords to innkeepers and others who had duties to protect individuals somewhat under their control from criminal acts.

Review Questions and Answers

Question: Louis Landowner dug a small pit for use in composting dead leaves. The pit was circular, about three feet deep and four feet wide. Willy Wanderer, a trespasser, fell into the pit and hurt his leg. Would Wanderer have a cause of action against Landowner if he claimed that the pit was unreasonably dangerous?

Answer: No. Landowner was not required to be reasonable with respect to injuries a trespasser might suffer; he was required only to refrain from intentional or wanton misconduct. It is highly unlikely that a court would find the construction of a compost pit to be wanton misconduct.

Question: If Louis Landowner saw a trespasser approaching a hidden pit and failed to shout a warning, would he be subject to liability if the trespasser fell into the pit and was hurt?

Answer: Yes. Landowner owed a duty of reasonable care to a discovered trespasser. Providing a warning about a concealed hazard would usually be considered necessary in the exercise of reasonable care.

Question: Hillary Homeowner invited Francesca Friend to visit her house. Friend went to the front door, and Homeowner invited her in. Homeowner warned Friend that the floor was slippery. She had waxed it recently and had put on three times too much wax because she had not read the product directions. Friend slipped and fell. Could she recover damages from Homeowner on a negligence theory?

Answer: No. Friend was a licensee (not an invitee, although invited). Homeowner was required to warn her of risks that Homeowner knew and Friend did not know, but Homeowner was not required to use reasonable care for Friend's safety. Since Homeowner warned Friend, Homeowner fulfilled her only obligation to Friend.

Question: Hillary Homeowner invited Conrad Contractor to visit her house to discuss making a bid on a renovation project Homeowner was considering. Homeowner had waxed the floor exactly as described in the question above. She gave Contractor a warning, and Contractor slipped and fell. Could Contractor recover from Homeowner on a negligence theory?

Answer: Yes. Contractor was entitled to reasonable care from Homeowner. A jury question would be presented as to whether providing a warning did or did not constitute reasonable care.

Question: Tim Tenant, who rented an apartment in a large apartment house owned by Larry Landlord, was hurt when a lighting fixture fell from the lobby ceiling and hit him. Would Tenant have a cause of action in negligence against Landlord?

Answer: Yes. Tenant's injury occurred in a common space on the landlord's property (the lobby was available to all tenants). Landlord owed Tenant a duty of reasonable care in maintaining common space.

EXAM TIPS

- The trespasser, licensee, and invitee distinctions are important mainly with regard to conditions on land. When a landowner has been active in some conduct, a duty of reasonable care usually applies to evaluating that conduct.
- Licensees are equivalent, usually, to social guests. Do not confuse the term *invitee* with the concept of social invitations.
- A duty to a licensee usually involves a warning about a hazard, but the duty does not require the landowner to make reasonable inspections. It only requires the landowner to disclose risks that are known to the landowner and unknown to the licensee.
- In modern one-category jurisdictions landowners still have opportunities to win cases against trespassers and licensees if the status of the plaintiff influences how the jury interprets issues such as foreseeability of harm and degree of care a reasonable person would exercise.
- The evolution in some states away from treating land entrant cases according to entrants' categories is parallel to the trend followed by some states to eliminate no-duty rules for landlords. This linkage is sometimes a subject for essay questions.

12 DAMAGES

CHAPTER OVERVIEW

- Tort damages are often categorized as either economic or noneconomic. Economic damages are primarily past and future medical costs and lost wages. Noneconomic damages are intangible losses such as pain and suffering or loss of the enjoyment of life.
- Damage awards must be supported by evidence in the trial record, often including expert testimony by actuaries.
- Jurisdictions have different approaches to reflecting inflation, taxes, and reduction to present value of awards to provide future income.
- The collateral source rule allows the plaintiff who has received compensation for an injury from sources other than the defendant to retain those payments and obtain full recovery from the defendant.
- Loss of consortium damages are awarded to the spouse (in all jurisdictions) and parents or children (in some jurisdictions) of the person initially injured by the defendant to compensate those close relatives for the losses imposed on their relationships by the defendant's conduct.
- Wrongful death and survival actions are statutorily created causes of action that allow redress for the death of an individual. Prior common law doctrines required that a cause of action be pursued by a live individual, so death terminated a cause of action for injury.
- Punitive damages are available in tort cases, subject to recently articulated constitutional limitations.

- The trial court can adjust damage awards downward through the procedure known as remittitur or upward through the procedure known as additur.

A. FUNDAMENTAL PRINCIPLES

The vast majority of tort cases involve money damages for harm to a person or property. Because recovering damages is the essential point of tort litigation, it is understandable that there are many detailed rules to control damages. The rules are both common law and statutory.

1. Actual Injury Required

In most cases the plaintiff must prove a genuine physical injury. This can be property damage (physical injury to something that belongs to the plaintiff) or personal injury (physical injury to the plaintiff's body).

2. Plaintiff's Burden of Proof

The plaintiff is required to prove damages. An award of damages is subject to reversal unless there is an adequate basis in the trial record to support each of its elements.

B. ECONOMIC AND NONECONOMIC DAMAGES DISTINGUISHED

In many states there is an important distinction between economic damages and noneconomic damages. Economic damages are losses that can be quantified by reference to past and anticipated earnings or costs. Noneconomic damages are losses for harms that are not tangible, such as pain and suffering or the loss of enjoyment of life. Tort reform legislation tends to restrict recovery of noneconomic damages.

1. Joint and Several Liability Limited to Economic Damages

In some jurisdictions joint and several liability applies only to economic damages.

2. Damage Caps for Noneconomic Damages

In some jurisdictions statutes set a ceiling or cap on the amount of noneconomic damages a plaintiff may recover.

C. CATEGORIES OF DAMAGES

Courts conventionally analyze damages by using specific categories. A plaintiff's interest is served by increasing the number of categories that apply to his or her case. A jury is likely to award more damages, in total, if it is invited to calculate amounts for a large number of separate categories of damages. When an appellate court reviews an award of damages that a defendant claims is excessive, the chance of affirmance is greater if the plaintiff has established a basis for damages in many separate categories at trial.

1. Economic Damages

The following are the conventional types of economic damages typically awarded to plaintiffs.

a. **Medical expenses.** Medical expenses are a common category of economic damages in personal injury cases. They can include all aspects of health care, including nursing and rehabilitation.

b. **Lost income.** If the effects of his or her injury decrease the plaintiff's earnings, that lost income is an element of economic damages.

c. **Substitute labor.** Another element of economic damages is the cost of employing people to perform functions of living that the plaintiff's injuries prevent the plaintiff from doing personally. Housekeepers and child-care providers are examples of this category of damages.

2. Noneconomic Damages

The following are the conventional types of noneconomic damages available to plaintiffs.

a. **Pain and suffering.** Plaintiffs who suffer physical pain and suffering are entitled to monetary compensation for that harm. This element of damages is crucial in many personal injury cases; it is also subject to significant criticism.

b. **Components of pain and suffering.** Pain and suffering damages can include amounts for physical pain, fright, shock, embarrassment, sadness, depression, worry, and anxiety.

   i. **Theoretical criticism.** Critics of pain and suffering damages point out that there are no familiar or reliable measurements for pain, since the experience of pain varies from person to person. Also, even if pain were susceptible of exact quantification, our society does not have a market for the infliction of pain, so there is no real basis for determining the right price for any specific amount of pain.

   ii. **Response to criticism: money is only available option.** One response to this criticism is that money is the best our society has to offer the victim of painful injuries. It is fairer to risk overpaying a victim (because of the lack of precise measuring tools for pain) than it would be to deny the victim all monetary redress for this aspect of the harm he or she has suffered.

   iii. **Response to criticism: damages help fund litigation.** Another response acknowledges the weak theoretical foundation for pain and suffering awards but rationalizes them as a response to the traditional American rule that each party pays his or her own lawyer's fees. In this view pain and suffering damages may be an approximate method of making sure that after a victorious plaintiff pays his or her lawyer, the amount of money the plaintiff has left comes close to equalling the amount of money the jury expected the plaintiff to have for lost wages, medical expenses, and other economic losses.

c. **Hedonic damages defined.** Hedonic damages is a term used to describe damages for loss of the enjoyment of life. If, for example, someone who once derived pleasure from playing a musical instrument suffered injuries preventing that activity, the loss of that recreation would be called a hedonic loss.

d. **Views on availability of hedonic damages.** Some jurisdictions allow hedonic damages as a separate category. In other jurisdictions they are considered part of pain and suffering. Treating them as a separate category favors plaintiffs by increasing the number of categories juries can use to specify dollar amounts of damages.

e. **Victim's awareness.** A requirement that a victim be aware of pain and suffering or hedonic damages is significant in many cases. For example, if a plaintiff is unconscious or in a coma, there is no proof that he or she has awareness of those effects of the injury.

   i. **Pain and suffering.** All jurisdictions require that a plaintiff be aware of pain and suffering to be entitled to damages for it. A victim who is in a coma, for example, is entitled to damages for pain and suffering only for any period during which he or she experienced the pain prior to becoming comatose.

   ii. **Hedonic damages.** Some jurisdictions allow hedonic damages regardless of the plaintiff's state of awareness. Others require evidence that the plaintiff is aware of his or her loss.

f. **Infants' pain and suffering.** Defendants sometimes claim that the concept of pain and suffering has no application to infants or other very young individuals. Courts usually reject this argument.

E&A

Example and Analysis

Money damages for tortious conduct usually involve four basic categories: past economic losses, future economic losses, past noneconomic losses, and future noneconomic losses. In a typical personal injury case economic losses are medical expenses and lost wages and noneconomic losses are pain and suffering.

D. CALCULATING PAST AND FUTURE LOSSES

A general rule for tort cases limits a plaintiff to only one lawsuit against a defendant; because of statutes of limitations, this single lawsuit cannot be postponed indefinitely. Thus, the plaintiff's proof of damages in a typical case is divided into two categories: past damages and anticipated future damages. The proof of past damages is fairly concrete. The proof of future damages often depends on expert testimony about the likelihood of future events.

1. Degree of Certainty Required for Future Losses

An award of damages for future harm must be based on evidence showing by a more-likely-than-not or a preponderance test that the future harm will occur. An expert need only testify that it is more likely than not that a certain consequence of the plaintiff's injury will occur, not that the consequence will definitely happen.

2. Typical Testimony About Future Losses

Predictions about an injured person's life expectancy are usually crucial in setting damages. If the jury believes that pain and suffering are likely to continue for the rest of the plaintiff's life, the jury must have an estimate of the duration of that life to determine an amount of money for that category of damages. Actuarial tables about life expectancies are usually used to satisfy this logical component of estimating future damages. For calculating future lost wages experts rely on various factors. These estimates also require an actuarial prediction of the plaintiff's life expectancy, as well as assessments of the career path the plaintiff would likely have taken if he or she had not been harmed.

3. Per Diem Argument

Some plaintiffs' lawyers have developed an argument called a "per diem argument" to encourage jurors to award large amounts for pain and suffering. This argument asks jurors to assign a small value to a minute or an hour of suffering and then to multiply that value by the number of minutes or hours in the victim's predicted life expectancy. Even a small amount for a minute or an hour usually leads to a huge sum, when the jurors do the arithmetic (there are 525,600 minutes in a year). Some jurisdictions prohibit the per diem argument on the theory that it is inherently misleading to jurors. Most jurisdictions allow it.

E. ADJUSTMENTS TO THE JURY'S DAMAGES FINDINGS

Damages for future losses are imprecise since no one can know the future. The usual requirement that the defendant pay the plaintiff at the present an amount of money to compensate the plaintiff for future losses raises additional complications.

Inflation may take place in the future. To have a person receive a certain amount of the money in a future year, it is only necessary to give that person a smaller amount now, since that sum will increase in value if it is invested until the year in which it is needed (this idea is known as the present value of money at a future time). The victim would have paid income tax on the wages he or she will lose due to the injury, yet personal injury judgments are free from taxation. Jurisdictions treat these issues in a variety of ways.

1. Inflation

Some courts allow expert testimony that attempts to give the jury a basis for estimating the future effects of inflation on the value of the plaintiff's future losses. Other courts reject this evidence.

2. Reduction to Present Value

Most courts require the jury to reduce its estimates of the plaintiff's future economic harm to present value. This means that, based on expert testimony or in some cases based on a prescribed percentage rate, the jury must award an amount that it estimates is the right size to produce future income to equal the future losses that it predicts the plaintiff will sustain. Some courts do not permit this type of calculation.

3. Disregard of Both Inflation and Present Value Reduction

Some courts instruct the jury to disregard both possible future inflation and the concept of reducing damages to present value, on the theory that the two errors these factors introduce into the calculation are likely to cancel each other out. Ignoring inflation makes the damages estimate too low, but ignoring the present value concept leaves the plaintiff with an award that is higher than is justified by that future estimate.

4. Taxes

Taxes can affect damages calculations in two ways. First, if part of a damage award involves the plaintiff's lost income, tort law must deal with the fact that the income would have been subject to taxation if the plaintiff had actually earned it. Second, personal injury damages (other than punitive damages) are free from taxation. Tort law must decide whether to have juries take that factor into account when they award damages.

a. **Lost income and taxation.** Juries are ordinarily instructed to consider income taxation when they calculate damages for past lost income. The jury can be informed about the tax rates and tax laws that would have applied at the time the plaintiff would have earned the income if he or she had not been injured. When the jury calculates damages for predicted future lost income, however, taxation presents a significant problem. A jury cannot be told what future tax rates or tax laws will be. For this reason most courts have juries ignore taxation when they calculate future lost income for typical plaintiffs.

i. **High-income plaintiffs.** In some instances, where the plaintiff's lost income damages are very high and the plaintiff can reasonably be predicted to have large tax liabilities, courts allow juries to estimate the impact of future taxes on the lost future earnings for which the plaintiff is being compensated.

ii. **Federal tort causes of action.** In cases tried in federal court on federal causes of action, such as railroad workers' injuries (covered by the Federal Employers' Liability Act), the jury must consider future taxation in calculating future income lost.

b. **Nontaxability of personal injury damage awards.** Personal injury awards have long been treated as nontaxable, although recent Supreme Court jurisprudence indicates a trend to define personal injury narrowly. (In Commissioner v. Schleir, 115 S. Ct. 2159 (1995), the Court treated as taxable the back-wages component of a plaintiff's judgment for the defendant's violation of the federal statute prohibiting age discrimination in employment.) Punitive damages are also subject to tax.

There are three views on whether the jury should learn that personal injury awards are nontaxable. Some jurisdictions require giving the jury this information, some allow it, and some forbid it.

i. **Require disclosure to jury.** In federal cases and in some other jurisdictions, the jury must be informed about the nontaxability of the plaintiff's damage award. The argument in favor of this position is that unless juries have accurate information about this fact, they tend to increase damage awards to make sure that the plaintiff will have the right amount of money after paying taxes. Another argument is that juries should have accurate information on this issue since they will otherwise just guess about it.

ii. **Allow disclosure to jury.** In some jurisdictions the court has discretion to inform or not to inform the jury about the nontaxability of damage awards. This discretion might be exercised in view of the specific facts of a case, perhaps with a preference for informing the jury in cases where damage awards are likely to be high.

iii. **Prohibit disclosure to jury.** Some courts prohibit informing the jury about the nontaxability of damage awards. There is no satisfactory reason for this position. It may be justified as a pro-plaintiff device that can sometimes increase plaintiffs' recoveries and thus partially compensate them for their lawyers' fees. It can also be supported by a belief that juries follow their instructions exactly, so they award the "proper" amount without regard to any guess about taxation of the amount the plaintiff receives.

5. Statutory Ceilings on Damages

In a number of states statutes set limits on the damages that a tort plaintiff may receive. The most common type of statute imposes this limit on noneconomic damages. If the statutory limit (or cap) is an amount such as $250,000, the plaintiff's judgment for noneconomic damages is never more than that amount, no matter how high an amount the jury specifies. In cases with punitive damages, some jurisdictions impose a statutory limit on the amount of punitive damages, usually relating them to the amount of compensatory damages.

a. **Informing the jury about a damages ceiling.** Jurisdictions differ on whether the jury may be informed about a ceiling on damages. Where there is a limit only on noneconomic damages, the plaintiff's lawyer faces a strategic problem if the jury is kept ignorant of the cap. The plaintiff's recovery is maximized if the jury awards only the ceiling amount for noneconomic damages, then gives generous awards for the categories of compensatory damages. The plaintiff's lawyer must motivate the jury to award noneconomic damages but must avoid a situation in which the jury feels that, because its noneconomic damages award is so high, it can properly be very cautious in setting amounts for economic (or compensatory) damages.

6. Payments from Third Parties (Collateral Source Rule)

Insurance companies, employers, friends, and other sources sometimes give victims economic benefits when they have suffered an injury due to a defendant's conduct. These benefits may be insurance payments, free medical care, sick pay, or nursing and housekeeping services. A common law rule, the collateral source rule, required that plaintiffs receive the full amount of any damages found by the jury, even if some component of that damage award was already paid to the plaintiff from some source other than the defendant. At present about half the states have rejected this rule. Under the influence of tort reform, those states require that a judgment be reduced to reflect any payments the plaintiff has received from sources other than the defendant to compensate for particular losses that the jury considered in reaching its decision on damages.

a. **Rationale supporting collateral source rule.** Common law courts justified the collateral source rule with a number of ideas. Mainly, judges thought that a prudent plaintiff who had paid for insurance in the past ought to be treated identically to a less prudent plaintiff who had never bought insurance. They therefore required a defendant to pay the full amount of damages found by the jury, even if the plaintiff had already been compensated by insurance.

i. **Windfall to defendant.** Some courts state that defendants should always pay for all of the damage they inflict, regardless of whether the plaintiff receives other payments, because a discount would give the defendant a benefit for which he or she had not paid, based on the plaintiff's own good fortune.

ii. **Insurance issues.** Some insurance policies allow the insurance company to be reimbursed by the policy holder for the benefits they have paid, if the policy holder receives a tort judgment. Where this is true, reducing the plaintiff's judgment to reflect insurance proceeds would penalize the plaintiff, since he or she would have to pay the insurance company from a judgment that had already been reduced by that exact amount.

b. **Rationale for rejecting collateral source rule.** The tort reform movement has had significant success in criticizing the collateral source rule. About half the states have abolished it or limited its application. These statutory approaches vary. In some the trial judge is given discretion about whether or not to reduce the plaintiff's award. In general the statutes seek to eliminate double recoveries.

i. **A tentative proposal by the American Law Institute would modify the collateral source rule.** A plaintiff's judgment would be reduced to reflect payments received by the plaintiff from insurance, but the defendant would be required to reimburse the plaintiff for some of the insurance premiums the plaintiff had paid to keep the insurance policy in effect.

EXAMPLE AND ANLAYSIS

What judgment would a plaintiff be entitled to receive from a defendant doctor found liable for malpractice if the plaintiff's damages were set at $250,000 but the plaintiff had been covered by insurance for $200,000 of the expenses reflected in that damages finding? The answer to this question depends on how the jurisdiction treats collateral source payments. The traditional collateral source rule would require the judge to enter a judgment for $250,000, ignoring the plaintiff's insurance benefits. Many jurisdictions would require a judgment of $50,000, reducing recovery to reflect the plaintiff's real out-of-pocket loss.

F. PLAINTIFF'S OBLIGATION TO MITIGATE DAMAGES

In tort law as in other fields of law, a plaintiff has an obligation to take reasonable steps to lessen the harmful effects of the defendant's wrongdoing. This is known as mitigation of damages.

1. Reasonable Actions Required

An injured plaintiff is required to act reasonably with respect to first aid or further medical treatment. The plaintiff may forego treatment that he or she has a good reason to reject. The defendant has the burden of establishing that some treatment the plaintiff did not receive would have had a significant effect on the plaintiff's condition.

Illustration: Zimmerman v. Ausland, 266 Or. 427, 513 P.2d 1167 (1973). The defendant's negligent conduct injured the plaintiff's knee. The defendant was entitled to argue that the plaintiff should have undergone surgery to decrease the harm caused by the injury. On appeal from a judgment for the plaintiff, it was held that the defendant's evidence created a jury question on the plaintiff's possible failure to take remedial actions that a reasonable person would have taken, but that it did not require a finding that as a matter of law the plaintiff's decision not to have an operation precluded a finding that she had suffered a permanent injury.

2. Failure to Use an Available Seat Belt

In some states, if a plaintiff who fails to use an available seat belt is injured in a vehicular accident, the plaintiff is not entitled to recover damages for any component of his or her injuries that the defendant shows would have been avoided by use of the seat belt.

a. **Statutory treatment of seat belt use.** In many states statutes control the impact a plaintiff's failure to use an available seat belt may have on the plaintiff's recovery. These statutes usually permit a decrease in the plaintiff's recovery through application of comparative fault principles and usually limit the amount of reduction to a fairly small percentage.

G. PERIODIC PAYMENTS

Statutes in some states allow a defendant to pay a judgment through periodic payments instead of the traditional, single, lump-sum payment. The plaintiff receives payments on a regular schedule for the remainder of his or her life. The payments stop when the plaintiff dies, and no payments are made to the plaintiff's estate.

1. Savings for Defendants

Defendants prefer the periodic payment option because it is usually cheaper to pay an insurance company for an annuity that will provide periodic payments to the plaintiff than it would be to pay a lump-sum judgment.

2. Critique of Periodic Payments

The periodic payment method gives defendants the benefit of the fact that some plaintiffs die prematurely. Because the payments to those plaintiffs cease when they die, insurance companies can reflect that probability in the prices they charge for all the annuities that all defendants may be required to purchase. Plaintiffs, on the other hand, are denied the ability to invest the proceeds of their damage awards according to their own preferences. Some plaintiffs argue that there is a lack of symmetry in the periodic payment statutes. While defendants pay less if a plaintiff's expenses stop early due to a plaintiff's death, there is no requirement that a defendant make extra payments if the plaintiff's needs increase during his or her lifetime.

H. LOSS OF CONSORTIUM

When a tortfeasor injures someone who has a spouse, children, or parents, the tortfeasor is liable to the person he or she injures for all types of damages already discussed in this chapter. The tortfeasor may also be liable to the injured person's spouse, children, or parents for loss of consortium damages. Spousal loss of consortium is the most widely recognized type of these damages.

1. Spousal Consortium

Damages for loss of spousal consortium are meant to compensate the husband or wife for the loss of companionship, sexual relations, household services, and other benefits previously received from the injured spouse.

a. **Early history: damages for husbands only.** This category of damages was originally reserved for a husband whose wife was injured. The common law courts treated the wife as property belonging to the husband and, thus, easily recognized an action by the husband seeking compensation for damage to his wife.

b. **Current status: equal treatment for husbands and wives.** At present the vast majority of states make consortium actions available to either a husband or a wife. A small number of states do not allow this category of damages for either a husband or a wife.

c. **Joinder of claims.** To prevent possibly multiple recoveries for the same losses, civil procedure rules usually require that the loss of consortium claim be presented in the same trial as the primary victim's main claim against the tortfeasor.

   i. **Duplicative claims.** An example of a duplicative claim involves an injured wife and a husband who curtails his employment to participate in her rehabilitation and nursing. The wife is entitled to damages for the value of those rehabilitation and nursing services. To allow those damages and simultaneously allow the husband to seek compensation for his lost income would, in effect, make the defendant pay twice for the same loss.

E&A Example and Analysis

A defendant whose negligence injures a husband is responsible for the damages directly inflicted on the husband and for the indirect harm that the husband's wife suffers. She is entitled to loss of consortium damages. Because those damages are meant to reflect losses in the quality of the marital relationship, evidence that the husband and wife previously had a happy relationship is relevant. Evidence that their marriage was unhappy and that they did not like to do things together is also relevant to assist the jury in assigning a monetary value to the loss of consortium.

2. Child's Loss of Parental Consortium

An action for a child's loss of parental consortium is meant to compensate the child for the loss of companionship, guidance, and other benefits previously received from the injured parent.

a. **Rejected by most states.** Most states reject loss of parental consortium actions brought by the children of individuals injured by tortfeasors. They base this rejection on a number of factors.

   i. **Large liability.** Parental loss of consortium actions present the risk of large liability for defendants. Allowing spousal consortium actions only makes defendants anticipate additional liability to one person, the spouse of the immediate victim. Allowing parental consortium actions might make defendants liable to a large number of additional plaintiffs, since an initial victim can have only one spouse but could have a large number of children.

   ii. **Duplicative recovery.** A parent's own damage award includes sums of money meant to replace the services the parent would have been able to provide to his or her children. This fact leads some courts to conclude that additional damages paid to the children are duplicative.

b. **Approved by minority.** Some states allow a child's cause of action for loss of parental consortium. They choose to recognize the independent loss suffered by a child as a consequence of injury to a parent. In emotional terms this loss is separate from the loss the parent suffers. For that reason some courts consider it worthy of compensation.

Illustration: Ferriter v. Daniel O'Connell's Sons, Inc., 413 N.E.2d 690 (Mass. 1980). Massachusetts recognized this action, specifying that it would be available only to a child who was a minor and who was dependent on the injured parent.

3. Parent's Loss of Consortium with Child

In some states the parent is permitted to recover for the emotional harm resulting from loss of companionship with the child if injuries make the child less able to participate in family life and familial emotional relationships. Note that this is separate from the cause of action a parent brings to recover the cost of payment for medical and other treatment the child requires because of an injury inflicted by a tortfeasor.

I. WRONGFUL DEATH AND SURVIVAL ACTIONS

Wrongful death actions and survival actions are suits to recover damages for a death caused by a defendant's tortious conduct. These actions were created by statute in each state to supplant an early common law doctrine. At common law, if the victim of a tort died, his or her suit seeking damages for that tort was terminated automatically. Any suit by another person to obtain damages such as loss of consortium damages was also terminated. It was cheaper, therefore, to kill someone than to injure someone.

1. Relationship Between Wrongful Death and Survival Actions

Wrongful death and survival actions are two separate approaches to providing causes of action when defendants' conduct produces death.

a. **Wrongful death action defined.** A wrongful death action can be brought against a tortfeasor by individuals specified in a wrongful death statute. The action seeks compensation for the harm that the death of the original victim has caused to the plaintiffs. These plaintiffs, or wrongful death beneficiaries, ordinarily are entitled to damages for loss of support and loss of companionship.

b. **Survival action defined.** A survival action is brought against a tortfeasor on behalf of the original victim's estate, seeking damages for claims that the original victim would have been allowed to make personally if he or she had not died.

c. **Overlap between wrongful death and survival actions.** Some states have only a wrongful death statute, and a small number of states have only a survival statute. In many states both types of statutes have been adopted. Where both statutes are in force, there can be some overlap of the types of harms they cover. Jurisdictions require that claims under either statute be brought in the same case, or they may require that claimants elect one cause of action.

Example and Analysis

A victim may lose earnings during the time between the injury and his or her death. Those earnings are typically an item of damages in a survival action, since they could have been sought by the victim personally had he or she not died. They are also a typical item in wrongful death recovery, since they represent a loss inflicted on the wrongful death beneficiaries. Jurisdictions use the variety of approaches described to prevent these types of double recoveries.

2. Beneficiaries

The beneficiaries of wrongful death and survival actions are defined in each state's applicable statutes.

a. **Wrongful death beneficiaries.** Wrongful death beneficiaries are usually the spouse and children of the victim. Step-children are ordinarily excluded from status as beneficiaries. In some states a victim's illegitimate children are excluded from recovery in a wrongful death action.

   i. **Unmarried or childless victim.** If the victim had no spouse or children, most statutes allow the victim's parents to be beneficiaries.

   ii. **Victim's nonspouse life partner.** No wrongful death statutes allow recovery for life partners or lovers.

b. **Survival action beneficiary.** The beneficiary in a survival action is the estate of the victim. Any judgment recovered by the estate is distributed according to the jurisdiction's general rules for decedents' estates.

3. Damages

Damages in all jurisdictions include medical and related expenses, funeral expenses, and the loss of the victim's future earnings. States are split on whether noneconomic damages should be available. Noneconomic damages provide compensation for grief and the loss of companionship with the victim.

a. **Statutory limits.** Early wrongful death statutes typically imposed ceilings on possible damage awards. Most statutes no longer contain these provisions, but some do limit total awards or the amount that members of a particular class of beneficiaries may receive.

b. **Death of a child.** Damages for the death of a child are affected by whether a jurisdiction recognizes noneconomic damages as well as economic damages.

i. **Only economic damages recognized.** In jurisdictions that allow damages only for economic losses, a child's death poses a significant problem, since straightforward analysis would probably support the conclusion that there has been no significant economic loss. The meaning of economic loss is sometimes stretched for these cases to recognize a monetary value in the loss of anticipated companionship. In some jurisdictions damages for the death of a child may include amounts that the parents anticipated the child would someday give to them, typically to help with their living expenses during their old age.

ii. **Economic and noneconomic damages recognized.** In jurisdictions that allow recovery for noneconomic losses such as mental anguish or loss of companionship, a case involving a child's death is similar to a case involving an adult's death. Even though the child had no earning power, the beneficiaries are likely to be awarded significant damages.

c. **Damages-to-estate rule.** A minority of jurisdictions calculate damages in terms of the loss to the decedent's estate. This method estimates the amount the decedent would have earned had he or she lived a normal time and deducts from that amount an estimate of the amount he or she would have spent personally. For people of low income, this calculation might not allow a finding of any damages at all, since they typically spend all that they earn.

d. **Spouse's remarriage.** Most jurisdictions prohibit informing the jury that a victim's widow or widower has remarried prior to the time of the wrongful death suit.

4. Defenses

The victim's own negligence, if any, is recognized in a wrongful death or survival action under the jurisdiction's usual comparative negligence principles. If a beneficiary had a role in the injury that caused the death, that beneficiary's negligence may also bar or reduce that beneficiary's recovery under the jurisdiction's standard comparative negligence principles.

J. PUNITIVE DAMAGES

In exceptional cases a jury is permitted to award punitive damages in addition to compensatory damages. Punitive damages are a sum of money taken from the defendant as a punishment; they are allowed only in cases where the defendant's conduct has been unusually bad. Usually the plaintiff must show reckless or willful and wanton conduct by the defendant. The punitive damages award is ordinarily given to the plaintiff. Some states now require that a portion of punitive damages be paid to the state.

1. Rationale

Punitive damages are a blend of policies from tort law and criminal law. They are similar to a fine imposed as part of the criminal law process; they are administered in the civil torts process, however, and have many attributes common to civil cases. A jury decides the amount, and the money is given to the plaintiff rather than to the state. Justifications for such penalties include that merely redressing the wrong may not be a strong enough deterrent for future misconduct, and that society demands significant punishment (in addition to deterrence) for some outstandingly bad conduct.

2. Current Controversies

The tort reform movement has devoted considerable attention to punitive damages. Recent scholarship and judicial decisions draw attention to several difficult issues concerning their fairness.

a. **Multiple judgments against a single defendant.** Especially in products liability suits, it is possible that a single defendant might be subject to multiple punitive damages awards in a series of cases brought by similarly injured plaintiffs. This possibility has led some manufacturers to use bankruptcy procedures as a way to manage that large risk.

b. **Constitutional challenges.** Critics of contemporary tort law seek to limit punitive damages through legislation aimed at establishing that they may be unconstitutional. The United States Supreme Court has ruled that, in general, punitive damages do not violate due process, in part because they have been an attribute of civil litigation since the earliest days of the nation. In a series of decisions, the Court has held, however, that some punitive damages awards may be too high to be constitutional.

Illustrations: Pacific Mutual Life Ins. Co. v. Haslip, 499 U.S. 1, 111 S. Ct. 1032, 113 L. Ed.2d 1 (1991). The plaintiff's insurance company was liable for an agent's fraudulent conduct that had led to the plaintiff's loss of money, loss of a favorable credit rating, and significant pain and suffering. The plaintiff won a judgment that included about $200,000 in compensatory damages and about $840,000 in punitive damages. The Court held that the size of the punitive damages award did not violate any constitutional principles, primarily because the state courts in which the award was made and affirmed had precise methodology for review and evaluation of the size of such awards.

BMW of North America, Inc. v. Gore, 116 S. Ct. 1589 (1996). The court invalidated a $2-million punitive damages award. The defendant automobile manufacturer had sold a car as new, even though the car had been damaged during shipping and then repaired. The jury assessed compensatory damages at $4,000 but set punitive damages at $4 million (reduced to $2 million by remittitur).

These decisions do not establish clear doctrines to separate legitimate and illegitimate punitive damages awards, but they do describe certain restrictions.

i. **Multiple-state conduct.** The Court has held that a state court jury may only consider a defendant's conduct in that state in assessing punitive damages. Considering the defendant's conduct elsewhere would represent an effort by a single state to control conduct outside its borders.

ii. **Reprehensible conduct.** Conduct that represents a good-faith choice among possible courses of action is not reprehensible enough to support a large punitive damages award, even if the conduct is ultimately judged to have been tortious. Harm that is merely economic is less reprehensible than harm that affects health or safety.

iii. **Compensatory to punitive ratio.** The ratio between compensatory and punitive damages must not be too large. In the *BMW* case the Court held that a 500-to-1 ratio between punitive and compensatory damages was too great.

iv. **Relationship to civil or criminal penalties.** A punitive damages award can be supported by a showing that it is similar in size to civil or criminal penalties that a state might impose for the defendant's type of conduct. In *BMW,* for example, the highest probable criminal or civil penalty for the defendant's conduct would have been about $2,000. This contributed to the court's finding that a $2-million punitive damages award was constitutionally improper.

3. Insurance for Punitive Damages

Some insurance policies explicitly exclude coverage for punitive damages. Where a policy appears to allow such coverage, courts are divided on whether social policies should allow a tortfeasor to be reimbursed through insurance for the cost of punitive damages. Some courts prohibit insurance coverage for punitive damages awards, on the theory that insurance coverage negates their punitive effect.

4. Statutory Restrictions

Some states have adopted statutes that control punitive damages awards. These statutes may require that certain portions of punitive awards be paid to the state rather than to the plaintiff. There are also a number of statutes that impose a ceiling on the amount of punitive damages that may be awarded or that heighten the evidentiary standard against which the jury must weigh the plaintiff's proof (for example, rejecting the usual preponderance-of-the-evidence standard and replacing it with the beyond-a-reasonable-doubt standard).

K. CONDITIONAL NEW-TRIAL ORDERS: ADDITUR AND REMITTITUR

Additur and remittitur are two procedural devices that can cause a plaintiff to receive a judgment different from the amount a jury specifies. They both involve the conditional grant of a new trial: the trial judge orders that a new trial will be held unless the party who opposes the motion for new trial accepts a judgment in a specific amount set by the judge.

1. Additur

A plaintiff who is unsatisfied with the amount of a jury verdict may move for a new trial or for additur. If the judge decides to use the additur procedure, he or she chooses a new, higher judgment amount and orders a new trial unless the defendant agrees to pay that new amount. Additur is not permitted in federal trials and has been limited in some states.

2. Remittitur

Remittitur is the mirror image of additur. A defendant who is unsatisfied with the amount of a jury verdict may move for a new trial or for remittitur. If the judge decides to use the remittitur procedure, he or she chooses a new, lower judgment amount and orders a new trial unless the plaintiff agrees to accept that new amount. Remittitur is permitted in federal trials and in most states.

REVIEW QUESTIONS AND ANSWERS

Question: Why would some jurisdictions have juries ignore both inflation and the principle of reduction to present value in calculating awards for future lost wages or future medical expenses?

Answer: The two factors, inflation and reduction to present value, work in opposite directions. Anticipating inflation, a jury necessarily awards more money to the plaintiff than it would if it thought that there would be no inflation in the future. Reduction of an award to present value, on the other hand, requires awarding less money at present than the plaintiff is thought to deserve in the future, since money can be invested and expected to increase in amount over time. Calculations based on both these two principles are inexact, since no one can know future interest or inflation rates. Some courts believe that ignoring both concepts is the fairest approach to handling our inability to apply them with full accuracy.

Question: If a plaintiff has incurred $35,000 in medical expenses due to the defendant's negligence but has received $20,000 in insurance benefits to pay those medical expenses, what award would the plaintiff receive for medical expenses in a jurisdiction that applies the collateral source rule?

Answer: $35,000. The collateral source rule requires the trial court to ignore payments the plaintiff has received from sources other than the defendant in computing the amount of damages to which the plaintiff is entitled.

Question: Would proof that a husband and wife had been experiencing serious marital difficulties be relevant to deciding the amount of loss of consortium damages one of them would be entitled to receive if the other were injured by a defendant's negligent act?

Answer: Yes. Since consortium damages are meant, in part, to compensate for the value of lost companionship, evidence that the companionship was of little value would be relevant to the jury's evaluation of the proper dollar amount to award for that damages category.

Question: What factors would be important in evaluating the constitutionality of a judgment that included $1,000 for compensatory damages and $2,000,000 for punitive damages, if the defendant's misconduct had exposed the plaintiff to economic harm but no physical risks, and the trial court and state appellate court had not evaluated the propriety of the size of the damages awards?

Answer: The Supreme Court has held that a state's appellate- and trial-court controls over punitive damage amounts are a significant factor. If there were no controls of that type, the punitive damages award might be improper. Also, in this problem the ratio between compensatory and punitive damages is 1 to 2,000, much higher than the ratio (1 to 500) found to be excessive in the *BMW* case. Finally, it is significant that the defendant's conduct exposed the plaintiff to economic but not physical harm. That factor makes a large punitive damages award less sustainable than it would be if the plaintiff had been exposed to a risk of bodily injury.

Exam Tips

- Exam questions often highlight the lack of logic in assigning dollar values to intangible harms like pain or loss of enjoyment of life. Two main responses to that lack of logic are important: 1. the logical flaw is genuine; and 2. money is all we have to work with in our society, so it is understandable that the tort system uses it for a wide range of damages categories.
- Factors that affect the size of an award include reduction to present value, future inflation, nontaxability of personal injury awards, and ceilings on allowable damages. If a question brings up the topic of probable total damages or the range of considerations that affect probable total damages, discuss as many of these concepts as possible.
- The collateral source rule is controversial at present, so it is a common topic for exam questions. The rule lets plaintiffs keep the benefit of any compensation they receive for their injuries (in addition to money paid to them by the defendant).
- Can consortium claims by children be distinguished from consortium claims by spouses? Most states think that the categories are different, mainly because a spouse can have only one husband or wife, while a parent can have an unpredictable number of children.
- Punitive damages awards are subject to very slight constitutional controls, but the details of the evolving standards are important. A ratio of 500 to 1 in a case of economic harm (not physical harm) was too high, in a recent Supreme Court analysis.

13 DEFENSES

CHAPTER OVERVIEW

- The contributory negligence doctrine treats any negligence by a plaintiff as a complete defense. A plaintiff who is negligent in any way that contributes to his or her injury is barred from recovery.
- Four states and the District of Columbia now apply the contributory negligence doctrine. All other jurisdictions use forms of comparative negligence.
- There are three main versions of the comparative negligence doctrine. All of them reject the concept that a plaintiff who is in any way negligent must be barred from recovery.
- Pure comparative negligence allows a negligent plaintiff to recover damages reduced by the percentage the finder of fact assigns to represent the plaintiff's responsibility for the plaintiff's injury.
- Modified comparative negligence allows a negligent plaintiff to recover damages if the plaintiff's share of responsibility assigned by the finder of fact is 50 percent or less (50-percent form of modified comparative negligence) or is 49 percent or less (49-percent form of modified comparative negligencc). Such a plaintiff is entitled to damages reduced by the percentage the finder of fact assigns to represent the plaintiff's responsibility for the plaintiff's injury.
- Under modified comparative negligence systems a plaintiff whose share of responsibility is more than the system's limit (more than 49 percent or more than 50 percent) is totally barred from recovery.

- Adoption of comparative negligence has led to the abrogation of the last clear chance doctrine and some other contributory negligence era approaches that lessened the anti-plaintiff effects of the contributory negligence rule.
- Assumption of risk prevents a plaintiff from recovering damages from a defendant in a case where the plaintiff expressly agreed that the defendant could inflict harms without liability.
- Some conduct by a plaintiff was formerly treated as supporting a finding of implied assumption of risk. This type of conduct is now analyzed identically to other conduct by a plaintiff that might reduce recovery under comparative negligence principles.
- Statutes of limitation bar remedies for stale claims. Doctrines that modify their effect include the discovery rule and the continuous treatment rule. Special treatment is sometimes provided for sexual abuse cases involving repressed memories.
- Immunities protect government bodies and government employees from liability for various types of conduct. Statutes allowing governmental liability provide access to remedies in many instances.
- Charities were once immunized from suit, but most jurisdictions now treat them as equivalent to for-profit entities for purposes of tort litigation.
- Intrafamilial litigation is sometimes prevented by immunities, but these immunities have been modified in certain circumstances.

A. PLAINTIFF'S NEGLIGENT CONDUCT

A negligent defendant is sometimes protected from liability to an injured plaintiff because of the plaintiff's own negligent conduct connected to the injury. The concepts tort law uses for taking account of a plaintiff's negligent conduct are contributory negligence and comparative negligence.

1. Contributory Negligence Defined

Under the contributory negligence doctrine a plaintiff whose own negligence contributes in any way to his or her injury is prohibited from recovering any damages from the defendant. In other words, any amount of negligence by the plaintiff is a complete defense.

Illustration: Butterfield v. Forrester, 11 East 60, 103 Eng. Rep. 926 (King's Bench 1809). The plaintiff, riding his horse in a negligent manner, rode into an obstruction that the defendant had negligently left blocking a road. A jury finding for the defendant was upheld on appeal. The court ruled that even if one person was at fault, another person was still obligated to use ordinary care for himself.

a. **Contemporary significance.** Contributory negligence applies now only in a single geographic cluster of jurisdictions: Alabama, Maryland, North Carolina, Virginia, and the District of Columbia. Except for those five jurisdictions, its importance is mainly historical. Understanding contributory negligence is sometimes helpful, however, in resolving issues about the application of its successor doctrine, comparative negligence.

b. **Rationales.** The basic rationale supporting the contributory negligence doctrine is that a person who has acted wrongly is not entitled to any redress from another person and is not entitled to have the government act in his or her behalf to make someone else pay for all or part of the harm. Another rationale sometimes offered for the contributory negligence doctrine is that the plaintiff's conduct is the proximate cause of the plaintiff's harm. This rationale is dubious, since it is generally understood that events can have more than one proximate cause.

EXAMPLE AND ANALYSIS

Under contributory negligence if a driver drove 30 miles per hour over the speed limit in a residential area and hit two people who were crossing a street, the victims would have no recovery against the driver if he or she could show that they had been negligent in any way. For example, if they had been talking to each other while walking and had failed to look carefully for traffic, their negligence would serve as a complete defense for the defendant driver.

c. **Application.** To apply the contributory negligence doctrine it is necessary to evaluate the conduct of the plaintiff. The plaintiff owes a duty to protect himself or herself. To determine whether the plaintiff breached that duty, essentially the same standards of care used to evaluate the defendant's conduct apply. Finally, proximate causation must be shown to link the plaintiff's negligence to the plaintiff's harm.

   i. **Child's standard of care.** Some scholars have suggested that the development of the special, child's standard of care was influenced by the contributory negligence doctrine. Since children are more often plaintiffs than defendants, establishing a lenient standard for evaluating their conduct makes it less likely that the contributory negligence doctrine will bar them from recovering damages for injuries they suffer. The lenient standard is not likely to work to the disadvantage of many plaintiffs, since children inflict injuries relatively rarely.

   ii. **Causation.** A defendant who sought to use the contributory negligence defense was obligated to show that the plaintiff's negligence had a cause-in-fact and a proximate-cause relationship to the plaintiff's injury. The same general rules for causation that apply to the link between a defendant's conduct and a plaintiff's injury also apply to the link between a plaintiff's conduct and a plaintiff's injury.

(a) **Pro-plaintiff application of causation rules.** Some courts in contributory negligence jurisdictions interpret proximate cause doctrines favorably to plaintiffs. Where the plaintiff's conduct risked causing a certain harm in a certain way, for example, but harm actually happened in some other way, some courts have permitted a finding that the plaintiff's conduct was not a proximate cause of the harm. This is opposite to the result that most courts reach in evaluating the causation issues related to a defendant's conduct.

d. **Plaintiff's responses to the contributory negligence defense.** The drastic consequence of the contributory negligence doctrine was total victory for the defendant in any case in which it applied. This fact influenced the common law courts to develop a number of exceptions to application of the doctrine.

i. **Last clear chance doctrine.** The last clear chance doctrine is an important doctrine available to plaintiffs to moderate the impact of contributory negligence. In a case where the defendant had the last clear chance to avoid an injury, the contributory negligence doctrine is withdrawn and the plaintiff is entitled to full recovery.

Illustration: Davies v. Mann, 10 M.&W. 547, 152 Eng. Rep. 588 (Exchequer 1842). The defendant's bad wagon driving injured the plaintiff's donkey, which the plaintiff had negligently fettered too close to a road. Recovery by the negligent plaintiff was affirmed on the theory that the defendant had the last clear chance to prevent the injury.

During the heyday of the contributory negligence doctrine, the last clear chance exception was the subject of a great deal of litigation. Cases usually involved characterizations of plaintiffs as helpless or inattentive and of defendants as aware or not aware of the dangerous situation. The following table shows how jurisdictions typically treated the last clear chance doctrine using these characterizations.

ii. **Unavailable as a defense to certain types of misconduct by defendants.** Another response to the contributory negligence doctrine was a set of doctrines rejecting its application where the defendant's conduct was especially bad. A plaintiff who had been negligent (and completely barred from recovery, ordinarily) was permitted to recover full damages in any case in which the defendant's conduct was an intentional tort, was reckless or willful and wanton,

APPLICABILITY OF LAST CLEAR CHANCE DOCTRINE ACCORDING TO CHARACTERIZATIONS OF PLAINTIFF AND DEFENDANT

	Aware Defendant	*Unaware Defendant*
Helpless Plaintiff	Last clear chance doctrine applies in all jurisdictions, withdrawing the contributory negligence doctrine and allowing plaintiff to recover.	Last clear chance doctrine applies in most jurisdictions, withdrawing the contributory negligence doctrine and allowing plaintiff to recover. This was called "unconscious last clear chance."
Inattentive Plaintiff	Last clear chance doctrine applies in most jurisdictions, withdrawing the contributory negligence doctrine and allowing plaintiff to recover.	Last clear chance doctrine has no application. Contributory negligence applies in all jurisdictions, since neither plaintiff nor defendant had last clear chance.

or was a violation of a safety statute adopted for the protection of individuals like the plaintiff.

2. Comparative Negligence

Under the comparative negligence doctrine a plaintiff's negligence is not automatically a bar to recovery. There are two main types of comparative negligence: pure comparative negligence and modified comparative negligence. Pure comparative negligence treats a plaintiff's negligence by reducing the plaintiff's recovery in every case to reflect his or her percentage of responsibility rather than by barring recovery completely. Modified comparative negligence also reduces the plaintiff's recovery to reflect his or her negligence but only applies in cases where the plaintiff's negligence is less than a particular percentage.

Illustration: McIntyre v. Balentine, 833 S.W.2d 52 (Tenn. 1992). The Tennessee supreme court surveyed the history of the development of comparative negligence and adopted the modified form, making Tennessee the 46th state to adopt it.

a. **Contemporary significance.** In 46 states comparative negligence is the main doctrine for dealing with a plaintiff's contribution to his or her own injury. Another name for the doctrine is comparative fault.

b. **Contrast with contributory negligence.** Comparative negligence is a significant contrast to the contributory negligence doctrine, which works on an all-or-nothing basis. Under contributory negligence, if the jury finds that the plaintiff was negligent, the plaintiff recovers nothing; if the jury finds that the plaintiff was free from negligence, then the plaintiff recovers full damages. Where comparative negligence applies, if a jury finds that the plaintiff was partly responsible for his or her injury, the plaintiff is not necessarily barred from recovery but may be entitled to damages that are reduced to reflect the plaintiff's responsibility.

c. **Application.** In all comparative negligence systems findings of fact must be made on two topics: the amount of the plaintiff's damages and the amount of the plaintiff's responsibility for those damages. Damages are stated in dollar amounts, and responsibility is stated as a percentage.

   i. **Meaning of "plaintiff's percentage."** Most jurisdictions have not developed a clear answer to the question of what the jury should compare in comparative negligence. Jurors are usually told to assign a percentage of negligence or responsibility to each party whose conduct they are required to evaluate. Their percentages must total 100.

      (a) **Quality of actor's conduct.** The percentage of responsibility may be based on the jury's conclusion about how bad the plaintiff's conduct was, from not at all bad (reasonable conduct) to extremely bad (highly unreasonable conduct).

      (b) **Causal significance of actor's conduct.** The percentage of responsibility may be based on a conclusion about causal significance. In a few jurisdictions this analysis is required. The jury must decide whether each actor was negligent in any degree. Then, for each actor who was negligent, the jury determines what percentage of the total causation of the plaintiff's injury is attributable to each actor's conduct, regardless of how bad the conduct was.

E&A Example and Analysis

A plaintiff might be judged to have suffered $100,000 in damages and to have been 20-percent responsible for those damages. The plaintiff would be entitled, under comparative negligence principles, to a judgment that is reduced to reflect his or her percentage of responsibility. The plaintiff's judgment would be for $80,000. That amount is calculated by subtracting 20 percent of the damages finding, to prevent the plaintiff from recovering money for the proportion of damages that his or her own negligence caused. The same result follows from calculating that the defendant or defendants were responsible for 80 percent of the negligence and, therefore, that they should pay $80,000.

---

d. **Types of comparative negligence.** Beginning in the late 1960s, states began rejecting contributory negligence and replacing it with comparative negligence (Mississippi had used the system since the beginning of the century, and Wisconsin had adopted it many years prior to the 1960s). In some states legislatures adopted it, and in others it was adopted by judicial decision. Comparative negligence is usually described as pure or modified. Modified systems are further characterized as either 50-percent or 49-percent systems.

   i. **Pure.** In pure comparative negligence a plaintiff is allowed to recover if his or her negligence is less than 100 percent of the total negligence involved in his or her injury. Total damages are reduced by the plaintiff's percentage of responsibility.

   ii. **Modified, 50-percent form.** In the 50-percent form of modified comparative negligence, a plaintiff is allowed to recover if his or her negligence is 50 percent or less of the total negligence involved in his or her injury. Total damages are reduced by the plaintiff's percentage of responsibility. A plaintiff whose negligence is 51 percent or more recovers nothing.

   iii. **Modified, 49-percent form.** In the 49-percent form of modified comparative negligence, a plaintiff is allowed to recover if his or her negligence is 49 percent or less of the total negligence involved in his or her injury. Total damages are reduced by the plaintiff's percentage of responsibility. A plaintiff whose negligence is 50 percent or more recovers nothing

e. **Distinctions between pure and both modified forms of comparative negligence.** The pure form allows any plaintiff to recover some amount of damages, unless he or she is responsible for all of the negligence involved in his or her injury. The 50-percent form allows a plaintiff to recover if his or her negligence is less than or equal to the negligence of the defendant. The 49-percent form allows a plaintiff to recover if his or her negligence is less than the defendant's.

   i. **Modified forms and 50-50 cases.** The difference between the 49-percent and 50-percent forms of modified comparative negligence is significant only in a case where the jury finds that the plaintiff and the defendant were equally at fault. This type of case is fairly common where there has been fault by both the plaintiff and the defendant or defendants against whom recovery is sought. If the jury finds that the parties were equally at fault (50 percent and 50 percent), the plaintiff recovers damages (reduced by 50 percent) in a 50-percent, modified comparative negligence jurisdiction but recovers nothing in a 49-percent, modified comparative negligence jurisdiction.

f. **Illustrative chart.** Organized according to possible jury determinations of the plaintiff's percentage of fault, the following chart shows the recoveries that would be granted to a plaintiff with $100,000 in damages under the various forms of comparative negligence.

	Plaintiff's percentage of responsibility		
Form	*0 to 49*	*50*	*51 to 100*
pure	$100,000 to $51,000	$50,000	$49,000 to zero
modified, 50-percent form	$100,000 to $51,000	$50,000	zero
modified, 49-percent form	$100,000 to $51,000	zero	zero

g. **Multiple party cases.** Some comparative negligence cases involve more than one defendant. These multiple party cases raise some issues not present in a simple case involving a single plaintiff and a single defendant.

   i. **Unit or individual rule.** In modified comparative negligence jurisdictions a plaintiff may recover only if his or her negligence is less than the defendant's (49-percent form) or is equal to or less than the defendant's (50-percent form). Courts adopting these forms of comparative negligence, and some legislatures, have failed to specify what comparison should be made in multiple party cases. There are two possibilities: comparing the plaintiff to each individual defendant separately or comparing the plaintiff to the total of negligence assigned to all the defendants. These methods are called the individual rule and the unit rule, respectively. The vast majority of jurisdictions use the unit rule, comparing the plaintiff's responsibility to the total of all the defendants' negligence.

E&A EXAMPLE AND ANALYSIS

In a two-defendant case, if a jury found that the plaintiff's share of responsibility was 40 percent and that each defendant's share was 30 percent, the plaintiff would recover nothing under the individual rule. Under the unit rule the plaintiff would recover 60 percent of the damages found by the jury. The plaintiff would be barred under the individual rule because his or her 40-percent share of responsibility is greater than each defendant's 30-percent share. The unit rule combines the defendants' shares to reach a total of 60 percent. That figure is greater than the plaintiff's 40 percent, allowing the plaintiff to recover.

---

ii. Consideration of nonparties' conduct. In the era of contributory negligence, any plaintiff who was found to have been negligent was completely barred from recovery. On the other hand, any defendant whose conduct was in any way negligent and causally related to the plaintiff's harm was responsible for the plaintiff's entire damages under the joint and several liability doctrine. A defendant had little incentive to have the jury consider the conduct of additional actors (unless it was likely that the jury would find someone other than the defendant entirely responsible for the plaintiff's harm).

Under comparative negligence some jurisdictions have eliminated or limited the joint and several liability doctrine. This gives defendants an incentive to offer proof about other parties' possible negligence, so the jury may assign percentages of responsibility to those other parties.

(a) **Jurisdictions that apply joint and several liability.** Adding additional defendants is possible, but it will not preclude the plaintiff's enforcing any judgment against the defendant the plaintiff originally selected to sue.

(b) **Jurisdictions that eliminate or restrict joint and several liability.** Adding additional defendants is very much to the advantage of any defendant originally selected for suit by the plaintiff, since there is a chance that the jury will assign some amount of responsibility to any actor whose conduct it considers. If the jury does assign a share of responsibility to parties the plaintiff chose not to sue, the share left for allocation to the original defendant is less.

(c) **Phantom parties.** In some states a defendant is entitled to give notice to the plaintiff that he or she will seek to have the jury consider the negligence of phantom, or nonparty, actors. A common scenario for this is a multi-car collision in which one of the drivers leaves the scene of the accident and is not identified. The jury is allowed to evaluate the conduct of the absent and unidentified actor and to assign a percentage of responsibility to that person. This reduces the original defendant's share of responsibility. The plaintiff is not able to collect damages from the unidentified actor. This means that the plaintiff receives a smaller amount of damages than he or she would have received in a system that precludes consideration of the conduct of individuals who are not parties to the litigation.

h. **Rationale for comparative negligence.** The strongest impetus for the adoption of comparative negligence was dissatisfaction with the total bar of contributory negligence. After long experience with that system, courts and legislatures became convinced that defendants who harm negligent plaintiffs should not always be totally free from financial consequences, particularly in a case where the plaintiff's negligence was less than the defendant's. Reluctance to reward careless plaintiffs was overcome by a belief that it was wrong to allow negligent defendants to avoid all the costs of the injuries they partly caused.

   i. **Fairness to plaintiffs.** The pure form of comparative negligence can be described as fair to all plaintiffs. A plaintiff who was negligent always bears some of the cost of his or her injury, since compensation from a defendant only covers part of its cost. The modified forms of comparative negligence fail to compensate plaintiffs whose own negligence exceeds those forms' 49-percent or 50-percent thresholds.

E&A Example and Analysis

Under pure comparative negligence a plaintiff who was 90-percent responsible for an injury valued at $100,000 receives $10,000 from the defendant but bears $90,000 of the cost personally. A plaintiff who was, for example, 55-percent responsible for an injury valued at $100,000 receives $45,000 but bears $55,000 of the cost personally. Under modified forms of comparative negligence, each of these plaintiffs recovers nothing, since in each case the plaintiff's negligence was greater than the defendant's.

   ii. **Serve the deterrence goal of tort law.** The pure form of comparative negligence deters all individuals from acting negligently. A plaintiff always suffers a reduction in recovery to reflect his or her negligence, and any defendant whose negligence caused harms pays for some of the cost of those harms. The modified forms of comparative negligence similarly provide deterrence to plaintiffs and defendants in all cases in which the plaintiff's negligence does not exceed the forms' threshold amounts. In a case where a plaintiff's negligence is greater than the threshold amounts, however, the plaintiff recovers nothing. Such a case provides no deterrence to defendants, even though the defendants may have been negligent. It may also be said that such a case provides too much deterrence to plaintiffs since a plaintiff who is only 51-percent responsible for his or her injury is required to bear its entire cost.

iii. **Increase compensation to deserving plaintiffs.** All forms of comparative negligence increase the availability of compensation to plaintiffs. Pure comparative negligence allows compensation to all injured plaintiffs except those who are 100-percent responsible for their injuries. The modified forms of comparative negligence make compensation available to many plaintiffs who would have been excluded from recovery by the contributory negligence doctrine, but they continue to treat some plaintiffs' negligence as a full defense (negligence that exceeds the systems' thresholds of either 49 or 50 percent).

i. **Effect on traditional contributory negligence doctrines.** Adopting comparative negligence has led many jurisdictions to reconsider certain doctrines developed under the contributory negligence system primarily to favor plaintiffs in cases where barring them from recovery due to their own negligence seemed particularly unwise.

i. **Last clear chance.** Every jurisdiction that has adopted comparative negligence and has considered the continued applicability of the last clear chance doctrine has rejected it. The facts that supported application of this doctrine—a plaintiff's helpless state or a defendant's awareness of a plaintiff's peril—are facts that a jury takes into account in assigning percentages of negligence.

ii. **Sudden emergency.** Jurisdictions are divided on whether the sudden emergency doctrine should continue under comparative negligence. The doctrine is essentially a special instruction to the jury, stating that people who confront sudden emergencies not of their own making may act with less care than would otherwise be required. While those factors can be assessed under comparative negligence, some jurisdictions continue to allow the use of a sudden-emergency jury instruction.

iii. **Defendant's willful and wanton or intentional misconduct.** Under the contributory negligence system a plaintiff's negligence was not a defense to liability based on a defendant's intentional tort or a defendant's reckless or willful and wanton conduct. A few comparative negligence jurisdictions continue this doctrinal approach and refuse to reduce a defendant's liability to a negligent plaintiff when the defendant's conduct fits one of these especially blameworthy categories. Many comparative negligence jurisdictions take the opposite approach and allow the jury to compare a plaintiff's negligence with a defendant's conduct, even if the defendant's conduct is worse than negligent.

iv. **Open and obvious danger.** A few jurisdictions have rejected the rule that an entrant on land has no cause of action against the landowner for an injury caused by an encounter with an open and obvious hazard. They have reasoned that this open-and-obvious-danger rule is essentially the same as contributory negligence as a matter of law. For this reason, having abrogated the contributory negligence doctrine, they reject the open-and-obvious-danger rule as well.

v. **Safety statutes.** In most states a defendant whose negligence involved violation of a statute enacted for the safety of a class of individuals that includes the plaintiff is prohibited from relying on the plaintiff's own negligence as a defense, even under comparative negligence.

j. **Nonuse of available seat belt.** Many tort cases involve vehicular accidents, and some of these involve a plaintiff who failed to use an available seat belt. Jurisdictions differ in how they treat this type of conduct by a plaintiff.

i. **Not relevant.** A few jurisdictions prohibit consideration of the plaintiff's failure to use an available seat belt.

ii. **Plaintiff bears total cost of avoidable injuries.** In some jurisdictions the plaintiff bears the total cost of the injuries he or she would have avoided through use of the available seat belt. It is the defendant's burden to show what part of the plaintiff's injuries can be attributed to the failure to use the seat belt.

Illustration: Spier v. Barker, 35 N.Y.2d 444, 363 N.Y.S.2d 916, 323 N.E.2d 164 (1974). The plaintiff was thrown from a vehicle in a collision, allegedly because she had failed to use an available seat belt. The court of appeals affirmed a judgment for the defendant, holding that the trial court had correctly instructed that there could be no recovery for any injuries that would have been avoided if the victim had used the seat belt.

iii. **Plaintiff's fault related to entire incident applies to all injuries.** Many jurisdictions instruct the jury to determine a percentage of fault that encompasses all aspects of the plaintiff's conduct. That percentage is used to reduce the plaintiff's recovery for all damages, including those that might have been avoided with use of a seat belt.

iv. **Plaintiff's fault related to nonuse of seatbelt applies only to avoidable injuries.** A minority of jurisdictions require the jury to make separate findings of plaintiff's fault, with one related to failure to use an available seat belt and another related to all other aspects of the plaintiff's conduct. The negligence percentage with regard to failure to use the seat belt is applied to damages related to that failure, and the other percentage is applied to all other damages.

v. **Statutes.** In many states statutes require the use of seat belts. These statutes often give explicit treatment to the role in tort litigation of a person's failure to use a seat belt. They typically set an upper limit on the percentage of negligence that the jury may assign for that conduct. In some of these statutes, the maximum percentage is a relatively low number, such as 5 percent or 10 percent.

B. ASSUMPTION OF RISK

A traditional doctrine, assumption of risk, completely protected a defendant from liability when the defendant established that the plaintiff's conduct met the doctrine's definitions. The doctrine is best understood historically. In the contributory negligence era the law recognized express assumption of risk and two kinds of implied assumption of risk. At present the majority of jurisdictions recognize express assumption of risk and only one kind of implied assumption of risk.

1. Overlap of Contributory Negligence and Assumption of Risk

In contributory negligence jurisdictions a plaintiff who was at all negligent was barred from recovery. Note that this consequence is identical to the consequence of a finding that the plaintiff assumed the risk. Because a defendant's victory was required under a finding of either contributory negligence or assumption of risk, some decisions in contributory negligence jurisdictions did not make clear distinctions between these two doctrines.

2. Express Assumption of Risk

Express assumption of risk is the legal description for the situation in which a plaintiff actually agrees to suffer the consequences of someone's negligence without seeking legal redress for any injuries. Courts are usually reluctant to enforce such agreements unless they are in writing. Even when they are written, courts tend to be strict in the analysis of their phraseology and the size and style of print that the defendant chose to use. Express assumption of risk is a complete defense under comparative negligence, as it was under the contributory negligence system.

Illustration: Winterstein v. Wilcom, 16 Md. App. 130, 293 A.2d 821 (1972). The plaintiff was injured in a collision while he was participating in a speed contest at a drag racing track. Judgment for the defendant, the operator of the track, was affirmed on appeal, since the plaintiff had signed a release prior to his injury. There were no public policy reasons to refuse enforcement of the release.

a. **Prohibited assumptions of risk.** Courts refuse to give effect to express assumptions of risk in some cases for public policy reasons.

   i. **Recklessness and intentional torts.** Courts refuse to enforce assumption of the risk agreements in which a plaintiff agrees not to seek damages for the defendant's willful and wanton, reckless, or intentional torts.

   ii. **Health care.** Health care providers are generally not allowed to have their patients assume the risk of negligent treatment. The rationale for refusing to allow health care providers to negotiate assumption of risk agreements with their patients is that there is a large disparity in bargaining power between those who need health care and those who provide it. Courts reason that an express assumption of risk would not really be voluntary. (Voluntariness is a standard requirement for establishing assumption of risk.)

   iii. **Public services.** Common carriers and public utilities are not permitted to rely on express assumption of risk agreements as defenses against liability to their customers. Courts have held that these entities have received a valuable benefit from society (the right to operate their particular businesses) and that inherent in that benefit is their obligation to compensate customers for the injuries they may cause due to negligence.

   iv. **Parking lots and similar facilities.** Parking lots and other facilities, such as coat-check rooms, may have an effective monopoly because of their locations. This leads courts to decline to enforce assumption of risk agreements with their customers. Courts generally honor assumption of risk arrangements made between businesses of this type and their customers, however, if these agreements are disclosed clearly, and if the prices they charged reflect the way the risks of loss are allocated between the businesses and their customers.

E&A EXAMPLE AND ANALYSIS

Charlie Customer joined GlamourGym, a health club, and paid monthly dues. Customer signed a release stating that he would not seek tort damages from GlamourGym for any injuries suffered while exercising due to inherent risks of exercise or due to GlamourGym's negligence. While Customer was working on a machine at the club, it suddenly increased its speed and the power of its resistance, breaking one of Customer's arms. GlamourGym had failed to maintain the machine properly. Customer has no cause of action against GlamourGym for this injury. The release is a valid assumption of risk that protects GlamourGym and is not against any of the public policies that can void such releases.

---

3. Implied Primary Assumption of Risk

The term *implied primary assumption of risk* is applied to a small group of situations concerning which courts hold that defendants owe either no duty or a reduced duty of care to plaintiffs. In these situations, because society has lessened the defendants' usual obligation to be careful, courts have sometimes said that plaintiffs assume the risk of injury. This doctrine applies in contributory negligence jurisdictions and in comparative negligence jurisdictions.

a. **Typical instances.** A common example of implied primary assumption of risk is the activity of attending professional sports games. In baseball, illustratively, the owner of a team has no obligation to protect a spectator from the risks of being hit by a batted ball or a thrown bat unless the spectator is seated in the area behind home plate. Some courts describe this result as assumption of risk, but others more accurately describe it as an example of limited duty. Other examples involve plaintiffs' active participation in sports. Skiers, illustratively, are usually prohibited from obtaining damages from the operator of a ski area for injuries caused by inherent risks of the sport. This is true whether or not they are aware of the particular risks. People who play recreational sports that involve contact with other players are often barred from seeking damages for injuries caused by negligent conduct of other players. This bar applies whether or not the prospective plaintiff is aware of the risk that ultimately injures him or her.

i. **Extent of defendants' obligations in recreational sports.** Under the implied primary assumption of risk doctrine, many jurisdictions hold that a plaintiff has no cause of action for injuries caused by a fellow player's negligent conduct within the ordinary course of the activity. There are two important consequences of this doctrinal position. First, negligent conduct that is outside the rules of the game or outside the ordinary conduct of the game can be a basis for a plaintiff's negligence claim. Second, conduct by a defendant that is reckless, willful and wanton, or intentionally tortious can also be a basis for a plaintiff's tort claim.

b. **Limited duty defines implied primary assumption of risk cases.** In cases such as the sports spectator cases, traditional assumption of risk analysis is not sensible, since it requires a showing that the plaintiff actually was aware of the full details of the risk encountered. In the sports spectator cases, however, all plaintiffs, regardless of their knowledge, are treated as being barred from recovery. This explains why those cases are better analyzed as limited duty cases, even though they are called "implied primary assumption of risk" cases.

4. Implied Secondary Assumption of Risk

A second type of implied assumption of risk is called "implied secondary assumption of risk." Particularly in the era of contributory negligence, courts decided many cases in which the crucial issue was whether a plaintiff's conduct should have been treated as implying his or her consent to injury. Implied secondary assumption of risk is the term used to describe the situation about which a jury was permitted to infer from the plaintiff's conduct that the plaintiff had chosen to assume the risks connected with the conduct the plaintiff had chosen to undertake. Most jurisdictions no longer treat implied secondary assumption of risk as a full defense.

a. **Elements of implied secondary assumption of risk.** Courts developed detailed requirements for establishing implied secondary assumption of risk, and insisted that defendants establish each element clearly. Courts were strongly motivated to do this, since they recognized that a defendant could establish a complete defense by showing that a plaintiff had assumed the risk.

The defendant must show that the plaintiff: 1. knew and understood the risk; 2. voluntarily subjected himself or herself to the risk; and 3. acted in a way that showed that consent.

Illustration: Hildebrand v. Minyard, 16 Ariz. App. 583, 494 P.2d 1328 (1972). The plaintiff's decedent parked a "bucket loader" in a narrow roadway, leaving it there after he had been warned that it presented a hazard. The defendant drove a vehicle into the bucket loader, killing the decedent. Judgment on a jury verdict was entered for the defendant but was reversed on appeal because of an error in instructing on assumption of risk. The appellate court found that an assumption of risk instruction was improper because there was inadequate evidence that the decedent had knowledge of the actual danger or that the decedent fully understood the consequences of his conduct.

i. **Knowledge.** To establish the assumption of risk defense the defendant must show that the plaintiff actually had knowledge of the particular risk he or she encountered.

(a) **Particular risk.** Courts sometimes have been very exacting in defining the particular risk the defendant must show that the plaintiff knew. A general showing that the plaintiff was aware of some risks in an activity does not satisfy this element of the doctrine.

(b) **Actual knowledge.** The defendant must show that the plaintiff's knowledge was actual, under a subjective standard that evaluates the individual plaintiff and what he or she knew. An objective, or general, standard is not used. In proving the plaintiff's real knowledge of a risk, the defendant is permitted to use circumstantial evidence.

ii. **Voluntariness.** The defendant must show that the plaintiff assumed the known risk voluntarily, acting out of his or her own free will.

(a) **Reliance.** If a plaintiff relies on a defendant's assurances of safety, he or she is not treated as having assumed the risks of the activity.

(b) **Necessity.** If a defendant's conduct creates a hazard that the plaintiff reasonably encounters, the plaintiff's choice to encounter that hazard is not treated as assumption of risk. For the idea of necessity to protect the plaintiff against the defendant's assertion of an assumption of risk defense, the plaintiff must show that the hazardous situation was created by the defendant and that the palintiff had no reasonable alternative to acting in a way that exposed him or her to the risk.

E&A Example and Analysis

Parkworld carelessly maintained a parking lot, allowing a large amount of greasy oil to collect on part of it. Paul Parker had to cross that hazard to reach his parked car. If Parker slipped and fell, his conduct in consciously walking across the slippery oil would not be treated as assumption of risk, since it was necessary to reach his car.

iii. **Manifestation of consent.** The plaintiff's conduct must manifest his or her consent. Applying this factor is problematic, since most conduct is meant to accomplish something, not to communicate a mental state like agreement to assume a risk.

(a) **Jaywalking.** Crossing a street against a light is a common example of conduct that fails to satisfy the requirement of manifestation of consent. Analysts of this situation usually say that the plaintiff does not mean to consent to being hit when he or she attempts to cross a street in a dangerous manner.

5. **Assumption of Risk Under Modern Comparative Negligence Doctrines**

Some assumption of risk concepts apply to a plaintiff's unreasonable conduct, which is precisely the type of conduct analyzed under comparative negligence doctrines. For this reason jurisdictions that have adopted comparative negligence have typically examined whether assumption of risk concepts should continue to be effective once another system of dealing with a plaintiff's unreasonable conduct has been adopted.

a. **Express assumption of risk.** The concept of express assumption of risk continues to apply in the context of comparative negligence.

b. **Implied primary assumption of risk.** The doctrine of implied primary assumption of risk continues to apply in the context of comparative negligence. Courts currently describe it as a type of limited-duty rule, so that the particular plaintiff's knowledge and other aspects of the plaintiff's conduct have no relevance to the protection that the doctrine gives to certain defendants.

c. **Implied secondary assumption of risk.** There are two types of implied secondary assumption of risk: reasonable and unreasonable. Implied secondary reasonable assumption of risk involves conduct by a plaintiff that was reasonable. Implied secondary unreasonable assumption of risk involves conduct by a plaintiff that was unreasonable.

E&A EXAMPLE AND ANALYSIS

A plaintiff fully aware of the risks might rush into a burning building to rescue a child or to protect a cheap hat from burning up. Juries would likely find that running the risk to save a child's life is reasonable and that running the risk for a hat is unreasonable. This illustrates the two varieties of implied secondary assumption of risk: 1. implied secondary reasonable assumption of risk, and 2. implied secondary unreasonable assumption of risk.

i. **Rejection of implied secondary unreasonable assumption of risk.** Conduct that involves a knowing and unreasonable encounter with a risk is treated as a full defense in contributory negligence jurisdictions. Comparative negligence jurisdictions reject that result. They have abolished the doctrine of implied secondary unreasonable assumption of risk.

Illustration: Blackburn v. Dorta, 348 So. 2d 287 (1977). The court rejected continued use of implied assumption of risk doctrines, due to the adoption of comparative negligence.

(a) **Differing treatment of similarly negligent plaintiffs.** Courts realized that the comparative negligence method of dealing with careless plaintiffs' conduct permits some careless plaintiffs to recover damages. However, the doctrine of implied secondary unreasonable assumption of risk prohibits certain careless plaintiffs from recovering damages.

(b) **Uniform treatment of similarly negligent plaintiffs through comparative negligence.** Courts reasoned that the type of negligence involved in a knowingly unreasonable encounter with a risk should be treated the same way as the negligence involved in a careless and poorly understood encounter with a risk. It seemed illogical to allow an unthinking plaintiff who had not noticed a risk to recover, while barring a thoughtful (but unreasonable) plaintiff under the doctrine of implied assumption of risk.

ii. **Rejection of implied secondary reasonable assumption of risk under comparative negligence.** The kind of conduct that involves a knowing and reasonable encounter with a risk is treated as a full defense in contributory negligence jurisdictions. Comparative negligence jurisdictions have rejected that result, with reasoning that is somewhat parallel to the reasoning for implied secondary unreasonable assumption of risk. If a plaintiff whose knowing and unreasonable encounter with a risk would no longer be barred automatically from recovery, it seemed wrong to impose that bar on a plaintiff whose encounter was actually reasonable.

iii. **Jurors' evaluations of conduct involved in secondary implied assumption of risk situations.** With comparative negligence jurisdictions rejecting the doctrine that treated a plaintiff's secondary implied assumption of risk as a complete bar to recovery, juries sometimes have to evaluate that type of conduct under comparative negligence principles. If the conduct really was reasonable, they are likely to assign no percentage of fault to the plaintiff for his or her action. If the conduct was unreasonable, they are likely to assign a percentage that is greater than zero, depending on their interpretation of its significance in the injury.

6. Summary of Modern Status of Assumption of Risk

The following table summarizes the forms of assumption of risk and shows their decreased recognition under comparative negligence.

STATUS OF FORMS OF ASSUMPTION OF RISK IN CONTRIBUTORY AND COMPARATIVE NEGLIGENCE JURISDICTIONS

Type of Assumption of Risk	*Contributory Negligence*	*Comparative Negligence*
Express (plaintiff actually agrees not to seek damages for any injuries caused by the defendant)	Full defense	Full defense
Implied primary (plaintiff has no cause of action for injuries from activity in which courts have held that defendant owes plaintiff limited duty or no duty of care)	Full defense	Full defense
Implied secondary unreasonable (plaintiff encounters risk voluntarily, with full knowledge of risk, for a purpose that makes encountering the risk unreasonable)	Full defense	Possible defense (conduct evaluated under comparative negligence doctrines)
Implied secondary reasonable (plaintiff encounters risk voluntarily, with full knowledge of risk, for a purpose that makes encountering the risk reasonable)	Full defense	No defense (conduct treated as reasonable under comparative negligence doctrines)

C. STATUTES OF LIMITATIONS AND REPOSE

A statute of limitations provides a defendant with a full defense if the plaintiff fails to commence suit within the time period specified in the statute. For statutes of limitations, the time at which the specified period starts to be measured is usually the time that the defendant injured the plaintiff. A statute of repose similarly provides a full defense to any action brought later than a time defined in the statute. Time periods in statutes of repose begin to run prior to any injury.

1. Statute of Limitations Examples

A typical torts statute of limitation requires that a suit in negligence be commenced within three years of the occurrence of the injury. In many states a shorter time is allowed for beginning a suit based on intentional tortious conduct.

2. Statute of Repose Examples

A typical torts statute of repose states that no relief may be granted on a claim related to injuries caused by alleged negligence in the construction of a building if the claim is made more than ten years after termination of the construction project. Statutes of repose in some states also apply to medical malpractice and products liability.

E&A EXAMPLE AND ANALYSIS

Limitations and repose statutes begin measuring their time periods at the occurrence of different events. The relevant period begins to be measured for a statute of limitations at the time the defendant injures the plaintiff. The period for a statute of repose begins to be measured prior to any contact between the plaintiff and defendant. For repose statutes the beginning of the relevant time period is some neutral event, like the end of a construction project or the termination of medical treatment.

3. Effect of Limitations and Repose Statutes

These statutes protect defendants from having to defend themselves in litigation concerning events that happened in the relatively distant past. Legislatures define how distant the past can be for the absolute defenses in these statutes to be available.

4. Rationales for Limitations and Repose Statutes

The rationales for these statutes are, in general, that litigation about old events should be discouraged because it is difficult for witnesses to remember accurately, and it is a hardship to require individuals and companies to maintain records indefinitely. It may also help the insurance market to have rational pricing if individuals and companies have certainty about freedom from liability for past actions after particular lengths of time have passed.

5. Expansions of the Time Limits in Statutes of Limitations

Because a statute of limitations can have a drastic effect on litigation (its complete termination), a number of doctrines have developed for recurring situations about which courts have ruled that a standard application of the statute would be unfair.

a. **Discovery rule.** For medical malpractice cases the discovery rule changes the ordinary application of a statute of limitations. Ordinarily the statutory time period starts to run at the time the defendant allegedly acted negligently. Under the discovery rule the time period starts to run at the time the plaintiff discovered or should have discovered the injury.

   i. **Foreign objects only.** Some states apply the discovery rule only for cases involving objects left in the plaintiff's body, excluding cases involving other types of negligent medical care.

   ii. **Discovery of harm and suspicion of negligence.** Some states apply a version of the discovery rule in which the statutory time period only begins to run when the plaintiff discovers or should have discovered a harm and suspects or should have suspected that it was caused by the defendant's negligence. This is more favorable to plaintiffs than the treatment in which the statutory time period begins to run when the plaintiff knows or has reason to know about the injury.

E&A EXAMPLE AND ANALYSIS

Dana Doctor treated Pat Patient in a jurisdiction that uses a three-year period for the statute of limitations applicable to medical malpractice. The following chronology illustrates the significance of various statutes of limitations doctrines.

1990	Doctor operates on Patient's arm.
1991	Patient feels strange pain in arm.
1992	Patient suspects the pain results from the operation.
1993	Last year suit is allowed under standard interpretation of statute of limitations.
1994	Last year suit is allowed under discovery rule.
1995	Last year suit is allowed under version of discovery rule that starts to run the limitations period when the patient is aware of a problem and is aware that it may have been caused by the defendant.

b. **Continuous treatment doctrine.** For a situation where a defendant doctor allegedly committed malpractice at a certain time but continued to treat the patient, the statute of limitations starts running at the conclusion of the period of continuous treatment (rather than at the earlier time when the defendant allegedly committed his or her negligent act).

c. **Minority or incapacity.** The statute of limitations is tolled (stopped from running) for any period of time during which a plaintiff was a minor or was incapacitated.

d. **Repressed memory cases.** In a case where a minor was a victim of a sexual assault, a conventional application of the statute of limitations starts the limitations period running on the day that the victim reaches the jurisdiction's age of majority. Some individuals have sought to bring suits alleging this type of injury at times later than this application of the statute of limitations allows, on the theory that they had repressed memory of the defendants' actions but filed their suits promptly upon recovering memory of the alleged conduct. Courts have varied in their approaches to these requests to modify the usual treatment of the statute of limitations.

i. **Discovery rule applies with corroboration.** Some courts treat these claims under the discovery rule if the plaintiff provides corroborating evidence of the alleged tortious conduct. In the absence of corroborating evidence these courts reject use of the discovery rule.

ii. **Discovery rule applies regardless of corroboration.** Other courts apply the discovery rule regardless of whether the plaintiff has corroborating evidence of the alleged tortious conduct.

iii. **Discovery of consequences of remembered sexual abuse.** There are a small number of cases in which courts have allowed suits to proceed under the discovery rule where the plaintiffs did not repress recollections of the defendants' alleged sexual abuse. In these cases the plaintiffs did not relate the remembered abuse to its alleged emotional consequences until a time which would have been too late for litigation under standard application of the statutes of limitations.

D. IMMUNITIES

Immunities protect their holders from all tort law responsibility for conduct that would otherwise be a basis for liability. Governmental immunities of various types shield all levels of government and protect certain government employees and officials. In some states charitable immunity applies to nonprofit entities. Familial immunity may protect a spouse from suit by the other spouse and may prevent a child from establishing a claim against a parent.

1. Governmental Immunity

Governmental immunity developed as an expression of the idea, "the king can do no wrong." For this reason it is sometimes called sovereign immunity. It can apply when the defendant is a governmental unit or when the defendant is a governmental official or employee. The details of immunity law vary depending on whether the defendant is a political subdivision (such as a town), a governmental entity (such as a school board), or a person (such as a public employee or official). Another factor that leads to variation in immunity law is the level of governmental entity. Federal, state, and local immunity apply differently.

2. Federal Tort Claims Act

A 1946 statute, the Federal Tort Claims Act (FTCA), allows individuals to seek tort damages from the federal government. Prior to adoption of the FTCA, individuals were prohibited from seeking tort damages from the United States under a traditional application of sovereign immunity. Special federal statutes were passed in many instances to provide payments to individual victims of injuries caused by governmental actions.

a. **Basic provisions.** The FTCA's basic provision is simple. When a federal employee negligently injures someone while acting within the scope of his or her employment, the victim may recover money damages from the United States if a private entity or person would be liable in a similar situation under the law of the state where the injury occurred. The FTCA's waiver of immunity is subject to some limitations described in this section.

i. **Respondeat superior.** The respondeat superior doctrine applies to FTCA actions. The federal government is liable for injuries only in circumstances in which a private employer would be liable. This requires a careful analysis of the scope of employment, since employers are usually free from responsibility for injuries inflicted by workers when workers are off duty or are acting in ways that differ from the typical descriptions of their duties.

ii. **Discretionary functions excluded from FTCA coverage.** The FTCA does *not* allow liability for injuries arising out of discretionary functions. The term *discretionary functions* means activities that involve significant judgment and policy making. Sometimes discretionary functions are defined by comparing them with operational functions.

(a) **Policy rationale for discretionary functions exemption.** The FTCA excludes discretionary functions from the conduct for which the government may be sued for two main reasons. One is based on separation of powers. Courts should not scrutinize executive-branch conduct that relates to political decision making. In this sense political decision making means choices based on allocation of governmental resources or choices about what types of government conduct best serve the public. The other reason for denying lawsuits about discretionary conduct is that juries may not be reliable evaluators of the wide range of choices inherent in most discretionary conduct. Government employees and officers should feel free to use their best judgment without expectation of later critiques in the civil justice system.

E&A EXAMPLE AND ANALYSIS

Deciding what kind of truck a government agency should buy for transporting hazardous materials is a discretionary function. Driving the truck is not a discretionary function. Thought and decision making are involved in driving the truck, but that type of thought is different from the thought involved in selecting the truck. Selection involves issues like allocating budgetary resources and analyzing how truck buying should relate to the overall work of a part of the government. Driving the truck involves decisions that have nothing to do with the types of judgment we expect government officials to exercise.

iii. **Negligent exercise of discretionary functions.** Even if the discretion involved in carrying out a discretionary function is exercised carelessly, the FTCA prohibits recovery for any resultant injuries.

iv. **Tests for defining discretionary functions.** One test for identifying discretionary functions is to distinguish between planning and operational work, with planning treated as discretionary and work involved in carrying out the plan treated as nondiscretionary. While this test may be helpful, it is difficult to apply and cannot be relied on as a rule of law. A more general inquiry into whether the conduct involves considerations of public policy is currently required under United States Supreme Court decisions.

Illustrations: Dalehite v. United States, 364 U.S. 15 (1953). This case involved liability for injuries caused by the catastrophic explosion of large quantities of fertilizer being prepared for shipping. The Court stated that the alleged negligence involved the exercise of discretion by individuals at the planning level on topics such as how to pack the fertilizer and how to ship it. For this reason the conduct was not subject to suit under the FTCA.

Berkovitz v. United States, 486 U.S. 531 (1988). A federal agency's own rules required that every batch of a vaccine be tested. An employee decided to skip testing one batch, and the plaintiff was injured by that batch. The Supreme Court held that the discretionary functions exemption of the FTCA did not apply, and that a suit was allowable. It stated that conduct must be "based on considerations of public policy'' to be within the FTCA's discretionary functions exemption. Failure to carry out an act is not discretionary if a statute, regulation, or policy requires that it be done.

v. **Reasonable enforcement of statute or regulation excluded from FTCA coverage.** The FTCA excludes liability for conduct by a government employee who acts reasonably to enforce a statute or regulation, even if the statute or regulation is later determined to be unconstitutional or otherwise invalid.

vi. **Intentional torts excluded from FTCA coverage.** Liability for intentional torts is excluded under the FTCA. The victim of a battery, for example, has no claim against the federal government. Other common intentional tort claims barred by this exception are: assault, false imprisonment, false arrest, malicious prosecution, abuse of process, libel, slander, misrepresentation, dcccit, and interference with contract rights.

(a) **Exclusion withdrawn for law enforcement officers.** Despite the general exclusion of intentional torts from potential federal government liability under the FTCA, certain intentional torts are allowed to be a basis for recovery when they are committed by law enforcement officers or investigative officers. A victim is permitted to obtain damages for the torts of assault, battery, false imprisonment, false arrest, abuse of process, or malicious prosecution if those types of conduct are carried out by law enforcement or investigative officers.

(b) **Employee's personal liability.** When a plaintiff seeks damages under the FTCA, no claim is permitted against the individual employee personally. If a claim may not be brought against the United States (if, for example, it involves an intentional tort), the plaintiff may seek redress from the federal employee as an individual.

vii. **Strict liability excluded from FTCA coverage.** The FTCA has been interpreted to forbid suits on strict liability theories.

3. States as Defendants

Traditionally, state governments were immune from suit under the same the-king-can-do-no-wrong theory that supported federal government immunity. Restricting suits against states is also sometimes justified by arguments that states have limited financial resources and that they need to be protected from the consumption of time and energy required to defend large numbers of suits. Currently, only a small number of states preserve full immunity. Others have rejected or limited immunity by statute or judicial decision. Factors leading to the erosion of immunity include the availability of insurance and a growing belief that all citizens, through taxation, should pay for the harms inflicted on particular citizens by the state.

a. **Discretionary functions.** Where immunity is abrogated, states usually limit the scope of litigation by continuing to reject suits based on discretionary conduct. This discretionary conduct immunity covers legislative and judicial acts as well.

b. **State tort-claims statutes.** States that have changed the traditionally full immunity by statute have adopted a variety of provisions.

   i. **Exposure linked to insurance.** Some statutes expose the state to suit only if the state has insurance that will cover any loss from the suit the plaintiff seeks to bring.

   ii. **Suit permitted for categories of conduct.** Some statutes expose the state to suit only for conduct in specific categories, such as operation of motor vehicles or operation of real estate.

4. Local Government Units as Defendants

Counties and cities may also be defendants. In the period when full immunity was common for states, local governmental units had immunity only for governmental functions. At present, in many states, even this narrower immunity has been lessened or eliminated.

a. **Governmental/proprietary distinction.** In limiting the immunity of local governmental units to governmental functions, courts have distinguished between governmental and proprietary activities. Proprietary functions are activities that a government might carry out but that a private entity could also carry out.

E&A

EXAMPLE AND ANALYSIS

Operating a hospital or an airport is a proprietary function. Even though these operations are often carried out by governmental units, private individuals or companies can also do them. Examples of governmental functions are maintaining roads or traffic lights and providing police or fire services.

b. **Immunity rejected for insured risks.** In some states local government immunity is rejected for conduct that is covered by insurance.

c. **Limited-duty rules as a substitute for immunity.** As municipalities have lost their general immunity from suit, courts have tended to develop alternative methods of shielding certain types of activity from scrutiny in the tort system. In particular, where claims are based on the theory that police protection should have been provided in some better way, courts are likely to define the duty to provide police protection quite narrowly. Summary judgment for the defendant may thus be available in most cases.

d. **Practices violative of federal rights.** A local government entity may be sued under a federal statute, the Civil Rights Act of 1871 (42 U.S.C. §1983), for a policy, custom, or practice that violates federally guaranteed rights. The statute establishes a cause of action for violation of civil rights under color of state law. Actions brought under this statute are commonly called "1983 actions."

Illustration: Owen v. City of Independence, 445 U.S. 622 (1980). No immunities exist in suits seeking damages for constitutional violations committed in the conduct of governmental functions.

5. Officials and Employees as Defendants

Government officials and employees often have immunity from tort liability. The policy that supports this is a belief that without such protection, well-qualified individuals would likely refuse public employment. See Restatement §895D, comment *b.* The extent of immunity may vary depending on the individual's rank and the type of activity for which a plaintiff seeks to impose tort liability on the individual.

a. **Legislators, judges, and prosecutors.** Legislators, judges, and prosecutors at all levels of government ordinarily receive absolute immunity for any conduct within the scope of their official duties. They have no liability for injuries they cause through negligence in connection with their work for the public.

i. **Application of scope-of-duties concept.** Since legislators, judges, and prosecutors have absolute immunity only for acts within the scope of employment or jurisdiction, defining that concept is important. In Stump v. Sparkman, 435 U.S. 349 (1978), a judge who ordered sterilization of a minor with no notice to the minor and without any statutory authority was entitled to immunity. This holding illustrates that courts are likely to avoid ruling that the conduct of a legislator, judge, or prosecutor was outside the boundaries of office. If an official has acted outside the scope of the official's duties, a qualified immunity may still be available (see below at b.ii).

b. **Federal executive and administrative officials.** The immunity of high executive and administrative officials in the federal government depends upon the nature of the claim brought by the plaintiff.

i. **Claims based on state law.** Federal officials have absolute immunity against claims based on state law for acts within the scope of their official duties. In recent years courts have begun to define the scope of official duties somewhat narrowly, but if an act does fit this definition, the federal official who committed it is absolutely immune from liability based on a state claim.

ii. **Claims based on federal law.** When a plaintiff claims that an injury was caused by a federal official's violation of his or her rights under the United States Constitution, the official has only a qualified immunity. The immunity is defeated with a showing that the defendant acted unreasonably. In this context it is unreasonable to take an action if no reasonable official would believe that the act does not violate a clearly established federal right. An exception to this doctrine protects the president of the United States from all liability for violations of constitutionally protected rights committed while in office.

c. **State executive and administrative officials.** The immunity of state executive and administrative officials is best understood by analyzing the type of claim presented by the plaintiff.

i. **Claims based on state law.** In most states there is no immunity for ministerial acts (acts that do not involve discretion). For acts that involve discretion, most states grant officials a qualified immunity. This means that a defendant is protected from liability unless the plaintiff shows that he or she acted in bad faith (sometimes called "malice").

ii. **Claims based on federal law.** Section 1983 (42 U.S.C. §1983) is the basis for most litigation against state officials based on federal claims. Legislators, judges, and prosecutors have absolute immunity from claims under this statute when acting within their legislative or judicial roles, but other officials have only a qualified immunity.

d. **Governmental employees other than officials.** At federal and state levels employees of lower ranks are generally subject to suit. Qualified immunity applies to all employees who are alleged to have violated a plaintiff's federal constitutional or statutory rights, however, unless the violation occurred in the context of purely ministerial functions.

The FTCA explicitly states that its remedy against the federal government is exclusive for motor vehicle injuries. This means that a plaintiff who seeks damages from the United States for a vehicular injury is prohibited from seeking damages for the same injury from any federal employee such as the allegedly negligent driver.

6. Charitable Immunity

Charitable institutions such as hospitals and schools once received immunity from negligence liability in almost all states. This was justified on theories that donors to charities intend their gifts to be used only for the organization's main functions, not to support tort liability, and that the beneficiaries of medical care or education implicity waive their rights to sue for negligence. Virtually all jurisdictions have now eliminated charitable immunity, so that a charitable or nonprofit hospital or educational institution is potentially liable for negligent conduct of its employees in exactly the same way that other such institutions may be liable.

7. Familial Immunity

Negligent conduct by family members may cause injuries to other family members. Immunity from suit applies in some of these situations, but the modern trend is to narrow the types of cases in which recovery is forbidden on immunity grounds.

a. **Claims against spouses.** A husband and wife were one legal being (the husband) at common law, so no litigation within that single being was permitted. Modern decisions and statutes have eliminated that doctrine, and the interspousal immunity that it supported has mostly been rejected or limited.

   i. **Rationale for rejecting immunity.** Courts have ruled that the risk of false testimony in suits between spouses can be controlled in the same way the legal system controls the risk of perjury in other settings. They have also reconsidered a theory that allowing litigation destroys the harmony between spouses.

   Illustration: Freehe v. Freehe, 81 Wash. 2d 183, 500 P.2d 771 (1972). The plaintiff husband sued the defendant wife for injuries he suffered allegedly due to her improper maintenance of a tractor. The trial court granted summary judgment to the defendant on immunity grounds, but the supreme court reversed in a decision that reviewed all the major arguments against maintaining the common law immunity.

   ii. **Doctrines to limit immunity.** Where interspousal immunity has not been eliminated, it has typically been rejected for cases involving: 1. intentional torts; 2. automobile accidents (because insurance is usually available); 3. injuries that occurred prior to the marriage; or 4. litigation commenced after the termination of the marriage.

b. **Litigation between parents and children.** Common law doctrines traditionally prohibited a parent from suing his or her child and prohibited a child from suing his or her parent. Many states, influenced primarily by the wide availability of insurance, have eliminated these immunities.

i. **Doctrines to limit immunity.** Where a general immunity is available, many states reject its application for cases involving: 1. intentional torts; 2. automobile accidents (because insurance is usually available); 3. business or property disputes; 4. wrongful death actions seeking damages for the death of a parent; and 5. actions brought by a child who has reached the age of adulthood.

ii. **Parental standards of care.** Where a parent no longer has immunity from suit by his or her child, a jurisdiction must establish a standard of care for typical parent-child interactions.

(a) **Reasonable parent standard.** Some jurisdictions adjust the usual reasonable prudent person test by instructing the jury to evaluate a defendant parent in terms of a reasonable prudent parent.

(b) **No duty to provide reasonable supervision.** Some courts have abrogated the parent-child immunity but have limited the effect of that action by stating that parents have no tort duty to provide reasonable supervision of their children. This means that there can be no negligence claim for damages from injuries allegedly caused by deficiencies in a parent's conduct of the ordinary supervision of children. Ordinary supervision usually is defined as providing food, shelter, clothing, education, and health care for a child.

REVIEW QUESTIONS AND ANSWERS

Question: Desperate to be admitted to a college fraternity, Paul Pledge decided to prove his bravery by putting on a blindfold and suddenly running across a busy highway. He was hit by a car and injured. Pledge discovered that the speed limit on the road was 55 miles per hour, the car was going at 80 miles per hour, and the driver would likely have been able to avoid Pledge if he had been driving within the speed limit. If Pledge sought damages for his injuries from the driver, how would his own conduct affect his chance for recovery under traditional contributory negligence doctrines?

Answer: He would lose. Even if the driver was negligent, Pledge's own negligent conduct would be a complete defense. Note that the last clear chance doctrine might have enabled Pledge to avoid the effect of the contributory negligence rule, but on the facts of this problem it is unlikely that the driver would be characterized as having had an opportunity to avoid the injury.

Question: On the facts of the question above, could Pledge win recovery against the driver under pure comparative negligence or modified comparative negligence doctrines?

Answer: Yes, under pure comparative negligence doctrines; maybe, under modified comparative negligence doctrines. A jury would determine the percentages of responsibility for Pledge and the defendant driver. Under pure comparative negligence, unless Pledge's share of responsibility was 100 percent, Pledge would be entitled to recover damages (reduced by whatever percentage of responsibility the jury assigned to him). Under modified comparative negligence systems Pledge would recover reduced damages so long as the jury found his share of responsibility to be 50 percent or less (under the 50-percent form of modified comparative) or 49 percent or less (under the 49-percent form of negligence).

Question: Paul Parker wanted to drive his car out of a parking lot onto a busy city street. The lot attendant, Sam Sleepy, motioned to Parker that it was safe to pull out. Parker did pull out but did not watch carefully enough to avoid being hit by a car that Sandra Surpriser was driving down the street. Parker sued Surpriser and Sleepy's employer for personal injuries and property damage to his car. A jury found the following facts:

Parker's responsibility	30 percent
Sleepy's responsibility	35 percent
Surpriser's responsibility	35 percent
Parker's damages	$100,000

What judgment would Parker receive in a comparative negligence jurisdiction?

Answer: Parker would be entitled to $70,000. That amount would represent his full damages reduced by 30 percent to reflect his share of responsibility. Since Parker's share of responsibility was not more than 49 percent or 50 percent, he would be entitled to recovery under any form of comparative negligence.

Question: Would Parker (from the question above) be entitled to judgment under a modified comparative negligence system if the jury had found the following facts?

Parker's responsibility	40 percent
Sleepy's responsibility	30 percent
Surpriser's responsibility	30 percent
Parker's damages	$100,000

Answer: Yes, in most places. Under modified forms of comparative negligence, Parker could recover only if his negligence was either less than (49-percent rule) or less than or equal to (50-percent rule) the negligence of the defendants against whom he sought recovery. If the jurisdiction follows the majority rule, it would combine the defendants' shares of responsibility (Parker's 40 percent would be less than the defendants' total of 60 percent) and Parker would be entitled to judgment. If Parker were compared individually to each defendant, Parker would receive no judgment, since his share was larger than the share assigned to each individual defendant.

Question: If Willy Watcher attended a professional hockey game and was injured by a puck that flew into the spectator's seating area, would any tort doctrine protect the arena or hockey team from liability for Watcher's injury?

Answer. Yes. Primary implied assumption of risk would define the arena and team as owing Watcher only a duty to provide the type of protection usually provided to spectators at such events. Watcher would be treated as having consented to his injury, or the potential defendants would be treated as owing Watcher only a limited duty.

Question: Ralph Runner ran from one aisle to another in a large clothing store, hoping to get to some sale items before other customers did. He slipped and fell while he was running. Runner sought damages from the store, claiming that it had designed its aisles without enough space for customers to move about safely. Would assumption of risk in one of its implied forms protect the store from liability?

Answer: No. Runner's conduct may have been negligent, but that factor would be analyzed under comparative negligence principles, not treated as a defense under an assumption of risk doctrine.

Question: Theresa Tourist slipped down a steep hill in a national park and was injured. Would immunity protect the federal government if Tourist sought damages claiming that the management of the park should have spent more money on guard rails?

Answer: Yes. Immunity would probably protect the government's budget decision from tort law scrutiny under the discretionary functions exception to the Federal Tort Claims Act.

Question: Theresa Tourist was hurt when a waiter in a national park restaurant spilled hot coffee on her. Would immunity protect the federal government if Tourist sought damages claiming that a waiter had been negligent?

Answer: No. The waiter's conduct is an example of the type of nondiscretionary conduct for which the Federal Tort Claims Act is intended to withdraw immunity and allow suit against the federal government.

EXAM TIPS

- Remember the contrast between the total bar of contributory negligence and the recovery-reducing function of comparative negligence.
- Be prepared to contrast the effects of pure comparative negligence with those of modified comparative negligence. The difference appears in any case where the plaintiff's share of responsibility is 51 percent or more.
- Do not treat old, contributory-negligence era defenses as complete defenses in the setting of comparative negligence. The factual backgrounds of those defenses (like last clear chance or assumption of risk) remain important, but they are only factors for a jury to consider in assigning percentages of responsibility.
- Where governmental immunity is an issue, be aware that the discretionary function exception to the Federal Tort Claims Act allows suits based on conduct that involves thought or discretion. The exception bars suits where the type of thought or discretion involves policy decisions, budgetary analysis, or other types of thought that deserve protection from tort scrutiny.

14 VICARIOUS LIABILITY

CHAPTER OVERVIEW

- Vicarious liability is one person's obligation to pay for the injuries another person has negligently inflicted.
- Employers are usually liable for the torts committed by their employees.
- Other vicarious liability possibilities involve: automobile owners and torts committed by people using their vehicles, joint venturers and torts committed by anyone in the enterprise, and (sometimes) parents and torts committed by their children.
- To establish that an employer is responsible for a worker's tort, the plaintiff must show that the worker's conduct was within the scope of employment at the time of the injury.
- To avoid liability for a worker's tort, an employer can show that the worker was an independent contractor.
- One who employs an independent contractor is usually free from responsibility for the contractor's torts, but this protection does not apply when the contractor's work involves inherently dangerous activities or a responsibility defined as nondelegable.

A. GENERAL DEFINITION

In some circumstances an individual who is free from negligent conduct is required to pay for the consequences of someone else's negligent conduct. This liability is called "vicarious liability," since it makes one person pay for another person's wrongdoing. The plaintiff proves that one person was negligent and is allowed to collect damages from a second person with no requirement to prove that the second person was negligent.

B. MAIN INSTANCES OF VICARIOUS LIAIBLITY

The most important setting for vicarious liability is the employer-employee relationship, where employers are responsible for the torts of their employees. A joint enterprise, where people work in concert, is another circumstance in which vicarious liability applies. Courts and legislatures have also used the idea of vicarious liability in a variety of situations related to vehicular injury cases. Finally, some states have statutes which make parents liable for the torts of their children (usually with a dollar limit on the amount of liability).

C. RATIONALE FOR VICARIOUS LIAIBLITY

Vicarious liability developed as a pro-plaintiff doctrine to make "deep pockets" available to victims, to provide deterrence to employers, and to spread the costs of injuries related to activities among all who benefit from the activities.

1. Deep Pocket Rationale

Without vicarious liability an injury victim has only the employee as a potential defendant. This is unsatisfactory because the employee is less likely than the employer to have enough money to pay a judgment.

2. Deterrence and Loss-Spreading Rationales

If the employee pays a judgment, the employer's finances are not affected by the occurrence of the injury. Courts believe that an employer should properly have to pay for injuries related to the business enterprise. This idea is based on the employer's ability to spread those costs to all customers and on a belief that the employer who receives the profits from the enterprise should also be the one who suffers losses related to injuries.

3. Ambiguity of Deterrence Rationale

Defendants who are vicariously liable pay judgments in circumstances where there is no proof that they have been negligent or blameworthy in any way. Therefore, it is difficult to claim, logically, that the vicarious liability doctrine works to deter carelessness or to encourage reasonable care.

E&A EXAMPLE AND ANALYSIS

If a restaurant's waiter carelessly spills hot coffee on a customer, the restaurant owner is liable for damages. That liability does not depend on any proof that the owner did anything negligent, such as bad hiring, bad training, or bad supervision. Since the plaintiff is entitled to damages from the owner without establishing that the owner was negligent, imposing this liability on the owner may not have any deterrent effect.

D. RESPONDEAT SUPERIOR

Respondeat superior is the name given to a doctrine that makes an employer liable for his or her employee's torts. In addition to this Latin phrase, older cases use the terms *master* and *servant* to mean employer and employee. The doctrine applies only when a plaintiff shows that the person who injured him or her actually was the defendant's employee and that the person committed the harmful act within the scope of that employment. Both of these issues, employment status and scope of employment, are subject to frequent litigation.

1. Tests for Employment Status

In any case where a plaintiff attempts to impose vicarious liability on a defendant, the plaintiff must show that the person who actually harmed the plaintiff was working for the defendant. There are, however, two possible relationships that the person who caused the harm might have with the defendant. One is the standard employer-employee relationship (which supports imposition of vicarious liability). The other is known as the independent contractor relationship. A person who employs an independent contractor is free from responsibility for harms that independent contractor may cause.

a. **Control test.** The basic distinction between an employee and an independent contractor is that an employee is subject to significant control and supervision, but an independent contractor has freedom to decide how to do his or her work. An employee is someone most people would assume is part of the staff of the defendant employer. An independent contractor may do work for many employers and is paid to accomplish a result rather than to work in any particular way.

b. **Factors in control test.** Courts commonly use a group of factors in applying the control test. They ask whether: 1. the worker conducted business in addition to the work done for the defendant; 2. the worker supplied his or her own tools and equipment; and 3. the defendant had the power to give specific instructions about the work with the expectation that they would be followed.

E&A EXAMPLES AND ANALYSIS

If a hotel guest is injured because of negligent conduct by a maid employed by the hotel, the hotel would likely be responsible, since a maid probably works only at that hotel, probably uses equipment and supplies provided by the hotel, and probably has to do the work exactly as required by the hotel.

If a hotel guest is hurt due to an elevator malfunction caused in part by negligent work by an elevator mechanic, the hotel would be free from liability if the mechanic works at many places with elevators, uses his or her own equipment and supplies, and is free to work on the hotel's elevators according to his or her own best judgment and choice of methods.

---

2. Scope of Employment

An employer is liable only for injuries an employee inflicts negligently or intentionally within the scope of employment. Courts generally define scope of employment as encompassing acts that further the defendant employer's business purpose.

a. **Range of interpretation.** The scope of employment concept is subject to a variety of interpretations. On the one hand, an employer might argue that it is against his or her company's rules for workers to be negligent and that, therefore, any negligence is outside the scope of employment. All courts would reject that argument. On the other hand, a plaintiff might argue that an injury occurred at the defendant's place of business and that, therefore, the worker who caused it must have been acting within the scope of employment. All courts would also reject that argument.

   Illustration: Fruit v. Schreiner, 502 P.2d 133 (Alaska 1972). A life insurance salesman attending a convention drove negligently and injured the plaintiff at about two o'clock in the morning as he was returning to the convention center after looking for fellow attendees at a bar. The plaintiff sought damages from the insurance company, claiming that the salesman had been within the scope of his employment at the time. The salesman had been told to mix freely with other salespeople at the convention. On appeal from a judgment for the plaintiff, the court held that a reasonable jury could have found that the salesman was acting within the scope of employment when he injured the plaintiff.

b. **Mixed business and pleasure.** If a worker's acts involve a combination of the employer's business and the worker's pleasure, courts usually define the acts as within the scope of employment.

c. **Travel to and from workplace.** Travel from a worker's home to the place of work is always defined as outside the scope of employment. Some courts have taken the opposite view of travel from the work site to a worker's home, defining that part of a worker's travel as within the scope of employment.

d. Side trips. Workers sometimes go places during working hours for purposes that are their own and that do not serve their employers' business needs.

i. Common law treatment. Common law courts used the expression *frolic and detour* for this type of side trip. They usually ruled that employers were free from responsibility for injuries their workers caused while en route for the workers' own purposes. They also ruled, however, that employers were responsible for injuries their workers caused when the workers finished their own purpose and were traveling on return to the functions for which they were employed.

ii. Current treatment. Modern courts use a foreseeability approach to this issue. If the distance involved in the worker's deviation is relatively small, an employer is usually liable for injuries inflicted during it. If the worker's own project is relatively large, the employer is usually free from responsibility except for injuries that occur quite close to locations where it is clear that the worker's presence furthers the employer's purposes.

EXAMPLE AND ANALYSIS

Denise Driver, a driver for Courierco, an overnight mail company, stopped at a shopping center after making a delivery elsewhere to check for stereo equipment she was thinking about buying. While parking her Courierco vehicle, she collided with Sam Shopper's car. Shopper would likely be entitled to damages from Courierco, because Driver's deviation from Courierco's business was slight and was probably foreseeable.

e. Smoking and other personal conduct. Modern courts usually impose liability on employers for negligent injuries employees inflict while smoking or while walking to bathrooms, even though it may be said that no one hires workers for those purposes.

f. Intentional torts. If an employee commits an intentional tort for the purpose of furthering the employer's enterprise, the employer is usually liable. The same intentional tort, however, is not a basis for the employer's liability if the employee commits it for personal motives.

i. Special employers. Some employers are liable even for personally motivated intentional torts by employees if the employers and the victims have a special relationship. The most common of these relationships is passenger-common carrier. A similar relationship may exist between a hotel guest and a hotel.

ii. **Facilitation of intentional tort.** Some businesses operate in ways that may facilitate the commission of intentional torts. For example, a company that sends salespeople into the homes of prospective customers might be held to have facilitated an attack on such a customer by one of its salespeople. Some courts impose liability for employees' intentional torts in these circumstances.

iii. **General foreseeability test.** A minority of courts make employers liable for intentional torts by employees if the torts are foreseeable.

iv. **Dangerous instrumentalities.** A minority of courts impose liability on employers for their employees' intentional torts if the employees commit the torts using dangerous instrumentalities related to the employees' work. Typical dangerous instrumentalities are firearms, explosives, and undomesticated animals.

E. INDEPENDENT CONTRACTORS: ALLOCATION OF RESPOINSIBILITY FOR THEIR TORTS

The client or employer of an independent contractor usually has no responsibility for harms that contractor may inflict. The victim of this type of harm has recourse only against the contractor.

1. Test for Independent Contractor Status

The test for independent contractor status is the mirror image of the test for employee status, discussed above in Section C.1.b.

Illustrations: Murrell v. Goertz, 597 P.2d 1223 (Okla. Ct. App. 1979). A newspaper company's control over the actions of a delivery person was not significant enough to justify classifying the latter as an employee rather than an independent contractor.

Hardy v. Brantley, 471 So.2d 358 (Miss. 1985). The defendant hospital was responsible for the negligence of an emergency-room physician despite language in a contract between the hospital and the group practice to which the physician belonged that seemed to establish an independent contractor relationship. The court relied primarily on its belief that patients of the hospital would assume that emergency-room physicians were part of that organization and that the hospital would be responsible for their work.

2. Injuries to Employees of Contractor

In most instances an independent contractor's employee who is injured in the course of employment is covered by workers' compensation. This means that the worker has no cause of action against the contractor. Most jurisdictions also hold that workers have no cause of action against the employers of contractors, even if exceptions to the usual rules of independent contractor liability make the employers of the contractors responsible for injuries the contractors or their workers inflict on other individuals.

3. Vicarious Liability for Independent Contractors' Torts

In two circumstances the employer of an independent contractor may be liable for the contractor's torts. These involve nondelegable duties and inherently dangerous activities.

a. **Nondelegable duties.** Some responsibilities that relate to the safety of strangers are considered so important that an individual who chooses to fulfill them by hiring a contractor is always responsible for injuries caused by the contractor's negligent acts. These responsibilities are called "nondelegable duties."

   Examples: Typical examples of nondelegable duties are the obligations to keep streets in repair and to make sure that a motor vehicle is in good working order. Anyone who has one of these duties is responsible for negligence on the part of an independent contractor that he or she hires to work on the street or maintain the vehicle.

b. **Inherently dangerous activities.** Some activities are defined as inherently dangerous. Under the Restatement definition they are activities that present a high degree of danger to others unless special precautions are taken. When a person employs an independent contractor to do work of this type, the contractor's employer is liable for injuries related to the activity's special risks if the contractor would be responsible for them under theories of negligence or strict liability.

   i. **Doctrine limited to special risks.** This doctrine imposes vicarious liability only for injuries related to the special risks that qualify the activity as inherently dangerous. Thus, if a contractor carries out a construction project that involves some inherently dangerous activities such as blasting and some ordinary activities such as driving, injuries related to the ordinary activity will not be a basis for imposing vicarious liability on the employer of the contractor.

      (a) **Injuries collateral to special risk.** Sometimes in connection with an inherently dangerous activity an injury: 1. is caused by a risk related to the activity's special dangers but 2. was not foreseeable to the person who hired the contractor. In a case like that, the contractor's employer is free from vicarious liability.

EXAMPLE AND ANALYSIS

Apartmentco, the owner of a large apartment house, hired a contractor to erect scaffolding around the building and to paint the building's window frames. If an apartment resident had been harmed because pigeons roosted in the scaffolding and the resident contracted a disease related to pigeon droppings, Apartmentco would be free from responsibility for this type of harm. Use of scaffolding would probably be defined as involving inherent dangers, but this particular harm would probably be defined as collateral and not foreseeable by Apartmentco.

---

ii. **Expanded category of inherently dangerous activities.** Modern courts tend to expand the category of activities characterized as inherently dangerous to cover any independent contractor's activity that becomes dangerous because of the lack of a safety precaution.

F. JOINT ENTERPRISES

People who collaborate for a particular purpose are sometimes called "joint venturers" with regard to that purpose. They are said to be involved in a joint enterprise. Each participant in a joint enterprise is responsible for any negligence by any participant.

1. Elements of Joint Enterprise

To establish the existence of a joint enterprise a party must show that the individuals involved had: an express or implied agreement, a common purpose, a common pecuniary or business interest in that purpose, and equal rights to control the enterprise.

a. **Social trips or gatherings.** Note that the monetary interest requirement precludes characterizing many social events as joint enterprises. For example, when one person allows a friend to ride in his or her car, the two individuals are not in a joint enterprise unless the arrangement includes some payment or other financial incentive.

b. **Common pecuniary or business interest.** Under Restatement §491, comment *i*, sharing expenses of a trip is not enough to satisfy the common pecuniary or business interest element of the joint enterprise definition.

c. **Equal rights to control.** Automobile passengers who have in common with the driver a business purpose for a trip and who ride with the driver under an express or implied agreement are usually found to have enough control over operation of the vehicle to satisfy the joint enterprise definition. Although they are not reasonably able to drive the vehicle, courts hold that they have substantial ability to control aspects of the driving such as choice of route and choice of speed.

G. VEHICULAR INJURIES AND VICARIOUS LIABILITY

The joint enterprise concept sometimes applies to vehicular accidents to increase the number of defendants available to an accident victim. Two other methods of imposing vicarious liability in vehicular injury cases are ''automobile consent'' statutes and the ''family purpose'' doctrine.

1. Automobile Consent Statutes

Many states have adopted automobile consent statutes. These statutes provide that if an automobile owner gives someone permission to use his or her car, the owner is liable for any injuries the driver may cause through negligence or other tortious conduct. This is vicarious liability, since it does not require a showing that the owner was negligent in giving the driver permission to use the car.

a. **Extent of owner's permission.** The owner's liability under an automobile consent statute is limited to injuries caused while the driver uses the vehicle within the scope of permission given the driver. The extent of permission can relate to times of day, purposes of driving, or types of roads or highways the driver might use.

b. **Third persons.** In some cases an owner gives someone permission to drive his or her car, then the person with permission allows a third person to drive it. Courts are divided on whether vicarious liability may be imposed on the owner under an automobile consent statute when a third person causes an accident through negligence. Since the basic purpose of the statutes is to increase the number of available defendants, courts tend to allow vicarious liability in this circumstance.

c. **Imputing contributory negligence.** A person driving an owner's car with permission may become involved in a collision with a second vehicle. If the owner then seeks recovery for damage to his or her car from the driver of the second vehicle, courts must decide how to treat the negligence of the person who was driving the owner's car. Some courts impute that negligence to the owner, making him or her responsible for it and thus decreasing recovery from the driver of the second vehicle. Other courts decline to do this, leaving it to the driver of the second car to seek contribution from the person who was driving the owner's car.

2. Family Purpose Doctrine

In some jurisdictions that have not adopted automobile consent statutes, a judge-made doctrine known as the family purpose doctrine serves a similar purpose. This doctrine applies when a vehicle owner allows members of his or her family to use the vehicle. It imposes vicarious liability on the vehicle owner in this situation.

H. PARENTAL LIABILITY FOR CHILDREN'S TORTS

At common law parents had no responsibility for their children's torts. Currently, many states have changed this doctrine by statute.

1. Limited Liability for Willful or Malicious Acts

Many statutes impose liability on parents for the consequences of their children's willful or malicious acts. These statutes usually have a ceiling on liability, set at amounts such as $1,500 (South Dakota), $2,000 (Wyoming), $5,000 (Connecticut), or $25,000 (California).

2. Liability for Negligent Acts

Some statutes make parents responsible even for their children's negligent acts. Hawaii and Illinois have statutes of this type with no ceiling on a parent's potential liability.

I. IMPUTED CONTRIBUTORY NEGLIGENCE

Imputed contributory negligence is a doctrine that applies in situations involving three or more individuals. Under the **both-ways test,** if someone would be vicariously liable for another person's negligence, the person subject to vicarious liability is charged with any contributory negligence by that other person in any suit where contributory negligence is relevant. In a simple scenario these individuals could be called "Boss," "Worker-driver," and "Stranger-driver." Boss is the employer of Worker-driver and would be vicariously liable for injuries caused by Worker-driver's negligence. Stranger-driver is a motorist with no relation to Boss or Worker-driver. The issue of imputed contributory negligence arises if there is an accident involving Worker-driver and Stranger-driver that causes damage to property that belongs to Boss. If Boss sues Stranger-driver for damages and Stranger-driver shows that Worker-driver was negligent, traditional doctrine imputes Worker-driver's negligence to Boss, reducing or preventing Boss's recovery.

1. Contemporary Significance of Imputed Contributory Negligence

The imputed contributory negligence doctrine is usually rejected in cases where vicarious liability is based on the family purpose doctrine or on an automobile consent statute. Its importance is diminished as jurisdictions develop comparative negligence principles that tend to restrict any party's liability to a proportion of the injury related to that party's fault. In the example above if Stranger-driver's liability for property damage is limited by his or her share of fault, it is irrelevant whether a doctrine says that Worker-driver's fault is imputed to Boss. The crucial fact is that Stranger-driver is protected from having to pay for Worker-driver's share simply by virtue of the jury's assessment of Stranger-driver's percentage of responsibility.

Review Questions and Answers

Question: Samantha Storeowner needed to have new carpeting in part of her store. She bought some carpeting and had one of her salesclerks attempt to install it. The clerk did the work poorly, and a customer tripped on some tools the clerk left scattered around as she was working on the project. Would Storeowner be responsible for the customer's injury?

Answer: Yes. The clerk committed the negligent act while employed by Storeowner. While laying carpet was not the clerk's main duty, it obviously was something Storeowner believed she could do and should do in her role as a store employee.

Question: Samantha Storeowner (from the question above) hired Carl Carpeter to install carpeting in part of her store. Carpeter was the sole proprietor of a carpet installation business. While Carpeter was working, he left tools scattered around. A customer tripped on the tools and was hurt. Would Storeowner be responsible for the customer's tort damages?

Answer: No. Carpeter was an independent contractor. His work involved many employers in addition to Storeowner, he supplied his own tools, and he would have been expected to install the carpeting according to his own techniques and methods rather than in accordance with detailed instructions from Storeowner.

Question: Samantha Storeowner (from the question above) hired Maxine Modern to install some carpeting in her store. Modern was the sole proprietor of a carpet installation business that competed with Carl Carpeter's business. Modern used a high-tech glue that was extremely combustible and could cause many serious allergic reactions. Two customers were injured in a small fire that started while Modern was working, and two others suffered serious skin rashes from the vapors of Modern's glue. Would Storeowner be responsible for the customers' injuries?

Answer: Yes. Although Modern was an independent contractor, it is likely that a court would characterize her work as inherently dangerous. The employer of an independent contractor is responsible for injuries inflicted negligently by the contractor if the contractor's work is inherently dangerous.

Question: Samantha Storeowner needed to employ a new collections manager for her store's credit department. She hired Frank Fighter, the first person who applied. She did not check Fighter's references and interviewed him for only five minutes. Fighter met with a customer to discuss the status of his charge account and agreed on how to resolve a credit problem. Then Fighter misunderstood something the customer said and punched the customer in the nose. If the customer sought damages from Storeowner, alleging that Fighter's battery was the responsibility of Storeowner and that Storeowner was personally negligent in hiring Fighter, how would the vicarious liability doctrines affect the suit?

Answer: Storeowner would probably be free from responsibility for Fighter's intentional tort. Since the punch happened after Fighter had resolved the credit problem, it is highly unlikely a court would find a jury justified in deciding that Fighter was furthering Storeowner's business when he hit the customer. Storeowner's own negligence, the tort of negligent hiring, was unconnected with any vicarious liability doctrines. If Storeowner owed a duty to be reasonable in her hiring decisions and if she breached that duty, her liability to the customer would be personal and direct, not vicarious.

EXAM TIPS

- Scope of employment is the key concept for vicarious liability in the workplace setting. Be alert for private excursions by employees.
- Distinguishing independent contractors from employees is also highly important, since the client or employer of an independent contractor has no liability for the contractor's torts.
- The loss-spreading, deep-pocket rationale for vicarious liability could be a factor in encouraging a court to define scope of employment broadly. If a problem's facts are hard to classify as establishing conduct within or beyond the scope of employment, explore whether the loss-spreading rationale might encourage a court to find that the scope of employment criterion was satisfied.

15 TRADITIONAL STRICT LIABILITY

CHAPTER OVERVIEW

- Strict liability is a rule of law that imposes liability without fault. A defendant whose activity is characterized as a strict liability activity must pay for the harms that the activity causes regardless of whether the defendant has used reasonable care.
- Damage caused by animals is a traditional category of strict liability. Strict liability covers property damage caused by grazing animals (subject to statutory changes in some states) and all injuries caused by a defendant's wild animals.
- Abnormally dangerous activities are subject to strict liability. Courts apply a six-part test to determine whether an activity is abnormally dangerous.
- Modern strict liability jurisprudence takes account of a plaintiff's negligence under whatever comparative negligence rules would apply if the basis of the plaintiff's claim against the defendant were negligence.

A. GENERAL DEFINTION

Strict liability is liability without proof of fault. A defendant who is strictly liable must pay for injuries related to the activity for which liability is strict regardless of how carefully he or she has carried out the activity. To recover, however, a plaintiff is required to prove causation and damages.

B. COVERAGE OF STRICT LIABILITY

Strict liability applies to cases involving animals, activities that are abnormally dangerous, injuries covered by workers' compensation statutes, and product-related injuries. This chapter covers animals and abnormally dangerous activities. Product-related injuries are covered in Chapter 16 (Products Liability), and workers' compensation statutes are covered in Chapter 17 (Workers' Compensation and Other Alternative Compensation Systems).

C. DISTINGUISHED FROM NEGLIGENCE

Strict liability causes of action and negligence causes of action are similar, but there is one important difference. In a negligence action the plaintiff must establish the elements of duty, breach, causation, and damages. In a strict liability action the plaintiff is freed from having to show breach of a duty: the fact that the injury occurred is treated as a substitute for the kind of proof of breach required in negligence cases. Alternatively, it might be said that the conduct of the activity to which strict liability applies is equivalent to the breach of a duty (a breach for which the actor has no financial responsibility until it causes an injury).

D. ECONOMIC ANALYSIS OF STRICT LIABILITY

Strict liability can be understood in comparison to liability for negligence. The negligence system deals with the risk of injury and the possibility of preventing injury by having society spend money on whichever choice (injury occurrence or injury avoidance) costs less. This means that enterprises will avoid only those injuries for which they will have negligence liability (the injuries that can be prevented for less than the cost they represent when they actually occur).

Strict liability, in contrast, makes an enterprise pay for all injuries related to its activities, even if preventing them would have cost more. This does not mean that a strict liability system necessarily reduces the number of accidents. An enterprise subject to strict liability will spend money to avoid accidents in all instances where the cost of avoiding them is less than the costs those injuries represent when they occur, but it will not spend money to prevent injuries in situations where it would cost more to prevent them than to pay for them. One major difference between negligence and strict liability involves the injuries for which the cost of prevention is larger than the cost of occurrence. Under negligence liability the cost of those injuries stays with the victims; under strict liability the enterprise pays for those injuries.

Some suggest that placing all the costs of injuries on the enterprise makes sense in situations where the enterprise is in the best position to evaluate all the costs and risks. The enterprise can control how much of the activity it wants to carry out and can make that decision based on its specialized knowledge.

E. HARMS CAUSED BY ANIMALS

Animals cause harm in two primary ways: by trespassing and harming land and by coming into contact with people and causing personal injury. Trespass and personal injury cases are both covered by strict liability, subject to a variety of conditions.

1. Trespassing Animals

The traditional rule makes the owner of animals strictly liable for property damage they cause on another person's land. This rule applies to almost all animals, with cases typically involving wandering livestock.

a. **Domestic animals.** Domestic animals such as cats and dogs are excluded from the strict liability rule.

b. **Statutes.** The common law rule has been superseded by statute in a number of states, primarily in the West. There are two general types of statutes, fencing-out statutes and fencing-in statutes.

   i. **Fencing out statutes.** A fencing-out statute provides that a plaintiff landowner has a strict liability action against the owner of trespassing animals only if the landowner has constructed a fence to keep animals out.

   ii. **Fencing in statutes.** A fencing-in statute provides that a plaintiff landowner has a strict liability action against the owner of trespassing animals only if the animal's owner has failed to construct a fence to keep his or her animals in.

   iii. **Rationale for statutes.** The fencing-in and fencing-out statutes both seek to give incentives for the building of fences. They vary, however, in their choice about which activity (farming or raising livestock) should have the burden of building the fences.

2. Personal Injuries Caused by Animals

Strict liability applies to personal injuries caused by animals, with an important distinction between wild animals and domestic animals.

a. **Classification of animals.** Domestic animals are those that are socially useful and traditionally used for "the service of mankind" (in the Restatement's definition). Examples of domestic animals are cats, dogs, cows, horses, and bees. Wild animals are any nondomestic animals.

b. **Liability for injuries caused by wild animals.** The owner or keeper of a wild animal is strictly liable for any harms the animal inflicts, as long as the harms are related to the general propensities of that type of animal or to the particular propensities, known to the owner, of that individual animal.

c. **Liability for injuries caused by domestic animals.** The owner or keeper of a domestic animal is strictly liable for any harms that the animal inflicts, if the owner knew or had reason to know of the animal's dangerous nature. This doctrine is often misunderstood as meaning that every dog is entitled to one free bite. In fact a dog that is known to be vicious is entitled to no free bites, since the dog's owner is strictly liable for any injuries the dog inflicts.

Some states have adopted statutes imposing strict liability on dog owners for their dogs' bites, precluding liability only if the owner can show that the plaintiff provoked the dog's conduct.

E&A EXAMPLE AND ANALYSIS

Dan Doglover owns Rover, a dog that always growls at strangers. When strangers pass Rover's yard, Rover always tries to escape from the yard. If Rover escaped from the yard and bit someone passing by, Doglover would be liable for the injury. Even if Rover had not bitten anyone in the past, Doglover had reason to know that Rover had a dangerous nature. If Doglover's state had a strict liability statute, the same result would be reached under that statute.

F. INJURIES CAUSED BY ABNORMALLY DANGEROUS ACTIVITIES

Courts use a multi-part test to determine whether a defendant's activity is abnormally dangerous. That determination is significant because strict liability applies to injuries caused by abnormally dangerous activities.

1. History: *Rylands v. Fletcher*

Applying strict liability to some activities because they present abnormal dangers has developed from the English case of Rylands v. Fletcher, L.R. 3 H.L. 330 (1868). The defendant hired a contractor to build a reservoir on his property. The project caused a flood on the plaintiff's land nearby by sending water through some previously unknown, old, abandoned mine shafts. Current legal doctrines protected the landowner from liability because he had been reasonably careful in selecting the contractor and because the respondeat superior doctrine had not yet been recognized for this type of situation. Nevertheless, the English court found a way to make the landowner responsible. It held that a person such as the landowner should be strictly liable for injuries caused by a "non-natural" use of his land.

2. Modern Definition

Currently, American courts apply strict liability by evaluating six factors, although there is no precise method of weighing the factors or deciding how to apply them when some of them fit a particular activity and some do not.

a. **High degree of risk.** To satisfy this factor there must be a high degree of risk of some harm to other people or their land or chattels. This concept is meant to focus on the likelihood that the danger that is risked will actually occur. It is equivalent to the odds that the event will happen.

b. **Risk of serious harm.** This factor requires a showing that the harm, if it occurs, will be great. Note the difference between this factor and the high-degree-of-risk factor. This factor explores how bad the event will be if it ever happens, while the high-degree-of-risk factor relates to the probability that the injurious event will occur.

c. **Cannot be eliminated by reasonable care.** This factor examines whether the risks of the activity could be eliminated by reasonable care.

d. **Not a matter of common usage.** This factor, directly taken from *Rylands v. Fletcher,* examines whether the activity is unusual or common.

e. **Appropriateness of location.** This factor evaluates the appropriateness of the activity to the place where it is carried out.

f. **Community value.** This factor is satisfied if the activity's dangers outweigh its value to the community. This factor must take into account that some activities are likely to be more valuable in some places than in others.

Illustration: Indiana Harbor Belt R.R. Co. v. American Cyanamid Co., 916 F.2d 1174 (1990). The defendant company shipped a dangerous chemical in a railroad car that passed over the plaintiff railroad's tracks. It leaked while it was there, and the plaintiff railroad was required to spend a large sum to decontaminate the area. The trial court granted summary judgment to the plaintiff on a strict liability theory. The court of appeals reversed. It applied the standard factors for classifying an activity as abnormally dangerous. It stated, in particular, that the risk involved could have been prevented by greater care and that the location of the incident (an urban area) was appropriate since railroad shipping usually involves routes that go through urban areas.

E&A EXAMPLE AND ANALYSIS

If someone driving on a highway were injured by an explosion at a nearby oil well, strict liability might be available against the oil well's operator. The risks involved in that activity are high, and if they do occur the harm they cause is likely to be severe. The risks are likely to be present regardless of the operator's level of care. The factors about common usage, appropriateness of location, and value to the community are very hard to apply in the abstract. A court is likely to be influenced by whether oil production is significant in the region's economy. In a state where the petroleum industry has only a small presence, these factors might well be found to work in favor of strict liability.

---

3. Rationale for Strict Liability for Abnormally Dangerous Activities

Sometimes courts say merely that an activity that presents abnormally dangerous activities should "pay its way." Another rationale looks at the lack of reciprocity inherent in abnormally dangerous activities. Because these activities are relatively rare, each represents a situation in which the operator imposes risks on others while there is only a tiny chance that he or she will ever be the victim of similar harms imposed by someone else. This is a marked contrast with common activities. For example, users of automobiles impose risks on others, but they are also subject to harm from that same type of risk. Those who operate abnormally dangerous activities do not usually run the risk of being harmed by the types of risks that they impose on a community.

4. Significance of Rationale

Understanding the social policies that support the application of strict liability is useful because it can be a basis for argument about activities that are difficult to classify as either abnormally dangerous or not abnormally dangerous.

E&A EXAMPLE AND ANALYSIS

Would conducting a professional fireworks display on the Fourth of July be an abnormally dangerous activity? With respect to common usage and value to the community, sensible arguments could be made in either direction. Choosing between them might be easier if one referred to the lack of reciprocity between fireworks professionals and all others in society. That would lead to a conclusion applying strict liability to the activity.

---

5. Typical Abnormally Dangerous Activities

While the factors used to identify abnormally dangerous activities are inexact and subject to regional variation, patterns have developed in court decisions about certain specific activities.

a. **Explosives.** The use and storage of explosives are almost always ruled to be abnormally dangerous.

b. **Fireworks.** Some decisions have found large-scale professional fireworks exhibitions to be abnormally dangerous.

c. **Crop dusting.** Crop dusting is almost always ruled to be abnormally dangerous.

d. **Nuclear power plants.** Nuclear power plants are likely to be ruled abnormally dangerous, although a federal statute imposes a ceiling on an operator's total liability for any accident.

e. **Transportation of hazardous materials.** Courts are divided on whether transportation of hazardous materials is abnormally dangerous. Typical cases involve gasoline tank trucks and chemicals shipped by rail.

f. **Aviation.** Suits involving injuries to passengers are treated as negligence actions. Injuries caused to people or property on the ground sometimes receive different treatment, with some courts treating aviation as abnormally dangerous with respect to risks of injury on the ground. Imposing strict liability for injuries to people or property on the ground may be justified on the theory that people on the ground receive no benefit from aviation and impose no reciprocal risks on the aviation industry, but the modern trend is toward treating all aviation-related injuries as negligence actions.

G. CAUSATION

The plaintiff in a strict liability case must establish cause in fact and proximate cause.

1. Cause in Fact

Cause in fact for strict liability is treated in exactly the same way as it is treated in negligence cases. See Chapter 7, Causation in Fact.

2. Proximate Cause

The proximate cause analysis for strict liability may differ somewhat from the analysis used in negligence cases. The plaintiff must show a link between his or her injury and the particular aspect of the defendant's enterprise that justified categorizing that enterprise as within the scope of strict liability.

Illustration: Foster v. Preston Mill Co., 44 Wash. 2d 440, 268 P.2d 645 (1954). The defendant conducted blasting operations that frightened mother mink owned by the plaintiff and caused them to kill their kittens. The plaintiff obtained judgment for this loss on a strict liability theory, but the judgment was reversed on appeal. Strict liability applied to blasting because of risks different from the one that caused the plaintiff's harm. For that reason applying strict liability was improper.

Some courts apply their proximate cause doctrines to strict liability cases with a more pro-defendant bias than they would use in negligence cases. This is justified, perhaps, as a balance to the general pro-plaintiff nature of the strict liability regime. The Restatement imposes liability for the same range of consequences in strict liability as it imposes in negligence cases.

E&A EXAMPLE AND ANALYSIS

A pedestrian who breaks a leg when hit by a truck filled with explosives is excluded from recovery based on strict liability since the enterprise of transporting explosives is classed as a strict liability enterprise because of the risk of explosions, not the risk of hitting pedestrians.

H. PLAINTIFF'S NEGLIGENCE

In the era of contributory negligence, strict liability cases were an exception to the general rule that any negligence by the plaintiff was a complete defense. When liability was based on a strict liability theory, negligence by the plaintiff was generally irrelevant. As jurisdictions have adopted comparative negligence, most have dealt with the issue of whether it is still sensible to ignore a plaintiff's negligent conduct when a defendant's liability is based on a strict liability theory. The majority position rejects the former approach and treats all aspects of a plaintiff's conduct as factors to be used by the jury in its assessment of comparative negligence.

I. PLAINTIFF'S ASSUMPTION OF RISK

In contributory negligence jurisdictions both reasonable assumption of the risk and unreasonable assumption of the risk were complete defenses to strict liability claims. Each of these theories required proof that the plaintiff was aware of the full details of the risk and chose to encounter it. Under comparative negligence the conduct that formerly served as a full defense when characterized as assumption of risk is now analyzed along with any other conduct by the plaintiff in the jury's assessment of comparative negligence. Note that the comparative negligence treatment of a plaintiff's conduct rejects both components of the traditional view (plaintiff's negligence was no defense and plaintiff's assumption of risk was a full defense).

REVIEW QUESTIONS AND ANSWERS

Question: Sara Stroller strolled by the front yard of Betty Beekeeper. Beekeeper raised bees as a hobby and as a service to farmers in her area. Some of Beekeeper's bees stung Stroller. Does Stroller have a good chance of obtaining damages from Beekeeper for her injury?

Answer: No. Strict liability applies to wild animals, not domesticated animals such as bees. This aspect of strict liability doctrine relegates Stroller to a negligence cause of action, but the facts provide no support for that possibility.

Question: Blast Brothers is a company that demolishes buildings with explosives. It blew up a building near a residential neighborhood, and two individuals were harmed by the blast. Harry Headwound was hit in the head by some debris that landed further away from the building than anyone would have expected. Paula Painter was finishing the design for a movie poster and was startled by the noise. It took her two days longer to finish the project than it would have had she not been startled. Can Headwound and Painter recover damages from Blast Brothers on a strict liability theory?

Answer: Yes for Headwound; no for Painter. The plaintiffs can establish that blasting is an abnormally dangerous activity. Each plaintiff must additionally show, however, that cause in fact and proximate cause doctrines are satisfied in their cases. They both can show cause in fact, since Headwound would not have been hit and Painter would not have been delayed if Blast Brothers had not demolished the building. For proximate cause, however, Headwound can show that his injury is a type of consequence predictably associated with blasting and is therefore one of the reasons why blasting is classified as a strict liability activity. This entitles him to a judgment. Painter cannot make a similar proximate cause showing and therefore has no strict liability claim.

Question: Barbara Busybody ignored some warning signs and entered a genetic research laboratory without required protective equipment. She suffered a physical harm by breathing in a new life form. If strict liability would usually apply to the activities in that lab, can Busybody recover damages for her injury even though she ignored the signs?

Answer: Maybe. Comparative fault principles control how Busybody's negligent conduct reduces or bars recovery. If a jurisdiction uses pure comparative negligence, her responsibility has to be set at 100 percent to bar recovery. If the jurisdiction uses a modified form of comparative negligence, she is allowed some recovery so long as her responsibility is not set at a percentage exceeding the maximum permissible for plaintiffs' recoveries.

EXAM TIPS

- "Every dog has one bite" is wrong. If a dog has shown signs of aggressive behavior, its owner is required to use reasonable care to avoid harms. Some jurisdictions have statutes that impose strict liability on dog owners for harms inflicted by their dogs.
- The owner of a wild animal is responsible on a strict liability basis for harms the animal inflicts.
- One who conducts an abnormally dangerous activity must pay for all the harms it causes, subject only to controls imposed by the cause in fact and proximate cause doctrines.
- In deciding whether an activity should be classified as abnormally dangerous, remember all six factors and be sure to write some common-sense ideas, based on your knowledge of the world, about how each factor might fit the activity that the question describes.

16 PRODUCT LIABILITY

CHAPTER OVERVIEW

- Three main theories allow recovery for product-related injuries: negligence, warranty, and strict liability.
- All the entities involved in the manufacture or distribution of products can be defendants in product liability suits.
- Negligence claims for product cases are identical to negligence claims for other types of injuries.
- Warranty claims are now controlled primarily by the Uniform Commercial Code (U.C.C.). Although they are based in contract law, they can sometimes provide a remedy for an injured victim who had no commercial relationship with the defendant.
- Most states use Restatement §402A as the source of governing doctrine for strict liability claims. Under strict liability a plaintiff's case must include proof of an injury, but the plaintiff is not required to establish a lack of due care by any defendant related to the occurrence of the injury.
- Product liability cases usually involve a flaw in: manufacturing (a product's failure to meet its own producer's specifications); design (use of a design that is not safe enough); or warnings (failure to provide adequate information about the product's hazards).

- Design defect cases often involve considerations of the reasonableness of a seller's design choices, so that despite the label "strict liability," concepts identical to those in negligence cases control the outcome.
- If a plaintiff's negligence contributes to his or her harm from a product, that negligence is compared with the defendant's responsibility, even if that responsibility is grounded in warranty or strict liability.

A. INTRODUCTION

Three overlapping legal doctrines apply to cases in which plaintiffs seek damages for injuries caused by products. They are negligence, warranty, and strict liability. Plaintiffs are often able to use all three theories.

1. Negligence

Negligence doctrines for product cases are the same as for other cases. The plaintiff must show that the defendant acted unreasonably. The concept of privity of contract was once a problem for plaintiffs in negligence cases. Privity refers to a direct relationship between the plaintiff and the defendant. Application of a privity requirement once prevented a victim from suing a product manufacturer if the victim's only direct relationship had been with a product retailer (different from a product manufacturer). Development in the common law eliminated this problem.

2. Warranty

Warranty law is rooted in contract and sales law. If a buyer can show that a product's attributes were not as good as its express or implied warranties required, recovery is allowed against the manufacturer or seller. The plaintiff does not have to show that unreasonable conduct was why the product failed to satisfy its warranties. Privity requirements apply in warranty cases and have not been modified as significantly as in the negligence context.

3. Strict Liability

Strict liability allows a plaintiff to recover without showing privity and without showing unreasonable conduct if the plaintiff shows that the defendant marketed a defective product. This combines the more pro-plaintiff aspects of both negligence and warranty law. The factor from negligence law that favors plaintiffs is a relaxation of the privity requirement. The factor from warranty law that favors plaintiffs is the requirement of proof only about the product rather than about the reasonableness of conduct by the manufacturer.

Illustration: This table shows that strict liability uses privity and proof of wrongdoing concepts from negligence and warranty law, selecting the theories most favorable to plaintiffs for each issue.

Required Proof of Product Characteristics, Manufacturer's Conduct, and Privity Negligence, Warranty, and Strict Liability, Compared

Topic	*Negligence*	*Warranty*	*Strict Liability*
Product characteristics	More dangerous than reasonable manufacture would produce	Worse than warranties require	Defective
Manufacturer's conduct	Manufacturer acted unreasonably	No required proof	No required proof
Privity between plaintiff and manufacturer	No required proof	Yes or no, varying among states	No required proof

B. NEGLIGENCE

A person who suffers a product-related injury can establish a negligence cause of action against a defendant who produced or marketed the product by showing that: 1. the defendant owed the person a duty of reasonable care; 2. the defendant breached that duty; 3. the person suffered an injury; and 4. the defendant's conduct was a proximate cause of the injury.

1. Privity Requirement

The concept of privity, meaning direct connection, was once problematic for victims of product-related injuries. At common law a plaintiff using a negligence theory had to show privity between the plaintiff and the defendant. A defendant owed a duty of reasonable care only to those with whom the defendant was in privity.

a. **Definition.** If a person buys a product from a retailer, the buyer and the retailer are in privity. The retailer and the manufacturer or wholesaler from whom the retailer obtained the product are also in privity. Note that the buyer and the manufacturer are not in privity, since they have no direct relationship.

b. ***Winterbottom v. Wright.*** In a famous case, Winterbottom v. Wright, 152 Eng. Rep. 402 (1842), a post office driver was injured because the coach he was driving broke down. He sought damages from the defendant who had failed to keep it in good repair. The plaintiff was denied recovery because the defendant's obligation to work on the coach arose from the defendant's contract with the post office. The defendant was protected from liability to the plaintiff because the plaintiff and defendant were not in privity.

c. ***MacPherson v. Buick Motor Co.*** The privity limitation was rejected in a very influential American case, MacPherson v. Buick Motor Co., 111 N.E. 1050 (N.Y. 1916). The plaintiff was injured in an accident involving a flaw in a new Buick. He sought damages from Buick, but the case was rejected at trial because he was in privity with the retailer but not with Buick. On appeal Judge Benjamin Cardozo reviewed some exceptions to the privity requirement that had already been recognized. These involved injuries from inherently dangerous products like poisons or scaffolds. He expanded that principle to reject the privity requirement in any case where something was "reasonably certain to place life and limb in peril when negligently made." *MacPherson* thus authorizes suits without privity in virtually all product injury cases.

d. **Modern range of allowable plaintiffs.** In every state a negligence action may be maintained against the negligent manufacturer of a product by any person who suffers a personal injury proximately caused by that negligence. Most states follow this rule for property damage as well.

2. Duty of Reasonable Care

Most negligence claims involve allegedly improper conduct by a manufacturer or a retailer. Each potential defendant owes a duty to act with reasonable care to any person who would foreseeably be affected by a deficiency in the product.

a. **Manufacturer.** The duty to act as a reasonable prudent person (the duty of due care) applies to all aspects of a manufacturer's actions. These include: designing a product, selecting its raw materials and component parts, examining or testing those materials and parts (if reasonable), manufacturing the product, inspecting and testing it, packing it, shipping it, and providing instructions or warnings needed by its user.

Illustration: Prentis v. Yale Manufacturing Co., 421 Mich. 670, 365 N.W.2d 176 (1984). The plaintiff sought damages from the manufacturer of a forklift that experienced a power surge that made him lose his footing and fall. Judgment was entered for the defendant on a jury verdict but was reversed by the intermediate appellate court because the trial court had failed to instruct on breach of warranty. The supreme court rejected strict liability theories for design defect cases, reasoning that the proper standard would be a negligence test that imposed liability for designs that incorporate an unreasonable balance of risk versus utility.

b. **Retailer.** The duty to act as a reasonable prudent person (the duty of due care) applies to all aspects of a retailer's actions. For retailers who sell things manufactured by others, however, the duty of due care is usually very easy to meet.

i. **Inspections.** In most jurisdictions a retailer is obligated to inspect a product only if there is a particular reason to think that the product may be dangerous. In some places if a simple inspection could be performed easily by the retailer and would be difficult for a customer to perform, a retailer may have a duty to carry out that type of inspection (as in the case of an automobile dealer).

   (a) **Negligent or omitted inspection does not protect manufacturer from liability.** A manufacturer who negligently produces a dangerous product is not protected from liability by showing that a retailer failed to inspect it. If a retailer gains actual knowledge of a product's danger and fails to communicate that danger to a buyer, however, this conduct may be considered so extraordinarily negligent that it becomes a superseding cause of any injury caused by the danger.

E&A

EXAMPLE AND ANALYSIS

Clara Cracker bought a box of saltines at a grocery store. One of the crackers contained a sliver of metal that injured Cracker seriously when she ate it. Cracker would have no cause of action against the grocery store for negligence in the sale of the crackers, since there was no reason for the operator of a grocery store to inspect the contents of a sealed package of crackers.

3. Proximate Cause

Each jurisdiction applies its proximate cause rules to negligence cases involving product-related injuries. A bystander who is injured by a defective product may be excluded from recovery if he or she is not a foreseeable plaintiff.

C. WARRANTY LIABILITY

Warranty liability is grounded in the law's regulation of the commercial relationship between buyers and sellers. If a seller sells something that turns out not to be as good as the seller claimed it would, the buyer has a contract-based remedy for that deficiency. There is no inquiry into why the product is deficient. Relief is based on proof of a discrepancy between the product as it is and the product as it was supposed to be. This discrepancy is called a "breach" of the warranty.

Warranty liability is strict liability because it applies regardless of how carefully the defendant acted. If a product is not as good as the seller said it would be, the seller is liable for injuries related to that shortcoming, even if the seller was as careful as any seller could have been.

1. Express Warranties

An express warranty is a seller's specific statement about a product's features or attributes.

Illustration: Baxter v. Ford Motor Co., 168 Wash. 456, 12 P.2d 409 (1932). The plaintiff was injured when the windshield of a car manufactured by the defendant shattered. The plaintiff sought damages on breach of express warranty theory, relying on brochures provided by the defendant that described the car's glass as "nonshatterable." At trial the defendant won a directed verdict. On appeal it was held that the plaintiff was entitled to proceed against the manufacturer despite a lack of privity between the plaintiff and manufacturer.

a. **U.C.C. provisions.** The Uniform Commercial Code covers express warranties in §2-313. Under this provision the following types of conduct by a seller can be the basis for a finding of express warranty: affirming a fact, promising something, describing the product, or showing a model or sample.

   i. **Reliance.** Common law required that a plaintiff show he or she had relied on an express warranty in order to use its breach as a basis for recovery. The U.C.C. only requires that the warranty be part of the "basis of the bargain," which usually means that the statement must have been made during or prior to the sale transaction.

2. Implied Warranty of Merchantability

The U.C.C. implies a warranty of merchantability in sales of goods by sellers who are merchants for that type of goods and who regularly sell that type of goods. The warranty requires the goods to be "fit for the ordinary purposes for which such goods are used." U.C.C. §§2-314(1) and (2).

a. **Transactions covered.** The implied warranty of merchantability applies to sales of food and drink as well as to sales of durable goods. It applies to sales by retailers and wholesalers, along with sales by manufacturers. Services are excluded from its coverage. Sales of used goods may or may not be covered, with variations among jurisdictions partly based on the particular attributes of the used product and its seller.

EXAMPLE AND ANALYSIS

Any significant flaw in a product constitutes a breach of the implied warranty of merchantability. Food with impurities is a prime example. Another example is a home appliance that gives someone an electric shock or starts a fire.

3. Implied Warranty of Fitness for a Particular Purpose

U.C.C. §2-315 implies a warranty of fitness for a particular purpose when: 1. a buyer wants goods for a purpose that is not typical; 2. the seller knows about that purpose; 3. the seller recommends certain goods; and 4. the buyer relies on the seller's recommendation.

4. Privity

As was true for negligence cases, warranty cases have traditionally involved a privity requirement. The requirement has been relaxed in two ways: judicial action and legislative adoption of U.C.C. provisions.

a. **Judicial action.** The landmark case, Henningsen v. Bloomfield Motors, Inc., 161 A.2d 69 (N.J. 1960), allowed the plaintiff, who had been injured in a vehicular accident, to sue the car's retailer and manufacturer on an implied warranty theory, even though she had been a passenger, not the purchaser of the car. Expanding a rationale from earlier cases involving sales of food, the court held that a warranty follows the item itself and is not restricted to purchasers.

i. **Vertical privity.** *Henningsen* involved two types of privity, vertical and horizontal. Vertical privity in warranty cases is the relationship between a purchaser and a remote defendant. The owner of the car had vertical privity with Bloomfield Motors but did not have vertical privity with Chrysler Corporation, which had manufactured the car. The court refused to enforce a vertical privity requirement.

ii. **Horizontal privity.** Horizontal privity in warranty cases refers to the relationship between a purchaser and a remote victim of product-related injury. In *Henningsen* the person harmed was not the purchaser but the purchaser's passenger (his wife). The court rejected a horizontal privity requirement.

b. **U.C.C. and privity.** The U.C.C. does not refer to vertical privity. Courts applying the U.C.C. generally reject that requirement, adopting the rationale of *Henningsen.* With regard to horizontal privity, the U.C.C. provides states with three options.

i. **U.C.C. privity alternative *A*.** A warranty claim that a purchaser would have may also be made by a member of the purchaser's household or a guest in the household if it is reasonable to expect that the person might be affected by the goods.

ii. **U.C.C. privity alternative *B*.** A warranty claim that a purchaser would have may also be made by any natural person who may reasonably be expected to suffer personal injury from the goods. Note that this extends warranty protection to foreseeable bystanders and others who are not members of the purchaser's family and are not guests in the purchaser's household.

iii. **U.C.C. privity alternative *C*.** Alternative *C* expands on Alternative *B* by adding non-natural plaintiffs (such as business entities) and property damage claims.

E&A EXAMPLE AND ANALYSIS

Barry Boater owned a boat and invited his friend, Frank Friend, to fish from it. The boat sprung a leak, and Friend was injured. For Friend to recover from the boat's manufacturer on a warranty theory, Friend would have to establish privity. Under the U.C.C. alternative *A*, Friend would have to show that he had been a guest in Boater's household when he was injured. It is questionable that being in the boat would be treated as having been a guest in the household. Under alternatives *B* and *C* Friend could establish privity, since a friend of a boat owner is a person whom one would reasonably expect to suffer an injury from a defect in a boat.

5. Defenses

A variety of defenses that were traditional in warranty cases have been rejected by the U.C.C., by federal law, and by courts.

a. **Disclaimers.** Under federal law if a warranty is given to a consumer, the warranty may not disclaim any implied warranty. The U.C.C. also limits a seller's ability to disclaim implied warranties.

b. **Limitations on damages.** Under the U.C.C. limitation of consequential damages (such as stating that damages will be limited to repair or replacement of goods) is forbidden in personal injury cases involving consumer goods.

c. **Notice of breach.** The U.C.C. requires a buyer to inform a seller of a breach. In cases where the plaintiffs are other than the buyers, courts usually refuse to impose that requirement.

D. STRICT LIABILITY

Strict liability for product-related injuries allows redress without requiring that the plaintiff prove unreasonable conduct. The plaintiff must show that the product was defective but need not show that the defendant acted unreasonably in producing or selling it. Defects are usually called: 1. manufacturing defects (products that do not meet the manufacturers' specifications); 2. design defects (products with designs that are not adequately safe); or 3. defects in warnings or instructions (products lacking information to make use less dangerous).

1. Comparison with Negligence Liability

Strict liability for product cases is highly similar to negligence liability, but some important differences may affect some cases.

a. **Relationship to *res ipsa loquitur* in negligence cases.** In most cases where defendants have marketed defective products, the defendants were probably negligent in some way. If the *res ipsa loquitur* doctrine were applied very freely, it would produce results identical to those reached through strict liability. The *res ipsa loquitur* doctrine allows a jury to infer negligence; the strict liability theory allows a jury to impose liability without finding that any negligence occurred.

b. **Range of defendants.** Strict liability allows plaintiffs to obtain redress from more defendants than would usually be subject to liability under a negligence analysis. Entities such as retailers or wholesalers who may not have committed any negligent acts or omissions are generally subject to strict liability for selling a defective product, even though they usually would be free from liability under a negligence analysis.

c. **Reasonably produced dangerous product.** In a rare case, a manufacturer might act reasonably and still produce a dangerous product. Recovery would be available only under strict liability.

E&A EXAMPLE AND ANALYSIS

A computer used in designing a component might have a defective chip that produces incorrect calculations. If a manufacturer used that computer to design a product, the product might have a dangerous flaw because of the miscalculation. A plaintiff who was injured by the product would have no negligence claim against the manufacturer, because the manufacturer acted reasonably. The plaintiff would be able to recover, however, under a strict liability theory.

---

d. **Defective designs.** The analysis of strict liability for defective designs in most jurisdictions uses concepts that are highly similar to negligence concepts.

2. **Restatement §402A**

California Supreme Court decisions were highly influential in the development of strict liability for product injury cases. Reflecting those decisions and some others, an extremely important provision of the Restatement (Second) of Torts, §402A, was promulgated in the mid-1960s. This provision was subsequently adopted in most states. It continues to provide the main doctrines for product cases at present, although states vary in their interpretations of its elements and some states have adopted statutes that differ from it.

a. **California precedents.** Two famous California cases foreshadowed the adoption of Restatement §402A.

i. **Escola v. Coca-Cola Bottling Co. of Fresno,** 24 Cal. 2d 453, 150 P.2d 436 (1944). The California Supreme Court affirmed a judgment based on use of the *res ipsa loquitur* doctrine in favor of a waitress who was injured by an exploding soft drink bottle. In a concurring opinion Justice Traynor argued that the court had stretched the *res ipsa loquitur* doctrine very far and that a better basis for decision would have been that fairness in a modern industrialized society requires making manufacturers pay for most of the injuries their products cause.

ii. **Greenman v. Yuba Power Products,** 377 P.2d 897 (Cal. 1963). About twenty years after *Escola,* Justice Traynor's position commanded a majority on his court. In *Greenman* the victim had been injured by a power tool, and it was unclear whether a jury verdict in his favor had been based on his negligence or warranty theory. The court held that the judgment should be affirmed despite the possibility that the plaintiff had failed to satisfy some of the usual requirements for warranty-based relief. Strict liability in tort was the proper doctrine for a case involving a user's injury caused by a defective product.

b. **§402A text.** Figure 16-1, p. 277, sets out the text of the Restatement section in the left-hand column. The right-hand column explains the main significance of each portion of the text.

FIGURE 16-1

Restatement Language	*Issues and Explanations*
§402A Special Liability of Seller of Product for Physical Harm to User or Consumer	The "special liability" is strict liability.
One who sells	The defendant must be one who sells the product. Manufacturers and wholesalers, as well as retailers, are product sellers.
any product	§402A covers products, not services.
in a defective condition unreasonably dangerous	"[D]efective condition unreasonably dangerous" is a term of art interpreted in a variety of ways.
to the user or consumer or to his property	Injury to a person or to property can be a basis for recovery.
is subject to liability for physical harm thereby caused to the ultimate user or consumer, or to his property, if	§402A applies only if an injury produces physical damages. It does not apply to a case with only economic damages.
(a) the seller is engaged in the business of selling such a product, and	The defendant must regularly sell the product. Sellers of used goods may be outside this definition if they sell many different types of goods.
(b) it is expected to and does reach the user or consumer without substantial change in the condition in which it is sold.	A seller is free from responsibility if injuries result from significant product alterations that the seller could not reasonably foresee.
(2) The rule stated in Subsection (1) applies although	The two statements following this introductory clause represent the two pro-plaintiff elements from negligence law and warranty law that §402A incorporates.
(a) the seller has exercised all possible care in the preparation and sale of this product, and	Liability is strict (as in warranty cases). Even the best possible care is no defense if the product was defective.
(b) the user or consumer has not bought the product from or entered into any contractual relation with the seller.	Privity between the victim and the defendant is not required (as in negligence cases after *MacPherson v. Buick*).

c. **Identifying the defendant or defendants.** The victim of a product-related injury must identify a defendant or defendants against whom to assert a strict liability claim. In most states any individual or entity with any role in the manufacture, distribution, or sale of a product is a potential defendant.

   i. **Different from negligence.** This is a significant difference between strict liability and negligence. Strict liability can attach to a wholesaler or retailer, for example, whose conduct in connection with the product was entirely blameless.

   ii. **Contemporary modifications.** Some states, through the process of tort reform, have narrowed the range of allowable defendants in strict liability cases. One approach allows a strict liability claim only against a product's manufacturer. Another approach applies that limitation generally but allows suits against wholesalers and retailers if the manufacturer is not solvent or is not subject to jurisdiction of the state's courts.

d. **Manufacturing defect.** A product has a manufacturing defect if there is a difference between its actual condition when it leaves the manufacturer's possession and its intended condition according to the manufacturer's specifications. When the product does not measure up to its own manufacturer's plans for it, and the discrepancy leads to an injury, the product is characterized as having a manufacturing defect.

   i. **Different from negligence.** Most of the times a manufacturer sells a product that fails to meet its own specifications, there was some negligence in the production process. Strict liability actions do not require the plaintiff to identify or prove that negligence. In an unusual instance a product may be produced with a flaw that even perfect manufacturing would not have prevented. In such a circumstance, negligence liability never attaches, but a strict liability theory makes the manufacturer liable.

   ii. **Rationale.** The rationale for this definition relies on a manufacturers' own decisions about product safety. The definition states, in effect, that a manufacturer may set its own standard but that the legal system will hold the manufacturer to that standard once the manufacturer picks it.

E&A EXAMPLE AND ANALYSIS

Stella Sitter was hurt when she sat on a chair made by Chairco and was cut by a sharp piece of metal that poked through the seat. Assuming that Chairco had not designed the chair to have this piece of metal as it was, Sitter could recover damages on a strict liability theory, claiming that the chair had a manufacturing defect. Sitter would not be required to show how carefully Chairco had made the chair, nor how many inspections Chairco had included in its manufacturing process. Proof that the chair did not conform to Chairco's specifications and that the discrepancy caused an injury would entitle Sitter to recovery.

---

e. **Design defect.** Most product liability cases involve products that were sold in exactly the condition that the manufacturer intended. The plaintiff must show that such a product was in a "defective condition unreasonably dangerous," in the language of Restatement §402A, because of its design.

Illustration: Cronin v. J.B.E. Olson Corp., 8 Cal. 3d 121, 104 Cal. Rptr. 433, 501 P.2d 1153 (1972). The court held that a plaintiff need only prove "defectiveness," since the word *unreasonably* introduced negligence concepts into a strict liability case.

i. **Consumer expectation test.** The consumer expectation test was the first test to achieve general use in strict liability product injury cases. It asks whether the product is dangerous "to an extent beyond that which would be contemplated by the ordinary consumer who purchases it, with the ordinary knowledge common to the community as to its characteristics." Restatement §402A, comment *i*.

(a) **Lack of community knowledge.** A problem with the consumer expectation test is that sometimes buyers or people in a community have no knowledge about the risks involved in a product. In such an instance the product satisfies their expectations because they have none.

(b) **Obvious hazards.** If a product has an obvious hazard (sometimes called a "patent" danger), consumers expect the hazard because they see it. Thus, the consumer expectation test does not impose liability where a product has an obvious danger, even if the manufacturer could have selected a different design that would have eliminated the danger.

ii. **Risk-benefit test.** Many jurisdictions use a risk-benefit test to ask whether the design selected was reasonable in light of its risks and benefits.

Illustration: Phillips v. Kimwood Machine Co., 269 Or. 485, 525 P.2d 1033 (1974). The plaintiff was injured using a sanding machine manufactured by the defendant. He sought damages claiming that its design should have incorporated safety features such as a guard to prevent materials from being thrown out of the machine toward its operator. The trial court granted a directed verdict to the defendant, but the supreme court reversed, holding that under a risk-utility balancing test the plaintiff had presented an adequate case for jury consideration.

(a) **Factors for risk-benefit balancing.** Courts use many different factors in applying a risk-benefit analysis. A seven-part test first suggested by the late John Wade is used in many jurisdictions. Its factors are:

- the product's usefulness and desirability as designed;
- likely occurrence and severity of injury;
- availability of safer alternative design or product;
- manufacturer's ability to eliminate danger without impairing its usefulness or making it too expensive;
- user's ability to avoid the danger;
- user's anticipated awareness of the danger; and
- feasibility of manufacturer's spreading the risk through insurance or pricing.

(b) **Different from negligence.** The risk-benefit test is quite close to an ordinary negligence test, except that it imposes liability where a design choice represents an unreasonable balance between risks and benefits even if the defendant acted reasonably in making that design choice. The defendant might have been reasonably unaware of a risk, for example, or might have made a reasonable error in some part of the design process.

iii. **Alternative tests: consumer expectation or risk-benefit.** In some states a plaintiff is permitted to show defective design with either the consumer expectation test or the risk-benefit test.

(a) **California burden shift.** In California these alternatives are available to plaintiffs. Additionally, in a method followed by a small number of states, the defendant has the burden of proof that its design was not defective if the plaintiff shows that an injury was caused by the product's design.

iv. **Feasible alternative test.** To prove that defendants' products were defective, plaintiffs in some jurisdictions must prove that they failed the risk-benefit test and that feasible safer alternatives existed. An

American Law Institute study, prepared as a possible replacement for the Restatement (Second) of Torts, adopts this view.

v. **Unavoidably unsafe products.** §402A, comment *k* on unavoidably unsafe products acknowledges that many dangerous products are socially useful, such as vaccines and other drugs. It states that their sellers shall be free from strict liability so long as: 1. the product's benefits outweigh its dangers; and 2. the seller provides adequate warnings along with the product.

Illustration: Brown v. Superior Court, 44 Cal. 3d 1049, 245 Cal. Rptr. 412, 751 P.2d 470 (1988). The California Supreme Court adopted the Restatement position in comment *k*, on the theory that subjecting drug manufacturers to strict liability would make them reluctant to do research or develop new drugs.

(a) **Historical rationale for comment *k*.** Comment *k* represents a particular application of the risk-utility test for product defectiveness. Its inclusion in Restatement §402A makes sense since the main definition of product defectiveness in the Restatement is the consumer expectation test. In jurisdictions using the risk-benefit test for defectiveness, comment *k* is redundant.

E&A Example and Analysis

Prescription drugs are the prime example of unavoidably unsafe products. Liability for injuries related to them is usually based on findings that their manufacturers failed to provide adequate warnings of their possible side effects.

f. **Warnings or instructions defect.** A product that is free from manufacturing or design defects may still be defective if its safety could have been increased by better warnings or instructions for use.

i. **Warnings and instructions for products with manufacturing or design defects.** If a product has a manufacturing or design defect, a plaintiff can recover under strict liability for injuries related to those defects, regardless of whether the product had warnings and instructions to reduce the danger.

ii. **Warnings for dangers in adequately designed and adequately manufactured products.** When a product's manufacturing and design meet the applicable standards for strict liability, the manufacturer has one more obligation: It must provide warnings or instructions for use if they will further reduce dangers or increase safety.

(a) **Standards for warnings and instructions.** The standard for adequacy of a product's warnings or instructions is essentially a negligence standard. If the cost of a warning or particular instruction is less than the cost of the injuries it might prevent, then the warning or instruction should be provided. Note that a manufacturer may sometimes show that too many warnings can reduce the effectiveness of each individual warning, so a choice to be silent about some risks may be defensible.

(b) **Learned intermediary doctrine.** For prescription drugs, where a consumer may not receive the product except through contact with a doctor, manufacturers are permitted to satisfy the obligation to warn by providing warnings to doctors. (A doctor is a learned intermediary.) In a small number of cases, where prescription drugs are dispensed without the usual personal attention that characterizes doctor-patient relationships, some courts have required that warnings be provided to the actual users of the drugs. These cases have involved birth control pills and drugs used for mass inoculations.

(c) **Heeding presumption.** In most jurisdictions juries are instructed to presume that the plaintiff would have heeded a proper warning or instruction if the manufacturer had provided it.

g. **Factual context for all cases: information at time of manufacture or time of trial.** In deciding whether a product's design struck the right balance between risks and benefits or whether a product's warnings and instructions gave proper information about risks, what knowledge should the judge or jury consider? There are two main answers to this question: knowledge that was available at the time the defendant manufactured the product, or knowledge available later, such as at the time of trial. In virtually all cases knowledge at the time of manufacture is the context in which the product will be evaluated.

i. **Responsibility for unknown and unknowable hazards.** There is a distinction between information that is unknown and information that is unknowable at the time the defendant makes its product. Unknown information is information that could be found or discovered but that the defendant does not obtain. Unknowable information is information that no one knows or would be able to know at the time, given the degree of scientific progress attained.

(a) **General rule: consider only facts knowable when product**

manufactured. The overwhelming weight of authority excludes from consideration information that was not within the scope of human knowledge at the time the defendant made the product.

Illustration: Anderson v. Owens-Corning Fiberglas Corp., 53 Cal. 3d 987, 281 Cal. Rptr. 528, 810 P.2d 549 (1991). In evaluating whether a defendant manufacturer should have provided a warning about a risk associated with its product, evidence of the state of the art with regard to that risk at the time of manufacture is relevant. There can be no liability for failure to warn of a risk that was unknowable at the time of manufacture.

(b) **Liability based on later-known facts.** Beshada v. Johns-Manville Products Corp., 90 N.J. 191, 447 A.2d 539 (1982). The court imposed responsibility on a defendant for its failure to warn about risks that were scientifically unknowable at the time the defendant marketed its product. This decision was justified in the sense that both the seller and the victims of product-related injury were reasonably ignorant of the risks. The court faced the choice of which of two innocent parties should bear the loss and chose to put it on the party that had made profits from the sale of the goods and had the ability to spread those losses.

h. **All defects: present when defendant released product.** A defendant has strict liability only for defects that were present at the time the defendant released the product into the stream of commerce. The main significance of this rule is that it protects defendants from liability for injuries related to products that other people have modified.

i. **Responsibility for anticipated modifications.** If a seller provides a product and knows that the user is likely to modify it in a particular way, strict liability may be imposed on the seller if that modification makes the product defective.

E&A EXAMPLE AND ANALYSIS

Power Press Company manufactures industrial presses that exert great force on dies to mold metal. To protect workers Power Press designs its machines so they will not function unless the operator is holding down two switches at once, guaranteeing that his or her hands are away from any dangerous part of the machine. If Power Press had knowledge that one of its customers was modifying the machine to allow it to function without both switches engaged, Power Press could be responsible for an injury a worker suffered from using a modified machine.

---

3. Compliance with State of the Art, Statutes, or Regulations

States vary in the treatment they give to proof that a defendant's product complied with the state of the art at time of manufacture, with statutes, or with regulations.

a. **Common law.** Most courts reject the idea that compliance with industry custom, regulations, or even statutes should be a complete defense. This is parallel to the usual position taken in negligence cases. The common law tradition allowed juries to reject the custom of an industry or reject a regulatory or statutory requirement and decide that under the applicable tort law standards the defendant should be liable.

b. **State statutes.** A number of states have adopted statutes that establish defenses of regulatory compliance and compliance with state of the art. Under these statutes defendants are protected from liability if their products complied with applicable regulations or statutes or with the state of the art at the time they were made.

   i. **Ambiguity in state of the art.** The phrase *state of the art* might mean the state of scientific and technical knowledge in a particular field. It might also mean the custom in an industry. For the purpose of a state-of-the-art defense in state statutes, the term usually means the first of these two definitions (scientific and technical knowledge). Legislatures generally intend not to allow compliance with industry custom to be a complete defense.

c. **Pre-emption by federal statutes and regulations.** As a matter of constitutional law, some federal statutes pre-empt the right of states to impose common law, statutory, or regulatory controls on certain activities. A federal statute pre-empts state law if it expressly states that it has that effect, if the statute is intended to occupy a particular field completely, or if a conflict between a state action and the federal statute makes it impossible to comply with both the state and the federal requirements.

   Illustration: King v. Collagen Corp., 983 F.2d 1130 (1st Cir. 1993). The plaintiff was harmed by a product manufactured by the defendant that was injected under her skin to smooth wrinkles. She sought damages from the manufacturer. The trial court ruled that her claim was pre-empted by a federal statute. The first circuit affirmed the trial court's summary judgment. Interpretation of the statute was the key to the court's decision, with the court finding express preemption applicable to this claim.

i. **Application dependent on statutory interpretation.** Application of the pre-emption doctrine is heavily dependent on statutory interpretation. In recent cases, for example, federal regulatory statutes have been held to pre-empt some but not all state-based remedies for injuries caused by cigarettes and pacemakers.

d. **Government contractor defense.** A defendant who supplies a product to the federal government for military use has no liability under any tort law theory for injuries the product may cause if the product complies with specifications approved by the government.

4. Causation

The plaintiff must establish that the product's defect was a cause in fact and a proximate cause of his or her injury.

a. **Pro-defendant application.** Some courts apply proximate cause doctrines like superseding cause with a slight pro-defendant bias in strict liability cases. They theorize that defendants who have not been proved to have been at fault deserve that benefit.

b. **Misuse as sole proximate cause.** When a plaintiff has misused a product, the defendant is likely to claim that the misuse was the sole proximate cause of the injury. If that analysis is accepted, the defendant is free from liability.

5. Plaintiff's Conduct

The plaintiff's conduct is often an issue in strict liability cases. Litigants often distinguish between ordinary negligence in the use of a product and misuse of a product. During the early period of development of strict liability for product-related injuries, ordinary negligence by a plaintiff was not a defense, but a plaintiff's misuse could protect a defendant from liability. The majority of states now apply comparative negligence principles to plaintiffs' negligence in strict liability product cases but still allow proof of misuse to protect defendants under certain circumstances.

Illustration: Daly v. General Motors Corp., 20 Cal. 3d 725, 144 Cal. Rptr. 380, 575 P.2d 1162 (1978). Despite the conceptual difficulty of comparing apples and oranges, plaintiffs' negligence should be compared with defendants' liability based on strict liability principles.

a. **Ordinary negligence.** The Restatement and modern comparative negligence jurisdictions differ on treatment of ordinary negligence by a plaintiff in a strict liability case.

i. **Restatement (contributory negligence era).** Restatement §402A states that ordinary contributory negligence is not a defense. It also states that assumption of the risk is a full defense. Denying the defense of contributory negligence was a significant step at the time §402A was promulgated, since the vast majority of jurisdictions still applied the traditional contributory negligence doctrine at that time.

ii. **Current treatment (comparative negligence).** Almost all jurisdictions now have replaced §402A's treatment of a plaintiff's negligence and assumption of the risk with comparative negligence doctrines. A jury is required to compare a plaintiff's negligence with a defendant's liability based on strict liability principles.

EXAMPLE AND ANALYSIS

Climbing a ladder while it is set on an uneven surface is an example of ordinary negligence in the use of a product. Modern jurisdictions allow recovery for a plaintiff injured this way if the plaintiff shows that the ladder was defective, but they reduce the plaintiff's recovery to account for his or her negligence.

b. **Misuse.** When a plaintiff has allegedly misused a product, that factor may relate to the seller's duty, to causation, or to a defense of comparative negligence. A defendant can argue: 1. there was no defect in the product since it only had shortcomings with respect to an unforeseeable misuse; 2. the product had a defect but the plaintiff's strange use of the product, not the defect, caused the harm; or 3. the product had a defect but the plaintiff was negligent in using the product so recovery should be reduced or barred.

i. **Duty.** A product seller has a duty to provide a product that is not defective for foreseeable uses. Thus, the decision about whether a product was defective necessarily includes a decision about the product's intended use. It is impossible to say that a design, for example, was safe enough or was too risky, without knowing what function the product was supposed to serve. Product sellers are required to anticipate both foreseeable uses and foreseeable misuses of their products. If a plaintiff only proves that the product was too dangerous when used in a way that was not reasonably foreseeable, the plaintiff has failed to establish a basis for strict liability. A seller has no duty to provide a product that is safe when used in a way that was not foreseeable.

(a) **Crashworthy vehicles.** Car manufacturers once claimed that cars were made for ordinary driving, not for crashes, so there was no obligation to design them in ways that would increase the safety of occupants in crashes. All courts currently reject that argument since crashes are highly foreseeable. They require cars to be crashworthy.

ii. **Causation.** In addition to showing that a product has a defect, the plaintiff must show that the defect caused the plaintiff's injury. A defendant may be able to show that the product's defect did not cause the injury, because the real cause of the injury was the plaintiff's misuse of the product. For example, a metal ladder might have been made with joints too weak for safe use when a person climbed it. If that same ladder failed when a person used it as a horizontal bridge across a space on a construction project, the defendant might escape liability by showing that the plaintiff's unforeseeable use of the product led to the injury.

iii. **Comparative negligence.** Although Restatement §402A states that contributory negligence is no defense and that assumption of risk is a full defense, the majority of jurisdictions now apply comparative negligence principles to both situations. Thus, some conduct that a defendant might characterize as misuse is treated as carelessness by the plaintiff. The effect is to bar or reduce recovery under the jurisdiction's ordinary comparative negligence rules.

E&A EXAMPLE AND ANALYSIS

Using a ladder as a horizontal bridge over an opening in the floor of a building under construction is an example of misuse of a product. A plaintiff injured while using a ladder that way might be unable to establish a strict liability claim for three different reasons. First, a flaw in the ladder that made it defective only for use as a bridge would probably not constitute a defect. Second, some courts would find that the plaintiff's unusual use of the product was the sole cause of the injury. Finally, some jurisdictions would apply comparative negligence principles to this circumstance but would reject any jury finding that failed to assign predominant responsibility to the plaintiff (in modified comparative negligence jurisdictions this would prevent recovery).

6. Evidentiary Issues

Two controversial evidentiary issues in strict liability cases involve the use of evidence of subsequent remedial measures and the role of epidemiological evidence.

a. **Subsequent remedial measures.** A nearly universal rule in negligence cases prohibits the use of evidence of a defendant's postaccident remedial measures to prove negligence. (Evidence of subsequent remedial measures is sometimes admissible to support inferences other than negligence, such as the defendant's ownership or control of the location or thing that harmed the plaintiff.) The rule is intended to encourage potential defendants to make safety improvements that they might otherwise postpone to protect their chances of winning a potential lawsuit. In strict liability cases most courts apply the same rule. A minority, however, allow evidence of subsequent remedial measures in strict liability cases as relevant to defectiveness. They reason that manufacturers have strong incentive to make their products safer all the time, and there is no need to increase that incentive by excluding information about improvements from products liability trials.

b. **Epidemiological data.** A few courts require plaintiffs to introduce epidemiological data to support claims that environmental hazards have caused them to suffer illnesses or that particular harms were related to drugs manufactured by the defendants. Most courts permit this type of evidence but allow juries to decide causation issues whether or not it is presented.

REVIEW QUESTIONS AND ANSWERS

Question: Mediocre Manufacturing Company was a large manufacturer of home appliances. To save money it fired all of its quality control inspectors and began shipping its products without checking to make sure they had been assembled properly. Charlotte Shocked bought a Mediocre toaster from a store called Kitchen Karnival. She plugged in the toaster, touched one of its switches, and suffered a severe electric shock (some of its wires were not properly insulated). Would Shocked have a cause of action in negligence against Mediocre?

Answer: Yes. A reasonable prudent manufacturer would have used some procedure for inspecting its products prior to selling them, especially if there was a risk that a defectively made unit could cause a serious harm.

Question: Charlotte Shocked (from the question above) had a brother named Sheldon Shocked. Injured by the Mediocre toaster, would Sheldon have a cause of action in negligence against Mediocre?

Answer: Yes. He was a foreseeable victim of Mediocre's negligent conduct, even though he was not the purchaser of the toaster.

Question: Would Charlotte Shocked (from the first question) have a cause of action in negligence against Kitchen Karnival for the shock she suffered from the defective toaster?

Answer: No. Kitchen Karnival did not act in an unreasonable way (assuming the toaster was delivered in a sealed package and there was no reason for Carnival to expect it to be flawed).

Question: Would warranty theories provide redress for Shocked (from the first question) against Mediocre?

Answer: Yes. The implied warranty of merchantability would be breached by an appliance with this defect.

Question: Would strict liability allow a cause of action by Shocked (from the first question) against Kitchen Karnival?

Answer: Yes. All sellers of a defective product are liable to the victim. Although Kitchen Karnival was not blameworthy, the majority of courts applying Restatement §402A would impose liability on it.

Question: If Shocked's toaster injured her not because Mediocre had skimped on quality control personnel but because Mediocre had decided to use a design that included much less insulation on the toaster's switch wiring than it had used on previous models, could Shocked use a consumer expectation test successfully to establish defectiveness of the toaster?

Answer: Yes. The consumer expectation test treats a product as defective if it is less safe than a typical consumer would expect. Mediocre's design decision did produce a toaster that was less safe than typical consumers would expect it to be.

Question: Could Shocked use a risk-utility test to establish defectiveness of the toaster in the preceding question?

Answer: Yes. The risk-utility test's seven inquiries would probably all point to defectiveness of the toaster design. For example, the product was not particularly useful as designed, the severity of the risked injury was great, and a user had no ability to avoid the danger.

Question: Charlotte Shocked bought another toaster, manufactured by Winner Company. She discovered that she could make the toaster's heating element stay on indefinitely if she used duct tape to press down one of its switches. She did that in an effort to change the colors of a small metal artwork that she had made. The toaster eventually caught on fire and caused Shocked's house to burn down. Could Shocked recover damages for loss of the house from Winner Company?

Answer: No. Winner Company did not have a duty to produce a toaster that could operate safely when its switch was disabled and it was used to heat a metal artwork rather than something edible.

Question: Charlotte Shocked bought another new toaster, manufactured by High-tech Homewares. It came with a remote control that operated all its features. Shocked lost the remote control and resorted to turning the toaster on and off by plugging it in and unplugging it. This repeated conduct caused power surges that made some of the toaster's microchips overheat, causing a fire that burned down Shocked's house. Could Shocked use a strict liability theory to recover damages for loss of the house from High-tech Homewares?

Answer: Yes. It is likely that a finder of fact would conclude that High-tech's design was not adequately safe. The unusual way in which Shocked used the toaster would be a full defense only if it was unforeseeable. If it was a kind of misuse that was foreseeable, then it was an aspect of the product's use that High-tech would have been required to consider in its design of the product. If a jury found that Shocked was negligent in choosing to operate the toaster as she did, her conduct would be evaluated under comparative negligence principles, probably leading to a reduced recovery.

EXAM TIPS

- The facts in product liability cases are always very important. Be creative in thinking about whether they show that a product was designed badly, manufactured badly, or marketed with deficient warning or instructions.
- Strict liability for design defects is a lot like negligence liability. One big difference is that retailers and wholesalers are liable under strict liability theories even though they are typically free from responsibility for design flaws under a negligence theory.
- Causation is sometimes a crucial factor in product liability cases. A product flaw is only a basis for liability if it has a causal connection to the plaintiff's injury.
- Strict liability applies to products, not to services. If a transaction seems to involve both a product and a service (like having copies made at a copy center), notice the issue and discuss it. Strict liability may apply just to the product

component of the transaction, or it may be that the sale of a product aspect of the transaction is especially predominant.

- The state of the art at the time a product was manufactured is usually relevant. An industry consensus on adequate safety relates to the risk-utility test. It is also important in warning cases, since there is usually no liability for a failure to warn about a risk that was not knowable at the time of marketing.

17 WORKERS' COMPENSATION AND OTHER ALTERNATIVE COMPENSATION SYSTEMS

CHAPTER OVERVIEW

- Workers' compensation statutes provide payments to injured workers or their estates without any litigation on the issue of negligence.
- For an injury to be covered by workers' compensation, the claimant must show that it occurred in the course of employment.
- Statutory schemes have adapted the administrative nonfault workers' compensation idea to other fields, notably injuries related to the use of automobiles and injuries related to the use of childhood disease vaccines.

A. WORKERS' COMPENSATION

State statutes covering almost all employees grant employers immunity from suits by employees seeking damages for workplace injuries but require them to pay specified amounts for particular types of injuries that occur in the course of and arising out of employment. This is a type of strict liability, since the worker is not required to show that the employer was negligent. Payment is required when there is proof of an injury arising out of or in the course of employment, without regard to fault by the employer or comparative negligence by the employee. Employers usually obtain insurance that satisfies their workers' compensation liability.

1. Types of Injuries Covered

The only injuries covered by the workers' compensation system are those that arise out of the employment or that occur in the course of the employment. Thus, injuries a worker suffers traveling to or from work are excluded.

Also, injuries a worker suffers in the workplace from conduct that has nothing to do with the job are outside the coverage of the system.

Illustration: Matter of Richardson v. Fiedler, 493 N.E.2d 228 (N.Y. 1986). The claimant's decedent was employed as a roofer. While he was on a job and was waiting for some materials to be brought up to a roof, he moved across the roof to get to some copper downspouts he was interested in stealing. He slipped and fell to his death. An award of workers' compensation was affirmed, rejecting the employer's contention that as a matter of public policy a death that occurs due to criminal conduct should be outside the coverage of the compensation system. The court noted that many employees stole copper and that the defendant employer had not attempted to stop the practice.

E&A

EXAMPLE AND ANALYSIS

Walter Worker worked for Warehouse Corporation in a large warehouse. If part of the ceiling there fell down and injured him, Worker would have no tort claim against Warehouse Corporation, because the injury would have occurred in the course of his employment. Worker would be entitled to benefits, however, under the workers' compensation system.

2. Intentional Misconduct Exception

An employee continues to have a right to seek redress from an employer under any common law theory for intentional misconduct. This intentional misconduct exception to the coverage of workers' compensation statutes is usually applied to instances of conduct that meet the definitions of traditional intentional torts. Courts usually reject efforts to characterize an employer's disregard of safety statutes as intentional misconduct.

Illustration: Blankenship v. Cincinnati Milacron Chemicals, Inc., 69 Ohio St. 2d 608, 433 N.E.2d 572 (1982). The plaintiffs contended that the defendant employer had intentionally failed to warn them about exposures to hazardous chemicals and had intentionally failed to report those conditions to certain government agencies. The trial court dismissed the claims on the ground that workers' compensation was the sole remedy. On appeal the supreme court rejected application of the compensation system to intentional misconduct and ruled that a jury should have been permitted to decide whether the defendant's acts had been intentional. A statute adopted after this decision expanded the workers' compensation system to cover intentional torts, providing for enhanced payments.

3. Actions Against Others Involved in Workplace Injury

Workers injured in accidents that involve equipment often seek to obtain damages from the suppliers of the equipment. Recovery against employers is limited to the statutory schedule of workers' compensation payments, but the workers' compensation statutes have nothing to do with possible recovery against others whose conduct contributed to injuries.

B. AUTOMOBILE INJURY COMPENSATION SYSTEMS (NO-FAULT SYSTEMS)

Many states have adopted statutes that attempt to bring the claimed efficiency of workers' compensation into the field of compensation for automobile injuries. Mandatory insurance provides benefits for injuries that are within the statutes' definitions of coverage, and there is no litigation to determine anyone's fault. These statutes apply to incidents with relatively small injuries.

C. CHILDHOOD VACCINE INJURIES

A federal statute provides a compensation system for victims of injuries related to childhood vaccines, with no requirement that the victims prove fault. The claimants are required to show that they suffered recognized adverse reactions to the vaccines and that the reactions occurred within specified time periods after vaccination. This relief is an alternative to litigation, although individuals may choose to sue rather than to seek compensation through the statutory system.

REVIEW QUESTIONS AND ANSWERS

Question: Paula Presser is employed by Maximum Metal company to operate a metal fabricating machine. If Presser's arm is caught in the machine and she is injured, Presser is entitled to workers' compensation benefits. Prior to the adoption of workers' compensation statutes, what kinds of proof would Presser have needed to develop to sustain a common law negligence action?

Answer: Presser would have been required to show that the employer had acted unreasonably in some way, perhaps in selecting the machine, maintaining it, or in organizing the work for which Presser used the machine. Presser would also have had to confront issues of her own possible contributory negligence.

Question: Workers' compensation applies to the injury suffered by Presser (from the question above). How does it simplify her effort to obtain redress for her injury?

Answer: Workers' compensation relieves Presser of the need to show fault or unreasonable conduct by the defendant. It also ignores contributory fault by the claimant. It should be noted, however, that Presser's total benefits from the administrative workers' compensation system are likely to be less than the damages she might have won in a jury trial, if workers' compensation had not been designed as the exclusive remedy for work-related injuries.

EXAM TIPS

- Alternative compensation systems are not frequent topics on torts exams, but you should be prepared to compare workers' compensation or any other nonfault system with the ordinary process of basing redress on proof of negligence.
- Strange scenarios sometimes test the extreme limits of the course-of-employment and arising-out-of-employment restrictions for workers' compensation.

18 NUISANCE

CHAPTER OVERVIEW

- Conduct that interferes with an individual's use or enjoyment of his or her land is a private nuisance.
- Conduct that interferes with the public's right to use or enjoy land is a public nuisance.
- To be actionable a nuisance must be a substantial and unreasonable interference with the plaintiff's right.
- Nuisance is a strict liability action. A defendant's conduct can subject the defendant to liability regardless of whether it is reasonable for the defendant to carry out that conduct.
- Even when a defendant's conduct is reasonable, its appropriateness to its location is a primary factor in considering whether the nuisance is actionable.
- Damages and injunctions are the remedies for nuisance.
- Coming to the nuisance does not, in itself, bar a plaintiff's action for damages or injunction.

A. DEFINITIONS

Tort law uses the term *nuisance* to describe two different situations, private nuisance and public nuisance.

1. Private Nuisance

A private nuisance is a thing or activity that substantially and unreasonably interferes with a plaintiff's use and enjoyment of his or her land or interest in land.

2. Public Nuisance

A public nuisance is an unreasonable interference with a right possessed by the general public.

3. Effect, Not Conduct

A nuisance is defined by its effect on the plaintiff's land or on a public right. It is not defined by reference to the actual conduct by the defendant that creates the effects.

4. Injury, Not Tort

A nuisance is a harm to a plaintiff's interest in land, but it is not a tort (conduct for which a remedy is provided) unless the plaintiff establishes the elements of duty, breach of duty, and causation.

Illustration: Philadelphia Electric Co. v. Hercules, Inc., 762 F.2d 303 (1985). The plaintiff owner of some polluted land sought damages from the successor to the entity from which the plaintiff had bought the land. The plaintiff argued that the defendant was responsible for the pollution under both private and public nuisance theories. Judgment for the plaintiff was reversed on appeal. The private nuisance theory could not support relief because the case did not fit the pattern of a defendant's infliction of harm on another's land. Having inflicted harm on its own land, the defendant then sold it to the plaintiff. The plaintiff should have dealt with this problem in the initial purchase transaction. The public nuisance theory also failed, because the plaintiff did not suffer a harm related to the exercise of a right common to the general public. The public's right was a right to clean water, but the plaintiff made no use of the water it claimed had been polluted by the defendant's predecessor.

B. PRIVATE NUISANCE: ELEMENTS

The plaintiff in a private nuisance case must show that: the defendant's conduct was intentional, reckless, negligent, or connected with an abnormally dangerous activity; the plaintiff suffered substantial and unreasonable interference with the enjoyment of his or her land or interest in land; and the defendant's conduct caused the interference.

1. Defendant's Conduct

Plaintiffs may use a wide variety of proof to show that the defendant's conduct involved an abnormally dangerous activity, was negligent, or was reckless. To establish that the conduct was intentional a plaintiff might show that the defendant continued the activity in question after being informed by the plaintiff about its effects on the plaintiff's land.

Illustration: Morgan v. High Penn Oil Co., 238 N.C. 185, 77 S.E.2d 682 (1953). The defendant's lawfully operated oil refinery could be characterized as a private nuisance because of the harm its gasses inflicted on the plaintiff's neighboring residence and restaurant. The plaintiff was not required to show that the defendant's conduct was negligent. Recovery could be based on a showing that intentional conduct led to an unreasonable invasion of the plaintiff's interest or that negligent conduct led to such an invasion.

2. **Substantial Harm**

The impact on the plaintiff's land or interest in land must be substantial. An impact is substantial only if it would be significant to a typical person in the community or would have a significant effect on land in the community being used in a typical way. A plaintiff whose use of land is unusually sensitive cannot base a nuisance claim on proof that the defendant's activity harmed the plaintiff's unusually sensitive use.

E&A Examples and Analysis

Noise and traffic from a drive-in movie theater could have a significant impact on the use and enjoyment of land next to the theater if that land is used for a residence. The impact might well be characterized as a nuisance.

If a drive-in movie theater claimed that light from a neighboring parking lot was a nuisance because it interfered with the darkness required for seeing movies, the drive-in might be classified as unusually sensitive. Under that analysis its claim that light from neighboring land was a nuisance would likely be rejected.

3. **Unreasonableness**

To determine whether the defendant's interference with the plaintiff's use of land is unreasonable, a court usually uses a balancing test, comparing the harm to the plaintiff with the utility of the defendant's conduct. The Restatement sets out an additional test: whether the defendant's activity would be economically feasible if the defendant had to pay for the activity's impact on the plaintiff.

a. **Traditional balancing test.** The traditional balancing test involves factors that guide the evaluation of the plaintiff's injury and of the utility of the defendant's conduct.

i. **Factors for assessing harm to plaintiff.** To assess the harm inflicted by the defendant's acts a court examines the type and extent of the harm, the social value of the plaintiff's conduct that the harm affects, the suitability of the plaintiff's conduct to the locale, and the burden to the plaintiff of avoiding the harm.

ii. **Factors for assessing utility of defendant's conduct.** To assess the utility of the defendant's acts a court examines their social value and suitability to the location and the practicality of preventing their impact on the plaintiff's land.

b. **Additional Restatement test.** Even if an activity passes the balancing test, under the Restatement a court could still award relief to the plaintiff if it finds that the harm is greater than one that the plaintiff should be required to bear without compensation. The Restatement refers to this concept in its definition of a nuisance as something involving substantial harm to the plaintiff for which the defendant could pay without making the defendant's activity infeasible. Restatement §§826, 829A.

In Carpenter v. The Double R Cattle Company, Inc., 108 Idaho 602, 701 P.2d 222 (1985), the Idaho Supreme Court refused to apply this Restatement principle. A jury had rejected a nuisance claim brought by a neighbor against the operator of a cattle feedlot. The intermediate appellate court reversed because the jury had not been instructed that, as the Restatement suggests, an activity can pass the injury-utility balancing test, but still be a basis for negligence liability. The Supreme Court affirmed the trial court result. It refused to allow damages to be awarded against a defendant whose conduct satisfied an injury-utility test, because it reasoned that such an outcome would be improperly burdensome to industries.

C. COMING TO THE NUISANCE

A defendant could formerly have a complete defense to a nuisance claim by proving that the plaintiff had come to the nuisance by buying land near the defendant's after the defendant had begun his or her allegedly unreasonable conduct. This doctrine has been abandoned on the theory that a single landowner ought not to have the power to impose conditions on the future use of nearby land. Courts continue to consider the plaintiff's choice to move into the neighborhood of an alleged nuisance, however, when they evaluate whether the defendant's activity is appropriate in its place.

D. REMEDIES FOR PRIVATE NUISANCE

The remedies for a private nuisance are damages and injunction. Courts occasionally employ these remedies innovatively in attempts to resolve conflicting factors in particularly difficult nuisance cases.

1. Damages

A plaintiff is entitled to money damages for the harm inflicted on his or her enjoyment of the use of the affected property. This remedy makes the most sense when the defendant's conduct has occurred only once or when it has occurred a number of times but has ceased at the time of the plaintiff's suit.

2. Injunction

An injunction is an order requiring the defendant to stop or modify the offensive activity. A plaintiff might obtain damages for past wrongs and an injunction to stop future improper conduct by the defendant.

3. Permanent Damages

Ordinarily, a plaintiff may seek and be awarded damages many times against the same defendant if the defendant repeatedly commits acts that satisfy the elements of a nuisance claim.

Illustration: Boomer v. Atlantic Cement Co., Inc., 257 N.E.2d 870 (N.Y. 1970). The court refused to enjoin the defendant's activities because they had the great social value of providing employment, and the court wanted to assure the defendant of freedom from future legal claims. It awarded a remedy of permanent damages. This was a damage award calculated to compensate the plaintiff for past and future harms from the defendant's activity.

4. Purchased Injunction

Another famous case with an unusual remedy involved a real estate developer who located a huge retirement community near vast cattle feed lots. The feed lots produced very bad smells (from one million pounds of manure each day). In Spur Industries v. Del E. Webb Development Co., 494 P.2d 700 (Ariz. 1972), the court rejected coming to the nuisance as a complete defense, but it found that it would be unfair to shut down the defendant's operation with an ordinary injunction. It resolved the problem by granting an injunction to the plaintiff real estate developer conditioned on the developer's payment to the defendant of the costs the defendant would incur in relocating its business. This remedy can be called a "purchased injunction," since it is effective only if the plaintiff pays for it.

E. PUBLIC NUISANCE: ELEMENTS

The plaintiff in a public nuisance case must show the defendant has interfered with a right common to the general public and that this interference has inflicted a type of harm on the plaintiff that is different from its harm to the general public.

1. Harms to Public Rights

Types of conduct that courts typically characterize as harming public rights include: maintaining a brothel, gambling den, or unlicensed bar; creating a health hazard; and blocking a street. Sometimes statutes define particular acts as public nuisances. An example is a statute prohibiting certain types of plants or grass over a certain height on private property.

2. **Plaintiff's Special Harm**

   An individual is entitled to damages for a public nuisance only if he or she has suffered harm of a type that is different from the harm that the nuisance inflicts on the general public. The plaintiff's harm and the harm suffered by the general public must both involve the exercise of the same general right.

   a. **Rationale for special harm requirement.** The requirement that the plaintiff's harm be different from the general harm inflicted by the defendant's nuisance protects potential defendants from being sued by a huge number of affected citizens.

E&A Examples and Analysis

An example of a plaintiff's harm that is different from the general harm created by a public nuisance is a plaintiff's personal injury from a defendant's conduct that obstructed a road. Another example is a plaintiff's loss of ability to pursue commercial fishing in a body of water that the defendant has polluted. The harm from polluting the water affects all citizens who cannot fish there, but the significance of the loss to commercial fishing enterprises is sometimes treated as different enough from the loss to the public in general to justify a public nuisance cause of action.

F. NUISANCE AND TRESPASS DISTINGUISHED

The trespass cause of action protects a plaintiff from physical invasion of the plaintiff's land. A nuisance action protects a plaintiff from interference with the use or enjoyment of the plaintiff's land. Sometimes a defendant's conduct constitutes both a trespass and a nuisance, but many cases are clearly either a nuisance or a trespass.

G. COMPARATIVE NEGLIGENCE DEFENSE

In cases of both private and public nuisance, comparative negligence principles generally apply.

Review Questions and Answers

Question: Max Music and Tommy Talker were neighbors in a suburban neighborhood. Music played classical music recordings on outdoor loudspeakers in his backyard most nights from 6:00 p.m. to about midnight. If Talker could show that the noise of the music made it very difficult to have conversations in Talker's backyard, would Talker be able to obtain a nuisance remedy against Music?

Answer: Yes. The impact is substantial in the sense that it would bother most people in that neighborhood. It is unreasonable, since its social value is very low and the harm it inflicts on Talker is substantial.

Question: Barbara Bookman set up a ten-foot-wide table on a street in a city's fanciest shopping district and used it to sell books to people who walked by. She set it up a few feet from the entrance to a bookstore called Readers' Roost. The table and the attention it attracted caused a lot of congestion in the street. Readers' Roost sought an injunction against Bookman, claiming that the congestion she caused made it harder for people to enter the Roost store and that her conduct in selling books made shoppers less likely to buy books at Readers' Roost. Would the plaintiff's claims likely be successful?

Answer: Yes, based on congestion, not on competition. Readers' Roost sought to enjoin a public nuisance. Bookman's blocking of the street affected a right generally possessed by the public. To have a cause of action to redress that nuisance, Readers' Roost would have to show that it suffered a distinct impact from the harm that affected the general public and that this harm involved the same interest that made the conduct a nuisance with regard to the general public. The harm was congestion, and the distinct impact was the lessened ability of customers to enter the store. Bookman's competition in the sale of books would not be a basis for Readers' Roost's remedy, since harm to that interest was not a harm that was inflicted on the public in general.

Question: Ralph Resident bought a new house near Gary's Garbage, a commercial garbage transfer station. The transfer station was a large field in which garbage trucks emptied their contents into larger containers that could be hauled on railroad cars to distant dump locations. The transfer station was very noisy and smelly. It also attracted large numbers of flies. Could Resident obtain an injunction to close the Gary's Garbage facility?

Answer: Authority is split on how to resolve a problem like this. Some jurisdictions would balance the utility of the defendant's conduct against the amount of harm it inflicted on the plaintiff's property. This balancing test might well lead to a finding that Resident is entitled to an injunction. Other jurisdictions might find that the activity passed the balancing test but could only be carried on if the defendant paid damages to Resident. Since Resident was aware of the garbage facility before buying his house, he might be entitled only to the opportunity to "purchase" an injunction, so the facility would be closed only if Resident paid Gary's Garbage damages to compensate it for the cost of closing and moving. Finally, Resident's claim would be denied in a minority of places where coming to the nuisance is a defense.

Exam Tips

- You usually do not have to decide how a harm-utility balance is resolved. You usually are required only to outline the factors and apply them to the facts.
- Be aware that a public nuisance is subject to a private party's remedy only when that party shows a particularly significant impact from the same type of harm that makes the action a nuisance in general.
- Professors interested in economic analysis often test the principles represented in *Spur* and *Boomer.* Be sure you understand how those decisions vary the usual results of injunction or damages.

19 MISREPRESENTATION

CHAPTER OVERVIEW

- Misrepresentation is a tort cause of action involving economic harm to a plaintiff because of a defendant's false statement or misleading silence.
- False statements that lead to physical harms are usually analyzed as satisfying the elements of other torts such as battery or negligence.
- The misrepresentation action requires proof of a false representation, the defendant's knowledge of its falsity or conscious ignorance of its falsity, intent to affect the plaintiff, justifiable reliance by the plaintiff, and damages.

A. INTRODUCTION

Misrepresentation is a cause of action to redress economic harm caused by a communication that conveyed false information to the plaintiff. A false statement, a half-truth, and a person's silence when that silence is reasonably understood to convey a meaning that is false can all be misrepresentations. A false statement that causes physical harm to a person or to property is usually redressed with an action in negligence, warranty, or strict liability.

EXAMPLE AND ANALYSIS

"This is a 1995-model car," spoken by a used car dealer to a customer about a car that is really a 1993 model is an example of a misrepresentation likely to cause economic harm. "When you drive this car, it's safer to slip the shoulder part of the seatbelt behind your back than to have it fit over your chest," spoken by a car dealer to a car buyer is an example of a misrepresentation likely to cause physical harm. The seatbelt statement, if it leads to harm, is a basis for recovery in either negligence or strict liability.

B. CATEGORIES

Actionable misrepresentations may be intentional, negligent, or non-negligent. At common law only intentional misrepresentation was recognized under the term of art *deceit.* Intentional misrepresentation continues to be the most common form of this category of tort cause of action. This chapter explains intentional misrepresentation and shows how the other two varieties of misrepresentation compare with intentional misrepresentation.

C. INTENTIONAL MISREPRESENTATION

The plaintiff must establish the following elements to maintain an intentional misrepresentation cause of action.

- False communication. The defendant must have made a false communication (a misrepresentation).
- State of mind. The defendant's scienter must be shown as either intentional or reckless with regard to the truth of the communication.
- Intent. The defendant must have intended to have the plaintiff rely on the misrepresentation.
- Justifiable reliance. The plaintiff must have acted in justifiable reliance on the misrepresentation.
- Damages. The plaintiff must have suffered actual damages from relying on the misrepresentation.

1. Types of False Communication

Many types of conduct and statement can underlie claims of misrepresentation.

a. **Words.** Written or spoken words are the most common type of communication that can be a misrepresentation. A half-truth, or statement that is literally true but actually conveys a false meaning, can be a misrepresentation. A half-truth might also be characterized as an ambiguous statement that has multiple meanings, some true and some untrue.

b. **Actions.** A defendant can communicate a false idea by actions, such as tampering with a scale so it displays an incorrect weight.

c. **Concealment.** A defendant who hides information or uses some other method to prevent the plaintiff from obtaining it is treated as though he or she has denied the existence of the information.

Illustration: Lindberg Cadillac Co. v. Aron, 371 S.W.2d 651 (St. Louis Ct. App. 1963). The defendant traded in a car at the plaintiff dealership. He had concealed cracks in the car's motor block. Although he said nothing about the car, the court held that the steps he took to hide its flaws amounted to a fraud.

d. **Nondisclosure.** At early common law silence was not actionable. Modern decisions establish a number of exceptions to this rule.

   i. **Fiduciary relationships.** In a fiduciary relationship there is often a duty to disclose material facts. These relationships include, for example, principal and agent, bank and depositor, attorney and client, and physician and patient.

   ii. **Incomplete statements.** When a defendant communicates a half-truth, he or she is obligated to furnish the supplementary information that allows the statement to be understood accurately.

   iii. **New information.** A defendant may obtain information subsequent to a communication the defendant has made to the plaintiff. If the new information makes the earlier communication untrue and the defendant believes the plaintiff is still acting on the earlier information, the defendant must communicate the new information to the plaintiff.

   iv. **Discovered reliance.** Recall that a statement cannot be a misrepresentation unless the defendant intends that the plaintiff rely on it. If a defendant discovers that a plaintiff is relying on a false statement that the defendant has made to the plaintiff, the defendant must disclose the untruth to the plaintiff.

   v. **Basic facts.** A defendant must disclose essential facts to a plaintiff if the defendant has special access to them, if nondisclosure is unconscionable, or if any other factors make the plaintiff reasonably expect their disclosure.

      (a) **Plaintiff's special access to facts.** In Swinton v. Whitinsville Savings Bank, 311 Mass. 677, 42 N.E.2d 808 (1942), the defendant house seller did not reveal to the plaintiff buyer that the house was infested with termites. This nondisclosure was not actionable. The court treated the defendant's silence on the topic of termites as different from a false statement. The ease with which a prospective buyer can have a house inspected may support the court's result.

e. **Opinions.** Under a traditional rule if a defendant says that something is his or her opinion, there is no liability even if the statement is false. The rationale for this rule is that plaintiffs ought not to rely on opinions but should rely only on statements of fact. This protection for opinion statements does not apply to statements that seem to incorporate or imply facts.

EXAMPLE AND ANALYSIS

Analyzing a statement like "In my opinion there's no better business in town than the one I'm trying to sell to you," a court might find that it implies the speaker's lack of knowledge of any serious shortcomings in the business. This could support a characterization of the statement as one of fact.

---

i. **Puffing.** The term *puffing* is used for commercial representations that are in the form of opinion. Courts refuse to base relief on false statements that are puffing on the theory that everyone knows sellers tell lies. "Best detergent ever made" is an example of puffing. If a plaintiff shows that reliance on such a statement was reasonable, a court may decline to permit the puffing defense.

ii. **Modern classes of actionable opinion statements.** Currently, a statement of opinion can be the basis of a misrepresentation claim if it can be said that the defendant was an adverse party to the plaintiff at the time the defendant made the statement of opinion. The adverse-party description applies in relationships such as buyer and seller.

(a) **Expert.** If the seller claims to have special knowledge on the topic, his or her opinion statements can be a basis for a misrepresentation claim.

(b) **Fiduciary relationship.** In a fiduciary relationship even statements of opinion can be treated as misrepresentations.

(c) **Plaintiff's reliance.** Opinion statements are subject to treatment as misrepresentations if the defendant has gained the plaintiff's confidence or if the defendant knows of the plaintiff's special vulnerability to false statements.

f. **Statements about law.** At common law statements about law were outside the scope of the misrepresentation action, since it was believed that they were always expressions of opinion. At present if a statement about a legal standard implies something factual, the statement can be a basis for a misrepresentation action. An example is "This car meets all the emissions requirements."

g. **Predictions.** Statements of predictions are equivalent to opinions and can support misrepresentation claims only if they are made in one of the contexts in which opinion statements in general can be actionable.

h. **Intentions.** Statements about the speaker's intentions are treated as statements of fact and are thus subject to misrepresentation claims.

2. Defendant's State of Mind

To establish intentional misrepresentation a plaintiff must show the defendant's scienter, or state of mind. Under the Restatement this scienter can be shown with proof that the defendant: 1. knew or believed his or her statement was false; or 2. did not have confidence in the accuracy of his or her express or implied statement; or 3. knew he or she did not have a basis for the statement.

Illustration: Derry v. Peek, 14 App. Cas. 337 (Eng. 1889). The court held that only fraud, not mere negligence, would support an action for deceit (now also called misrepresentation).

3. Allowable Plaintiffs

A defendant who makes a misrepresentation can be liable to any individual to whom the defendant makes the misrepresentation. Under modern doctrines there can sometimes be liability to third persons, also.

a. **Commercial documents.** If a defendant makes a misrepresentation in a commercial document, he or she can be liable to anyone who justifiably relies on the statement.

b. **Foreseeable reliance.** Under the Restatement a defendant who makes a misrepresentation in any context can be liable to a third party harmed by that misrepresentation. The third party must show that he or she is a member of a class that the defendant had reason to expect would rely on the misrepresentation. The third party must also show that the type of transaction in which the third party was involved was the type of transaction that the defendant should have expected would involve such reliance.

4. Reliance

The plaintiff must show justifiable reliance.

a. **Causation.** If a plaintiff acts in response to a misrepresentation, the causation question is straightforward: can the misrepresentation be found to have caused the plaintiff's action?

i. **Multiple causes.** More complicated cases arise when the plaintiff acts due to the misrepresentation and some other information. If the misrepresentation is a substantial factor in the plaintiff's choice of action, the causation requirement is satisfied. If the plaintiff relies totally on information he or she has obtained independent of the misrepresentation, then the misrepresentation is irrelevant and cannot be a basis for relief.

b. **Materiality.** The topic of a misrepresentation must be material in order for a cause of action to be allowed. Thus, a false statement about some unimportant aspect of a transaction is not a basis for relief. To determine whether a topic is material, a court asks whether a reasonable person would consider it important in making a decision about the transaction in question.

c. **Justification.** The plaintiff is required to show that his or her reliance was justified reliance. Reliance is not treated as justifiable if the defendant's statement was an ordinary opinion or a prediction. There is no general duty to investigate the truthfulness of a defendant's representations. Reliance, however, cannot be established if a statement's untruth would be obvious to someone who makes a "cursory examination or investigation." Restatement §541, comment *a*.

5. Damages

Damages for intentional misrepresentation are measured in terms of either reliance or benefit of the bargain. Some courts allow reliance damages: the plaintiff is awarded the difference between what the plaintiff paid for and the value of what the plaintiff received. A greater number of courts allow benefit-of-the-bargain damages: the plaintiff is awarded the difference between what the plaintiff really received and the value that whatever the plaintiff received was supposed to have had.

E&A EXAMPLES AND ANALYSIS

Where reliance is the measure of damages, if a defendant's misrepresentation induces a plaintiff to pay $100 for something that was worth only $80, the plaintiff is entitled to damages of $20.

Where the benefit of the bargain (or expectation) is the measure of damages, if a defendant's misrepresentation induces a plaintiff to pay $100 for something that is worth only $80, and the item would have been worth $120 if it really had the attributes the defendant said it had, the plaintiff is entitled to damages of $40. The plaintiff's damages are set at an amount that fulfills the plaintiff's expectation, in this case an expectation of $120 (provided by adding together the $80 value of the item and a $40 damages award).

D. NEGLIGENT MISREPRESENTATION

While at common law there was no cause of action for negligent misrepresentation, modern courts allow this cause of action in a variety of situations. The basic elements of a cause of action in negligent misrepresentation are identical to those for intentional misrepresentation, with the exception of the scienter, or intent, requirement. Instead of proving intention the plaintiff in a negligent misrepresentation case must prove action by the defendant that fails the reasonable prudent person test for negligence. The following categories describe the limited classes of cases in which courts now permit recovery for negligent misrepresentation.

1. Defendant's Pecuniary Interest

The defendant must have a pecuniary interest in the transaction or must have made the representation in the course of his or her employment.

2. Allowable Plaintiffs

The defendant may be liable to any individual to whom he or she meant to give the incorrect information. In many jurisdictions additional individuals are permitted to recover if they are in a limited group that the defendant knew would receive and rely upon the defendant's statement.

a. **Distinction from fraudulent misrepresentation.** In fraudulent misrepresentation a defendant is potentially liable to anyone who the defendant should expect will rely on his or her statement. In negligent misrepresentation liability to third partics is limitcd to individuals to whom the defendant gives the false statement or individuals the defendant knows will receive the false information from those to whom the defendant gives it initially.

b. **Liability to third parties.** There are a number of recurring situations in which defendants who have made negligent misrepresentations have been held liable to third parties.

   i. **Public weigher.** In Glanzer v. Shepard, 135 N.E. 275 (N.Y. 1922), a public weigher who reported the wrong weight for a commodity was responsible for the monetary injury to a purchaser who relied on that weight report, even though the defendant did not have any direct contact with the plaintiff.

   ii. **Land surveyor.** Land surveyors can readily anticipate that their information will be passed on to others beyond those for whom they conduct their surveys.

iii. **Will-drafting lawyer.** A lawyer who drafts a will and makes a negligently incorrect representation about its effect can be liable to an individual who would have inherited money were the will drafted to produce the result the lawyer had says it will have.

iv. **Accountant.** An accountant who makes a negligent misrepresentation in a report prepared for a client may be liable to others who receive that information from the client if the accountant has reason to anticipate that the report will be given to others by the client.

Illustrations: Citizens State Bank v. Timm, Schmidt & Co, 113 Wis. 2d 376, 335 N.W.2d 361 (1983). Liability of accountants for financial losses suffered by a plaintiff in reliance on a negligently prepared financial report will be governed by ordinary foreseeability principles.

Credit Alliance Corporation v. Arthur Andersen & Co., 65 N.Y.2d 536, 493 N.Y.S.2d 435, 483 N.E.2d 110 (1985). Where the plaintiff and a defendant accountant had no privity of contract, the plaintiff would be permitted to recover for damages related to the accountant's negligently prepared report only if the accountant was aware that the plaintiff was expected to rely on the accountant's work and there was some conduct by the accountant that showed the accountant understood that party's reliance.

3. Physical Harm

If a defendant's negligent misrepresentation causes physical harm, the plaintiff may bring a cause of action under ordinary negligence principles.

Illustration: Winter v. G. P. Putnam's Sons, 938 F.2d 1003 (9th Cir. 1991). The plaintiffs were injured when they ate poisonous mushrooms allegedly described as edible in a book published by the defendant. They sought damages on a misrepresentation theory. The trial court granted summary judgment to the defendant. On appeal it was held that First Amendment principles precluded imposing liability on a publisher for its publishing of false information.

E. INNOCENT MISREPRESENTATION

Liability for innocent misrepresentation is a type of strict liability, since it involves no proof of fault. This cause of action is not recognized universally, but the Restatement provides it in two classes of cases: physical harm from products and monetary loss in a sale, rental, or exchange transaction.

1. Physical Harm from Product

Under Restatement §402B (a rarely invoked companion to the famous strict liability provision, §402A) a defendant who is in the business of selling a product is strictly liable for physical harm caused by a misrepresentation made to the public about the product.

2. **Monetary Loss in Sale, Rental, or Exchange**

Another Restatement provision, §552C, applies strict liability for an innocent misrepresentation when it is made by someone in the negotiation of a sale, rental, or exchange transaction. Damages are limited to the difference between what the plaintiff paid for and what the plaintiff actually received.

Review Questions and Answers

Question: Maximum Motors, a used car dealership in a town located within 100 miles of Delaware, Maryland, and Virginia, sold a car to Frank Fastbuyer. Maximum's salesman said, "This car is guaranteed to pass the emissions inspection." The salesman knew that it could pass the test in one of the nearby states but that it would not pass the test in the other two. Was the salesman's statement false?

Answer: Yes. An ambiguous representation is treated as a false statement if the maker of the statement means it to be understood in a way that is false or if the maker of the statement has no belief about how it will be understood.

Question: Fran Franchise owned a franchise for a popular fast-food restaurant called Tomato Town. She offered to sell the restaurant to Nat Newbuyer, telling Newbuyer that the parent company of Tomato Town had promised not to open any additional Tomato Town restaurants in the same county as Franchise's restaurant. After giving that information to Newbuyer, Franchise learned that the parent company of Tomato Town had decided to open four new Tomato Town restaurants near Franchise's restaurant in Franchise's county. Franchise did not reveal this information to Newbuyer. If Newbuyer bought the restaurant and discovered it was less profitable than he had expected it to be, could Franchise's communications to Newbuyer be treated as false statements?

Answer: Yes. Franchise told the truth to Newbuyer when they first negotiated, but Franchise's failure to tell Newbuyer about Tomato Town's change of plans made the overall communications from Franchise to Newbuyer false.

Question: Henry Homebuyer was shopping for a new house. As he was deciding whether to buy a particular house, he asked Sarah Seller, a real estate agent representing the owner of the house, if she knew whether the neighborhood had any problems with soil settling. She said, "I don't think there's a safer neighborhood in the state as far as soil problems go." Homebuyer bought the house. It soon needed expensive repairs for cracks in its walls caused by soil settling. If the neighborhood in fact had serious problems with settling soil, would Seller's statement to Homebuyer be treated as false?

Answer: Yes. It was expressed as an opinion but would probably convey to most people the idea that the neighborhood did not have soil problems. Because the speaker could be considered an expert, even if her statement were characterized as an opinion, it could be a basis for a misrepresentation claim.

Question: Bob Buyer bought a used car from Sally Seller, a person who lived in his neighborhood. While negotiating for it, Buyer asked Seller, "Does the car have anti-lock brakes?" and Seller told him it did. Seller had heard someone at an automobile repair shop talking about her car's brakes and thought the person had said the car had anti-lock brakes. If Seller was wrong, could Buyer obtain a remedy for misrepresentation?

Answer: Yes. Buyer would have a cause of action for negligent misrepresentation. Seller made a false communication, Seller's basis for the statement was not reasonable, Seller intended Buyer to rely on it, and Buyer's reliance was justifiable. Buyer's damages would be measured by the difference in value between the car with the described attributes and the car with its actual attributes.

EXAM TIPS

- Be creative in interpreting the truth or falsity of statements that might be misrepresentations. Remember that half-truths are lies.
- The causation element is easy to overlook in misrepresentation. There is no liability unless the plaintiff relies on the defendant's false statement.
- The plaintiff's reliance must be reasonable.
- Facts that justify a defendant's liability to someone with whom the defendant does not deal directly usually involve the foreseeability of that other person's reliance on the defendant's false statement. Be alert for situations that are parallel to the established cases of public weighers, land surveyors, and accountants (in some circumstances).

20 DEFAMATION

CHAPTER OVERVIEW

- Defamation provides a remedy for a person about whom a defendant has communicated a statement that could harm the person's reputation.
- A defamatory statement must be false to permit recovery. Usually the plaintiff must show the falsity of the statement.
- Occasionally a person is privileged to communicate derogatory information about another person.
- Communications are interpreted with a number of common-sense techniques. A statement that conveys a defamatory meaning only to people who already know some other information can be characterized as defamatory if there is proof that the people to whom it was communicated knew that contextual information.
- Slander is a spoken defamation. Ordinarily a plaintiff must prove actual damages to recover for slander.
- Libel is a written or printed defamation. A plaintiff may be entitled to presumed damages for libel.
- Constitutional doctrines meant to protect the right of free speech require that state defamation law include a number of protections based on whether the allegedly defamed person is a public official or public figure and on whether the topic of the challenged statement is a public topic.

- A public official or public figure may recover defamation damages only with a showing that the defendant acted with actual malice.
- For a private figure allegedly defamed in connection with a public topic, a state may not allow a strict liability cause of action. To allow recovery of actual damages the state must require the plaintiff to show at least that the defendant acted with negligence.
- For a private figure allegedly defamed in connection with a public topic, if presumed or punitive damages are sought, the plaintiff must show that the defendant acted with actual malice.
- For a private figure allegedly defamed in connection with a private topic, constitutional requirements are unclear. It is possible that states may allow liability without fault for any type of damages.

A. INTRODUCTION

Under common law the tort of defamation (incorporating libel and slander) has the following elements: 1. a defamatory statement and 2. communication of the statement to someone. There is strict liability with no requirement that the plaintiff show that the defendant was at fault. In many circumstances presumed and punitive damages are available in addition to any actual damages the plaintiff may prove.

United States Supreme Court decisions have held that certain common law defamation doctrines concerning strict liability, damages, and burdens of proof are unconstitutional in some cases. The decisions have primarily involved cases with public attributes, such as a plaintiff who is a public official or a defamatory statement about a topic of public concern.

This chapter begins by setting out the common law of defamation in the context of suits where the plaintiffs are private individuals and the topics of the defamations are private matters that are not subjects of public importance. The Supreme Court has not yet ruled on whether the constitutional restrictions on the defamation cause of action apply to these cases. The chapter then explains the ways in which those restrictions change the common law in the cases to which they apply.

B. COMMON LAW DEFAMATION IN CASES WITH NO PUBLIC ATTRIBUTES

For some types of cases the Supreme Court has not ruled on the constitutionality of traditional common law doctrines. In those cases states are free to develop their own standards on topics such as duty, strict liability, damages, and burdens of proof. These cases must involve: 1. a plaintiff who is not a public official or public figure and 2. a statement on a topic that is not a matter of public concern. A third criterion may apply, requiring that the defendant in such cases be a nonmedia defendant. Whether the nonmedia status of the defendant is required in order for a state to be free of constitutional restrictions in defining its defamation doctrines is currently a subject of controversy.

Restatement §558 defines four elements for liability for defamation:

- false and defamatory statement about another,
- unprivileged publication to a third party,
- fault, and
- damages.

1. Defamatory Statement

A defamation case must include proof of a defamatory statement. This involves issues about what types of statements are defamatory and how to interpret vague or incomplete statements.

a. **Injury to reputation.** A defamatory statement is a statement that has a tendency to harm the plaintiff's reputation.

i. **Reputation in small group.** A statement might have the capacity to injure the plaintiff's reputation only within some relatively small group in society. If the group is respectable, damage to reputation in that group is adequate to satisfy the damage-to-reputation element of defamation.

ii. **Derogatory statement.** To be defamatory a statement must be derogatory or must relate to some aspect of reputation that involves disgrace.

E&A EXAMPLES AND ANALYSIS

A statement that harms the plaintiff's reputation among bank robbers, for example, is not defamatory because tort law does not seek to confirm or reinforce the social standards of bank robbers through the vehicle of defamation law.

A statement that someone does not recycle glass bottles is not defamatory, since it is unlikely to cause any people to scorn or ridicule the object of the statement.

iii. **Living person.** A statement must refer to a living person to be defamatory. The estate of a person defamed when alive can bring a defamation action to redress the harm inflicted while the person was alive.

iv. **Legal entity.** A legal entity such as a corporation or partnership can be defamed if the subject matter of the statement deters people from dealing with the entity or harms it in its activities.

b. **Judge and jury roles.** The judge has a screening role in defamation cases that is particularly important where an allegedly defamatory statement is ambiguous. The judge decides whether there is at least one reasonable interpretation of the statement as defamatory. If one such meaning is reasonably possible, then the jury will have the task of deciding whether any individual actually did interpret the statement as having a defamatory meaning.

c. **Defamatory only in context of additional information.** A statement that "the plaintiff is a thief" is defamatory on its face. Other statements are only defamatory if the people to whom they are communicated have additional information that identifies the subject of the statement and may give a full understanding of the statement's explicit words. The common law uses technical terms for the process of providing context for an allegedly defamatory statement.

i. **Inducement.** The inducement is a statement of extra facts that are relevant to understanding the statement.

ii. **Innuendo.** The innuendo is a statement explaining how the inducement makes it possible for the statement to have a defamatory meaning.

iii. **Colloquium.** Proof that the statement is subject to interpretation as being about the plaintiff is known as the colloquium.

E&A EXAMPLE AND ANALYSIS

A statement that "the manager of the Ajax Hotel has the original Mona Lisa in his living room" would only defame the plaintiff if the Mona Lisa had been stolen and the plaintiff were the hotel manager. In this example the inducement would be a statement that the Mona Lisa had been stolen from a museum. The innuendo would be a statement that any private person who possessed the painting was a thief or a receiver of stolen property. Finally, the colloquium would be an allegation that at least one person understood that "manager of the Ajax Hotel" referred to the plaintiff.

d. **References to groups.** References to large groups of people are outside the scope of the defamation tort. A reference to a relatively small group, however, may be a defamation of a single member of the group, particularly if the defamatory statement seems to refer to all the group's members.

Illustration: Neiman-Marcus v. Lait, 13 F.R.D. 311 (S.D.N.Y. 1952). A derogatory statement about 382 saleswomen at a store was held to cover too many people to be treated as defamatory about any one of them, but a statement that "most" of the store's 25 salesmen had an attribute that was considered disgraceful did constitute a defamation against each salesman.

e. **Statements of opinion.** A statement that only expresses an opinion is never defamatory. A statement of opinion that seems to contain a representation about a fact may be defamatory, however. In Milkovich v. Lorain Journal Co., 497 U.S. 1 (1990), the Court held that a statement expressed as an opinion can be a basis for a defamation claim if it implies an assertion of an objective fact.

   i. **Implied statement of fact.** "In my opinion John Jones is a liar" contains an idea that could be proved true or false (Jones is a liar). It therefore is subject to control under defamation doctrines.

   ii. **Opinion free from implied fact.** "In my opinion John Jones is stupid because he watches a lot of MTV," by comparison, is exempt from a defamation suit, because the idea that people who watch MTV are stupid cannot be proved true or false.

   iii. **Style of expression.** In deciding whether a claimed statement of opinion can reasonably be interpreted as incorporating an implied statement of fact, the style of expression is relevant, since extreme statements are relatively unlikely to be taken as implying facts.

2. Truth

The truth of a statement is a full defense to defamation. A statement that is substantially true is treated as true for the purpose of this defense. A defamatory statement that accurately reports some fact about the plaintiff but makes an error about some minor aspect of the fact is treated as substantially true. If a defendant falsely says that a plaintiff has acted in a particular way, however, proof that the plaintiff has actually done other things that are worse is not a defense.

E&A EXAMPLE AND ANALYSIS

A statement that the plaintiff has committed extortion against three people would not be actionable even if the plaintiff had only committed that act against two people. The difference between doing that act to two people and doing it to three is not significant. A statement that the plaintiff has committed extortion would be an actionable defamation, however, if the plaintiff had never committed extortion, even if the plaintiff had done other acts that were as bad or worse.

---

a. **Burden of proof.** At common law the defendant bears the burden of proving the truth of the statement.

b. **Minority rejection of truth defense.** In a small minority of states, a truthful derogatory statement can be defamatory if the speaker's motive meets a common law standard of maliciousness.

3. Publication

The plaintiff in a defamation case must prove that the statement was published. In defamation law "publication" means communication of the statement to at least one person. It does not mean publish in the sense of printing and selling a book or magazine. Publication must be negligent or intentional (common law defamation has a strict liability component, but there is no strict liability with regard to the publication requirement).

a. **Defendant communicates with the plaintiff.** Communicating a defamatory statement about the plaintiff to the plaintiff does not satisfy the publication requirement. The defamatory information must be conveyed to someone other than the plaintiff.

b. **Special cases of defendant's communication.** The publication requirement is met in both of these situations: the defendant dictates a defamation to a stenographer; a person includes a defamation in his or her will and an executor reads the will.

c. **Publication by the plaintiff.** When circumstances force a plaintiff to convey to a third party a defamation the defendant made directly to the plaintiff, that communication can satisfy the publication requirement.

E&A Examples and Analysis

If a blind person receives a written defamatory statement and has someone read it aloud, the publication requirement is satisfied, since the information has been conveyed to the reader.

If an employer fires the plaintiff, saying something defamatory about the plaintiff to the plaintiff, there is no publication. If the plaintiff repeats the defamatory statement in response to a question from another prospective employer, however, that repetition satisfies the publication requirement in many jurisdictions.

---

d. **Repeater.** A person who repeats a defamatory statement is subject to liability for defamation, even if he or she claims not to believe the statement. Newspapers and broadcasters can be repeaters of defamatory statements when they quote statements in their news reports.

e. **Distributor.** A distributor of material that contains a defamatory statement is liable only on proof that he or she had reason to know that the material was defamatory at the time of distribution.

f. **Single publication rule.** A single edition of a book, newspaper, or magazine is treated as a single publication. This is significant for procedural issues such as applying a statute of limitations.

4. Intent

Defamation is a strict liability tort under the common law, although constitutional decisions now restrict the ability of states to impose strict liability in many cases. A state may continue the common law strict liability aspect of defamation in a case where the plaintiff is a private individual (not a public official or public figure) and the topic of the defamation is a matter of private concern. Even if a defendant has a reasonable belief in the truth of his or her statement about the plaintiff, under strict liability the defendant is liable if the statement is defamatory. The constitutional rejection of strict liability for certain cases is described below in Section C.

5. Damages and the Libel/Slander Distinction

The common law recognizes two types of defamation: libel and slander. The distinction between libel and slander can be significant because of doctrines that control damages. Damages for most types of slander require a showing of pecuniary harm, while damages for most types of libel can be presumed.

a. **Definitions.** In general a defamatory statement that is printed is a libel, and a defamatory statement that is spoken is a slander. Slanders are any oral defamations that fail to fit the definition of libel. They are ordinarily words spoken by one person to another. A defendant who utters a slander may be responsible for the effects of repetition of that slander by others if he or she authorized it or should reasonably have expected it.

b. **Physical form required for libel.** The statement that constitutes a libel must exist in some tangible form, such as a writing or a computer record.

i. **Dictation to stenographer.** Words spoken to a stenographer who writes them down constitute a libel.

ii. **Broadcasts.** Words broadcast on radio or television are libels if they also are present on a written script for the broadcast. The Restatement classifies all defamatory broadcast statements as libels, but statutes in some states reject that position and classify them as slanders.

c. **Presumed damages for libel available at common law.** A private person harmed by a private defendant's libel may recover presumed damages. This means that a jury can estimate the likely harm the plaintiff has suffered and award damages even if the plaintiff has introduced no proof to substantiate an award.

d. **Pecuniary harm required for some slander damages.** The general rule for slander damages is that the plaintiff is entitled only to actual damages. Actual damages are defined as the pecuniary (or monetary) value of loss of reputation or association due to the defendant's defamation. The plaintiff must introduce evidence to support a claim of actual damages.

e. **Pecuniary harm requirement waived for specified slanders.** Certain types of slander are considered so harmful by the common law that the pecuniary harm requirement is withdrawn. These types of slander are called "slander per se."

i. **Crime.** A statement that the plaintiff was involved in criminal conduct punishable by imprisonment or otherwise involving moral turpitude is slander per se.

ii. **Loathsome disease.** A statement that the plaintiff has a venereal or loathsome disease is slander per se.

iii. **Fitness for business or trade.** A statement that the plaintiff has characteristics or behaves in ways that are incompatible with the plaintiff's business or trade is slander per se.

iv. **Unchastity.** At common law a statement that a woman is unchaste is slander per se. Some states have expanded this category to include all statements related to sexual misconduct by a man or a woman.

f. **Punitive damages.** At common law punitive damages are available for libel or slander in a case where the defendant's conduct is particularly reprehensible.

6. Defenses

A defendant is free from liability if the plaintiff consents to the defendant's statement, if the defendant is privileged to make the statement, or if the statement is true. In most cases at present, falsity is a factor that the plaintiff must establish. Consent and privilege continue to be treated as defenses the defendant bears the burden of establishing.

a. **Consent.** If a plaintiff asks a defendant to say something or repeat something and the defendant complies with that request, the defendant's statement cannot be a basis for recovery in defamation, since the plaintiff consents to it. It is important to note that a plaintiff's request to a defendant to say or repeat something is not a consent to any previous statement by the defendant.

b. **Privilege.** A defendant who would otherwise be liable for defamation may be immune from liability because of a privilege. Privileges are either absolute or conditional. An absolute privilege is a full defense under all circumstances. A conditional privilege is a full defense only if the defendant acts consistently with the purpose for which the privilege is recognized. The holder of a conditional or qualified privilege bears the burden of showing that the privilege is applicable.

   i. **Absolute privileges.** The following absolute privileges provide total protection for conduct that would otherwise subject the actor to liability for defamation.

      (a) **Executive communications.** Most officials of the federal and state executive branches are absolutely immune from defamation liability for statements they make within the scope of their duties.

      (b) **Legislative communications.** Absolute immunity attaches to statements made by legislators in legislative debate and other legislative proceedings.

      (c) **Judicial communications.** All participants in judicial proceedings are absolutely immune from defamation liability for statements made in connection with litigation. This immunity covers judges, attorneys, witnesses, and parties. It begins with the filing of a complaint and ends with the conclusion of the litigation.

      (d) **Spousal communications.** A statement made by a person to his or her spouse can never be a basis for defamation liability.

   ii. **Conditional privileges.** A conditional privilege, sometimes called a qualified privilege, protects a beneficiary unless the beneficiary has acted in a way that causes the privilege to be withdrawn.

      (a) **Report of public proceedings.** There is a privilege for fair and accurate reports of public proceedings.

      (b) **Public interest.** A privilege covers a statement made by a defendant about a matter of public interest to a person authorized to protect that interest.

(c) **Publisher's interest.** Statements a person makes to protect his or her own interest can contain defamatory material as long as it is relevant to the primary purpose of the person's communication.

(d) **Recipient's interest.** If a defendant answers someone's request for information, a conditional privilege protects the defendant from liability. A letter of reference supplied to someone at that person's request is an illustration of this situation.

(e) **Common interest.** Communications by a defendant to someone with whom the defendant has a shared interest, such as membership in an organization, can contain defamatory material without exposing the defendant to liability if the information is relevant to the common enterprise or interest.

iii. **Loss of conditional privilege.** The plaintiff bears the burden of showing that the defendant should be denied the benefit of a privilege. The following reasons require withdrawal of a privilege.

(a) **Lack of belief in truth of statement.** The holder of a conditional privilege must believe in the truth of the statement he or she seeks to shield with immunity. At common law some states have held that this requirement is satisfied if the defendant has an honest belief in the truth of the statement. Other states have required that the defendant have an honest and reasonable belief in the truth of the statement.

If the privilege is lost when there is proof that the privilege claimant was negligent, the privilege has little practical value under current constitutional principles. In the usual case, recovery is never allowed without proof that the defendant was negligent. Thus, non-negligent defendants are protected from liability whether or not there is a privilege. Some states respond to this by requiring proof of recklessness to deny application of the privilege. This allows the privilege to continue to have effect in favor of defendants even in addition to the protection most defendants receive under the constitutional doctrines.

(b) **Inconsistency with purpose of privilege.** A communication may be inconsistent with the purpose of a privilege if it is made with a malicious motive or if it is unnecessary for satisfying the purpose for which the privilege was established.

C. CONSTITUTIONAL REQUIREMENTS

The famous case of New York Times v. Sullivan, 376 U.S. 254 (1964), introduced First Amendment concepts to the law of defamation. The Court's analyses have been complicated, and it has decided some important cases with plurality (not majority) decisions. It is clear, however, that a defamation case must be analyzed in terms of the type of plaintiff and the topic of the allegedly defamatory statement. Supreme Court decisions have not rejected operation of the common law doctrines in one category: cases with a private plaintiff and a private-interest topic. Constitutional modifications have changed the common law for two other categories: cases with a private plaintiff and a public-interest topic and cases with a public-figure plaintiff. The Court has reserved judgment on whether some of its requirements announced in cases where the defendants were media defendants might apply only to defendants of that type.

1. Actual Malice Requirement for Public Official Cases

In New York Times v. Sullivan the plaintiff was a public official whose duties included some supervision of a police department. He won defamation damages from the defendant on a showing that it had printed an advertisement that made false representations about that police department and civil rights demonstrators. The Supreme Court held that the First Amendment prohibits strict liability in this type of case. The plaintiff must show that the defendant acted with actual malice.

a. **Actual malice: primary definition.** *New York Times v. Sullivan* defined actual malice as "knowledge that [the statement] was false or with reckless disregard of whether it was false or not."

b. **Altered quotation as proof of actual malice.** Masson v. New Yorker Magazine, Inc., 501 U.S. 496 (1991). The plaintiff sought to establish that because the author of a magazine article knew she had altered statements she presented as quotations from the plaintiff, the author knew the quotations were false. The court rejected this attempt to establish actual malice through a per se rule about altered quotations. For an altered quote to be a basis for liability, the Court held, the plaintiff must establish that the altered version materially changed the meaning of the plaintiff's words.

2. Actual Malice Requirement for Public Figure Cases

In Curtis Publishing Co. v. Butts and Associated Press v. Walker, reported together at 388 U.S. 130 (1967), the Court applied the actual malice requirement to cases where the plaintiffs were not public officials but were public figures. The plaintiffs were a college football coach who was very well known and a retired general who had become famous for opposing desegregation of a southern university. The defendants were publishers. The Court held that a public figure is someone who is intimately involved in the resolution of important public questions or who has so much fame that he or she shapes events in areas of concern to the public.

a. **Unlimited public figure.** An unlimited public figure is a person who is so famous that he or she is a public figure in all contexts.

b. **Limited public figure.** A limited public figure is a person who has voluntarily become involved in a particular public issue. To be defined as a limited public figure a person must have sought public attention or voluntarily entered "the vortex of thc public issue."

   Illustration: Gertz v. Robert Welch, Inc., 418 U.S. 323 (1974). Unless a person has general fame or notoriety or has pervasive involvement in the affairs of society, the person is not an unlimited public figure.

3. Fault Requirements for Private Figure Cases Involving Public Issues

In *Gertz v. Robert Welch, Inc.,* the plaintiff was a private figure and the defendant was a magazine publisher. The case involved a public issue. The Court held that even a private-figure plaintiff cannot be allowed to recover for defamation on a showing of strict liability. It held that states must require such a plaintiff to show negligence, recklessness, or actual malice, whichever showing a state might choose to require. The Court held, additionally, that to recover presumed or punitive damages in addition to compensatory damages based on proof of actual harm the plaintiff must be required to show actual malice.

4. Fault Requirement for Private Figure Cases Involving Private Issues

In Dun & Bradstreet v. Greenmoss Builders, 472 U.S. 749 (1985), the plaintiff and defendant were both private parties. The topic of the defamation was a credit report about the plaintiff sent to five clients of the defendant. The Court held that where the topic of the defamation was of no public interest, it would not apply the *Gertz* requirement of a showing of actual malice for presumed or punitive damages. Because the plaintiff had established the defendant's negligence, the Court did not have to decide whether strict liability could be a basis for recovery in this class of cases.

5. Burden of Proof on Truth or Falsity

In Philadelphia Newspapers v. Hepps, 475 U.S. 767 (1986), a private figure plaintiff sought defamation damages from a newspaper. The Court held that the plaintiff was required to establish that the statement was false. This rejected the common law position requiring a defendant to prove that a statement was true. This ruling would certainly apply to public-figure cases, but it is not clear whether it would apply to a case involving a private figure and a nonmedia defendant.

6. Illustration

This chart illustrates the consequences of Supreme Court decisions for defamation cases involving public and private plaintiffs and public and private topics. The court has not yet clarified whether standards should vary according to whether the defendant is a media defendant or a nonmedia defendant, so the chart does not show those possible categories.

Summary of Constitutional Aspects of Defamation Law

Type of Plaintiff	*Topic of Statement*	*Proof for Actual Damages*	*Proof for Presumed Damages*	*Proof for Punitive Damages*
Public official or public figure	Public topic	Actual malice	Actual malice	Actual malice
Private figure	Public topic	State's choice of negligence or more pro-defendant requirement	Actual malice	Actual malice
Private figure	Private topic	State's choice, not currently restricted by Supreme Court decisions	State's choice	State's choice

Review Questions and Answers

Marla Mother told several of her neighbors that they should avoid sending their children on errands to Carl's Convenience Store because an employee there, Sam Strange, had sexually molested several children in the past. Strange sued Mother for defamation.

Question: Would Strange's suit involve libel or slander?

Answer: Strange's suit would involve slander, because the defamation was spoken, not printed or written.

Question: Under common law what harm would Strange be required to show in order to recover damages?

Answer: For most slander the common law requires proof of actual damages. Mother's words, however, fit two of the special categories of slander per se that allow recovery of presumed damages. The statement described Strange as having committed sexual misconduct and, by those same acts, as having committed a serious crime. Therefore, Strange would not have to show any specific harm in order to recover damages (under common law).

Question: Would Mother be entitled to summary judgment if Strange admitted that Mother had only repeated information she had heard from others and had indicated that she did not personally believe it?

Answer: No. A repeater is subject to liability exactly as is the original maker of a statement. The repeater's claim that she did not believe the statement would provide no protection from liability for disseminating it.

Question: Would Mother be entitled to summary judgment if she had made her statements to a local police officer instead of to several neighbors?

Answer: Maybe. There is a qualified privilege for statements in the public interest made to a person who is authorized to protect that interest. A court might find that informing a police officer about a former child molester's employment in contact with children fits this category of qualified privilege. The answer is maybe because Mother would lose the benefit of the qualified privilege if she did not believe the statement when she made it or (in some jurisdictions) if she was negligent with regard to its truth or falsity.

Question: If Strange proved that he had molested only two children, would that proof establish the falsity of Mother's statements?

Answer: No. The difference between the truth (two children) and Mother's statement (several children) was slight. Mother's statement was accurate in naming the type of conduct and was accurate in conveying the idea that the conduct had happened more than once. In the context of this type of criminal behavior, the discrepancy between the statement and the truth would not seem significant to most people.

Question: Would constitutional principles restrict Strange's cause of action?

Answer: Strange was not a public official or a public figure. He was a private figure. If the topic of a defamation is a private topic, the current status of constitutional limitations is unclear. It may be that states are free to impose whatever common law doctrines they choose for that category of defamation case. If the topic of the defamation was one of public interest, to be entitled to actual damages Strange would be required to establish that Mother had been negligent (his state would also be permitted to impose a more defendant-protective burden than requiring a showing of negligence). If the topic was a public-interest topic, to recover presumed or punitive damages Strange would have to show actual malice. It is unclear whether Strange's past conduct was or was not a public topic. One factor that could influence a court's characterization of the topic as public is whether there was widespread interest in it, in contrast to the plaintiff's credit status (which was a private topic in *Dun & Bradstreet*), for example.

Connie Conserver put up posters in several prominent downtown locations of her city. The posters said that local city council member, Barry Builder, voted to turn a local nature preserve into a parking lot because Builder's vote was "either paid for in advance or bought on credit." Builder sought defamation damages from Conserver.

Question: Would constitutional principles restrict Builder's cause of action?

Answer: Yes. Builder was a public figure, and the topic of Conserver's statement was a topic of public interest. To recover any damages Builder would be required to show that Conserver acted with actual malice.

Question: If Conserver stated in a deposition that she put up the posters without knowing anything about Builder's reasons for voting but that she criticized him as she did because she wanted to attract attention to the conflict between urban growth and conservation, would Conserver's description of her conduct satisfy the actual malice requirement of Builder's suit?

Answer: Yes. A plaintiff can show actual malice with evidence supporting a conclusion that the defendant knew the statement was false or that the defendant acted with reckless disregard of whether it was false or not. Conserver did not know that her statement was false, but she admitted she had absolutely no basis for believing it.

Question: If Builder's case satisfied the actual malice standard and Builder showed that there was no element of bribery in connection with his vote, could Conserver avoid liability by arguing that her posters stated an opinion and, thus, were not defamatory?

Answer: No. An opinion that implies a proposition that can be proved true or false is treated as a statement of fact under modern defamation principles. If Conserver's poster had been more extravagant in its terminology, an opinion defense might have worked, but saying that a vote was paid for in advance or on credit was not so extreme that a reader would have understood that the statement was not intended to be taken as true.

Exam Tips

- A defamation plaintiff must show that the defendant's statement can harm the plaintiff's reputation. Two common, tricky cases involve a plaintiff with a horrible reputation and a plaintiff with an incredibly good reputation. If either plaintiff appears in an exam question, write about the possibility that the defendant's statement will have no effect on the plaintiff's reputation.
- Be alert for statements that seem to be opinions but are treated under modern concepts as factual statements.
- Most defamation cases involve public officials or public figures. If an exam question has a private individual as a plaintiff, you can apply all the common law doctrines. Even strict liability is theoretically available when the case involves a private figure and a private topic.
- Actual malice, the state of mind required for defamation liability when the defendant's statement concerns a public official or figure, does not mean angry, vindictive, or meaning to harm. It means acting with knowledge of the statement's falsity or with reckless disregard of its truth or falsity.

21 INVASION OF PRIVACY

CHAPTER OVERVIEW

Tort law provides remedies for the following types of conduct that can invade a plaintiff's privacy:

- Using a person's identity, usually for commercial purposes;
- Disclosing private (true) facts about a person if they are the kind of facts people usually consider private;
- Intruding on a person's zone of privacy;
- Making false statements about a person that are not defamatory but that would be objectionable to a reasonable person.

A. FOUR CAUSES OF ACTION

Invasion of privacy cases are usually analyzed in the framework of four causes of action. These are: 1. appropriation, 2. public disclosure of private facts, 3. unreasonable intrusion, and 4. false light in the public eye.

B. APPROPRIATION

The elements of the tort of appropriation are a defendant's use without authorization of the plaintiff's identity for a commercial purpose. This tort is sometimes called "misappropriation of identity" or "invasion of a right of publicity." In some states statutes forbid the use of a person's likeness for commercial purposes.

1. Definition of Use of Identity

Courts have held that defendants have used plaintiffs' identities in various circumstances. In one clear case the defendant used a photograph of the plaintiff in an advertisement for its product. In a number of cases courts have allowed celebrities to recover when defendants have used vocal or visual impersonators to evoke the celebrities' identity.

Illustration: Flake v. Greensboro News Co., 212 N.C. 780, 195 S.E. 55 (1938). The defendant newspaper negligently used the plaintiff's photograph in an advertisement. While a libel cause of action was not available (due to a lack of special damages), the supreme court recognized a cause of action for invasion of privacy.

2. Damages

Compensatory and punitive damages are available for appropriation of identity. Compensatory damages are measured by the value of the appropriated use.

E&A EXAMPLE AND ANALYSIS

A person who looks like a celebrity or someone who hires that person to impersonate a celebrity is the usual defendant in appropriation cases. A living celebrity's ability to profit from his or her fame and characterization is protected by the appropriation cause of action.

C. PUBLIC DISCLOSURE OF PRIVATE FACTS

The elements of the tort of public disclosure of private facts include a defendant's disclosure to the public of private facts about the plaintiff. The disclosure must be "highly offensive to a reasonable person" (Restatement §652D) and must not be a subject of legitimate public interest.

1. Disclosure to Public

The disclosure must be to the public, not just to a limited number of individuals. Disclosure to the public includes a storekeeper's posting of a sign listing the plaintiff as one who passed a bad check.

2. Private Facts

This tort applies only to facts that are private. First Amendment considerations limit a state's ability to characterize some facts as private and therefore subject to tort law protection from disclosure.

3. Public Interest

If a person's life has become a matter of public interest, then disclosure of facts that are private is not a basis for recovery. Illustratively, in Sidis v. F-R Publishing Corp., 173 F.2d 806 (2d Cir. 1940), the defendant had no liability for publishing a magazine article describing private facts about its subject's life, since the subject had been a famous prodigy in earlier years, and members of the public had a legitimate interest in his current status.

4. Constitutional Limits on Recovery

The First Amendment imposes limitations on the public disclosure of private facts cause of action.

a. **Public record facts.** There is no cause of action for disclosure of facts that are a matter of public record. In Cox Broadcasting v. Cohn, 420 U.S. 469 (1975), the Supreme Court held that the First Amendment precluded any tort penalty for disclosing facts that were on the public record, even where the fact involved was the name of a person who had been raped and murdered.

b. **Newsworthy facts not on public record.** In Florida Star v. B. J. F., 491 U.S. 524 (1989), the defendant violated a state statute that prohibited publication of the name of a rape victim. The Court reversed a recovery for the plaintiff but did so stating that if there is a "state interest of the highest order," a state does have the right to punish dissemination of this type of information. On the facts of the case, the Court held that no such high-order state interest was present, in particular because the statute applied only to media and had no effect on others who might communicate the specified information.

E&A Example and Analysis

In an effort to discourage women from having abortions, publishing the name of a woman who underwent an abortion would probably subject the publisher to liability for public disclosure of private facts. Regardless of the woman's point of view and feelings about abortion, there is no doubt that the procedure is personal and intimate, involving aspects of life that are ordinarily kept private.

5. Damages

Damages include compensatory and punitive damages. Mental distress is an allowable component of these compensatory damages.

D. UNREASONABLE INTRUSION

The elements of the tort of unreasonable intrusion are an intrusion into a plaintiff's seclusion that would be highly offensive to a reasonable person.

1. Types of Intrusion

This tort covers intrusions such as planting electronic listening devices or obtaining ordinarily private information about plaintiffs from third persons. It also covers conduct like repeatedly making telephone calls to a plaintiff.

2. Seclusion

The conduct must affect the plaintiff in some private place. A defendant may take a picture of a plaintiff on a public street but might commit the tort of unreasonable intrusion by taking a picture of the plaintiff in the plaintiff's house. The Restatement suggests that some right of privacy sometimes continues to be present even when a person is in a public place: If an amusement park fan blew a woman's skirt up and exposed her underwear, it would be an unreasonable intrusion to take a photograph of the plaintiff at that time. Restatement §652B, illustration 7.

3. Damages

Damages include compensatory and punitive damages. Mental distress is an allowable component of these compensatory damages.

E. FALSE LIGHT IN THE PUBLIC EYE

The elements of the false light tort are public presentation of the plaintiff in a false light in a way that would be highly offensive to a reasonable person.

1. Different from Defamation

Information that presents a person in a false light need not be defamatory. Typically, this information might ascribe political views to a person that are different from his or her own real views, or it might describe the person as having done things that he or she has not done.

E&A EXAMPLE AND ANALYSIS

A movie about a war hero might depict him in a romantic relationship that never occurred. While this would not be defamatory, it could be found highly offensive by a reasonable person and could be a basis for recovery under the false light in the public eye theory (Restatement §652E, illustration 5).

2. Constitutional Limits on Recovery

Current doctrine requires that a false light plaintiff show actual malice to be entitled to recovery, even if the plaintiff is a private figure.

Illustration: Time, Inc. v. Hill, 385 U.S. 374 (1967). The Court held that a plaintiff was required to show a defendant's actual malice to recover for the false light tort. Actual malice was defined identically to actual malice in *New York Times v. Sullivan*. The plaintiff was obligated to show that the defendant knew its representation was false or had a reckless disregard of its truth or falsity.

Cantrell v. Forest City Publishing Co., 419 U.S. 245, 95 S. Ct. 465, 42 L. Ed.2d 419 (1974). The defendant newspaper published an article describing the plaintiff as having shown grief in particular ways; the reporter had not seen the plaintiff act in those ways, and there was evidence that the description was false. Judgment was entered for the plaintiff on a jury verdict that rejected a punitive damages claim but awarded compensatory damages. On appeal it was argued that the absence of punitive damages indicated that there had been no jury finding of actual malice. The Supreme Court rejected that analysis, stating that actual malice is different from the common law malice required for punitive damages.

a. **Argument for relaxing the actual malice requirement.** In defamation cases the *New York Times* actual malice requirement has been rejected where the plaintiff is a private figure. A similar evolution of the actual malice requirement may occur for false light cases.

b. **Argument for retaining the actual malice requirement.** Although the actual malice requirement for private figure cases has been rejected for defamation, it could be retained for false light cases. Different treatment of the malice issue may be justified because of differences between defamation and false light. The defendant's conduct in a defamation case is likely to be worse, in general, than in a false light case. This distinction could justify lightening the plaintiff's burden in defamation cases while allowing the plaintiff's burden in false light cases to continue to include the actual malice requirement.

Review Questions and Answers

Question: School Shots Company, a business that took class and individual pictures of school children, used a picture of Glenn Goodlooker in a brochure that described the prices charged for various types of photographic prints. Would Goodlooker have a cause of action against School Shots for its use of his picture?

Answer: Yes. This is a classic example of appropriation of the plaintiff's identity. The fact that the defendant did not use Goodlooker's name would have no bearing on the strength of Goodlooker's claim.

Question: Weekly Watch, a suburban newspaper, obtained copies of essays written by participants in a group therapy program for people with antisocial impulses. It published an article about the therapy group, quoting an essay written by Sally Sicker, a member of the group. Sicker's essay described her fantasies about killing elderly people. Would Sicker have a cause of action against Weekly Watch for its report about her?

Answer: Yes. Weekly Watch would likely be liable for invasion of privacy under the public disclosure of private facts cause of action. A reasonable person would find such a disclosure highly offensive. Constitutional limits on this cause of action likely would not prevent Sicker's claim, since her essay was not a public record and her fantasies were not a newsworthy subject of general public interest.

Question: Alan Actor, a reporter for a college newspaper, impersonated a student named Gary Goodgrades to obtain a copy of Goodgrades's transcript from the college registrar's office. Actor studied the transcript, hoping to find evidence of fraud by Goodgrades. Actor found no such evidence and threw away the transcript. Would Goodgrades have a cause of action against Actor for his conduct?

Answer: Yes. Actor committed an unreasonable intrusion into the private concerns of Goodgrades. The fact that Actor did not publish the information would not preclude liability.

Question: Regina Rightwing, a person active in conservative politics, asked Laura Leftish, a person active in liberal politics, to sign a nominating petition for a candidate for public office. Rightwing tricked Leftish into believing that the petition was for a person who supported liberal positions. In fact the petition was for an extremely conservative person. Leftish discovered the fraud and told Rightwing to remove her signature from the petition. Rightwing continued to use the petition and to show people Leftish's signature. Would Leftish have a cause of action against Rightwing on these facts?

Answer: Yes. Rightwing committed the tort of placing Leftish in a false light in the public eye. There was nothing defamatory about communicating the idea that Leftish supported the extremely conservative person, but it was untrue. False descriptions of a person's political beliefs are likely to be objectionable to a reasonable person, so Rightwing could be liable to Leftish.

EXAM TIPS

- When a plaintiff is a public figure, constitutional issues are usually present. A state must have a very strong interest to impose a sanction on disclosures of information about public figures or about events of public interest.
- Intrusion can be accomplished with any technique that enables the defendant to see, hear, or know about something that would otherwise have been protected from the defendant's perception. Problems can involve, for example, electronic listening devices or low-tech means such as bribery.
- False light and defamation are closely related. If a professor has stressed constitutional issues, an exam question might ask whether the actual malice requirement can continue to be justified in false light cases with private plaintiffs.
- Not all disclosures of private facts are actionable. The fact must be something that a reasonable person would keep secret.

22 MISUSE OF LEGAL PROCEDURE

CHAPTER OVERVIEW

- Malicious prosecution is a cause of action that redresses a defendant's wrongful role in instigating a criminal case against a plaintiff.
- Wrongful institution of civil proceedings is a cause of action that redresses a defendant's wrongful role in instigating a civil case against a plaintiff.
- Abuse of process is a cause of action that redresses a defendant's wrongful use of legal procedures, such as the subpoena power, against a plaintiff.

A. CAUSES OF ACTION

Three tort causes of action treat misuse of legal procedures: malicious prosecution, wrongful institution of civil proceedings, and abuse of process.

B. MALICIOUS PROSECTUION

Malicious prosecution is the institution of a criminal proceeding by the defendant for an improper purpose and without probable cause. Additional elements of the tort are malice, resolution of the criminal proceeding in favor of the plaintiff, and proof of damages sustained by the plaintiff.

1. Institution of Criminal Proceedings

The defendant must take a significant action that brings about a criminal prosecution of the plaintiff.

a. **Significant actions.** A defendant's role in a criminal prosecution is significant enough for the tort of malicious prosecution if the defendant signed an affidavit for a warrant, persuaded a prosecutor to begin a case, or knowingly gave false information to a prosecutor.

b. **Lesser actions.** A defendant can have a small role in the instigation of a criminal prosecution without being exposed to liability for malicious prosecution. Illustratively, a defendant has no liability for only giving information to authorities if the defendant limits his or her role to furnishing the information and refrains from attempting to influence the prosecutor's actions in response to the information.

2. Improper Purpose

Improper purpose can be shown if the defendant's main purpose in instituting the criminal proceeding is other than a desire to bring the offender to justice. Lack of probable cause supports an inference that the defendant has some additional motive.

E&A EXAMPLE AND ANALYSIS

Walter Welsher wanted to withdraw from a business deal with Neville Nice. If Welsher instigated a fraud prosecution of Nice to try to influence Nice to rescind their agreement, that would be an improper motive for instituting criminal proceedings.

3. No Probable Cause

A defendant has probable cause to instigate a criminal proceeding only if he or she reasonably believes that the plaintiff committed acts that constitute the charged crime.

a. **Objective test.** The plaintiff can seek to establish that the defendant did not have probable cause with an objective test that asks whether a reasonable person with the same information the defendant possessed would have believed the plaintiff had committed the crime.

b. **Subjective test.** A subjective test is also available to the plaintiff. It asks whether the defendant actually believed that the plaintiff was guilty.

c. **Consultation with lawyer or prosecutor.** When defendants institute criminal proceedings in response to advice from lawyers or prosecutors, most jurisdictions treat this advice as conclusive evidence that the defendants had probable cause.

4. Outcome Favorable to Plaintiff

The plaintiff must establish a favorable outcome of the criminal proceeding. This outcome may be dismissal by a magistrate, refusal of a grand jury to indict, or an acquittal at trial.

5. Relationship of Outcome to Probable Cause

An outcome favorable to the plaintiff is usually relevant to the question of whether the defendant had probable cause.

a. **Dismissal or refusal to indict.** A magistrate's dismissal of charges or a grand jury's refusal to indict is treated in most jurisdictions as prima facie evidence that the defendant did not have probable cause.

b. **Acquittal.** If the plaintiff is acquitted, that fact has no relevance to the question of probable cause, since acquittals can occur for many reasons that do not contradict the existence of probable cause. A defendant has the right to litigate the issue of the malicious-prosecution plaintiff's guilt to show that probable cause really did exist. In the tort trial the issue of the plaintiff's guilt is decided on a preponderance of the evidence standard.

6. Damages

At common law presumed damages are permitted for malicious prosecution, they are traditionally available in defamation cases; the injuries in defamation and wrongful prosecution are similar. It is unconstitutional to permit presumed damages in some defamation cases now, but it is unclear whether that limitation will be imposed on malicious prosecution cases.

C. WRONGFUL INSTITUTION OF CIVIL PROCEEDINGS

The tort of wrongful institution of civil proceedings is similar to the tort of malicious prosecution.

Example: Friedman v. Dozorc, 412 Mich. 1, 312 N.W.2d 585 (1981). The defendant lawyer had represented a client against a physician. The case against the physician had ended with a directed verdict in the physician's favor. The physician then sued the plaintiff's lawyer, alleging abuse of process and malicious prosecution. The supreme court held that no cause of action was presented on these facts. Representation of plaintiffs would be hampered too much if their lawyers were required to anticipate tort damages for bringing cases that ultimately fail.

1. Institution of Civil Proceedings

Civil proceedings include lawsuits and other actions such as administrative cases or bankruptcy proceedings.

2. Improper Purpose

If the defendant had a purpose other than securing adjudication of the actual civil claim, that additional purpose was improper. The plaintiff must show the existence of some such improper purpose.

3. No Probable Cause

The plaintiff must show that the defendant lacked probable cause. In the civil context a finding of probable cause can be based on weaker evidence than is required in the malicious prosecution context.

4. Outcome Favorable to Plaintiff

The plaintiff must show that the proceeding ended with an outcome in the plaintiff's favor. Such an outcome is conclusive, in contrast to the case of malicious prosecution. Because the prior proceeding (about which the plaintiff claims wrongful institution of a civil proceeding) had to be adjudicated undcr a prcpondcrancc of thc cvidcncc standard, and sincc that is thc same standard used in the wrongful institution suit, there is no basis for relitigating the subject matter of the prior proceeding.

D. ABUSE OF PROCESS

Abuse of process is the intentional misuse of a judicial process for a purpose different from the purpose for which that process is intended. Examples of abuse of process include serving a subpoena on someone for the purpose of harassment rather than the purpose of obtaining information, and causing an arrest warrant to be issued by giving false information to the police.

1. Favorable Termination Not Relevant

Abuse of process cases do not involve an element of favorable termination of an earlier proceeding, because the harm alleged need not have occurred in the context of a proceeding.

REVIEW QUESTIONS AND ANSWERS

Question: Carla Cautious noticed her next-door neighbor, Sam Skulker, unloading what seemed to be about fifteen identical cartons of stereo equipment from a van into his garage. Cautious called the police to tell them about this, suggesting that Skulker might be receiving stolen goods. The police investigated and found that Skulker was planning to give each of his fifteen cousins a CD player for Christmas. Would Skulker have a cause of action against Cautious for these events?

Answer: No. Skulker never was prosecuted, so criminal proceedings never occurred. Also, Cautious's contact with the police was fairly slight. Even if a prosecution had followed from the police investigation, a court might find that Cautious had very little responsibility for it.

Question: Max Monopoly operated a chain of food stores in a large city. To make trouble for a competitor, Nancy Newstore, Monopoly had investigators collect information about Newstore's business practices. The investigators obtained videotapes that apparently showed Newstore engaging in a pattern of bribing weights and measures inspectors. Monopoly gave the tapes to prosecutors and had his lawyer call the prosecutors several times to ask whether they were evaluating them carefully. Prosecutors did obtain an indictment of Newstore, but she was acquitted at trial. On these facts would Newstore have a successful malicious prosecution action against Monopoly?

Answer: No. A successful malicious prosecution suit must satisfy all the elements of the tort. Monopoly had an improper motive, here, and Newstore was acquitted. Those factors help Newstore. The lack of probable cause element, however, would be hard for Newstore to satisfy. The videotapes apparently showed bribery. A reasonable person who saw them would have believed that a crime was taking place.

Question: Larry Loyal, Jr., arranged to have his wealthy father, Larry Loyal, Sr., examined by psychiatrists. Junior believed that Senior had become incompetent. Junior was also very interested in obtaining control over Senior's assets. The psychiatrists agreed that Senior should be institutionalized. Junior instituted civil commitment proceedings because his father resisted being institutionalized. Senior was committed. Could Senior be successful in an abuse of process action against Junior?

Answer: No. Despite the fact that Junior had a strong desire to control his father's money, his actions did not constitute abuse of process. Junior used the process for the purpose for which it was designed. If he had used the process as a mode of extortion, for example, liability might be imposed.

EXAM TIPS

- Watch all the elements of malicious prosecution and wrongful institution of civil proceedings. If criminal charges lead to a conviction, there is no cause of action for malicious prosecution. If civil litigation leads to a judgment for the plaintiff, there can be no cause of action for wrongful institution of civil proceedings.
- Remember the relationship between an acquittal and the question of whether a person who instituted the criminal process had probable cause. Acquittal and probable cause can be consistent: acquittal in a criminal case does not mean as a matter of law that there was no probable cause for the criminal proceedings.

23 INTERFERENCE WITH ADVANTAGEOUS RELATIONS

CHAPTER OVERVIEW

- Interference with contract, interference with prospective advantage, and injurious falsehood are three torts that redress economic harms suffered in commercial contexts.
- Intentionally interfering with the performance of a contract between the plaintiff and another party can subject a person to liability for interference with contract.
- Intentionally interfering with the someone's prospective business advantage can subject a person to liability for the tort of interference with a prospective advantage.
- Privileges allow defendants to take many actions that may harm another's contractual or prospectively advantageous relationships.

A. INTERFERENCE WITH CONTRACT

Interference with contract cases always involve at least three parties: a plaintiff who had a contract with a second party, and a defendant who is alleged to have induced the second party to breach the contract that the second party had with the plaintiff. A defendant who intentionally causes someone to breach a contract with the plaintiff is liable to the plaintiff for the monetary losses the plaintiff suffers due to breach of the contract.

Illustration: Lumley v. Gye, 2 El. & Bl. 216, 118 Eng. Rep. 749 (Queen's Bench 1853). The plaintiff had a contract with a famous opera singer, requiring her to sing at his theater and also requiring her to refrain from professional appearances for other producers. The defendant, a rival producer, allegedly persuaded the singer to refuse to perform for the plaintiff. The plaintiff sought damages for this action. The trial court granted a demurrer. On appeal the court recognized a cause of action by analogy to an action already known on behalf of a master against one who induced a servant to leave his service unlawfully.

1. Elements

The plaintiff must establish that: 1. the plaintiff and the second party had a valid contract; 2. the defendant knew about the contract; 3. the defendant intended to interfere with the contract; 4. the defendant did interfere with the contract; and 5. the plaintiff suffered damages.

2. Applicability to Certain Contracts

The cause of action for interference with contract is recognized for most contracts, but special rules apply for the following types of contracts.

a. **Illegal contract.** If the contract in question is illegal, there is no cause of action for interfering with it.

b. **Contract to marry.** Interference with a contract to marry cannot be redressed through the interference with contract cause of action.

c. **At-will contract.** The common law did not recognize an action for interference with an at-will contract on the theory that it was liable to be terminated at any time. The Restatement and many modern courts take the opposite position, holding that inducing the breach of this type of contract does support a cause of action, since the contract expresses valid obligations until a party decides to terminate it.

d. **Unenforceable contract.** The cause of action for interference with contract does not apply to a contract that would be unenforceable in a suit between its parties because of a problem with the statute of frauds or another contract defense.

3. Defendant's Conduct

A defendant is privileged to protect his or her own prior financial interests and to protect the financial interests of others.

a. **Prior financial interest.** Action to protect a prior financial interest does not constitute interference with contract, even if it leads to someone's breach of a contract with another party.

E&A EXAMPLE AND ANALYSIS

A component-part supplier might have contracts with the plaintiff and defendant to supply parts for their use but might be unable to manufacture enough parts to satisfy its obligations to both. The defendant would be free to induce the supplier to honor its contract with the defendant and to breach its contract with the plaintiff; in doing so the defendant would only be protecting a prior financial interest.

---

b. **Interest of others.** A person who gives advice that helps someone decide to breach a contract to protect his or her financial interest has no liability to the party who suffers a loss due to the breach.

c. **Routine business solicitations.** A person who makes a routine business solicitation that has the effect of inducing someone to breach a contract has no liability for the tort of interference with contract. This rule applies also to the act of offering someone a price that is better than the price he or she is obligated to pay under a contract. A person does commit the tort of interference with contract, however, by recommending breach of a contract in the context of offering a better price.

4. Knowledge and Intention

The plaintiff must show that the defendant knew about the contract that someone breached and that the defendant intended to influence that person to breach it. Negligent conduct does not support a cause of action for interference with contract.

B. INTERFERENCE WITH PROSPECTIVE ADVANTAGE

The tort of interference with prospective advantage is similar to the tort of interference with contract, except that it applies to business dealings that have not yet developed into a contract.

Illustration: Leigh Furniture and Carpet Co. v. Isom, 657 P.2d 293 (Utah 1982). The defendant sold a retail furniture business to the plaintiff in a transaction that included a lease for the plaintiff's use of a store. The defendant then made frequent visits to the store to confront and question the plaintiff about the business. The defendant also undermined the plaintiff's relationships with customers, suppliers, and potential business associates. This conduct satisfied the intentional interference element of the tort. The element of improper purpose may not have been satisfied, since the defendant had a legitimate interest in regaining control of the leasehold. The means by which the defendant sought to achieve that purpose were improper, however, and that was an alternative ground for a finding of improper purpose.

1. Elements

Interference with prospective advantage has the same elements as interference with contract, except the plaintiff must show an economic expectancy between the plaintiff and a second party, not a contract. The defendant must have knowledge of that expectancy, not of a contract between the plaintiff and the second party.

2. Privilege to Protect Defendant's Interests

A significant doctrinal difference between interference with prospective advantage and interference with contract is that the privilege to protect one's financial interests is applied more favorably to defendants when what is at stake is prospective advantage rather than continued compliance with contractual obligations.

3. Privilege to Compete with Plaintiff

A defendant has a privilege to seek to obtain a prospective advantage for himself or herself, even if the defendant knows that the plaintiff is also anticipating having the benefit of that advantage.

C. INJURIOUS FALSEHOOD

A defendant who makes a false statement to someone about a third person's business or property with the intention of causing economic injury to the third person is liable for the tort of injurious falsehood. This tort is sometimes called "trade libel" when the statement involves the plaintiff's business or product.

Illustration: Ratliffe v. Evans, 2 Q.B. 524 (C. A. 1892). The defendant newspaper published a false report that the plaintiff's business was no longer in existence. The plaintiff won damages at trial without proving special damages. On appeal it was held that proof of general damages was adequate to support the plaintiff's judgment.

1. Attributes of Statement

The plaintiff has the burden of proof on the issue of falsity of the defendant's statement. The plaintiff must also show that the statement referred to the plaintiff.

2. Distinct from Defamation

A falsehood need not be defamatory to be actionable as an injurious falsehood. For example, a statement that a certain business does not sell a type of product is not defamatory. It could be an injurious falsehood, however.

3. Damages

The plaintiff must show economic harm from the defendant's statement. Modern courts tend to accept proof of general loss of business as equivalent to proof that the defendants' statements caused specific losses.

4. Defenses

Consent is a full defense. Additionally, the privileges applicable to defamation apply to injurious falsehood (such as the privileges for statements made by legislators and statements made to protect the public interest). There is also a privilege for fair competition. This privilege allows general (or puffing) statements of comparison between the plaintiff's and defendant's businesses or products.

Review Questions and Answers

Question: Clever Cleaners, a company that provided office cleaning services, wrote a letter to several large businesses in its city, stating, "We will clean your offices for 20-percent less than the price you pay to whatever service you have a contract with now." One of those businesses breached a contract with Classic Cleaners (Clever's competitor) and hired Clever. Would Classic have a valid cause of action against Clever for interference with contract?

Answer: No. Offering a competitive price for a service or product would not be treated as inducing someone to breach a contract he or she had with another to provide the same product or service.

Question: Clever Cleaners (from the question above) added the following language to its letter: "Don't be afraid to breach your contract with your current cleaning company. Litigation takes years, and your savings from dealing with us will more than pay for any loss you might have." If Classic lost a customer to Clever based on this letter, would Classic have a valid cause of action for interference with contract?

Answer: Yes. This version of Clever's letter crossed a significant line. In addition to offering a competitive price, it recommended contract breach explicitly. Tort law prohibits that type of solicitation.

Question: Genetic Grass Company developed a type of grass that never needed to be mowed (growth over a certain height turned into mulch). Would Genetic Grass be subject to liability in suits by lawn mower manufacturers and lawn mowing companies for the harm that the Genetic Grass product caused to their businesses?

Answer: No. Genetic Grass had a privilege to compete with the plaintiffs, even if it could predict that its business would hamper or ruin theirs.

EXAM TIPS

- Lots of competitive conduct is nontortious. Be careful to remember the various privileges that protect defendants who are aggressive in business dealings.
- Interference with contract and interference with prospective advantage are intentional torts. Look for and discuss the issue of the defendant's willful intent or substantial certainty with regard to the impact of the defendant's conduct on the plaintiff's contract or prospective advantage.
- For the tort of injurious falsehood, the privilege for puffing is important. A defendant's statements about a plaintiff competitor must seem highly specific or authoritative in order to subject the defendant to liability for injurious falsehood.

SAMPLE EXAM QUESTIONS

Question: Ralph Rancher saw Wally Walker walking on a road near his ranch. Meaning to frighten him, Rancher shouted, "Get away or I'll shoot you." He then pointed a shotgun at Walker and fired it. Rancher was a bad shot and he missed Walker. Rancher was unaware that Edgar Extra was also on the road. Unfortunately, Rancher's shot hit Extra, wounding him. Discuss whether Extra can recover damages from Rancher for his injury.

Answer: Rancher is liable to Extra for the intentional tort of battery. Extra can recover compensatory damages and may be entitled to punitive damages as well.

Battery is an intentional tort. Extra can satisfy the intent element with the doctrine of transferred intent. Under that doctrine an intent to commit the tort of assault is equivalent to the required intent for battery. Rancher's conduct definitely satisfies the intent requirement for assault. Firing the shotgun was a volitional act, and he did it with the purpose of scaring Walker. Thus, Rancher had the intent to commit an assault. That intent satisfies the battery intent element.

To recover for battery Extra must show that he suffered a harmful or offensive touching. Extra was wounded, so he suffered a harmful touching.

Rancher had no privilege and Extra was not negligent in any way. Thus, Rancher is liable for the tort of battery. Extra is entitled to compensatory damages, which include medical expenses and lost income if his wound prevented him from working. Depending on local standards, Rancher's conduct may seem outrageous enough to justify an award of punitive damages.

Question: Oliver Owner, the owner of a small store, set up a heavy vending machine on a slanted ramp at the store's entrance. The machine tipped over and injured Cathy Customer. Customer sued Owner for damages, alleging that Owner had been negligent in placing the machine on the slanted ramp. Discuss whether Customer's suit is likely to be successful, assuming that Owner can establish each of the following representations with credible evidence:

1. He did not understand that a very heavy machine could tip over if it was set up on an inclined ramp.
2. He was partially paralyzed and therefore could not move the machine to a more stable location.
3. He thought that an outer-space creature would hold the machine steady.
4. He was not smart enough to understand that the machine might tip over.
5. He was drunk when he decided where to put the machine.
6. Many store owners put their machines on slanted floors and ramps.
7. He would have lost sales if he had put the machine on a level location, because the slanted location was the only place passed by most of his customers.

Answer: Customer has an excellent chance of recovery. Owner's conduct in selecting the location of the machine and deciding to let it stay at that spot would be evaluated under a reasonable prudent person test, since Customer was an invitee on the store's premises and was owed a duty of reasonable care. A jury could well decide that the risk of injury to someone like Customer was significant enough to have made it imprudent for Owner to keep the machine at that place. The machine was heavy, and usually such machines are placed on level surfaces.

None of Owner's arguments is helpful. His failure to understand the risk has no relevance, since the reasonable prudent person test is objective, not subjective. The claim that he was disabled and therefore could not move the machine is unavailing, since he was capable of having someone else move it. Even if Owner really did think a creature from space would take care of the machine, the traditional tort treatment of delusional behavior is to evaluate it under the reasonable prudent person test. Under that test it was not sensible to rely on a creature to keep the machine steady.

Owner's proof that he was not smart enough to understand the risk is not relevant, since tort law requires someone like Owner to act with the typical intelligence of an ordinary person, whether or not he possesses that intelligence. Owner's "defense" of intoxication is also of no avail, since an intoxicated person is expected to act as carefully as a sober person.

The fact that many machines are placed on slanted floors is not conclusive. Common experience shows that more machines are kept on flat surfaces than on slanted ones. Even if most storekeepers put machines on ramps, a jury is not obligated to treat compliance with that custom as a defense. It could evaluate the reasonableness of that practice independently.

Owner's last representation involves costs and benefits. Focusing on the opportunity to increase sales from the machine, it unfortunately does not include in its calculation the likely occurrence and cost of injuries. Higher sales do not typically justify the higher risks involved in locating a machine in a precarious position.

Question: Assume the following two situations. First, if a plaintiff slipped and fell on the dance floor in a hotel banquet room and sought damages from the hotel for negligence, claiming that the floor had been treated with wax that made it too slippery, the professional standard of care would not apply. The hotel's conduct would be judged according to the reasonable prudent person standard. Second, if a plaintiff had a hip replacement operation that was unsuccessful because the new hip failed to stay firmly attached to the plaintiff's bone structure and the plaintiff sought damages from the surgeon for negligence, claiming that the surgeon had used adhesive cement that was not strong enough, the professional standard of care would apply. Compare these two cases in terms of differences in the plaintiffs' required proof and in the way the juries will evaluate the defendants' conduct.

Answer: In the surgeon case the plaintiff must introduce evidence that shows the professional standard of care. This will have to be testimony from experts who know what kind of adhesive cement typical surgeons use in that operation, either in the locality where the surgeon operated or in the nation, depending on whether the trial jurisdiction uses the locality rule or a national standard. The jury will be instructed that in order to win the plaintiff must have persuaded it that the defendant's conduct did not comply with the professional standard. In the hotel case the plaintiff does not have to use expert testimony (although he or she might choose to do so as a matter of strategy), and the jury will be free to use its own judgment about what degree of slipperiness is all right for a dance floor.

Question: The defendant gas station had an automatic car wash; to use it a customer deposited money or entered a code number into a control unit and drove his or her car into the enclosure that contained the car-washing apparatus. Machinery then moved over and around the car to wash it. The plaintiff seeks damages for a dent the machinery allegedly made in the plaintiff's car. Discuss whether the *res ipsa loquitur* doctrine should be available to the plaintiff in this situation.

Answer: Probably. The plaintiff must persuade the judge that this type of injury usually occurs due to negligence. The plaintiff can likely do that. The machine might have malfunctioned because it had not been installed, inspected, or maintained correctly, it had been damaged by some other customer, or it had been temporarily affected by some unpredictable problem like lightning or a power surge from the electric company that supplied its power. Most of these possible causes involve negligence.

The plaintiff must also persuade the court that the type of negligence that probably caused the harm was probably the fault of the defendant. Note that the plaintiff was inside the car wash and had turned the machine on, suggesting that the defendant was not in control of the machinery when it caused the harm. Most courts treat this problem by asking who was in control of the machinery at times when the negligence probably happened. If the negligence was likely to have been bad inspection, bad maintenance, or bad installation, it is easy to conclude that the defendant was in control of the apparatus when that occurred.

If the jurisdiction still requires plaintiffs to show freedom from responsibility to be entitled to the benefit of the doctrine, the plaintiff must satisfy that element by testimony about his or her conduct. A court that focuses on the probable times and locations of any negligence might conclude that the plaintiff could not have had anything to do with poor maintenance, inspection, or installation, regardless of any testimony about the plaintiff's conduct at the time of the actual damage to the car.

Question: Defendant Duplicating Company made 200 copies of a poster for Plaintiff. Flakes of copier ink came off the posters and injured Plaintiff. Discuss the significant issues in a negligence suit by Plaintiff against Defendant. Also discuss the significant issues that would arise if Plaintiff sought damages from Defendant on a theory of strict liability.

Answer: Under a negligence theory the Duplicating Company owes a duty of reasonable care to Plaintiff. It might have failed to meet that duty if it used ink and processing that it should reasonably have known were not of good quality. If incidents of this type had happened previously, it is likely that the company's conduct in continuing to use the same ink and processing would additionally be found to have been unreasonable. Issues of cause in fact and proximate cause are simple: the victim suffered a type of harm that is predictable, and the victim was actually known to Defendant, so issues of remoteness or an unforeseeable plaintiff do not arise.

For a strict liability claim, an initial question is whether Defendant sold a product or performed a service. If it is characterized as having provided a service, strict liability does not apply. While some aspects of the company's business seem individualized, it can also be said that it manufactured pieces of paper with ink on them. Applying strict strict liability would be consistent with the main ideas supporting the doctrine, that enterprises should spread the costs of possible injuries and that enterprises have better access to information about safety than their customers have.

Under either a risk-utility test or a consumer expectation test the copies were probably defective. Buyers do not expect copies to make them sick. The risk-utility test would probably favor Plaintiff also, since it is hard to imagine that the defendant's choices were sensible in terms of the possibility of avoiding the harm, the availability of economically viable alternatives, and Plaintiff's ability to avoid the harm. Causation issues are the same as for the negligence claim.

Glossary

Abnormally dangerous activity. An activity, defined with a six-part test from the Restatement, to which strict liability applies.

Additur. A provisional grant of a plaintiff's new-trial motion conditioned on the defendant's acceptance of an increase in the judgment.

Appropriation. A cause of action for invasion of privacy involving use of the plaintiff's name or identity.

Assault. The intentional tort of causing someone to apprehend an imminent battery.

Assumption of risk. A doctrine characterizing certain types of conduct by a plaintiff as equal to consent to be harmed and treating that conduct as a complete defense.

Attractive nuisance. A theory imposing a duty of due care owed by a landowner to certain child trespassers.

Battery. The intentional tort of causing a harmful or offensive touching of another person.

Burden of proof. The requirement that a party produce sufficient evidence on each element of a cause of action or a defense to persuade a jury by a preponderance of the evidence that each element exists.

Cause in fact. An event that satisfies a but for test or a substantial factor test relating it to a second event is a cause in fact of the second event.

Collateral source rule. A rule requiring a jury or judge, in setting the size of a damage award, to ignore payments a plaintiff may have received for elements of damage that would ordinarily be the responsibility of a defendant.

Colloquium. Facts that link a defendant's allegedly defamatory statement to the plaintiff.

Comparative Negligence. Pure comparative negligence is a system of treating negligence by a tort plaintiff as a factor that reduces but does not bar the plaintiff's recovery. Modified comparative negligence treats negligence by a tort plaintiff as a factor that reduces recovery if the plaintiff's negligence is equal to or less than a specified percentage and bars recovery if the negligence is above a specified percentage.

Compensatory damages. A monetary award to pay a plaintiff for past and future harms suffered due to a defendant's tortious conduct.

Concerted action. Conduct by two or more people to accomplish a common plan.

Concurrent tortfeasors. Tortfeasors whose conduct affects the plaintiff at a single time.

Consent. Agreement to a defendant's conduct or to an encounter with a risk created by a defendant that precludes tort recovery for the consequences of the conduct or risk.

Consumer expectation test. In a product liability case a test for defect based on what an ordinary consumer with knowledge of a product's characteristics would expect.

Contributory negligence. A system of treating negligence by a tort plaintiff as complete defense.

Contribution. A cause of action in which an overpaying defendant seeks reimbursement from another defendant who underpaid a judgment.

Conversion. The intentional tort of inflicting significant interference with a plaintiff's chattel.

Defamation. A communication that could have the effect of impairing a plaintiff's reputation or influencing others against associating with the plaintiff.

Discipline. A privilege to act toward a plaintiff for the purpose of imposing discipline in a way that would otherwise be an intentional tort.

Duty. An obligation recognized in law for a certain type of person or entity to act in a certain way in a certain situation.

Eggshell plaintiff. A person with an unusual weakness. A defendant may not rely on that weakness as a defense if the defendant's conduct would have been tortious toward a typical person but harms the eggshell plaintiff more severely.

False imprisonment. The intentional tort of confining the plaintiff.

False light. The privacy tort related to presenting a plaintiff to the public in a non-defamatory but false and offensive way.

Fault. Blameworthy conduct, sometimes required for imposing tort liability.

Immunity. A doctrine that protects an actor from tort liability to another. An example is governmental immunity.

Impact rule. A former requirement in negligent infliction of emotional distress cases. The plaintiff was not permitted to recover unless the defendant's conduct had caused some physical touching of the plaintiff in addition to the allegedly resultant distress.

Indemnity. A defendant's right to have the entire cost of a judgment shifted to another actor.

Inducement. A defamation allegation showing how extrinsic facts might give a statement an interpretation that is defamatory.

Innuendo. A defamation allegation explaining a defamatory meaning inherent in a statement.

Intent. A state of mind (for one who commits an intentional tort) characterized by willful action with the purpose of accomplishing a result or with substantial certainty that the result will occur.

Intervening cause. A cause of an injury that occurs after another cause occurred.

Intrusion. An invasion of privacy tort involving conduct that intrudes on a plaintiff's private life in an offensive way.

Invitee. A person who enters land for a business purpose or a purpose for which the public is generally invited.

Joint and several liability. The obligation of each of a group of joint tortfeasors to pay the plaintiff's entire judgment.

Joint tortfeasor. A person whose conduct and the conduct of others jointly caused a plaintiff to suffer an indivisible harm.

Last clear chance. A doctrine that defeats the contributory negligence defense when a defendant had an opportunity to avert a harm that was partly caused by a plaintiff's prior negligent conduct.

Legal cause. A synonym for proximate cause.

Libel. Communication of a defamation in writing or another permanent form.

Licensee. A person who enters land as a guest but who does not have the qualifications required for the status of invitee.

Misrepresentation. False statement of fact. The tort action for misrepresentation provides redress for intentional, negligent, and innocent misrepresentations.

Misuse. A product liability plaintiff's use of a product for a purpose other than the one for which it was designed.

Mitigation. Reduction, alleviation, abatement. A plaintiff is ordinarily obligated to take reasonable steps in mitigation (or reduction) of damages.

Necessity. A privilege permitting the use of another's land or property.

Negligence. Failure to act as a reasonable and prudent person would act in the circumstances.

Nuisance. An unreasonable and substantial interference with another's use and enjoyment of his or her land.

Prima facie case. The elements about which a plaintiff must introduce sufficient evidence to support a jury finding that they exist in order to be entitled to recovery of damages.

Privilege. A defense to a tort cause of action.

Product liability. Theories under which a plaintiff may recover damages for a product-related injury. The theories include negligence, warranty, and strict liability.

Proximate cause. A required element of a plaintiff's cause of action, expressing the legal system's control over the range of consequences of a defendant's acts for which the defendant is responsible.

Public disclosure of private facts. A privacy tort covering publicity given to private facts of the plaintiff's life.

Punitive damages. Damages awarded to a plaintiff to deter a defendant from especially blameworthy conduct. Punitive damages are awarded in addition to compensatory damages.

Reasonable prudent person. A hypothetical concept used to define the quality of care required of most people in most situations. They must act as a reasonable and prudent person would act.

Recklessness. Quality of acting with conscious disregard of the risk of physical harm.

Remittitur. A provisional grant of a defendant's new-trial motion conditioned on the plaintiff's acceptance of a decrease in the judgment.

Res ipsa loquitur. A procedural device to establish a plaintiff's prima facie negligence case in a situation that presents a high likelihood of negligence by the defendant.

Respondeat superior. An employer's liability for torts committed by an employee in the course of employment.

Risk-utility test. In a products liability case a test for defect evaluating design choices in terms of the balance struck by the manufacturer between risks and utility.

Self-defense. A privilege to use force or other reasonable means to resist an unprivileged tort against a person.

Slander. Defamation conveyed by speech or gestures.

Strict liability. Liability without fault. Examples are strict liability for product-related injuries and for injuries from abnormally dangerous activities.

Superseding cause. An intervening cause sufficiently unforeseeable to justify insulating a previous actor from liability for the consequences of a harm caused by the previous actor's conduct and the intervening actor's conduct.

Trespass. A cause of action for intentional entry on land or interference with a chattel.

Vicarious liability. Liability for the conduct of another.

Wrongful birth. An action by parents of an unwanted child born with a birth defect against a health care provider who allegedly was negligent in connection with a sterilization procedure or prenatal treatment.

Wrongful life. An action by a child born with a physical defect against a health care provider who allegedly was negligent in connection with a sterilization procedure on one of the child's parents or with prenatal treatment of the child's mother.

Zone of danger. Location in which a defendant's conduct could possibly have caused physical harm to another. The concept is used in negligent infliction of emotional distress cases.

TABLE OF CASES

Table of Restatement (Second) of Torts Sections

Index